BEYOND THE LIBERAL CONSENSUS

IWAN W. MORGAN

Beyond the Liberal Consensus

A Political History of the
United States since 1965

ST MARTIN'S PRESS, NEW YORK

First published in the United States of America in 1994

Printed in Hong Kong

ISBNs
0–312–10747–1 (*Cloth*)
0–312–12015–X (*Paper*)

Library of Congress Cataloging-in-Publication Data

Morgan, Iwan W.
   Beyond the liberal consensus : a political history of the United
States since 1965 / Iwan W. Morgan.
     p.   cm.
   Includes bibliographical references and index.
   ISBN 0–312–10747–1 (cloth). — ISBN 0–312–12015–X (paper)
   1. United States—Politics and government—1945–1989. 2. United
States—Politics and government—1989– I. Title.
E839.5.M64 1994
973.92—dc20   93–44098
                                               CIP

To Humphrey and Eleanor
creators of consensus (usually)

Preface

This book seeks to provide a broad overview of the recent political history of the United States for students and other readers with an interest in contemporary America. It is premised on the notion that one era of American political history ended in the mid 1960s and another began. Its main arguments can be summarized as follows: (1) a "liberal consensus" shaped America's political development in the two decades after World War II, but this collapsed in the second half of the 1960s; (2) since the mid 1960s American politics has been characterized more by political dispute and conflict than by consensus over the role of government in the economy and society, over values, and over foreign policy; and (3) notwithstanding the electoral success of Ronald Reagan, nothing resembling a conservative consensus came into being in the 1980s.

This study makes no claim to being a comprehensive narrative of American politics in the last quarter-century or so. The material is organized around three principal themes: political debate over foreign policy; the shifting currents of economic policy; and political trends reflected in domestic policy changes, party politics and election results. Occasional references are also made to British political development, partly to make American political developments more intelligible to British readers but also to highlight for American readers some of the political parallels between the recent pasts of our countries.

Because this is a work of synthesis, I am heavily indebted to many scholars and journalists, whose works have influenced my perspectives of American politics and are duly acknowledged in the bibliography. I am also grateful to have had the opportunity to present some of my ideas to Professor Tony Badger's American History seminar at the University of Cambridge and the annual colloquium of the Center for the Study of Political Change, London Guildhall University. My greatest debt is to my family, who have had to put up with the long and obsessive hours that I spent writing this book. My wife Theresa and my children Humphrey and Eleanor — to whom the book is dedicated — have sustained my spirits throughout this time and kept me aware of what is truly important.

I.W.M.

Contents

Preface   vii

Chapters

1. The Liberal Consensus of the Postwar Era   1

   People of plenty   3
   Government and the economy   8
   The New Deal political order   12
   The Cold War consensus   20

2. The Unraveling of the Liberal Consensus, 1965–1968   28

   The Vietnam war   28
   The rise and fall of the "new economics"   35
   The Great Society and a divided society   41
   The 1968 presidential election   52

3. Beyond Dominion: a New Foreign Policy for a
   Changed World, 1969–1976   58

   Nixon, Kissinger and the concept of detente   58
   Vietnamizing the Vietnam war   63
   Detente at high tide, 1971–1973   70
   Detente in decline, 1973–1976   76
   Beyond the Cold War consensus   84

4. Beyond Eden: the Political Economy of Stagflation,
   1969–1976   87

   The ailing economy   88
   "Nixonomics"   95
   The Great Inflation, the Great Recession, and Party Politics,
   1974–1976   104

5. Beyond Roosevelt: Parties, Politics and Domestic Issues,
   1969–1976   109
   Nixon and a new Republican majority   109

Domestic politics of the first Nixon administration   112
Democrats in disarray   124
The 1972 election   128
The resurgence of the Republican right   130
Return to Roosevelt?   133

6. Malaise: the Politics of the Carter Era, 1977–1980   138

From detente to confrontation   138
The battle against inflation   150
The end of the New Deal order   157

7. True Believers: Conservatives and the Conservative
   Agenda of the 1980s   171

Reagan   171
The revived right   174
The Republican party   183
The political agenda of Reaganism   187

8. Incomplete Revolution: Politics and Policy in the Reagan
   Era, 1981–1988   198

"Reaganomics"   199
Reducing the colossus of government   207
Race and gender issues   215
Reagan and the world   219
Parties, elections and voters in the Reagan era   228

9. The Morning After: the Politics of the Bush Era,
   1989–1992   240

New world order   240
Economic malaise   248
Race, rights, and riots   253
Rise up, women   258
Mandate for change?   261

Conclusion: Beyond the Liberal Consensus   271

Select Bibliography   277

Index   285

1
The Liberal Consensus of the Postwar Era

The political history of postwar America underwent significant change in the middle years of the 1960s. For two decades after World War II American politics was shaped by the existence of a liberal consensus. This consensus rested on three foundations: a strong economy that generated unprecedented prosperity; the New Deal political order; and the Cold War commitment to contain the expansion of communism on a global basis. During the second half of the 1960s domestic, economic and international developments undermined these foundations and brought about the decline of the liberal consensus. In consequence the American polity of the 1970s, 1980s and early 1990s has been markedly different to that of the postwar era.

Consensus has not been the norm in America's history. The political experience of the United States has more often been characterized by conflict — rich against poor, labor against industrialists, farmers against bankers, whites against blacks, rural dwellers against urban dwellers, old-stock Protestants against new immigrants, and North against South. Nevertheless a liberal consensus took shape in the decade following World War II and was at its peak from the mid 1950s to the mid 1960s. It was the product of the historical circumstances of the postwar era. In Godfrey Hodgson's words, the liberal consensus was "the operational creed of a great nation at the height of its confidence and power".

At the time, however, "liberal consensus" was not a term employed by anyone to describe the state of American politics. The nature of the liberal consensus was far easier to perceive when it no longer existed than during its heyday. The postwar era had its share of conflict and controversy, notably the McCarthyite Red Scare, the violent response of the white South to the emergence of the civil rights movement, and the "missile gap" issue of the late 1950s. To contemporaries, the political disputes of the period may well have appeared more significant than its consensual issues. Nevertheless there was broad agreement on important matters and this molded the fundamental character of

1

American political history between 1945 and 1965. In essence there was consensus about the capacity of American capitalism, assisted by a moderate degree of economic management by government, to create widespread prosperity; the desirability of preserving and modestly extending the New Deal legacy; and the necessity of combatting the threat of world communism.

In reality, of course, the liberal consensus was basically centrist. As Godfrey Hodgson observed, "It was born of a fusion of certain elements from both liberal and conservative tradition. Specifically it came into existence . . . when most conservatives came to accept some of the economic and domestic policies of Rooseveltian liberalism, while many liberals adopted a foreign policy whose major premise was the kind of anticommunism that had once been the mark of conservatives." It should also be emphasized that the liberal consensus set narrower limits for the role of government in domestic affairs than did the social democratic consensus which developed in postwar Britain. This difference was inevitable in view of Britain's stronger collectivist traditions, the egalitarian ideals about postwar society that infused the government and people of Britain during the nation's darkest hours in World War II, and the fact that Britain possessed in the Labour Party a far more left-wing mainstream political party than existed in the United States.

The moderate nature of the liberal consensus can be highlighted by a brief description of the social democratic consensus that prevailed in Britain and was accepted by the main political parties from 1945 until the late 1970s. Its core elements were: Keynesian management of the economy by government to ensure full employment; a mixed economy in which certain strategic industries like coal, utilities, and railways came under public ownership and other enterprises remained in private hands; development of the welfare state (including establishment of the National Health Service and expansion of free education, public housing, sickness benefits, and family allowances) to ensure universal and free welfare benefits; conciliation of trade unions by government; progressive taxation to reduce income inequality and redistribute wealth; and in foreign policy, decolonization of the British empire, support for the United States in the Cold War, and (more tenuously) acceptance that Britain should be in the European Community.

America's liberal consensus had more in common with the kind of social market consensus which developed in West Germany in the early 1950s and still exists (perhaps less securely) in the unified Germany of the early 1990s. The West Germans regarded the private market system as the motor of economic advance. In practice, however, their governments pursued somewhat more interventionist economic and social policies than those of postwar America in order to ensure the social responsibility of the market. This has involved a policy of steering rather than planning and of working through market forces rather than attempting to set them aside in order to promote full employment and spread the benefits of prosperity.

The postwar consensus survived much longer in West Germany and even Britain than in the United States, where the early collapse of the liberal consensus was due in large part to the fact that it rested on flawed assumptions. American capitalism was not as successful as was believed. It could not eliminate poverty, economic inequality, and social conflict at home. Furthermore, the United States exaggerated the danger of world communism and overcommitted itself abroad in its efforts to contain it. To make matters worse, America's political, economic, intellectual and media elites defined the limits of political debate during the two postwar decades in such a way as to leave the United States unprepared for the problems that confronted it at home and abroad in the second half of the 1960s.

People of plenty

Prosperity was the most important prop of the liberal consensus. Paradoxically, at the end of World War II many Americans had been worried that the return of peace would be accompanied by high unemployment. Memories were still strong that it had been the onset of war which revitalized American industry and ended the Great Depression of the 1930s. However, popular anxiety about a peacetime slump proved groundless. The US economy experienced inevitable contraction in the period of reconversion to civilian production but this was short-lived. Gross National Product (GNP) soon rose again and surpassed its wartime high in 1950. The next decade was a time of unprecedented prosperity, consumerism, and economic optimism. Never before in America's history, or any other nation's, had so many people enjoyed such a high standard of living.

In 1960 the United States, which had only 6 per cent of the world's population, was producing and consuming over a quarter of the world's goods and services. Measured in constant 1958 dollars, GNP rose from $227 billion in 1940 to $355 billion in 1950 and to $488 billion in 1960.

As the economy reached new heights, Americans brought home bigger pay packets and had more money to spend than ever before. Real purchasing power increased by 22% between 1946 and 1960. By 1956 the real income of the average American was more than 50% greater than it had been in the pre-Depression year of 1929, and by 1960 it was 35% higher than in 1945. The good times got even better in the 1960s. Real purchasing power grew by 38% during this decade. The proportion of families and unattached individuals with an annual income of $10,000 or more (in 1968 values) stood at 33% in 1968, compared with 9% in 1947.

A number of factors underlay this economic miracle. The United States enjoyed preeminence in world trade in large part because it had escaped the physical ravages of World War II suffered by other industrial nations. Moreover, much of the money earned by American workers in the full-employment war economy had gone into savings accounts because of the unavailability of consumer goods. The peacetime release of pent-up consumer demand gave the reconverted economy an immense boost, and the easy availability of low-interest credit kept the boom going long after wartime savings had been spent. Massive demand for housing placed the construction industry at the forefront of the postwar economy. Very little homebuilding had taken place during the depressed 1930s and the war years, even though the number of households had increased by 8 million (26%) between 1929 and 1945. The postwar baby boom added to the pressure for new family homes. As a result over 13 million new dwelling units — 11 million of them in the suburbs — were built in the 1950s. By 1960 a quarter of the nation's housing stock was less than a decade old. Suburban development required new roads, schools, shopping malls, public buildings, all of which kept construction on the crest of a long boom. It also generated demand for automobiles, another cornerstone of the postwar economy. From a low base in the final year of the war, the sale of new cars climbed steadily to reach a peak of 7.4 million in 1955.

Prosperity encouraged business to increase investment, which further boosted economic expansion. Research and development expenditure nearly quadrupled between 1953 and 1964 and did much to boost new growth industries, particularly electronics, chemicals and plastics. It also spawned technological innovation which resulted in increased automation in the workplace. Business plowed some $10 billion a year into new plant and equipment (especially computers) between 1946 and 1958. The result was a 35% increase in total productivity in the ten years after the war. By 1960 it took only 160 man-hours to produce a car, compared with 310 in 1945. Many of these innovations were only affordable to big business, so technological development inevitably promoted the concentration of industrial ownership. By 1968 the 200 largest manufacturing corporations held the same proportion of manufacturing assets as the largest thousand had in 1941.

Yet as the historian William Leuchtenburg noted, "[I]f corporations played a stellar role in promoting economic growth, they had to share the limelight with government." The Servicemen's Readjustment Act of 1944, better known as the GI Bill of Rights, helped to underwrite postwar prosperity. It provided returning veterans with benefits that included living allowances and tuition payments for those who wanted a college degree or technical training, guaranteed loans of up to $2000 for those seeking to establish a small business, and — most importantly — furnished assistance with homebuying. The GI bill thus fueled the post-war housing boom and made possible the education of a generation of professionals, managers, and skilled workers who went on to take well-paid jobs in the booming economy.

Moreover, the public sector did not shrink back to its pre-New Deal/World War II size with the advent of peace and prosperity. Government jobs — at federal, state and local levels — comprised the fastest growing segment of the postwar labor market. More than 8 million people were employed in this work by 1957, double the number in 1940, and the bulk of these were in white-collar jobs. In 1955 government (all levels combined) was responsible for one-fifth of total purchases in the private sector, making it by far the largest buyer, and overall public spending accounted for 25% of GNP, compared with 10% in 1929. This development was partly due to the legacy of the 1930s but it also reflected the needs of the Cold War. By far the biggest item in the federal budget was defense. The Korean war caused military spending to rise from $13 billion in 1949 to $50 billion in 1953. Peace brought about some reduction in defense expenditure, but it remained on a high plateau of $35–40 billion for the remainder of the 1950s and escalated sharply early in the next decade. By 1960 Washington was financing about half of all research and development undertaken in the United States because of the need for ever more sophisticated weaponry to wage the Cold War. The main beneficiary was the electronics industry, which rose from the nation's forty-ninth largest industry in 1939 to fifth largest by 1956.

Nevertheless, extreme disparities of wealth remained a feature of

American society. Low-income groups were substantially better off than in the past, of course, but the distribution of wealth between each quintile (fifth) of income earners was more or less the same in 1970 as it had been in 1947. In effect, everybody's income had risen at approximately the same rate, leaving their ratios unaffected. Moreover, only a minority of Americans enjoyed true affluence in the so-called affluent society. By 1967 just one in eight families had an annual income of $15,000, the level defined by the Bureau of Labor Statistics as the lower limit of affluence. The majority of Americans had a comfortable standard of living, but did not wallow in the lap of luxury. Some three out of five families who could be classified as near-affluent depended on more than one wage earner to achieve this status. Americans who were neither truly affluent nor poor relied on credit to give them access to the accoutrements of affluence. The estimated annual installment credit oustanding skyrocketed from $4 billion in 1946 to $34 billion in 1957 and to over $89 billion in 1969. By the 1960s American families were on average saving only 5% of their income, compared with savings levels of 10–20% in most other industrialized nations.

Meanwhile, poverty not affluence was the way of life for nearly a quarter of the nation. In 1962 about 42.5 million Americans lived in poverty (defined as an annual income below $4,000 for a family of four, or below $2,000 for a single person). Poverty affected both ends of the age scale. Senior citizens living on inadequate pensions made up a quarter of the poor, and youngsters aged under eighteen constituted a third. Many of the young lived in female-headed families, whose members accounted for a quarter of the poor. Race and racial discrimination were also powerful factors in poverty. One-fifth of the poor were non-white, including nearly half of all black Americans and more than half of all Native Americans. In an age when education was increasingly necessary to advance in the job market, two-thirds of the poor lived in households headed by a person with an eighth-grade education or less. Finally, poverty afflicted the victims of economic modernization, notably low-skilled workers displaced by automation, residents of depressed areas like the Appalachians, and small farmers and farm workers at a time when mechanization and large farm units increasingly dominated agriculture.

Whatever the limitations of affluence, popular satisfaction with the economic system was strong. Public opinion surveys showed that Americans in the postwar era had only one major concern — fear of another war — and generally exuded confidence about the state of the nation and a way of life that promised continued betterment. The fact that so many people were willing to go into debt in order to finance their consumption was an indication that they expected the good times to last and the pain of repayment to be eased by rising wages. The optimism of younger Americans was buttressed by marked improvements in their educational status. A college degree was the key to advancement in the mushrooming management and professional sectors of the labor market. By 1970, three out of every four students graduated from high school (three out of four failed to get beyond eighth grade in 1920), and five times as many Americans were studying for a college degree as in 1940. The economic perspective of the majority of adult Americans in the postwar decades was also conditioned by memories of the 1930s. Few of them could have doubted that the late 1940s and 1950s were very good times by comparison. Even those living in poverty were poor only by American standards rather than global ones. At the end of the 1960s, for example, 41% of poor families had cars, 62% had central heating, and 99% had refrigerators.

The mood of satisfaction was exemplified by the trade unions. The labor militancy of the 1930s became a historical relic. Prosperity was one reason for this, but there were other factors. The union movement largely purged itself of communist and radical influences during the early stages of the Cold War. The Taft-Hartley Act of 1947 rescinded some of the gains made by unions under the New Deal, and made it much more difficult for them to organize new industries that were developing in the emergent Sunbelt economy of the South and Southwest. The consequences of economic modernization also worked against organized labor. Union membership rose by 40% in numerical terms between 1945 and 1970, but it declined as a proportion of the even more rapidly growing total work force. By 1956 white-collar workers, who were resistant to unionization, outnumbered blue-collar workers.

In these circumstances the larger unions abandoned social activism and integrated into the postwar corporate economy to pursue improved conditions and benefits through a private, depoliticized system of collective bargaining. Most of them (notably the automobile, construction, electrical, rubber, steel, and Teamsters unions) succeeded in winning long-term contracts which gave members job security and a guaranteed annual wage in return for a no-strike pledge. They also took collective bargaining into the realm of "welfare bargaining" to secure healthcare benefits and pension agreements from employers. All this led *Fortune* magazine to conclude that unions had "made the worker, to an amazing degree, a middle class member of a middle class society".

Government and the economy

The liberal consensus acknowledged that government had a significant role in managing the economy and maintaining prosperity. The economic activism of the state was a legacy of the New Deal. During the Great Depression of the 1930s the Democratic administration of Franklin D. Roosevelt had departed from the American tradition of limited government and instituted economic recovery measures that were broadly (though not explicitly) Keynesian in their concern to use the powers of the state to boost consumption and spread the fruits of capitalism more widely within society. Nevertheless, contained within the New Deal were different varieties of economic liberalism, which some scholars have conceptualized as "social Keynesianism" and "commercial Keynesianism". The eventual ascendancy of "commercial Keynesianism" had immense significance for the political economy of postwar America.

Proponents of so-called "social Keynesianism" advocated government regulation of business practices, redistribution of wealth, and expansion of the public sector economy to compensate for the inadequacies of the depressed private sector. However, the interruption of economic recovery by the Roosevelt Recession of 1937–8 persuaded other New Dealers that government had to make greater use of its fiscal and monetary powers to stimulate the private economy. Roosevelt, it should be noted, had hitherto run deficit budgets in every year of his presidency, but these were regarded as stop-gap measures to finance emergency needs while the foundations of economic recovery were being laid by the structural and social reforms of the New Deal.

The "commercial Keynesians" wanted fiscal policy to be the core element of economic strategy. In essence, as historian Alan Brinkley observed, they believed that the role of the state should be to "compensate for capitalism's inevitable flaws and omissions without interfering with its internal workings". This credo eschewed wealth redistribution and lauded a high consumption economy as the key to prosperity. In its view government programs that pumped spending power into the economy — whether through public works, social security, minimum wage legislation, tax cuts, credit relaxation, and so forth — were the most efficient means of creating the requisite level of demand. Such thinking became the new Democratic orthodoxy in World War II, when confidence in American capitalism was revitalized by full employment and the production miracles routinely performed by industry.

By 1945 the liberal wing of the Democratic party was largely committed to the view that economic growth was a more effective guarantor of social progress than regulation and redistribution. It envisaged that the federal government would use its fiscal powers of spending and taxation to ensure full employment in the peacetime economy, as Roosevelt had promised in the 1944 election campaign. However, efforts to promote a legislative commitment to this end were thwarted by a coalition of Republicans and conservative Democrats in Congress and the lobbying activities of big business. Instead, a compromise measure, the Employment Act of 1946, established the Council of Economic Advisers (CEA) to assist the president in the task of economic management and prescribed in vague terms that government should expedite the process by which business maximized investment, production, employment and income levels within society.

The United States was one of only two industrial democracies (Canada was the other) which did not institute a postwar economic policy formally giving priority to continued full employment. Liberal Democrats swallowed their disappointment at this outcome because it soon became apparent that the economy did not need to be underwritten by government guarantees of full employment in the postwar years. In 1945 sixty million jobs had been considered the hallmark of a full-employment economy, but total employment stood at 64 million by 1952. The economic policies of the Democratic administration of Harry S. Truman became fully attuned to the successful operation of a high-consumption capitalist economy. CEA chairman Leon Keyserling preached the gospel of economic growth and reassured the corporate community that the Democrats wanted to enlarge the economic pie rather than reslice it. Truman's budgets provided a massive boost to purchasing power. Their scale dwarfed Roosevelt's spending in the depressed 1930s, thanks in the main to increased defense expenditure, but also in part to expanded domestic commitments. The Truman administration also sought to ensure harmony between supply and demand. Faced with a mild recession in 1949, it ran compensatory budget deficits which helped to limit the decline in consumption and boost rapid recovery. Conversely, when inflation rose sharply because of tight supply conditions during the Korean war, Truman imposed wage and price controls, tighter credit and tax surcharges to douse demand.

The election in 1952 of Dwight D. Eisenhower, the first Republican president since Herbert Hoover, did not produce a marked change of course in economic policy. In contrast to the 1930s, the parties were no longer divided on the issue of whether government should manage the economy. Eisenhower recognized that a strong economy was vital to wage the Cold War. He was also anxious to rescue the Republican party from its politically crippling Depression-era image of Hooverite do-nothingism. His use of budget deficits to combat the post-Korean war recession of 1953–4 signified the relaxation of traditional Republican insistence on balanced budgets and placed a bipartisan seal of approval on the use of compensatory deficits to reverse economic decline. Eisenhower repeated this medicine when a more serious recession hit the economy in 1957–8. The fiscal 1959 budget deficit of $12.4 billion was by far the biggest to date in peacetime.

This did not mean that the Eisenhower era was free from political dispute over the economy. In the late 1950s controversy developed over the issues of inflation and growth. Eisenhower regarded an inflation-free economy as the prerequisite for sustainable economic growth. In the opinion of most Democrats, however, growth was linked with increased productivity and was therefore the best safeguard against inflation. This view was shared by liberal Republicans, like Governor Nelson A. Rockefeller of New York, and even some members of Eisenhower's own administration, notably Vice-President Richard M. Nixon. The debate was fueled by the Soviet launch of the Sputnik satellites in 1957, which prompted concern that Russia was forging ahead of the United States in missile development. Republicans like Nixon and Rockefeller basically agreed with the Democrats that only a faster growing economy could keep America ahead in the arms race. Though less concerned about social justice than the party of Roosevelt, they also recognized that GOP electoral prospects would benefit if the Republicans could harvest the political fruits of expanded prosperity.

The annual inflation rate in the 1953–60 period hovered around 2%. This was minute in comparison with what the United States later experienced in the 1970s, and was well below the inflation rate of the 1980s, supposedly a low-inflation era. Yet Eisenhower worried, almost to the point of obsession, about the long-term impact of "creeping inflation" on prices and the value of the dollar. As a result the fiscal and monetary policies of his administration tended to be modestly restrictive rather than expansionary. Except in times of recession, Eisenhower was anxious to keep public spending under tight rein in order that federal demand for goods and services did not strain the economy. He succeeded in balancing the budget on three occasions, a feat that none of his successors has come close to emulating. Nevertheless, fiscal restraint helped to slow down the annual rate of economic growth from 4.3% in the 1947–52 period to 2.5% in 1953–60. This development had implications for the global position of the United States. By the late 1950s the Soviet Union's growth rate was more than three times as high as America's, (though, of course, this reflected the very low base from which its economy had started to expand). More ominously, the United States faced a renewed challenge in world trade from Western Europe and Japan, whose economies had made a rapid recovery from World War II. Meanwhile, recurrent recessions in 1957–8 and 1960–1 aroused concern at home that sluggish growth was eroding the economy's capacity to sustain full employment.

Slow growth left Eisenhower economics politically discredited. In the 1960 presidential election both the Democratic and Republican candidates, respectively John F. Kennedy and Richard Nixon, ran on platforms promising government action to boost the rate of economic growth. For the Democrats, in particular, growth was the key to all good things. Under this banner, they promised social justice to low-income Americans, greater material abundance to the expanding middle class, the replenishment of public services, and a build-up of military power to strengthen the nation's security. Kennedy synthesized all these goals into a single pledge to get the country moving again in the 1960s.

The Kennedy administration pursued an economic policy that CEA chairman Walter H. Heller described as "Keynes cum growth". It sought not only high rates of utilization of manpower and available capacity, but also continuous expansion of capacity and the closing of the gap between actual income and the economy's expanding potential. The priority was no longer full employment *per se* but the expansion of potential output (the supply side) and the achievement of balance between income (the demand side) and output. In essence, the new economics of the 1960s represented the ultimate expression of the "commercial Keynesianism" which had become the guiding principle of Democratic economics during World War II.

The New Deal political order

The importance of the New Deal to the liberal consensus extended beyond political economy. Its legacy shaped domestic policy and party politics during the postwar era. As historians Gary Gerstle and Steve Fraser observed, the New Deal had created a political order which possessed "an ideological character, a moral perspective, and a set of political relationships between policy elites, interest groups, and electoral constituencies". New Deal liberalism (in the form that developed in World War II) engendered the ideological assumptions of the liberal consensus about the prospects for the widespread distribution of prosperity within an expanding capitalist economy. The New Deal's moral commitment to social activism on behalf of lower-income groups continued to mold public policy in the postwar era. Finally, for nearly a quarter-century after World War II, American politics was dominated to a large extent by the Democratic political coalition that the New Deal had created.

Notwithstanding its many limitations as a reform program, the New Deal did seek to improve conditions of life for low-income Americans. Among other things, it established the rudiments of an American welfare state, it gave assistance to hard-pressed farmers, it provided federal aid for public housing construction to rehouse slum dwellers, and it enacted legislative guarantees of workers' rights. Many of these initiatives may have been modest in scope, but they constituted a distinct break from the American traditions of limited government, and they laid foundations that would be built upon by postwar administrations.

Roosevelt's programs also changed the partisan loyalties of millions of voters, and mobilized the support of millions of others who had previously been nonvoters. As a result the Democrats replaced the Republicans as the majority party. Traditionally strong in the rural South and West, the party became increasingly identified with new power bases in the urban-industrial states of the North in the 1930s. The New Deal made the Democrats into a party of mass strength on mass issues. It created a new voter coalition that included trade unionists, blue-collar workers, Roman Catholics, ethnics of southern European and eastern European descent, Jews, blacks, and white southerners. The groups who made up this polyglot coalition were mainly urban and working class — except for white southerners, whose loyalty to the Democrats dated back beyond the Civil War and cut across socioeconomic and demographic lines. The changed nature of the Democratic party was indicated by the new relationship that it developed with organized labor, particularly the industrial unions that formed the CIO in 1936. The unions became a virtual adjunct to the party, helping to finance it and gaining influence in return within Democratic policymaking circles.

The Democratic party continued to be a New Deal party in the postwar era. For a quarter-century after Roosevelt's death in 1945, every serious candidate for the Democratic presidential nomination claimed to be his political legatee. The support of congressional Democrats from northern states for the New Deal and its legacy actually strengthened in the postwar era. Older, conservative northern Democrats, who had frequently opposed Roosevelt's programs in the 1930s, were replaced in the 1940s and 1950s by a new generation of younger, liberal-inclined Democrats. The newcomers included Senators Paul Douglas (Illinois), Hubert Humphrey (Minnesota), John F. Kennedy (Massachusetts), and Edmund Muskie (Maine).

The Democrats also remained the majority party because of the continuing electoral popularity of the New Deal. They won three out of five presidential elections from 1948 to 1964, and only surrendered control of Congress for two brief periods, in 1947–8 and 1953–4. During this era the party identification of the electorate remained remarkably similar to what it had been in the late 1930s. On average, nearly half of voters identified themselves as Democrats, 30% as Republicans and 20% as independents. Nor was there a decline in the proportion of voters identifying themselves as strong rather than weak partisans. What did decline in the postwar era was the class basis of partisanship. Democrats made gains among young middle-class voters from Republican families who were more receptive than their elders to the activist philosophy of the New Deal. They also retained the support of most of those Americans — or their children — who made the transition from the working class to either the blue-collar middle class or the professional/managerial middle class in the boom years of the 1940s and 1950s. Nevertheless the bedrock of Democratic support came from voters in the lower half of the income distribution. In 1948 Harry S. Truman was backed by 57% of white voters of low socioeconomic status (ses), 43% of middle ses whites, and 30% of high ses whites. Twelve years later John F. Kennedy's support among these groups was 61%, 53%, and 38% respectively.

The typical Democratic voter of the postwar era had a job, was neither affluent nor poor, and had a higher income than anything he or she had previously enjoyed. The strong emotional loyalties formed in the 1930s constituted one reason for continuing identification with the party of Roosevelt. Rational considerations were also significant. Millions of blue-collar voters, whether part of the working class or lower middle class, were grateful to the Democrats for their prosperity and looked to them for the preservation of it. This was certainly true of organized labor. The increasingly cosy relationship that the unions developed with business in the 1950s did not mean that they had forsaken a political role. In fact the links between labor and the Democrats grew ever closer in the postwar years. One reason for this was the anxiety of union leaders to prevent further erosion of labor rights, following the enactment of the Taft-Hartley bill by a Republican-controlled Congress. They also recognized that some matters of direct concern to workers, such as healthcare, employment safety, disability pensions, and unemployment insurance, could not be resolved solely through collective bargaining, and had to be addressed in the legislative arena. Finally, the unions were anxious to ensure that government would promptly implement Keynesian compensatory measures whenever the economy was threatened by recession.

The New Deal's enduring appeal compelled its acceptance by the GOP. Moderate and liberal Republicans had come to this conclusion in the late 1930s. Dominant in the presidential wing of the party, they nominated presidential candidates (Wendell Willkie in 1940 and Thomas E. Dewey in 1944 and 1948) who were not hostile to the New Deal. It took another ten years before the Republican right, which was dominant in the congressional wing of the party, resentfully came to terms with political reality. Conservative Republicans had commenced what they hoped would be a roll-back of much of the New Deal during the 80th Congress of 1947–8, but this assault came to an abrupt halt with Harry S. Truman's upset reelection victory in 1948. Though every opinion poll predicted that he would lose, Truman won because he convinced voters that the New Deal would not be safe in Republican hands. The electorate also rejected the record of the 80th Congress by restoring the Democratic majority in the House and Senate.

After this debacle the Republicans took care not to make themselves vulnerable again to the kind of "bloody shirt" campaign waged by Truman. In the 1952 elections the New Deal was no longer an issue. The Democrats lost because voters were disillusioned by the Korean War stalemate, the communists-in-government issue, and corruption scandals in the Truman administration. They could elect Dwight D. Eisenhower president secure in the knowledge that neither he nor his party would threaten Roosevelt's legacy. The GOP had come to offer voters an echo not a choice with regard to the New Deal. It departed from this new orthodoxy only once, with predictably disastrous consequences. In 1964 frustrated right-wingers succeeded in nominating Senator Barry M. Goldwater (Arizona), an unreconstructed anti-New Dealer, as Republican presidential candidate. In the ensuing election the Democrats went on to win the largest share of the popular vote (61.1%) in US history.

The enmity of big business towards the New Deal also declined. The process of accommodation had began during the Depression, at the very time that many corporate leaders were denouncing Roosevelt's expansion of governmental power as socialistic and being denounced by him in turn as "economic royalists". Many capital-intensive industries (notably corporations engaged in electronics, oil, and communications), investment banks, and internationally-oriented commercial banks aligned themselves with the Democrats from 1935 onwards. Firms in these sectors did not feel threatened by the pro-union stand of the New Deal because they were not labor-intensive, and they recognized that meliorative social reforms constituted the best means of restoring political stability and subduing radical influences. What attracted them to the New Deal above all else, however, were Roosevelt's efforts to stabilize the dollar and his commitment to replace Republican protectionism with free trade. These policies were in fundamental accord with their own interests in an expanded international economy.

Representatives of the pro-New Deal business bloc, such as Averell Harriman, James Forrestal, and Robert Lovett gained important positions in the Truman and Kennedy administrations. They were particularly influential in shaping the foreign policies and the international economic policies of these governments. Their voices were also raised in support of expansionary economic policies. Similar views began to be expressed on this score by corporate leaders in labor-intensive manufacturing industries, formerly the main source of business hostility to the New Deal, when economic growth slowed down at the end of the Eisenhower era. These businessmen were also reassured by organized labor's new moderation, and by the Democratic party's retreat from regulatory liberalism, signaled by its toleration of the postwar trend towards concentrated ownership of industry. As a result, it was hardly surprising that the majority of the corporate community came out in support of Lyndon B. Johnson in the 1964 election.

Widespread acceptance of the New Deal did not mean that there was broad support for an expanded reform agenda in the postwar era. The fate of the Fair Deal, Truman's second-term program, made this clear. It had considerable success in broadening the furrows already plowed by the New Deal, but it did not produce a harvest of new governmental activism. Truman's greatest achievement was the Social Security Act of 1950, which extended the coverage of the New Deal-created social insurance programs to an additional ten and a half million Americans and raised benefit levels by an average of eighty per cent. He also enacted a far more substantial public housing program than FDR had ever managed. Other successes that extended the New Deal legacy included an improved wages and hours statute, conservation measures, and natural resource development. However, Truman was unable to enact new reforms, most notably civil rights, federal aid to education, the Brannan farm program combining low consumer prices with high farm income, and a national health insurance plan. All these measures fell foul of the congressional coalition of Republicans and conservative Democrats. Meanwhile, public opinion was at best apathetic towards the Fair Deal. In contrast to the 1930s, most Americans did not feel that new programs were needed.

In spite of these defeats, political debate over domestic reform continued to focus on the unfinished agenda of the Fair Deal for the next decade and a half. Most of Truman's new proposals constituted a logical progression of the New Deal heritage of social activism by government. This was even true of civil rights, about which the New Deal had been silent. Blacks had joined the Democratic coalition in the 1930s out of gratitude for Roosevelt's relief and welfare measures, but their desire for civil rights could not be ignored for long. Their numbers swollen by wartime migration from the South, black voters had become crucial to Democratic success in many northern industrial states by 1948. In recognition of this, and out of a sense of moral idealism, Truman committed himself to the black cause. In 1949 he proposed legislation to outlaw the poll tax, make lynching a federal crime, end segregation in interstate transport, and establish a permanent Fair Employment Practices Commission, but this was defeated in Congress. In spite of this failure, Truman had succeeded in bringing civil rights into the mainstream of the nation's political agenda for the first time.

The expansion of the liberal consensus to include much of Truman's agenda proved a slow process. Eisenhower, who characterized his political philosophy variously as "conservative progressivism" and "dynamic conservatism", initially drew the line against new reforms, but built on the New Deal in a manner that embodied his concerns with efficiency and cost-effectiveness. His administration created the Department of Health, Education and Welfare to administer federal social services, sanctioned another major expansion of Social Security (a self-financed program), and raised the minimum wage (which did not cost government a cent). It also initiated the interstate highway system (financed by new taxes on road users), the largest public works program in US history. Slowly but surely, however, Eisenhower also came under pressure to move in the direction defined by the Fair Deal.

The Soviet technological triumph in launching the Sputniks led directly to the first federal-aid-to-education legislation, the National Defense Education Act of 1958, which provided funds to improve the quality of science education. Meanwhile, the bulge in the school-age population caused by the postwar baby boom put increasing pressure on the resources of the states, who were traditionally responsible for managing and financing the nation's schools. By 1960 the leadership of both parties accepted that general federal aid to education was necessary, but disagreement over the details impeded the enactment of legislation. Eisenhower would only support emergency funding for school construction, but most Democrats favored long-term assistance that included aid for teachers' salaries.

The Republicans also shifted their position on health insurance in response to growing public concern about the escalating costs of medical care. As with education, the Eisenhower era ended with both parties agreed in principle about the need for federal health insurance for the aged but unable to agree on legislative details. The GOP wanted a voluntary scheme for private insurance, financed through a combination of personal premium payments and federal subsidies, while most Democrats favored a compulsory program, financed through social security contributions. Meanwhile, the emergence of black protest in the mid-1950s increased pressure for civil rights. New laws were enacted with bipartisan support in 1957 and 1960 to protect black voting rights in the South. These were limited measures that lacked effective enforcement mechanisms, but they were significant as the first federal civil rights legislation since the 1870s. In essence they opened the way for the eventual enactment of more comprehensive laws.

Contrary to the expectations of most Democrats, Kennedy's election as president did not enable them to bring the emergent consensus on these issues to legislative fruition. The main obstacle to further reform in the early 1960s was the congressional coalition of right-wing Republicans and conservative Democrats, whose existence dated back to the Roosevelt era. This informal alliance had previously stymied the expansion of the New Deal after 1938 and had limited Truman's success as a reformer. Though its ranks had thinned out over time, it was still powerful. Conservative Republicans, who had very reluctantly acceded to Eisenhower's modest reform proposals in the late 1950s, were not willing to go along with the more liberal measures now sought by a Democratic president. Meanwhile, their Democratic counterparts, who had formerly included northerners, had become almost entirely southern in composition during the postwar era. It was the latter who were the mainstay of the conservative coalition in the early 1960s.

White southerners had grown increasingly disenchanted with the national Democratic party after 1945. Having accepted federal activism as the only hope of economic salvation in the 1930s, the states of the old Confederacy reasserted their customary Jeffersonian preferences for limited national government in the postwar era. Preservation of states' rights was deemed essential to safeguard Dixie's racial system. In 1948 the inclusion of a civil rights commitment in the Democratic national party platform prompted the formation of a southern splinter party, the States' Rights Democrats. Its hope was to prevent Truman from winning the South's electoral college votes, thereby ensuring the election of a Republican president. Although this tactic failed and the new party was quickly disbanded, the 1948 election marked the beginnings of the steady defection of a core constituency from the New Deal presidential coalition.

Nevertheless the South's alignment with the Democratic party at congressional level remained solid. In 1960, 94% of its seats in the House of Representatives and all its Senate seats were held by Democrats. Not all southern congressmen were unreconstructed conservatives on racial issues, of course, but those who were constituted a powerful impediment to the enactment of a strong civil rights bill and of other measures which impinged on racial issues, notably aid to education. Moreover, thanks to the seniority system that rewarded unbroken tenure of office, many long-serving congressmen from the one-party South held the chairmanships of important congressional committees. As a result conservative southerners, like Representative Howard Smith (Virginia), and Senators James Eastland (Mississippi), Richard Russell

(Georgia), Harry Byrd (Virginia), and Willis Robertson (Virginia), wielded great power over legislation.

On the other hand blacks were no longer prepared to endure their status as second-class citizens in the South. In 1954, under the leadership of new Chief Justice Earl Warren, the Supreme Court had ruled in its landmark judgement, *Brown* v. *Topeka Board of Education*, that segregated schools were inherently unequal and that segregation was a denial of equal protection of the laws. This decision reversed the "separate but equal" doctrine that had legitimized segregation since the *Plessy* v. *Ferguson* judgement of 1896. It therefore brought into question the constitutionality of the "Jim Crow" state laws that underpinned segregation in the South. It also encouraged blacks to become more assertive in demanding civil rights. Black protest, which began with the Montgomery bus boycott of 1955, reached new peaks in the early 1960s, with student sit-ins at segregated lunch-counters, the Freedom Rides, and the demonstrations in Birmingham, Alabama. A hesitant Kennedy had sought to defer civil rights legislation until his second term, in the hope that his reelection would give him a clear mandate on the issue. However, the violent reaction of the white South to peaceful black protest activities eventually compelled him to propose a new bill in 1963. Kennedy was assassinated before the measure became law, but Lyndon Johnson was able to mold a broad consensus in the nation and Congress that it should be enacted in honor of the dead president's memory.

In many respects the Civil Rights Act of 1964 marked the high point of the liberal consensus. It also laid the foundations of a new federal activism on racial issues that would eventually do much to unravel this consensus. In addition to sweeping away the South's apartheid system, this measure empowered the Attorney-General to end school segregation, and it outlawed discrimination in employment on the grounds of race, gender, and national origin. Segregated schools were not confined to the South, of course. They existed on a *de facto* basis throughout the nation, because black communities remained trapped in impoverished inner city ghettoes at the time that many whites were migrating to the suburbs. Discriminatory employment practices were also widespread. Consequently, the new racial agenda of US politics would no longer be confined to issues that could be treated as a regional aberrance.

The ongoing black struggle for civil rights would increasingly become a quest for economic equality. As a result it became entwined with the problem of poverty within the affluent society. Renewed concern about poverty raised questions about the adequacy of public welfare. The New Deal had bequeathed a two-tier federal welfare state. One tier consisted of social insurance programs (unemployment compensation, widows and survivors' pensions, old age pensions, and — from 1956 — disability insurance), financed by social security taxes on employers and employees. Everyone covered by these programs qualified for payouts, even though many recipients were neither poor nor needy. The other consisted of "categorical" public assistance programs, whereby the federal government gave funds to the states on a "matching grant" basis to assist specified groups among the needy, notably the blind, aged, and families with dependent children. Such a system made recipients dependent to a significant extent on the ability, and indeed the willingness, of the states to provide generous assistance that Washington could match. Even so, they were better placed than those among the poor who did not qualify for categorical aid and had to rely on "general assistance" programs financed entirely by states and localities.

The difference between what became known as "social security" and "welfare" was clear — one rewarded people for working, the other paid them for not working. Roosevelt had anticipated that the social security system, established in 1935, would eventually become the mainstay of the welfare state. This was effectively achieved by the Social Security Act of 1950. For the next decade and a half the public assistance programs experienced what can best be described as a period of benign neglect. During this time the liberal consensus about the welfare state rested on what Edward Berkowitz has described as "an idealized picture of a person who maintained a steady relationship with his employer and the state". New thinking was required before social welfare policy could truly improve the lives of the poorest groups in society.

The Cold War consensus

The liberal consensus also embraced foreign affairs. The isolationist mood of the 1930s, which had made American entry in World War II both reluctant and late, had evaporated in the crucible of global conflict. The United States emerged from the war with a new sense both of its power and its international responsibility. Its leaders enthusiastically embarked on the task of shaping the world to American preferences. They soon came to regard the Soviet Union as a threat to freedom, liberty, and prosperity throughout the world. As a result the dominant characteristic of postwar American internationalism was anticommunism.

Scholars have long debated which side was responsible for the Cold War. The orthodox view is that the United States responded to Soviet aggression, while revisionists blame what they perceive as America's drive to establish hegemony over a capitalist world order. Other historians see Soviet-American tensions as rooted in mutual misperceptions about each other's motives. Regardless of where blame really lay, the indisputable fact is that postwar foreign policy debate in the United States centered on how best to deal with the threat of communism, rather than whether communism actually posed a threat.

The Cold War was more than just a conflict between two powers. It was also a struggle between diametrically opposite belief systems. Truman's address to Congress in March 1947, which formed the basis of what became known as the Truman Doctrine, was the seminal declaration of US purpose in the Cold War. The president avowed: "At the present moment in world history nearly every nation must choose between alternative ways of life. The choice is too often not a free one. . . . I believe that it must be the policy of the United States to support free peoples who are resisting subjugation by armed minorities or by outside pressures". The ideological nature of the conflict heightened confrontation and reduced the prospects for conciliation and compromise. America viewed itself as the leader of the "free world" and saw communism as a monolithic, Soviet-dominated force, intent on world domination. This vision of a global battle between good and evil meant that the advancement of communism anywhere was perceived as a defeat for the United States. It also made "free peoples" and "anticommunist" interchangeable terms in the American vocabulary. The Truman Doctrine, historian Stephen Ambrose has observed, "came close to shutting the door on any revolution" because all any dictatorship had to do to get American aid "was to claim that its opponents were Communist."

The willingness of American policymakers to undertake a crusade against communism also reflected their confidence that the United States had the resources to wage the Cold War. In the second half of the 1940s not only did the country possess an atomic monopoly but its conventional force superiority was also awesome. American military power was grounded in the wealth and productivity of the American economy. The war had ravaged the industrial capacity of other nations, including the Soviet Union's, but it had given America's a massive stimulus. In 1947 the United States produced about one half of the world's manufactures. Its lead was greatest in those industries which were vital to modern warfare, namely aviation, chemical engineering, and electronics. Nor did there seem any reason to believe that things would change in the near future, in view of the immense capital resources that American industry had available to invest in productivity-boosting modernization.

The Truman Doctrine of 1947 unveiled the strategy of containment that shaped US foreign policy for the next quarter-century. Containment was not a roll-back policy. According to State Department policy analyst George F. Kennan, who formulated its theoretical rationale, the aim was to prevent the expansion of communism in the expectation that this would cause the Soviet Union either to collapse under the pressure of its own internal weaknesses or to mellow as a regime. Containment doctrine, as Charles Kegley Jr and Eugene Wittkopf indicated, was based on the following corollary assumptions: the Soviet Union was inherently expansionist and sought to maximize communist power through military conquest and revolution; the Soviet goal of world domination was permanent and would succeed unless vigorously resisted; only the United States had the means to repel Soviet aggression; accordingly, the United States had to increase its power relative to the Soviet Union in order to ensure its capacity to contain Soviet expansion; appeasement could not work — to stop Soviet expansion, force had to be met with force; and the fate of the world was determined by Soviet-American relations — US relations with other nations were subordinate to the priority of competing with the Soviets.

A new national security apparatus was created to implement containment policy. The necessity for effective policy coordination and for speedy — often secret — decisionmaking ensured increasing presidential preeminence in foreign affairs. The National Security Act of 1947 institutionalized the "Cold War state" within the executive branch of government. It recognized the army, navy and air force as co-equal branches of the military and brought them under the control of a unified Department of Defense. It also created three new agencies: the National Security Council (NSC), to advise the president on security-related affairs; the National Security Resources Planning Board, to advise the president about the effect of security policy on the economy; and the Central Intelligence Agency (CIA), to coordinate overseas intelligence activities and analyze information acquired from these.

The Cold War also furthered the development of an "imperial presidency" that transgressed on congressional foreign policy powers. Troops were sent abroad without consultation, and in the cases of the Korean and Vietnam wars without a formal declaration of war by Congress. Executive agreements were entered into with foreign governments, and congressional efforts to limit presidential power to make such agreements were thwarted by the defeat in 1954 of the proposed constitutional amendment known as the Bricker Amendment. Finally, the doctrine of "executive privilege", established by Eisenhower in 1954, was used to legitimize presidential withholding of information from Congress.

Despite the Truman Doctrine's sweeping language, containment policy in its early stages did not entail global commitment. Between 1947 and 1949 the Truman administration prioritized the defense of Western Europe, the Middle East, Latin America and Japan, but held back from unlimited commitment to the imperilled Nationalist regime in China. Truman also kept defense spending within limits that he thought the nation could afford (about $12–14 billion annually), because the US monopoly in atomic weapons ensured security against Soviet attack. What changed things were the Soviet development of an atomic bomb in 1949, and the emergence of Asia as a Cold War battleground, following China's fall to communism in 1949 and the onset of the Korean war in 1950. The blueprint for the globalization of containment was NSC memorandum 68, approved by Truman in September 1950. This document reassessed America's security needs in response to the new international circumstances. It called for development of the hydrogen bomb to maintain America's nuclear superiority, a massive increase of conventional forces to meet the threat of communism wherever it occurred, and new aid programs and alliances to strengthen other free-world nations. The costs of all this would be immense. The authors of NSC-68 estimated that global security needs would require annual expenditure of some $50 billion, but they were confident that huge defense outlays would stimulate rather than weaken the US economy.

Truman's acceptance of the NSC-68 recommendations ended whatever prospect there had been of keeping the Cold War limited. The commitment to develop thermonuclear weaponry initiated a new and frightening arms race with the Soviets, which saw both sides eventually develop "nuclear overkill" capability. The American concept of a monolithic world communism was now carved in stone. Although the United States had adopted a friendly posture to communist Yugoslavia, which adopted an independent line from Moscow in 1948, it spurned further opportunities to sow divisions among communist nations. The new communist regime in Beijing was fearful of Soviet domination, and had raised the possibility of establishing ties with the United States as a counter to this. However, the Truman administration saw it as an agent of Soviet imperialism and continued to treat the deposed Nationalist regime, which took refuge on the island of Taiwan, as the sole government of China. The Korean war extinguished any prospect of rapprochement. For the next twenty years Sino-American relations would be characterized by extreme bitterness. US anticommunist involvement in Asia took another fateful step in 1950, with the decision to aid the efforts of the French colonial regime to crush the communist insurgency in Vietnam.

Containment strategy in its initial and expanded versions led the United States to give aid, economic or military, to over one hundred nations, and to enter into mutual defense treaties with more than forty countries. It also spawned a series of US-created regional alliances, notably the North Atlantic Treaty Organization (NATO), the Organization of American States, the Southeast Asia Treaty Organization, and various Middle East arrangements, such as the Baghdad Pact. America's naval forces patrolled the globe, and it deployed about a million soldiers in some four thousand bases in thirty countries. Intervention in the affairs of other nations became normal practice for the United States. Its involvement was overt and militaristic in Korea, Lebanon, the Dominican Republic, Laos, and South Vietnam. It took the form of covert operations by the CIA in many other countries, notably Italy, Iran, Guatemala, Cuba, the Philippines, and Indonesia.

Despite this global activism, containment entailed acceptance of communism where it already existed, and recognition of the realities of Soviet military power, especially its possession of atomic weaponry. The Cold War was different to any previous conflict in the history of mankind because both sides possessed weapons of mass destruction. Accordingly, efforts were made from time to time to relax Cold War tensions and reduce the dangers of nuclear war. Brief periods of detente occurred in 1955–6, 1959–60, and 1963–5. These did not result in progress towards resolution of fundamental Cold War problems, but some advancement was made in controlling the arms race. In 1963 the United States and the Soviet Union finally signed a treaty limiting nuclear tests to those areas which could be monitored without on-site inspection (the atmosphere, outer space, and underwater). This modest accomplishment was significant as the first arms control agreement of the nuclear age. Containment abroad was underpinned by consensus at home. There was an extraordinarily high degree of domestic agreement about the necessity of preventing communist expansion. Few groups or individuals raised their voices against the Cold War. Support for it came from all sections of society, including the media, business, labor unions, and the academic community. The Cold War consensus embraced all social groups, whether based on class, ethnicity, religion, region, race, or gender (though men were consistently more hard-line than women). Truman's 1947 address to Congress had been intended to arouse popular concern about the menace of communism, and it succeeded in doing so. From this time onwards opinion polls revealed strong public backing for containment, but it should be noted that most Americans were far more concerned about the Soviet Union as a threat to national security than on ideological grounds. Support for armed involvement abroad formed part of this consensus. Americans worried about the dangers of nuclear war more than anything and did not approve of military action against Soviet satellites, but they were willing to back military containment. Despite popular disillusion with the military stalemate in Korea, opinion polls conducted in 1951–2 found that most Americans (over 60%) believed that it was more important for the United States to keep communism from spreading than to stay out of another war like Korea.

Containment also had the support of both political parties. It was one of the few things on which conservative and liberal Democrats agreed. A group of the most left-wing Democrats, who wanted a conciliatory policy towards Russia, did mount a brief challenge to the Cold War consensus under the leadership of Henry Wallace, FDR's wartime vice-president. They formed a peace party, the Progressives, to contest the 1948 election, but this made little impact and quickly faded away. On the Republican side, the main dissent came from midwestern and western conservatives, who were traditionally skeptical of US involvement in Europe. Though trenchantly anticommunist, they voiced concern that the Marshall Plan and other costly forms of Truman Doctrine aid to Western Europe would bankrupt the nation. Their leader, Senator Robert A. Taft (Ohio), advocated reliance on air-atomic power to deter the Soviets, a strategy that various critics denigrated as "bargain-basement" containment and the "new isolationism". Nevertheless the Republican right became more belligerent when the

Cold War was extended to Asia. Appalled by the so-called "loss" of China, its supporters demanded a reallocation of American resources from Europe in favor of an "Asia First" policy that pursued liberation rather than mere containment. This conservative challenge faded away after Taft lost the 1952 Republican presidential nomination to the representative of the eastern-internationalist wing of the party, Dwight D. Eisenhower. As president, Eisenhower sustained Truman's policies, and was largely successful in converting recalcitrant Republicans to acceptance of Cold War globalism.

Bipartisan support for the Cold War did not prevent foreign policy from being a major bone of party contention. Accusations by the opposition party that the administration in office was losing the Cold War were a normal feature of US politics from the late 1940s onwards. The most virulent of these attacks was launched by Senator Joseph McCarthy (Wisconsin) against the Truman administration. He went so far as to question the loyalty of top officials, including Secretary of State Dean Acheson and Secretary of Defense George Marshall, and alleged that communist sympathizers in government were responsible for the loss of China and the lack of victory in the Korean war. Partisan calculation induced Taft and other GOP leaders to support these reckless charges. In turn the Republicans were embarrassed by Democratic charges that defense cuts made by Eisenhower in pursuit of a balanced budget had weakened America's security and undermined its global position. The choice facing the nation, John F. Kennedy said in 1960, was "which gamble . . . we take, our money or our survival".

Kennedy's determination to regain the global inititative that he accused Eisenhower of surrendering led to a hotting-up of the Cold War in the early 1960s. He presided over a new build-up of US military power, risked direct confrontation with the Soviets over Berlin and Cuba, and stepped up American efforts to combat communist influence in Third World countries. Yet Kennedy's actions were guided by the inherited doctrine and policies of containment. In spite of his grandiose rhetoric and his claims to stand for a new generation of leadership, he did not take US foreign policy in new directions. As Henry Kissinger later remarked, the Kennedy period should be seen as "the last flowering of the previous era rather than as the beginning of a new era".

*   *   *

American politics were to change markedly shortly after Kennedy's death in 1963. In the two decades following World War II, US economic power and international influence had been at their peak, and the New Deal legacy remained strong. National self-confidence had been at an all-time high. The liberal consensus was an outgrowth of this sense of wellbeing. In the mid 1960s, however, America entered an era of turmoil and uncertainty. This new era saw the relative decline of American economic and military power, and the advent of political problems that New Deal-influenced liberalism could not resolve. As a result the political economy of prosperity, the New Deal political order, and the Cold War consensus ceased to shape American politics. In other words, the liberal consensus became a historic relic.

2
The Unraveling of the Liberal Consensus, 1965–1968

At the start of 1965 few Americans could have realized that their nation was approaching a turning point in its postwar history. The liberal consensus that had shaped the course of US politics since 1945 was at high tide. America's international preeminence, its economic wellbeing, and the New Deal legacy seemed stronger than ever. John F. Kennedy's military build-up and his facing down of the Soviets over Cuba in 1962 had strengthened confidence in America's global superiority. Thanks to the tax-cutting "new economics" of the Kennedy-Johnson administrations, the economy was on the crest of its postwar boom. Finally, Lyndon B. Johnson's landslide victory in the 1964 election had destroyed the challenge of the Republican right and paved the way for the enactment of an ambitious program of liberal reforms. Nevertheless the decline of the liberal consensus from its zenith was rapid. By 1968 it had unraveled as a result of the Vietnam war, the onset of inflation, and the divisive impact of the Great Society on the New Deal political coalition.

The Vietnam war

The United States had been involved in Vietnam since 1950 but this commitment did not become a focal point of the Cold War until much later. At the time that Lyndon Johnson became president few Americans knew anything about this small Southeast Asian country. In 1965, however, Vietnam became the ultimate test of America's capacity and will to sustain global containment by military means.

Johnson's Vietnam policy was a natural progression of the anticommunist strategy pursued by his predecessors. Despite Truman's commitment of economic aid, the French colonial regime had been unable to withstand a nationalist uprising by Vietnamese communists. Vietnam's independence was eventually recognized by France in the Geneva Declaration of 1954, but this accord partitioned the country into two temporary zones — the communist north and non-communist south —

28

as a prelude to final unification under a government to be chosen through internationally-supervised elections in 1956. Anticipating a communist victory at the ballot box, the Eisenhower administration sought to ensure that Vietnam remained permanently divided. With US economic assistance, Ngo Dinh Diem established a government in South Vietnam and sabotaged the scheduled elections. In 1959–60, however, the Diem regime lost control of many rural areas to a Vietcong communist insurgency backed by North Vietnam. In response Kennedy increased the number of US military advisers in Vietnam from less than a thousand to 16,000 and sanctioned their use in combat-support roles. America was drawn deeper into the Vietnam mire by Kennedy's decision in October 1963 to support a coup by the South Vietnamese military against Diem, whose authoritarian, inefficient, Catholic-dominated regime had failed to win the hearts of the peasantry and had alienated Buddhist factions.

The new regime proved as ineffective in both political and military terms as its predecessor. In early 1965, with South Vietnam seemingly on the verge of collapse, the Johnson administration decided that the only way to prevent a communist victory was to Americanize the Vietnam war. Operation Rolling Thunder, a policy of gradually intensified air attacks against North Vietnam, was launched in February. Six months later Johnson took the fateful decision that committed the United States to involvement in a land war as well. He had followed the course that Kennedy himself would probably have taken had he not been killed. Notions that Kennedy would have avoided the Vietnam trap seem fanciful at best. Both he and Johnson were guided by the same set of Cold War assumptions. The policy of global containment required the preservation of a non-communist South Vietnam. By mid 1965 Johnson and his top advisers were convinced that only the use of military force could achieve this end. As Paul Conkin observed, "[T]hey never expected all the consequences that followed, never quite realized the extent of the risk that lay behind their policies. But even had they known this, it is doubtful that their choices would have been all that different."

America's war aim was a limited one — it wanted North Vietnam to stop all forms of aid to the Vietcong. The Johnson administration was confident that the communist insurgency would not survive for long without such support. Of course this specific goal was entwined with a broader concern to preserve the credibility of containment strategy. Johnson was upholding a global policy, which had been pursued since the late 1940s and which he still considered valid in the world of the mid 1960s. Administration officials identified the threat being contained in Vietnam sometimes as Soviet-supported wars of liberation in the third world and at other times as the expansionist pro-clivities of Communist China, but they had no doubts that failure in Southeast Asia would weaken America's international influence and encourage communist aggression elsewhere in the world. As Johnson told Congress in 1965, "The aim [of the communists] in Viet-Nam is not simply the conquest of the South. . . . It is to show that the American commitment is worthless. Once that is done, the gates are down and the road is open to expansion and endless conquest."

America's strategy was to fight a war of attrition that would inflict sufficient damage on the North Vietnamese and Vietcong to force them to negotiate peace terms. No one in the Johnson administration anticipated a painless victory, but the dominant view — questioned by only a few dissenters — was that communist will to sustain the war would quickly collapse in the face of America's military might. After all, the most powerful nation in the history of the world was taking on "a raggedyass little fourth-rate country", as the president once described North Vietnam.

However, US strategy was misconceived for a number of reasons. Firstly, military power could never resolve the fundamental political problem of establishing a viable regime in South Vietnam. Secondly, the United States used air power in a much more restricted manner than in Korea, initially confining attacks to military targets and later extending them to war-related economic facilities. This was partly because Johnson was anxious not to provoke military intervention by Russia or China, and partly because he assumed that the mere application of US air power would be enough to destroy enemy morale. As a result, the air war never imposed back-breaking damage on the enemy, the gradual build-up of the attacks gave the Hanoi regime time to develop potent anti-aircraft defenses, and the material losses that North Vietnam did suffer were more than offset by increases in Soviet and Chinese aid. Thirdly, although the United States rapidly expanded its troop levels in Vietnam from 75,000 in mid 1965 to 265,000 a year later and to over 500,000 by early 1968, it failed to inflict losses on enemy forces at a rate that exceeded their ability to recruit additional soldiers. Some 200,000 communist troops had been killed by late 1967 — but an estimated 200,000 North Vietnamese reached draft age every year, so Hanoi was able to replace communist losses and match every American troop escalation. Finally, and most significantly, Johnson and his top advisers underestimated the enemy's willingness to bear heavy losses in pursuit of a communist Vietnam.

The war quickly developed into a stalemate: American involvement prevented South Vietnam's collapse but could not force North Vietnam's withdrawal. This situation became politically disastrous for Johnson at home, because he had done almost nothing to prepare Americans for a long and costly conflict. The United States was never placed on a war footing comparable with that of the Korean war, when Truman had called up the reserves, imposed economic controls, and slashed domestic spending. As George Herring observed, Johnson's policy reflected his "determination to achieve his goals in Vietnam without sacrificing the Great Society and his certainty that he could accomplish both things at once". Mindful of the McCarthyite assault on the Fair Deal after the loss of China to communism in 1949, LBJ feared that the fall of South Vietnam would result in his domestic reforms being stymied by a new "red scare". Nevertheless, his commitment to the Great Society shackled his war policy. Johnson could not afford to go onto a full war footing because this would have aroused concern that the United States was likely to be involved in a lengthy conflict in Southeast Asia. As a result conservative congressmen would have been able to argue that the nation could ill afford expanded domestic commitments as well as a costly war.

Johnson based his authority to expand American involvement on the Gulf of Tonkin Resolution, which Congress had approved in August 1964 in response to reported North Vietnamese torpedo attacks on US warships. This empowered the president to take all "necessary measures to repel armed attack against the forces of the United States and to prevent further aggression". Despite such sweeping language, Congress intended the measure as a warning to North Vietnam rather than as authority for eventual full-scale war. However, Johnson used the resolution as a blank check to escalate the war in mid-1965, thereby avoiding debate about the possible costs of the conflict. The manner in which he had maneuvered the nation into war therefore made rapid victory politically essential for Johnson. When this was not forthcoming, he continued to issue optimistic statements about the light at the end of the tunnel. In essence, he sought to deceive the American people by portraying what was in reality a military stalemate as a situation promising eventual victory in Vietnam.

The initial escalation of the war generated a rally-round-the-flag patriotism. In December 1965, one opinion poll reported that 82 percent of Americans believed that US troops should remain in Vietnam until the communists accepted terms. Nevertheless antiwar opinion grew in strength as the war dragged on throughout 1966 and 1967. It was mainly voiced by intellectuals, New Left radicals, student activists, some civil rights activists like Martin Luther King, and sections of the big business community, the media and both political parties.

Some critics condemned the war on grounds of morality, citing in particular the air attacks against North Vietnam, which claimed many civilian casualties in spite of efforts to focus on military targets. More radical voices denounced the conflict as a manifestation of American capitalism's intent to destroy third-world socialism and protect potential markets and raw materials. By contrast, the politicians who opposed the war did so largely on practical grounds. They included many northeastern liberal Democrats like Senator Robert Kennedy (New York), some moderate southern Democrats like William Fulbright (Arkansas), and a number of liberal Republicans like Senator Thruston B. Morton (Kentucky). Hitherto supporters of global containment, they now doubted whether the costs of the war could be justified in view of Vietnam's peripheral significance to American security. The liberal Democrats also expressed concern that the war had undermined the administration's moral and material commitment to the Great Society. Meanwhile, some business elites, particularly those involved in international-oriented finance, feared that the war had distorted and inflated the economy. They worried, too, about its alienation of college youth, who would make up the next generation of the managerial-professional class. Concern about the costs of the war and the divisions that it had bred within society also caused sections of the press, including some metropolitan dailies like the *New York Times* and the influential *Time-Life* publications, to undergo a change of heart towards administration policy in 1967.

Nevertheless a gulf continued to separate opponents of the war from the mass of Americans, who showed much greater constancy in backing Johnson's policy in Vietnam than had been the case with Truman in Korea. Pragmatic critics of global containment failed to rally the mass public to their cause, largely because they disagreed among themselves whether the best solution to the Vietnam dilemma was immediate withdrawal, gradual de-escalation, or a negotiated settlement. Meanwhile, the most visible form of antiwar activism — the student protests and peace rallies — became enmeshed with a youth counterculture that questioned patriotism, authority, and materialism. As such, the campus peace movement represented an attack on what most people still cherished as the American way of life. Class divisions within society also limited its appeal. Troops serving in Vietnam were disproportionately of low-income background. To them — and their parents — antiwar protesters were a privileged, cosseted elite, who had draft deferment because they were rich enough to go to college. Typifying this view, one soldier complained, "I'm fighting for those candyasses because I don't have an old man to support me."

Not until the latter part of 1967 did public support for the war fall sharply. By then 13,000 US soldiers had died in Vietnam, draft call-ups exceeded 30,000 a month, and Johnson had finally been forced to request a tax surcharge to pay for the war. Polls now indicated that for the first time a majority of Americans considered intervention a mistake and doubted that US forces were making progress. But they also showed that the public was not yet ready to abandon the cause. In response the White House stepped up its efforts to convince Americans that the war was being won. There appeared to be realistic cause for such optimism: more areas of South Vietnam were pacified than at any time since 1964, enemy casualties were escalating, and the Vietcong had won no significant victories in over a year. But Johnson's hopes of staying the course were thwarted by the Tet offensive in January 1968.

Tet was one of the few conventional attacks launched by communist forces against the Americans and their South Vietnamese allies. In two weeks of heavy fighting they regained control of much of the countryside and captured eight provincial capitals. Though US forces eventually repelled them and inflicted severe casualties (estimated at over 58,000 killed), the North Vietnamese and the Vietcong had demonstrated that they still retained enormous strength and vitality. The light at the end of the tunnel was shown to be an illusion. General Earle Wheeler, chairman of the Joint Chiefs of Staff, and General William Westmoreland, military commander in Vietnam, informed the president that an additional 206,000 troops were now needed. The latter believed they could be used for an expanded war to crush the enemy finally after the Tet reverse, but the former pessimistically forecast that they would be needed to hold back renewed communist attacks. This request forced the Johnson administration to make a critical reevaluation of its Vietnam policy.

Doubts about the war were already surfacing in the administration and the broader foreign policy establishment. Secretary of Defense Robert McNamara had resigned in disillusionment in late 1967. His successor, Clark Clifford, supposedly a hawk, had also become skeptical of the possibilities of victory following Tet. The so-called "Wise Men", an informal advisory group of senior former national security officials whom Johnson periodically consulted on the war, shared this view. One of these, Dean Acheson, the architect of military containment as Truman's Secretary of State, avowed that the United States could "no longer do the job we set out to do in the time we have left and we must begin to take steps to disengage." Johnson's Vietnam policy now lacked substantive support. Since he was unwilling to escalate the war as the military wanted for fear of alienating public opinion and arousing even greater levels of antiwar protest, the president had only one option. On March 31 he announced that he would stop the bombing north of the demilitarized zone in Vietnam in order to facilitate peace talks. In addition, he told Americans that he would not seek reelection as their president, in order to concentrate on negotiating a settlement. The policy of gradual escalation in Vietnam had ended; the policy of gradual disengagement had started.

The Cold War consensus had spawned the Vietnam War but the progeny was responsible for the demise of its creator. The effect was most immediately apparent at leadership level. For nearly a quarter of a century the nation's political, economic, and intellectual elites had been largely united in support of global containment. However the Vietnam war produced divisions among them that were to survive until the end of the Cold War itself. Many liberal Democrats and a section of the foreign policy establishment — the network of past and present government officials, internationally-oriented businessmen, and academic advisers — believed that Vietnam had demonstrated the limits of American power. In their view a more selective activism in international affairs was now essential. They advocated that the United States should decide its priorities, take risks only to protect its most important interests, and aim for better balance between means and ends. In contrast, others within the foreign policy establishment, the military, the trade union leadership, and many on the right of the political spectrum insisted that Vietnam raised questions not about America's power but its will to use it. Accordingly, they demanded that global containment should be sustained.

Meanwhile the disillusionment of the mass public with the war was growing. By mid 1968 polls showed that more than three out of four

Americans believed that the nation was hopelessly bogged down in Vietnam. As yet there was no popular consensus in favor of withdrawal or escalation, but the seeds of what became known as the "Vietnam syndrome" — opposition to further military involvement abroad — had clearly been sown. The public's mood of outright hostility to the war would eventually crystallize in the early 1970s as a result of the Nixon administration's continuation of the conflict in search not of victory but an acceptable peace.

The rise and fall of the "new economics"

The Vietnam war also had immense consequences for the liberal political economy of postwar America. Johnson's decision to go to war in Southeast Asia coincided with the high point of optimism in the ability of government to manage the economy. The doctrines of the "new economics" had seemingly furnished the nation's leaders with the elixir for economic growth. There was now widespread confidence, within both government and the community of professional economists, that the technical problems of the modern economy could be resolved by enlightened politicians guided by experts. In 1966 Walter Heller exulted, "Economics has come of age in the 1960s. Two Presidents have recognized and drawn on modern economics as a source of national strength and Presidential power. Their willingness to use, for the first time, the full range of modern economic tools underlies the unbroken US expansion since 1961". However the halcyon days of the new economics were already numbered when these words were written. The limitations of this doctrine were exposed when it was faced with the inflationary pressures created by the Vietnam war.

The new economics had been conceived to redress the slack economy inherited from Eisenhower. Kennedy was anxious to follow through on ambitious plans at home, abroad, and in space, but stronger economic growth was essential for this. Charged with resolving the problem of how to convert potential output into actual output were the Keynesian economists who had been drawn from the top universities to serve in Kennedy's Council of Economic Advisers (CEA). Their solution called for the use of fiscal policy to "fine-tune" the economy to ensure maximum growth, high employment and low inflation. When the economy required stimulation to boost growth and employment, taxes were to be cut and government spending increased; by contrast, when it showed signs of overheating, the reverse policies would be implemented to douse inflationary pressures. In essence, the new economics envisaged an active, positive and continuous use of the instruments of modern economics to keep demand at levels that would make full use of the economy's potential and keep that potential growing without a corollary rise in inflation.

What was "new" about the new economics was its willingness to sanction deficit budgets even though the economy was not in recession. Instead of seeking to balance the actual budget, it placed more emphasis on balancing the economy, by calculating federal expenditures in relationship to the hypothetical receipts that would accrue if the economy were operating at full potential. The so-called hypothetical full-employment budget provided license for growth-inducing tax cuts and federal spending increases. Johnson's CEA chairman, Arthur Okun, proudly proclaimed, "The big tax cut [of 1964] was the first major stimulative measure adopted in the post-war era at a time when the economy was neither in, nor threatened imminently by, recession. And unlike US tax reductions in the 1920s, late 1940s, and 1954, the 1964 action was taken in a budgetary situation marked by the twin facts that the federal budget was in deficit and federal expenditures were rising."

Concern for growth did not blind the new economists to the dangers of inflation. The Phillips curve had become an integral element of Keynesian doctrine in the late 1950s. This demonstrated a statistical relationship between unemployment, wages and prices, whereby a fall in the first of these caused the second to rise, which pushed up the third. Heller and his colleagues recognized that expansionary measures would have to be reversed if the economy showed signs of overheating, but they were confident that a benign trade-off could be managed between unemployment and inflation. Their goal became to keep the former at four percent and the latter at two percent.

Kennedy and Johnson became enthusiastic backers of the new economics. The former promoted substantial tax benefits for business in 1962, and the latter secured enactment of a massive $10 billion income tax cut — initially proposed by his predecessor — in 1964. These measures gave the economy a huge boost. Between 1961 and 1966, over 7 million new jobs were created, the nation's real output increased by a third, and the $50 billion gap between actual and potential production was closed. In 1965 annual economic growth exceeded 6% and unemployment fell to 4.1%, effectively the full-employment level. Meanwhile, the Consumer Price Index (CPI) rose by less than 2% a year from 1963 to 1965. As a result the new economics enjoyed a brief apotheosis. John Maynard Keynes finally made the front cover of *Time*, and the magazine ran a story headed "We are all Keynesians now".

In the second half of the 1960s, however, inflation replaced growth as the dominant economic issue. What the United States now experienced was a classic case of "demand-pull" inflation, which occurs when aggregate demand for goods and services rises faster than supply, and thereby bids up prices of scarce commodities. By late 1965 the expansionary measures of the Kennedy-Johnson administrations had largely succeeded in squeezing the slack out of the economy. There were already signs that private demand, fueled by high employment, low taxes, and rising incomes, might soon outstrip production potential. At this juncture demand pressures intensified as a result of two new developments within the public sector.

The first of these was the launch of the Great Society, which substantially increased federal expenditure on social programs. The second and by far the more significant impetus for increased spending was the escalation of American involvement in Vietnam. The total costs of the war to the public purse from fiscal 1966 through fiscal 1968 neared $52 billion, with the annual bill skyrocketing from a mere $103 million in fiscal 1965 to $26.5 billion in fiscal 1968. In addition, the diversion of production from civilian goods to military goods necessitated by the war fueled inflationary pressures because it increased the relative scarcity of consumer products.

With public and private demand shooting ahead faster than production could be expanded, the result was the most significant upward movement in price trends since the first year of the Korean war. The CPI rose steadily by nearly 3% in 1966, by over 3% in 1967, by 4.7% in 1968, and by more than 6% in 1969. Taking account of additional indices like wholesale prices and interest rates, the overall rate of inflation rose from an annual average of 1.5% in 1960–4 to 3.5% in 1965–9. Viewed from the present day this level of inflation appears minimal, but it aroused great concern in the 1960s because Americans were accustomed to the almost zero inflation of the postwar era.

Inflation had real as well as psychological effects. In a Gallup poll of late 1967, 60% of respondents named the high cost of living as their most urgent problem. First to feel the pinch were blue-collar workers, whose average weekly take-home pay had risen steadily from $68 to $78 (in constant dollars) between 1958 and 1964. From 1965 onward, however, the real value of their wages hardly increased at all because of inflation. Taking up the cudgels on behalf of their beleaguered members, trade unions pressed for bigger and bigger wage increases, but their actions forged another link in the inflationary chain. Higher wage bills for business meant higher production costs, which were passed on to the consumer in the form of higher prices. Pay increases also reduced profit margins in some industries, thereby discouraging investment. Total business after-tax profits, which had grown by 71% between 1962 and 1965, rose by only 9% from 1966 to 1969. It was hardly surprising, therefore, that many corporate leaders came to voice doubts about a war that had done little to benefit them. As Bank of America chairman Louis B. Lundborg commented in 1970, "[P]rotestations of the new left to the contrary, the fact is that an end to the war would be good, not bad, for American business."

The failure of the new economics to keep the lid on inflation was rooted in Lyndon Johnson's insistence that the nation could simultaneously afford both the Vietnam war and the Great Society without recourse to tax increases. In essence the president was right: the economy could afford guns and butter. However this was not true of the federal budget. Failure to transfer funds from the private economy to the public sector to pay for its increased commitments resulted in growing budget deficits. In fiscal 1965, thanks to the extra revenues generated by economic growth, the budget was only $1.6 billion in the red. This prompted confidence among the new economists that the nation was entering a new era of balanced budgets, in which an expanding economy would generate more than enough revenues for the federal government to pay for its growing domestic commitments. Instead the budget deficit widened once more, rising to $3.8 billion in fiscal 1966, $8.7 billion in fiscal 1967 and a record $25.2 billion in fiscal 1968.

Running deficits when the economy was more or less at full-employment level was a sure way of aggravating inflation. Well aware of this, the CEA had urged Johnson in December 1965 to propose a tax increase, but its pleas were rejected for political reasons. The president's stand on taxes exposed a major weakness of the new economics and its reliance on fiscal "fine-tuning". The architects of this doctrine failed to appreciate that political considerations could militate against the speedy implementation of restrictive measures to combat inflation because sensitive questions of social equity and government priorities would be at issue. Being accountable to voters, politicians are reluctant to raise taxes at the best of times. In this instance Johnson knew that Congress would only support a tax increase if it was presented as a war tax. But such a proposal would be the cue for conservative demands for cutbacks in Great Society programs and would arouse liberal concern that the war was placing social reform in danger. The president's desire to preserve consensus therefore led him to reject the advice of his economic experts.

To make matters worse for the new economists in the CEA, Johnson's political need to sustain popular confidence that the war would be short-lived led him to deliberately underestimate its costs to the federal budget. This inevitably made their task of economic forecasting extremely difficult. The fiscal 1967 budget, submitted to Congress in January 1966, earmarked $10.3 billion for the war. This figure represented a combination of wishful thinking and deceit. Congress was informed that the estimate of costs was based on the assumption that the war would be over by mid 1967, but no-one involved in Vietnam decision-making within the administration truly expected this. The actual cost of the war in fiscal 1967 turned out to be close to $20 billion. To the proponents of the new economics, this was the budget that opened the floodgates to inflation and destroyed the foundations of the liberal political economy.

It also became evident that the advocates of fiscal fine-tuning had underestimated the significance of the money supply as an instrument of economic management. In mid 1966 the Federal Reserve engineered a credit crunch to douse inflationary demand and applied the monetary brakes so hard that the economy nearly tipped over into recession in early 1967. Nevertheless, at this juncture too little was known about how monetary policy actually worked for it to be used with confidence for purposes of short-run stabilization. Coordination of fiscal and monetary policies was also difficult, because the latter was under the control of the independent Federal Reserve Board. Owing to the unexpectedly harsh effects of the credit squeeze on the housing market, the Federal Reserve went to the opposite extreme in early 1967 and began pumping overgenerous quantities of monetary reserves back into the banking system. As a result the inflationary pressures temporarily stiffled by its previous policy were reignited.

The resurgence of inflation finally compelled Johnson to come clean and ask Congress for a ten percent temporary tax surcharge in August 1967. However, conservatives enjoyed considerable influence within the congressional committees responsible for tax legislation, and the administration had to wage a long and bitter battle before the measure was finally enacted in June 1968. The victory was a costly one for

Johnson, because the legislation also mandated corollary cuts of $6 billion in Great Society expenditures. It was largely due to this measure that federal finances moved into the black in fiscal 1969, when the budget recorded a surplus of $3.2 billion. This was a feat of some historic significance, for the budget has never been in balance since. But the tax increase came too late to douse inflation, which had already established a firm grip on the economy. In fact the surcharge did little to curtail private spending, partly because its temporary nature did not affect consumers' long-term income expectations, and partly because cheap credit was available for most of 1968 as a result of the Fed's easy money policy.

The eminent Keynesian James Tobin ruefully acknowledged, "In 1966 and subsequently it became painfully clear that economists do not have enough tools of foresight, analysis, and policy to enable their government to avoid or offset shocks to the economy". The optimism of the new economics that the economy could be managed to ensure high employment, low inflation, and strong growth evaporated because of the failure to deal with the economic consequences of the Vietnam war. This failure had significant implications for the commercial Keynesianism that had shaped the political economy of postwar America.

Confidence that government could redress the instabilities inherent in the private economy was one of the props of the liberal consensus, but this had been severely jolted because it was government actions that destabilized the economy in the 1960s. Moreover, the notion that a benign trade-off could be made between unemployment and inflation in a rapidly growing economy could no longer be sustained. Due to the experience of the 1960s, Keynesians and their allies in the Democratic party grew disillusioned about the possibilities of a full-employment economy and accepted instead the existence of a so-called "natural unemployment rate". The new orthodoxy held that government efforts to peg joblessness below this level, which retrospective estimates put at above five percent in the Kennedy-Johnson years, only served to drive up inflation to unacceptable levels. In essence the inflation generated by Vietnam spelled doom for the growth economics that the Democrats had pursued since the end of World War II. The liberal political economy of the postwar years had promised growth, jobs, and stable prices. In future painful choices would have to be made between the goals of high employment and low inflation. The political economy of prosperity would give way to the political economy of limits.

The Great Society and a divided society

The liberal consensus had emerged triumphant from the 1964 election. Faced with a choice between Lyndon Johnson and Barry Goldwater, the most conservative Republican presidential candidate since Herbert Hoover, a large majority of Americans endorsed Roosevelt's heir. One out of every five people who had voted Republican in 1960 changed sides in 1964. There was widespread satisfaction about the economy, about Johnson's achievements in fulfilling the legislative agenda of the dead Kennedy, and about the state of world affairs. As a result business and middle-income voters deserted the GOP in droves to join labor, ethnics, blacks, and blue-collars under one big Democratic tent. The coat-tail effects of Johnson's mammoth victory also enabled the Democrats to win huge majorities of 155 in the House of Representatives and 36 in the Senate (compared with majorities of 81 and 34 respectively in the previous Congress). For the first time since the mid-1930s a Democratic president now had enough support in Congress to enact a wide-ranging reform program over the opposition of Republicans and the conservative wing of his own party.

The scale of the Democratic victory persuaded some political commentators that conservatism and the Republican party itself were moribund. This was a gross misconception. Goldwater's politics were too radical for most Americans in 1964, but many of his campaign issues — reducing the welfare state, cutting taxes to encourage individual initiative and wealth creation, greater say for states in how they spent federal grants, and tough law-and-order policies — foreshadowed the mainstream concerns of the 1970s and 1980s. Moreover, his message did strike a chord with one part of the New Deal coalition. The defection of the white South from the presidential wing of the Democratic party, which had begun in 1948, gathered pace in 1964. Goldwater was the first Republican presidential candidate to carry all five states of the Deep South. His strong advocacy of states' rights had great appeal in the region. The white South rallied to him as a voice of protest against the increased social activism of the federal government. It was not long before other groups in American society focused their resentment on the same target.

An examination of why voters handed the Democrats a landslide victory in 1964 makes more understandable the swift decline thereafter of the liberal consensus on domestic policy. As Allen Matusow observed, the 1964 election "was a referendum on the policies of the past four years — indeed, the liberal policies of the past generation". With considerable assistance from his opponent's loose rhetoric, Johnson had been able to portray Goldwater as a man who would demolish the welfare state and the Keynesian political economy inherited from Roosevelt and extended by all his successors. The election was not a referendum on the new direction in which the Democratic administration would take liberalism. The Johnson campaign muted debate on social innovation and emphasized instead the president's experience, responsibility, and moderation. This strategy was well-suited to winning a landslide against a candidate so out of touch with the national mood as Goldwater, but it did little to build up real popular support for change. Nevertheless, Johnson seized the opportunity to launch the Great Society. For a brief moment the factors that had long made the American political system resistant to rapid change — fear of big government, party divisions, congressional obstructionism, and middle-class apathy — were in abeyance. But Johnson knew he had to move quickly before these reasserted themselves. "Hurry, boys, hurry," he told White House aides, "Get that legislation up to the Hill and out. Eighteen months from now ol' Landslide Lyndon will be Lame-Duck Lyndon." Driven along by the president's enthusiasm and energy, the 89th Congress of 1965–6 outdid the New Deal Congresses of 1933–4 and 1935–6 in terms of legislative output.

Johnson's vision of the Great Society was inspired not only by the New Deal's material concerns to ensure widespread prosperity but also by his own vision of the qualitative betterment of people's lives. Speaking at the University of Michigan in 1964, he committed his administration to build the foundations for a future in which Americans "were more concerned with the quality of their goals than the quantity of their goods". The legislative record of the 89th Congress testified to the Great Society's diffuse concerns. It enacted measures to expand the provision of social welfare, to improve the quality of education in schools and universities, to enhance environmental protection and natural resource conservation, to revitalize inner cities, to improve urban mass transit, to protect the rights of consumers, to terminate discriminatory immigration restrictions inherited from the 1920s, and to sweep away the restrictions on black voting rights imposed by southern states since the 1890s.

In spite of this diversity, the Great Society drew its political identity above all else from Johnson's determination to secure his reputation in history as a great president by eradicating poverty from American society. His predecessor had already established task forces to investigate ways of dealing with this problem. It is not clear how rapidly Kennedy would have moved to implement their recommendations, but Johnson decided that a crusade against poverty should be the centerpiece of his administration. In 1964 he secured enactment of the Economic Opportunity Act, which established the Office of Economic Opportunity (OEO) to oversee and coordinate a host of programs collectively designated as the War on Poverty. These included VISTA (a domestic equivalent of the Peace Corps that provided community services to the poor); the Job Corps (residential centers offering vocational training for unskilled youngsters); and the Neighborhood Youth Corps (providing training and work experience for high school drop-outs). The OEO's most innovative venture was the Community Action Program (CAP), which pursued neighborhood solutions to poverty and encouraged "maximum feasible participation" by the poor themselves in the process of developing local antipoverty projects. Between 1965 and 1970 it funded about a thousand community agencies, some focusing on educational programs like Head-Start (for pre-school children) or Follow-Through (for elementary school pupils), and others on provision of services like legal aid, family planning advice, and day care centers for children of working mothers.

A host of other antipoverty measures was enacted following Johnson's reelection. The Medicare program of health insurance for the aged was added to social security in 1965. Increased concern for the aged was also reflected in improvement of social security benefit levels. Medicaid, enacted as a corollary to Medicare, provided federal matching funds for states operating health programs for recipients of Aid to Families with Dependent Children (AFDC). Changes made in the matching grant formula in 1965 also encouraged many states to widen eligibility for AFDC assistance. Henceforth the federal government guaranteed to pay at least half of whatever total sum each state paid out to AFDC families, providing the state also offered Medicaid. To combat malnutrition among the poor, the existing food stamps and school lunch programs were substantially expanded. Meanwhile, the Appalachian development program was launched in 1965 to revitalize one of the nation's poorest rural regions, and the Model Cities program of 1966 targeted development aid toward depressed urban areas. A rent supplement program for impoverished tenants was created in 1965, and the most ambitious program of low-income housing construction since the Fair Deal was enacted in 1968. Educational deprivation was addressed by the 1965 Elementary and Secondary Schools Act, which provided federal funds to local school districts through a formula involving the number of low-income residents in the county.

The Johnson administration presided over the greatest expansion of social welfare in American history to date. Spending on social insurance and income-transfer welfare programs doubled during the second half of the 1960s to $61 billion, representing a rise from 4.6% to 6.1% of GNP. The fastest growing program in expenditure terms was social security (including Medicare), which distributed $54 billion to 29.9 million citizens by 1974, compared with $16.6 billion to 20.8 million people in 1965. Meanwhile, noncontributory welfare grew more rapidly in terms of recipients. Due entirely to the expansion of AFDC, the numbers on categorical public assistance grew from 7.8 million in 1965 to 11.1 million in 1969, and rose again to 14.4 million in 1974.

According to official estimates the number of poor fell from 32 million (17% of the population) in 1965 to 23 million (11% of the population) by 1973. However the real decline in poverty was smaller than these figures suggest because they were based on an unrealistically low definition of the poverty line ($3,700 for an urban family of four in 1969). It is also difficult to separate out the impact of economic expansion and the effects of social policy on the actual reduction that did occur. In spite of such caveats, the Great Society's achievement was substantial. At the very least it deserves credit for vastly increasing the proportion of disadvantaged Americans assisted by their government, guaranteeing them a minimally adequate diet and health care, and lifting many of them, especially the elderly, out of extreme poverty. Johnson did indeed succeed in building a more equitable society. Of course this judgement does not preclude recognition that he fell far short of his grandiose aims.

While praising Johnson's use of the state to benefit the underprivileged, most historians tend to regard the war on poverty as being little more than a skirmish. Neither in terms of its taxation nor business regulation policies did the Great Society seek to correct the maldistribution of wealth and power in the United States. The most significant social welfare improvements were in social security (including Medicare), on which federal expenditure rose in the 1960s by almost three times as much as the increase in categorical welfare assistance. As a result there was a marked improvement in the economic status of the aged. By 1970 only 25% of elderly people were poor, compared with 40% in 1959. With their exception, however, the social insurance programs did not aid the neediest groups in society. Meanwhile, categorical assistance programs were not adequate by themselves in any state, even liberal ones, to raise families out of poverty, and the federal government still gave the states and localities no money for general assistance programs. It was hardly surprising, therefore, that there was no reduction in poverty among female-headed families, the largest group among the poor, between 1963 and 1969.

Federal spending on the Great Society's new antipoverty programs was also inadequate. The rent supplement and housing construction programs suffered particularly in this respect. Aid to education did not provide for teachers' salaries or for renovation of urban schools, which continued to deteriorate. Only one out of every three pupil recipients of its antipoverty assistance were poor, because local officials tended to use the funds to benefit low educational achievers irrespective of their economic status. Meanwhile, OEO annual expenditures only averaged $1.7 billion in 1965–8, equivalent to between $50 and $65 a year per poor person, and much of this inadequate money went on program administration rather than directly on the poor. As the costs of the Vietnam war rose, Johnson would not enlarge the budget deficit further by spending more generously on social programs. His obsession with the war also doused his passion for the crusade against poverty during his final two years in office. In 1968, following a wave of ghetto riots the National Advisory Commission on Civil Disorders called for massive federal intervention to combat unemployment, bad housing and racial discrimination in the inner cities, but Johnson ignored the recommendations of the body that he himself had appointed.

The much ballyhooed War on Poverty launched by the OEO was also based on misconceptions about poverty. Its emphasis on a services approach to combatting poverty assumed that poverty was a largely cultural problem, rather than a predominantly economic one. The Johnson administration antipoverty strategy aimed to foster employability of the poor rather than to guarantee jobs. From its perspective, the problem was that the poor lacked the values, incentives, and skills to exploit the opportunities available in the expanding economy. In essence, the poor themselves, rather than the flaws of society and the economic system, were held responsible for their own predicament. Accordingly, the OEO set out to boost their ability to achieve economic self-improvement.

Scholarly opinion is generally agreed that the War on Poverty would have been far more successful had poverty been tackled head-on through a New Deal-style program of public employment and a guaranteed income program. Its most famous critic, sociology professor and government official Daniel P. Moynihan, lamented that "an immense opportunity to institute more or less permanent social changes — a fixed full employment program, a measure of income maintenance — was lost while energies were expended in ways that very probably hastened the end of a brief period when such options were open, that is to say the three years from the assassination of Kennedy to the election of the Ninety-first Congress."

Whether this opportunity actually existed in the Johnson era is debatable. The measures envisioned by Moynihan were more attuned to the social democratic consensus that existed in Western Europe. The degree of state control over the economy which they would have required was alien to the fundamental credo of the liberal consensus that an expanding consumer capitalism was the best guarantor of prosperity for all Americans. The fiscal costs would also have been far greater than those of the War on Poverty, and would have had to be financed through redistributive tax increases on the middle classes and big business.

Such an approach would have spelled the end of the liberal consensus, but it would probably have established a more stable basis of political support for the Democratic party than the Great Society achieved. A social democratic strategy would have strengthened the unity of the working class constituency that had kept the Democrats in power since the 1930s. All the subgroups within the Roosevelt coalition, regardless of their race, ethnicity, gender, and age, would have benefited as working-class Americans from the guarantees of economic security offered by a full-employment program. The experience of the 1930s had already underlined the political effectiveness of class-based programs. Despite its economic failures, the New Deal — in Ira Katznelson's words — "understood poverty as anchored in class relations as it aimed to put the working class back to work." Ironically, by eschewing a class-based poverty program in an attempt to operate within the confines of the liberal consensus, the Great Society helped to destroy what it sought to conserve. The racial, social, and cultural changes associated with its programs created tensions among the different groups within the Roosevelt coalition. The result was to undermine the Democratic domination of American politics that was an integral element of the liberal consensus.

In essence the antipoverty strategy of the Great Society was interlinked with and a natural outgrowth from the two other major domestic innovations of the Kennedy-Johnson administration. Its emphasis on equipping the poor to take advantage of economic opportunity was a corollary to the confident assumption of the new economics that government manipulation of the economy would ensure strong growth and high employment. The Great Society was also entwined with the civil rights revolution because it conceived poverty principally as a matter of race rather than class.

Even though the number of white poor was almost double that of black poor, poverty was disproportionately concentrated among blacks. In 1966, 41% of blacks lived beneath the official poverty line compared with some 12% of whites, black unemployment was double that of whites, and black *per capita* income was just over 57% that of the white average (the ratio had changed little in the postwar era). Of course the poverty programs cast their net far wider than just the black poor, but Johnson's public statements tended to emphasize the link between race and poverty above all else. Speaking at Howard University in 1965, he acknowledged the "burden that a dark skin can add to the search for a productive place in society" and the reality that "unemployment strikes most swiftly and broadly at the Negro". However Johnson's efforts to uplift the black poor aroused racial animosities that weakened the New Deal political coalition in the North as well as the South.

It is important to understand that the antipoverty programs grew out of the optimism of policy elites within the Kennedy-Johnson administrations that poverty could be abolished in the prosperous conditions of the 1960s. Carried along by the conviction that the federal government now had the tools to dispose of a longstanding problem, these elites took the initiative to define a new policy agenda. Unlike the New Deal, the Great Society's war on poverty was not a response to an immediate crisis. Nor was it prompted by popular demand for action. Social security expansion and Medicare apart, the antipoverty programs elicited little interest from the trade unions. Similarly, they were peripheral to the concerns of the Democratic mayors and political organizations that ran the big cities. Meanwhile, despite Michael Harrington's 1962 best-selling study of poverty, *The Other America*, and unprecedented media interest in the problem, the public continued to hold unflattering stereotypes of the poor as lazy and underserving.

Bereft of popular support from the start, the Great Society's war on poverty soon encountered a backlash of resentment as the feeling grew among whites that it was intended to aid only blacks. A Harris poll in 1966 found that 85% of white respondents believed that blacks were seeking too much, too fast, whereas two years previously only 34% had taken this view. Polls also revealed that the majority of the white poor felt they had been overlooked. More significant was the hostility of whites who were neither poor nor affluent. These composed the bulk of the amorphous group that came to be dubbed as "middle Americans" by journalists and scholars.

During the second half of the 1960s, according to US Bureau of Labor Statistics calculations, about 65% of white families lived above the poverty line and beneath the level of affluence, respectively defined as annual family incomes of $5,000 and $15,000. Almost two-thirds of these had incomes beneath $10,000, the level for a "modest but adequate standard of living" for an urban family of four. Also, over 60% of white families needed two or more earners to reach an income of $5,000 or more. Life was a struggle for many middle Americans to keep up mortgage payments on their homes, to run a car (usually a second-hand one), to finance basic family needs, and to get their children through school. About 65% of families with annual incomes between $5,000 and $10,000 carried installment debts (compared with 48% of families with incomes over $15,000). Few could afford so-called luxuries, most had inexpensive leisure pursuits, and less than half took vacation trips lasting longer than five days.

As a *Newsweek* poll confirmed in 1969, most middle Americans believed that blacks now had a better chance than whites of getting a decent standard of living because of the government assistance they received. Typifying this view, a blue-collar ethnic who lived in Milwaukee — a city where most welfare recipients were black — complained, "People on relief got better jobs, got better homes than I've got. . . . The colored people are eating steak, and this Polack bastard is eating chicken. Damn right I'm bitter." Similar sentiments were voiced to the journalist Studs Terkel by a Chicagoan of Czech extraction: ". . . the Negro is going to make great strides by virtue of the fact that he has the force, the militant force, of the government behind him. This is the only reason he is going to make these strides."

Middle America's resentment was the product of complex motives and fears. It did not spring from racist desire to hold blacks back, but mainly reflected concern that blacks were gaining an unfair advantage. AFDC was a particular source of grievance because blacks, who comprised 46% of recipients by 1967, were the principal beneficiaries of its expansion. Many nonaffluent whites saw themselves as victims of "reverse discrimination", particularly in states like California, Michigan and New York, which had swelling welfare rolls and high taxes. Accepting the necessity for hard work, self-reliance and thrift to improve their own lot, middle Americans took offense that blacks seemed to be getting ahead without having to observe the same rules. This sense of grievance was compounded by the belief, expressed by 79% of respondents in the *Newsweek* poll cited above, that the majority of people on welfare could earn their keep if they wanted to.

Of course the benefits that blacks gained from federal programs were infinitely smaller than middle Americans imagined. Economic injustice, from which blacks suffered nationwide, proved far more difficult to eradicate than the legal injustices of the South's Jim Crow system. Frustrated at the slow rate of progress, blacks outside the South became increasingly active in demanding more forthright measures to improve their socioeconomic conditions. In doing so, blacks were posing their own challenge to the liberal consensus and its fundamental assumption that incremental reform could put right inequalities based on race. In 1966 Martin Luther King organized demonqtrations in Chicago to demand open housing policies, but this effort to transplant the non-violent tactics of the southern civil rights movement to the North did not prove effective. Black activists turned increasingly to more militant strategies under the banner of Black Power, which rejected traditional concerns of racial integration in favor of empowering blacks to run the political, economic, and cultural affairs of their own communities. However, the most evident expression of black anger and frustration was the worst outbreak of ghetto rioting since World War I.

There had been several relatively small disorders in 1964, but the first serious riot took place in the Watts section of Los Angeles in August, 1965. The National Guard only restored order after five days of violence, burning, and looting, which left 34 dead, over 1,000 injured, and over 800 buildings damaged or destroyed. There was relative calm in 1966, but eight major riots (and 156 "minor" ones) occurred in 1967, the worst in Detroit and Newark, where the dead respectively numbered 43 and 24. In 1968 riots broke out again following the assassination of Martin Luther King in Memphis on April 4,, with the worst disorder occurring in Washington DC.

These events were a manifestation of black rage against entrapment in impoverished inner-city ghettoes and the limited results of government action to date in redressing their situation. While the Johnson administration and liberal Democrats disavowed the violence, they tended to blame it on the socioeconomic discrimination that blighted the lives of black ghetto dwellers. Reflecting this view, the National Advisory Commission on Civil Disorders declared in its 1968 report, "White racism is essentially responsible for the explosive mixture that has been accumulating in our cities." Most middle Americans took a different view. Unable to understand or sympathize with the problems of ghetto dwellers, they blamed the riots on the lawlessness of blacks and their unwillingness to rely on traditional methods of self-improvement. Television scenes from Watts and other places of rioting blacks shouting "Get Whitey" and "Burn, Baby, Burn" also generated fears among many whites that their own neighborhoods, lives, and property might come under attack.

The outbreak of rioting coincided with a huge increase in urban crimes like muggings, robberies, and rape, much of it committed by blacks against other blacks. These two developments merged together in the minds of many whites and reinforced stereotype views that blacks often resorted to criminal actions to get what they wanted. Law and order concerns consequently became entangled with racial issues. Many of those who called for stronger government action against crime and disorder perceived the black community as the main source of lawlessness. In their view the Johnson administration's emphasis on solving ghetto problems through social programs merely encouraged black law-breaking. Republican rhetoric also helped to strengthen popular convictions that the Democrats were soft on the law and order issue. House minority leader Gerald R. Ford (Michigan) avowed in 1967, "The war at home — the war against crime — is being lost. The Administration appears to be in full retreat. The homes and streets of America are no longer safe for our people." Such attacks hit home. In September 1968, 81% of respondents to a Harris poll felt that law and order had broken down, and 84% believed that strong presidential action was needed to combat lawlessness.

Compounding the Democrats' image problem on this issue was the unpopularity of recent judicial decisions in criminal justice cases. Though an independent body, the Supreme Court was linked in the public mind with the Democrats during the Kennedy-Johnson era. According to legal scholar Martin Shapiro, it was engaged under the leadership of Chief Justice Earl Warren in incorporating into constitutional law "the implications of the victory of the New Deal coalition and the dominance of the New Deal consensus." This may well have been the case regarding its civil rights, political representation, and welfare eligibility judgements. But the Supreme Court entered different territory in expanding the rights of the accused in such cases as *Mapp v. Ohio* (1963), which restricted police right of search and seizure, and *Escobedo v. Illinois* (1963) and *Miranda v. Arizona* (1966), both of which defined suspects' rights that law enforcement authorities had to observe in order to obtain a conviction. Opposed by 65% of respondents in a 1966 Harris poll, these decisions aroused popular outrage that the police were being prevented from effectively fighting crime.

Underpinning critical attitudes towards welfare, crime and social reform was a moral traditionalism. Middle Americans felt engulfed by a sense of cultural crisis because of what they perceived as the rejection of traditional values by so many groups in society. Their dislike of the war on poverty drew force from stereotype images of the black ghetto as a place where crime, violence, drug addiction, sexual license, illegitimacy and female-headed families were the norm. Their sense of patriotism was offended by the anti-Vietnam war demonstrations. Their respect for authority and conventional mores was at variance with the emerging youth culture of the 1960s, which celebrated sexual freedom, personal liberation from traditional discipline, and drugs. Their regard for law and order was scandalized by the ghetto riots and the rising crime rate. Finally, their belief in the family and in the strong delineation between the roles of men and women was threatened by the rise of feminism from the mid 1960s onwards.

In moving beyond the bread and butter liberalism of the New Deal to deal with the related problems of economic inequality and race, the Great Society had opened a Pandora's box of troubles for the New Deal political order. Johnson had launched his reform program with excessive expectations of what could be achieved. The wide imbalance between rhetoric and reality in the Great Society's final ledger helped to undermine the optimism in government's ability to resolve social problems that had sustained Democratic party support for the expansion of federal responsibilities since the 1930s. Johnson's policies had also weakened the emotional bonds that had tied so many voters to the Democrats since the days of Roosevelt. Many middle Americans felt betrayed by the social and political changes that the Great Society had unleashed. Their concerns appeared to have been overridden by the needs of racial and social minorities in the post-1965 agenda of the national Democratic party. As a result many blue-collar and middle-income Democrats came to see liberals as adversaries rather than allies. This became evident in the volatile politics of the 1968 presidential election.

The 1968 presidential election

The most divisive and traumatic presidential election of the twentieth century took place in 1968 against a background of violence, assassinations, and mass protests. It was also the pivotal election in the political development of postwar America. The build-up to it laid bare the stresses and strains that had developed within the liberal consensus over America's role in the world and its domestic policy priorities. At one stage it seemed that forces dedicated to peace and cooperation abroad and social justice at home could mount a serious challenge for popular support. Instead, the outcome laid the foundations for retreat from the traditional means, but not the ends, of Cold War globalism and from the Great Society's efforts to improve the lives of the underprivileged. It also signified that with regard to presidential elections the once-dominant New Deal voter coalition was in serious decline.

Few could have foreseen this outcome at the beginning of the year. Although antiwar Democrats were restive, Johnson was widely expected to be renominated and reelected. Only the eloquent and intellectual Senator Eugene McCarthy (Minnesota) was bold enough to set aside party regularity to run as a peace candidate against LBJ for the Democratic presidential nomination. A month before the first primary in New Hampshire his cause seemed hopeless. No twentieth-century president had failed in the quest to be renominated. Johnson controlled the party machinery and still commanded the loyalty of habitual Democratic voters, only 17% of whom voiced support for McCarthy in a nationwide poll taken in January 1968.

But the communist Tet offensive changed the political landscape by undermining the credibility of Johnson's claims that victory in Vietnam was imminent. New Hampshire Democrats, many of them hawks who wished to voice protest against the administration's discredited war policies, responded by giving McCarthy 42.4% of the primary vote, compared with 49.5% for Johnson. Though defeated, the antiwar candidate had done much better than had seemed possible a few weeks earlier, so his challenge began to be taken seriously. Many peace activists and students now deemed it possible to achieve their end through the instrument of party politics and flocked to join McCarthy's campaign. With money pouring into his coffers and campaign workers aplenty to assist him, the challenger looked set to win the next primary in Wisconsin. The realization that he would be beaten in this contest precipitated Johnson's decision not to seek renomination.

In the meantime the New Hampshire primary result induced a change of heart in Senator Robert Kennedy, whose conviction that Johnson had the nomination sewn up had deterred him from mounting a challenge. Though a critic of the war since late 1965, Kennedy's belated declaration of his candidacy came under fire from peace supporters for having exploited the opportunity created by McCarthy's courage, and he never regained their trust. The two senators squared up against each other in the Democratic primaries to decide which of them should head the insurgency that was seeking to win the party leadership. McCarthy kept his support among middle class Democrats, peace campaigners, and college youth, while Kennedy found his constituency among the poor and racial minorities.

McCarthy had an undistinguished record of legislative action on behalf of the underprivileged, but Kennedy had taken up their cause after the assassination of his brother. In a way he had traveled to the same political destination as Martin Luther King, but from a different starting point. By 1968 King had metamorphosed from being a civil rights campaigner into a human rights campaigner, a critic of the Vietnam war, and a spokesman for impoverished Americans whatever their race. Recognizing that class inequalities were as significant to blacks as racial inequality, he devoted the last year of his life to organizing the Poor People's Campaign to undertake a mass march to the nation's capital. Robert Kennedy, once a hard-nosed pragmatist dedicated above all else to John Kennedy's interests, had developed a passionate commitment to abolish racism and poverty, and had come to realize that the Vietnam war had to be ended in order to achieve a more equitable society at home. Together, Kennedy and King embodied the best hope of forging a movement that would pursue peace and social justice outside the confines of the liberal consensus but within the structure of the existing political system. The possibility that America would move in this direction was tragically cut off, first by King's assassination, and then Kennedy's in Los Angeles on the night of his victory in the California primary of June 4.

It must remain a matter for debate whether Kennedy could have fulfilled his ideals under the pressures to compromise that he would inevitably have faced had he become president. What is undeniable, however, is that his nomination would have given the Democrats their best prospect of keeping the New Deal coalition intact and retaining the presidency. The antiwar constituency, blacks, and the poor would have rallied to Kennedy. Moreover, his victory in the Indiana primary showed that the Kennedy name still held an aura for labor and ethnic voters, and that his record as a former crime-fighting Attorney-General reassured them of his sensitivity to their law-and-order concerns. After winning the California primary, Kennedy could also have reached out to the Democratic party's power brokers as a proven vote winner. McCarthy, who was essentially a single-issue peace candidate, lacked such broad appeal, and his efforts to rally Kennedy's supporters to his cause following the latter's death had limited success.

At the Democratic convention in Chicago in August the presidential nomination eventually went to Vice-President Hubert Humphrey, who had the support of delegates controlled by the traditional powers within the party, notably state party bosses, big city mayors, and trade union leaders. Although he had not entered the primaries, opinion polls showed him the favorite of registered Democratic voters. Tracing his political identity to the New Deal, Humphrey had forged an outstanding record on social welfare issues and civil rights. Nevertheless, many peace Democrats now saw him as the toady of Johnson and party chieftains.

Vietnam was the albatross around Humphrey's neck. Initially skeptical about the war, he had been bullied into supporting it by Johnson, who maintained his grip over him during the convention. In negotiations with peace Democrats led by representatives of Senator Edward Kennedy (Massachusetts), the Humphrey camp had agreed a compromise plank on the war that called for an unconditional end to all bombing of North Vietnam. However he reneged on this under pressure from the president, and the convention eventually voted by 3 to 2 for a Vietnam plank that upheld administration policy. This was hardly an overwhelming endorsement. Never before in time of foreign war had any president's party been so bitterly divided over war policy at its nominating convention.

By contrast the Republicans had healed their wounds after the internecine strife of 1964 between the conservative and liberal wings of the party. In 1968 former Vice-President Richard Nixon, who ran in the primaries as a moderate, easily captured the GOP presidential nomination. Unlike Goldwater four years earlier, neither before nor after his nomination did Nixon campaign as an enemy of the New Deal. The constituency that he targeted was the middle Americans who had become disenchanted with Great Society liberalism, ghetto riots and peace demonstrations. Appealing to the sociocultural conservatism of those he called the "forgotten Americans", he pledged to uphold law and order and traditional mores, and vowed not to penalize working Americans who had earned the fruits of success through their own striving. Symbolizing this commitment, Nixon chose as his running-mate Governor Spiro Agnew of Maryland, the son of a poor Greek immigrant family and a politician best known for urging that rioting looters should be shot. On Vietnam Nixon promised to seek peace with honor, eventually telling the nation that he had a "secret plan" to achieve this.

In view of the Democrats' problems, Nixon seemed certain to win, and he initially led Humphrey by 16 points in the polls. However the race became much closer than expected thanks to the third party candidacy of George C. Wallace, the Democratic governor of Alabama. Wallace, who had made his name as an archsegregationist, had campaigned on openly racial themes in the Democratic presidential primaries of 1964. In 1968, as American Independence Party candidate, he adopted a broader strategy and ran as a new type of right-wing populist who articulated the resentment of many white Americans against the racial, social and cultural liberalism of the 1960s.

Like Nixon, Wallace focused his attack on Great Society liberalism rather than New Deal liberalism. His platform endorsed social insurance programs and the collective bargaining rights of labor unions, but condemned social engineering to enforce equality at the expense of average working men and women. Unlike Nixon, whose implicit emphasis was on containment of the social changes of the 1960s, Wallace promised roll-back. He also succeeded in fixing in the public mind the distinctive image of a liberal cabal of northern Democrats, bureaucrats, judges, intellectuals, and newspaper editors bent on imposing a new social agenda on the nation. Over half the respondents in a 1968 Harris poll shared Wallace's view that an unrepresentative liberal elite had run the country for too long. This pointed to the long-term significance of his campaign. According to Thomas and Mary Edsall, "Wallace brought into mainstream presidential politics a new political symbol, a vilified Democratic establishment that replaced as an enemy of lower-income voters the Republican establishment of corporate America and the rich."

Nixon, who had expected to take the South and challenge Humphrey for the votes of blue-collar whites in the North, found Wallace eating into both these constituencies. The Alabaman had no chance of winning, of course, but hoped to deny either main party candidate a plurality in the electoral college. This outcome would have placed the decision about which one became president in the hands of the House of Representatives, ensuring that Nixon or Humphrey would need

Wallace's endorsement in order to get the votes of southern congressmen. Opinion polls put Wallace's support at 21% in late September, but it quickly slipped from this peak. The Vietnam issue initiated the slide. The Wallace platform emphasized patriotic support for the war. This responsible position was undermined when his vice-presidential running mate, former Air Force chief of staff General Curtis E. LeMay, declared that he would support the use of nuclear weapons if necessary to end the conflict. As a result Wallace's candidacy became saddled with a damaging "mad bomber" image.

In the meantime Humphrey's fortunes rose after he broke free from meek obeisance to Johnson's war policy. In a nationally televised speech on September 30, he declared that if elected he would stop all bombing of North Vietnam as an acceptable risk for peace. Though a guarded statement with conditions attached, this seemed to meet the enemy's demands for a total bombing halt as a precondition to progress in peace negotiations. As a result many peace Democrats now felt able to back Humphrey (though others did not, and abstained from voting in sufficient numbers to help account for his eventual narrow defeat). Having neutralized the Vietnam issue, the vice president was free to campaign on domestic issues and made stirring appeals about the need to build a better society. Trade union leaders also mounted a propaganda campaign against Wallace that stemmed the defection of their members to him.

In the end Humphrey came tantalizingly close to victory, taking 42.7% of the popular vote, compared with Nixon's 43.4% and Wallace's 13.5%. Only 9 percent of white manual workers in the North backed Wallace, but this was enough to deny Humphrey victory in some states. On the other hand the only electoral college votes that Wallace won were from four Deep South states that would otherwise have gone to Nixon. Had Wallace not run in 1968, Nixon and Humphrey would probably have received roughly the same proportion of the two-party vote that they actually achieved.

Humphrey's comeback, the partial healing during the campaign of the party's bitter divisions over Vietnam, and the fact that they retained control of both houses of Congress in the 1968 elections seemed to indicate that the Democrats were still in good shape. Nevertheless the presidential vote had ominous significance for the party. Humphrey, who polled twelve million fewer votes than Johnson in 1964, ran badly among white voters regardless of their class. He won the backing of just 38% of low socioeconomic status (ses) whites, 39% of middle ses whites, and 36% of high ses whites. Only the overwhelming support of blacks and Jews had kept him in contention. His weak showing partly reflected disillusion with Johnson administration policy in Vietnam. Above all it indicated the divisive impact of racial and social issues on the class solidarity of the New Deal coalition.

Polls in the 1950s revealed that the American public identified the economic welfare cleavage as the main difference between the Democrats and Republicans. The parties' positions on civil rights were regarded as broadly similar. By the end of the 1960s, however, a dramatic change had occurred. Polls now showed that the two parties were most distinctive to the public in their stand on race-related issues. The profound impact of this change on voter loyalties was initially manifested in the 1968 presidential election, which marked the end of the era of Democratic party majority status that had began in the 1930s.

*   *   *

By 1968 the liberal consensus had passed into history. Within a period of three years the assumptions that had shaped US foreign, economic, and domestic policies in the postwar era had been undermined. America's leaders had lost confidence in the capacity of the United States to contain communism on a global basis, in the ability of government to manage the economy so as to produce strong growth, full employment, and low inflation, and in the state's potential to resolve social problems. At popular level, Vietnam had created deep divisions within society, many Americans were becoming concerned that inflation posed a threat to the perpetual improvement in living standards that they had enjoyed since World War II, and disenchantment with Great Society liberalism had eroded the unity of the New Deal political coalition. It remained to be seen whether a Republican president could pick up the pieces of a fragmented consensus and remold them into new political patterns.

3
Beyond Dominion: a New Foreign Policy for a Changed World, 1969–1976

For twenty years or so after 1945 the United States had been confident of its ability to shape the world's destiny. By the end of the 1960s, however, the limits of American dominion were evident. Failure in Vietnam, the growth in Soviet military power, and the rising economic challenge of Japan and Western Europe heralded the need for a new foreign policy which recognized the reality that US power was in relative decline. This adjustment to a changed world was to prove a painful and difficult process for the United States during the 1970s.

The task of reassessing America's international role initially fell to President Richard M. Nixon. Counseled by his National Security Adviser Henry A. Kissinger, he sought to relax Soviet-American tensions and develop a new equilibrium between the two superpowers through the process known as detente. Together Nixon and Kissinger engineered the most important changes in US diplomacy since the idea of containment was first mooted two decades earlier. Their new foreign policy entailed a modification rather than an abandonment of globalism. It aimed to contain Soviet power in the world arena by new and cheaper means. However the gap between the promise and reality of detente made it politically vulnerable at home. As a result domestic opinion remained divided about foreign policy following the breakdown of the Cold War consensus.

Nixon, Kissinger and the concept of detente

According to historian John Gaddis, the Nixon-Kissinger policy of detente consisted of five interrelated elements. Its central concern was to develop a new US-Soviet relationship based on recognition of the superpowers' legitimate security interests and mutual restraint where these were not involved. Related to this was Kissinger's concept of "linkage", a carrot-and-stick policy that tied gains made by the Soviets in one area to their good behavior in another. The third element of detente grew out of linkage. This was the effort to improve relations with the People's Republic of China (PRC) and form a new Sino-American axis to block Soviet ambitions in Asia.

Befriending China lessened the number of adversaries facing the United States and paved the way for implementation of the fourth feature of detente: the phasing down of America's commitments, particularly in Asia. The Nixon Doctrine, first presented in mid 1969, avowed that the United States would honor existing obligations to provide allies with economic assistance and military equipment but would otherwise expect them to be responsible for their own defense. As Kissinger put it, "America cannot — and will not — conceive all the plans, design all the programs, execute all the decisions and undertake all the defense of the free nations of the world." The Nixon Doctrine sent the world a signal that the United States would in future be highly selective in deciding whom it would defend and on what terms. Finally, lest the reduction of American commitments appeared a sign of weakness, Nixon and Kissinger favored tactical escalations in some areas in order to create uncertainty in the minds of adversaries by demonstrating that the country could still act if it chose to do so.

The two men who presided over the making of detente made an unlikely team. Nixon was a California-born WASP of lower middle-class origins, a professional politician whose roots lay in the Republican right, and whose McCarthyite past had made him something of a pariah to the foreign policy establishment. Kissinger was a Jewish refugee from Nazi Germany, but had been accepted into the very circles from which Nixon felt excluded. He was professor of government at Harvard University, had worked with the elite Council of Foreign Relations, and had been foreign policy adviser to Governor Nelson A. Rockefeller of New York, the dean of eastern liberal Republicanism. Despite their different backgrounds, Nixon and Kissinger were alike in many ways. Their similarities made their partnership well-suited to undertake an innovative foreign policy, but also made it prone to flout some fundamental principles of the American Constitution. Both were risk-takers who were contemptuous of the slow-moving procedures of the State Department. Both shared a love of secrecy and surprise, and both had a cynical attitude towards democracy. In their view the successful conduct of international affairs required the concentration of foreign policy-making powers in the White House. As a result they marginalized the role of Secretary of State William P. Rogers and tried to do the same to Congress.

In their respective memoirs Nixon and Kissinger each portrayed himself as the dominant partner, but the truth was that they needed each other. Nixon relied on the academically prestigious Kissinger to endow his policies with legitimacy in the eyes of foreign affairs experts and of opinion-makers in the media. The professor's skill as a diplomat and negotiator were also essential in the process of implementing detente. Furthermore, his willingness to use the National Security Council (NSC) as a quasi-State Department within the White House abetted Nixon's intention of increasing presidential control over foreign policy. In turn, Kissinger relied on Nixon for his entree into power and his unique relationship with the president opened the doors for his diplomatic successes with foreign governments. But he never dominated Nixon, who was personally responsible for conceiving the basic thrust of detente.

Nixon's political persona manifested an unusual combination of ideology and pragmatism. His meteoric rise from freshman Congressman in 1947 to Senator in 1951 and to Vice-President in 1953 at the age of 39 had been largely due to his vigorous anticommunism. Having come to prominence initially as a hunter of domestic subversives, he soon became more interested in the international dimensions of the Cold War. From the "loss" of China in 1949 until the mid-1960s, he was the most prominent and persistent advocate of global engagement against communism. Had he won the presidency in 1960, he would almost certainly have stepped up US activism abroad in the way that Kennedy and later Johnson were to do. Nixon had no doubts at this juncture that America had the power to maintain military supremacy over the Soviets and put down communist insurgencies in the Third World. But his outlook had changed by 1968.

Excepting Eisenhower and George Bush, no incoming president since 1945 has been better prepared than Nixon to conduct foreign policy. His transformation from ardent Cold Warrior to architect of detente resulted from his hard-nosed assessment of American power, based on extensive study, a substantial knowledge of foreign countries gained from widespread travel (including three trips to the Soviet Union), and long experience of international affairs. The metamorphosis was easier for him than it would have been for Hubert Humphrey, who would have been harried by criticisms of being soft on communism, particularly from Nixon himself, had he won the presidency in 1968 and then tried to implement detente. Given his impeccable anticommunist credentials, Nixon had greater freedom of action than anyone else to change American policy, and his flexibility took on the guise of statesmanship.

Nixon appointed Kissinger as National Security Adviser to help him articulate his foreign policy goals and integrate them into a conceptual framework for managing world affairs. Kissinger's ideas, outlined in a number of books written in the late 1950s and 1960s, reflected the realist approach to international relations. This school of thought contended that US foreign policy was excessively shaped by ideological precepts, had failed to respond to the diffusion of power away from the two superpowers, and lacked a coherent strategy for establishing a relationship between means and ends.

Detente was a response above all else to the relative decline of US power, but it also recognized that other developments favored bold diplomacy. America's Cold War illusion that the communist world was a Soviet-dominated monolith was no longer tenable. Simmering tensions between the Soviet Union and China, the result of longstanding territorial and ideological disputes, finally erupted into border fighting in 1969. This prompted the Beijing regime to seek friendly relations with the West. Signaling this change of course, in 1969 it terminated the three-year-long purification process known as the Great Cultural Revolution, which had plunged China into internal chaos and self-imposed isolation. In spite of its growing military power, marked by the achievement in 1969 of nuclear parity with the United States, the Soviet Union also had reason to welcome better relations with its capitalist rival. The huge military build-up launched in the mid 1960s had imposed a debilitating burden on the badly organized Soviet economy. The Kremlin was anxious to avoid the ill-effects of a prolonged arms race and regarded increased trade with the West, especially the importation of American high-technology products, as the best hope for economic revitalization.

The Nixon-Kissinger foreign policy viewed the world in geopolitical rather than ideological terms. It sought to create a new global equilibrium based on recognition that both American and Soviet power was limited, that a multipolar world was emerging, and that different ideological systems could have similar interests. Containment strategy had failed to distinguish between areas of vital and peripheral significance to US security. Hence the Kennedy-Johnson administrations had made Vietnam a symbolic test case of American power and commitment to combat communism on a global basis. In contrast, Nixon and Kissinger favored a more flexible conception of American interests based on a worldwide balance of power.

Detente rested on the assumption that neither the United States nor the Soviets had the resources to pursue ambitious goals simultaneously in different parts of the world. One outcome of this was the tacit revival of the spheres-of-influence concept accepted by Franklin D. Roosevelt at the end of World War II and then abandoned with the onset of the Cold War. More significantly, Nixon and Kissinger recognized that setbacks for one side in one place, such as the Americans had experienced in Vietnam, could be compensated for by gains elsewhere. It was the global balance of power that was deemed important, not defeats or victories in theaters of competition. Detente was not based on the expectation of immediate global reconciliation with the Soviets, nor did it entail a US retreat from a global foreign policy. Instead, it sought to achieve old ends by new means. Containment would still be pursued, but on a selective basis, by political and economic means rather than military ones, and through mutual concessions. The aim was to manage competition between the two superpowers so as to preserve global equilibrium and prevent the development of a suicidal nuclear confrontation.

Another cornerstone of detente was the conviction that the increasingly fragmented nature of power made possible a multipolar equilibrium, even though all the nations involved were by no means equal in terms of their power. While recognizing that America and the Soviet Union remained the only military superpowers, Nixon and Kissinger believed that Western Europe and Japan could now wield influence through their rising economic power, and that China's rivalry with the Soviets for the leadership of international communism made it a political power of note. In their view the multipolar system would allow for a more stable balance of power, because the primary burden for maintaining it would not fall on one nation.

Unlike its postwar predecessors, the Nixon administration did not make anticommunism a cardinal principle of its foreign policy. "[W]e have no permanent enemies", Kissinger declared in 1969, "We will judge other countries, including communist countries, . . . on the basis of their actions and not on the basis of their domestic ideology." Statements of this kind signaled the abandonment of efforts to reform the internal nature of other societies and export the American version of democracy that had been a hall-mark of previous Cold War policy. Nixon and Kissinger's principal goal was the development of a stable world order that was mutually acceptable to the United States and the Soviets. According to Walter LaFeber, they "most feared not communism, but disorder — especially revolutionaries who wanted to destroy order". Of course this did not mean that ideology played no part in US foreign policy during the era of detente. Third World revolutionaries who were regarded as the enemies of order were often Marxists, and American opposition to them had anticommunist overtones. Nixon and Kissinger would not tolerate the establishment of new Marxist regimes, whether independent from Moscow or not, because further victories for communism were deemed incompatible with the preservation of the global balance of power.

Detente was a dazzling concept, particularly when articulated by Kissinger, but there were weaknesses in its intellectual foundations. The implicit assumption that by acting together the superpowers could control political developments in the Third World was the most serious miscalculation. Nixon and Kissinger never appreciated that revolutionary governments and movements in Africa and Asia were not Soviet pawns and were resistant to outside manipulation. They also overestimated Soviet willingness to assist in controlling political developments in the Third World. Confident of their new military power, the Russians actually sought to expand their interests in Africa and Asia during the 1970s. Finally, Kissinger's concept of linkage mistakenly assumed that diplomatic pressures and inducements could be tightly coordinated through presidential control over the policymaking machinery. Already disillusioned by Johnson's misuse of presidential power in Vietnam, Congress grew increasingly hostile to Nixon's efforts to expand the "imperial presidency" and eventually asserted its constitutional right to share in the making of foreign policy. All these problems would surface when the Nixon-Kissinger foreign policy faced its first test — how to extricate the United States from Vietnam.

Vietnamizing the Vietnam war

According to Raymond Garthoff, an honorable exit from Vietnam was Nixon's dominant preoccupation during his early years in office. Improving relations with Moscow and Beijing were "at that time seen as much as means to that end as they were ends in themselves". The concept of detente was by no means fully developed at the outset of Nixon's presidency and its gradual evolution was partly a subsequent rationalization for a series of maneuvers undertaken to help get the United States out of Vietnam. The war denied American diplomacy the flexibility to capitalize on changing world developments. It was a huge drain on national treasure and diverted resources from other security needs. Its effects on the economy were increasingly evident. Last and by no means least, it was creating domestic turmoil unparalleled in the twentieth century.

The question that perplexed the new administration was not whether to pursue peace, but how to do so. Peace through military victory was evidently impossible. Johnson's limited war had been a failure, but public opinion would no longer support a long-term escalation of the war effort in pursuit of final victory. Atomic diplomacy, such as President Eisenhower had practiced to bring about a cessation of hostilities in Korea in 1953, was not a feasible option. The United States no longer possessed nuclear superiority, so Nixon could not risk provoking the Russians and Chinese into making counter-threats in aid of Hanoi.

Of course the easiest way out was through immediate unilateral withdrawal. This was not an option given serious consideration by Nixon and Kissinger. Their goal of "peace with honor" required American withdrawal to take place on terms that would preserve the existence of a noncommunist Republic of South Vietnam. Only this outcome, they believed, would enable the United States to maintain its credibility as a military superpower in the eyes not only of the Soviets and Chinese but also of its allies. At stake was more than merely saving face. Nixon and Kissinger deemed the perception of US power to be as important as the reality of US power if they were to succeed in building a stable international equilibrium. Their policy in Vietnam remained tied, just as Johnson's had been, towards global ends.

As reported by the White House chief of staff, H. R. (Bob) Haldeman, Nixon was initially optimistic of capitalizing on his anti-communist reputation to convince Hanoi that "I've reached the point where I might do anything to stop the war." This "Madman Theory", as the president labeled it, required him to demonstrate that he was willing to go further than Johnson to secure acceptable peace terms. Accordingly, US bombing of communist-held areas of South Vietnam was stepped up in the spring of 1969. Nixon also ordered intensive air attacks on communist sanctuaries in neutral Cambodia, which were kept secret from both the State Department and Congress. When these actions had no effect on North Vietnam's determination to prolong the struggle, Nixon and Kissinger toyed with a plan, code-named "Duck-Hook", to escalate the war still further. This would have entailed massive bombing of North Vietnam, the destruction of its dike system, a possible invasion of the country, and the optional use of nuclear bombs against the Ho Chi Minh Trail (along which military supplies were moved to communist forces in South Vietnam). However, news that such a scheme was being contemplated revitalized the antiwar movement in the fall of 1969, so Nixon had to abandon the plan for the sake of domestic harmony.

Unable to pursue the "Madman Theory", Nixon fell back on a multipronged strategy intended to secure a negotiated ceasefire and mutual withdrawal of American and North Vietnamese troops from South Vietnam. Its core element was the Vietnamization program to build up the self-sufficiency of South Vietnam's army (ARVN) and enable it to bear the brunt of the fighting while a phased withdrawal of American troops took place. In conjunction with this, Nixon planned a short-term escalation of US military action to put pressure on the communists to negotiate. Finally, guided by Kissinger's concept of linkage, he hoped that the carrot of improved political and economic relations with the United States would induce the Soviets to use their influence with Hanoi on behalf of peace.

Nixon anticipated that the American withdrawal, which began with the announcement in June 1969 that 25,000 troops were being brought home, would be completed by the end of 1970. Instead, it was a long-drawn-out process that finally ended in early 1973 with a peace settlement that was neither honorable nor lasting and whose terms were little better than could have been negotiated four years earlier. During this period more than half a million enemy soldiers, over 107,000 South Vietnamese troops, and nearly 21,000 Americans (almost 40% of total US losses in the war) were killed, civilian casualties mounted, and American bombing laid waste to large areas of North and South Vietnam, Cambodia and Laos. US actions also helped to destabilize Cambodia and Laos with dreadful consequences for their citizens. At home, meanwhile, all the existing problems caused by the war were exacerbated and several new ones came into being. Small wonder, therefore, that Nixon's principal biographer Stephen Ambrose has characterized the Vietnamization policy as "one of the worst decisions ever made by a Cold War President" and the "worst mistake of his Presidency".

It was a strategy riddled with flaws. Like LBJ, Nixon and Kissinger failed to understand that the North Vietnamese were motivated by nationalist concerns, which precluded acceptance of a compromise peace recognizing the legitimacy of the Saigon regime. Nixon's announcement of phased troop withdrawal, made without extracting any concessions in return, only increased communist determination to continue the war. Hanoi's incentive to negotiate was reduced and its confidence in ultimate victory was correspondingly increased by the knowledge that the Americans were pulling out. Reliance on linkage also proved misplaced. The North Vietnamese were not puppets of international communism. Moreover, the Soviets were happy to see the United States tied down and did little to promote a settlement until detente took concrete form with the Moscow summit of 1972. Thereafter, they regarded Vietnam as a sideshow and urged Hanoi to make peace, but continued to send it economic assistance and military equipment.

Nor did the Vietnamization program address the political and military character of the war itself. The United States was seeking to preserve an inefficient, corrupt and dictatorial government that lacked widespread popular support. The massive influx of American money and weaponry enabled the Saigon regime to order a huge mobilization that increased ARVN personnel from 700,000 to 1,100,000, over half the able-bodied male population. Of course, this did nothing to resolve issues like land reform, economic development, and political rights that would have given the people of South Vietnam a cause worth fighting and dying for. As a result the effectiveness of the ARVN as a fighting force continued to be impeded by low morale among its rank-and-file soldiers and junior officers. In addition, Vietnamization primarily equipped the ARVN for a high-fire-power war against a conventional enemy, such as the United States had tried to fight with limited success in 1965–8. It did not provide the means to counter the highly effective guerilla tactics employed by communist forces.

Although Vietnamization was not making satisfactory progress, Nixon had to continue the withdrawal of US troops for domestic political reasons. In these circumstances he decided on another tactical escalation to buy more time for the ARVN and "show the enemy that we were still serious about our commitment in Vietnam". A coup d'état in Cambodia in March 1970 brought to power a trenchantly anticommunist government, whose efforts to prevent the North Vietnamese from moving supplies across its territory to communist forces in South Vietnam resulted in a number of bloody military skirmishes. These events provided Nixon with the justification for one of the most controversial acts of his presidency. In April US and South Vietnamese troops invaded Cambodia to destroy communist supply lines and base areas.

The results were disastrous. The invasion did little damage to the enemy's military capabilities and the United States acquired another weak client regime that it could not protect against a communist insurgency. North Vietnam stepped up its own support for the Khmer Rouge rebels, who gained control of Cambodia in 1975 and instituted a bloody rule of terror that claimed the lives of between one and two million people. Nixon's actions in Cambodia also did much to undermine domestic support for the administration's policy in Vietnam.

By late 1969 Nixon had succeeded in mobilizing a constituency of support for the Vietnamization program as a means of winning an honorable peace in Southeast Asia at relatively little cost to the United States. Polls showed that most Americans were still reluctant to accept anything resembling defeat in Vietnam, even though they were equally reluctant to increase US commitments there. Largely dormant since the 1968 election, the antiwar movement did revive briefly to protest against the Duck-Hook plan but was soon put on the defensive. In a televised address to the nation on November 3, Nixon urged the "great silent majority" of Americans to back him, and warned that failure in Southeast Asia would encourage communist aggression elsewhere. Dismissing peace protesters as irresponsible and naive, he claimed: "North Vietnam cannot humiliate the United States. Only Americans can do that." This appeal to Cold War patriotism elicited widespread support. Nixon's Gallup poll approval rating soared to 68% and both houses of Congress endorsed resolutions supporting his policy.

However, the invasion of Cambodia pitched America into turmoil once more. Nixon again used television to appeal for patriotic unity, but antiwar activities on college campuses reached new peaks. This volatile situation had tragic consequences. On May 4 the Ohio National Guard fired on protesters at Kent State University, killing four students. Ten days later, Mississippi state police shot dead two students during protests at the all-black Jackson State College. These events threw the campuses and the nation at large into chaos. Symbolizing the divisions that had arisen, prowar construction workers beat up antiwar protesters in New York, but business leaders flew to Washington to warn the president that the expanded war and the resultant turmoil were close to causing a financial panic. To quieten the situation, Nixon announced that American troops would be withdrawn from Cambodia by the end of June. Nevertheless the invasion had brought about a considerable erosion of the short-lived consensus that he had created for Vietnamization. Not only had the peace movement revived, the media had grown increasingly hostile to the administration's Vietnam policy

and — most significantly — congressional opposition to the war had
hardened.

The invasion of Cambodia prompted Congress to challenge presidential ability to make war in Southeast Asia for the first time since the
United States had become involved in the region. In June 1970 the
Senate repealed the Gulf of Tonkin Resolution, which Johnson had
originally used as a mandate to Americanize the Vietnam War, and the
House of Representatives followed suit in December. This was a largely
symbolic act of defiance since Nixon argued that the Resolution was
not necessary to continue the war. More importantly, the Senate also
enacted an amendment to cut off all funds for American military
involvement in Cambodia after June 30. Though defeated in the House
of Representatives, this motion marked the first significant effort by
Congress to use its appropriations power to limit presidential war-
making power since the onset of the Cold War in the late 1940s. Many
congressmen were still wary about the electoral consequences of voting
against military funds that the Commander-in-Chief adjudged necessary
to preserve the lives of American soldiers fighting in Vietnam. Nevertheless, as public dissatisfaction with the war rose, Congress grew correspondingly bolder in challenging the president. In late 1970 both
houses voted to proscribe the use of appropriated funds for the rein-
troduction of ground troops into Cambodia.

Nixon stubbornly persisted with Vietnamization despite its lack of
military, diplomatic or political success. In 1971, as the pace of US troop
withdrawal was accelerated, he stepped up the use of air power to aid
South Vietnam. The bombing of military targets in North Vietnam was
resumed and air attacks on communist supply-routes in Cambodia and
Laos were increased. Air support was also provided for the ARVN's
incursion into Laos to hit enemy bases. However this episode only
underlined that South Vietnam was nowhere near achieving military
self-sufficiency. Faced by well-armed and battle-hardened adversaries,
the ARVN took a bad beating, suffering a casualty rate as high as 50%,
and retreated home after six months of heavy fighting. As in Cambodia,
the expansion of the war destabilized Laos and set the scene for communist insurgents to gain ground with North Vietnamese aid.

By the summer of 1971 popular disillusion with Nixon's policy was
widespread, even among former supporters. A Gallup poll indicated
that 71% of Americans now regarded US involvement in Vietnam as
a mistake and 58% deemed it morally wrong. For the first time a
substantial majority was in favor of withdrawing US troops even at

the cost of a communist takeover of South Vietnam. The nation's will to sustain the war had almost evaporated. On two occasions the Senate actually approved resolutions fixing a deadline for complete withdrawal, but the House defeated both measures.

To make matters worse a siege mentality had taken hold of the embattled Nixon White House. The presidential aide and Watergate conspirator Charles Colson recalled, "It was now 'us' against 'them'. Gradually, as we drew the circle closer around us, the ranks of 'them' began to swell." After the Kent State killings, Nixon ordered the FBI and CIA to cooperate in a massive counterintelligence project to investigate whether antiwar groups were connected with communist subversives. The original scheme was torpedoed by FBI director J. Edgar Hoover, who objected that it was excessive and illegal. It was revived in the form of a secret White House operation after onetime Department of Defense employee Daniel Ellsberg leaked the so-called "Pentagon Papers" to the *New York Times* in 1971. Commissioned in 1967 by Robert McNamara, this 7,000-page study of US involvement in Southeast Asia since 1945 provided clear evidence of important discrepancies between the policies and public statements of successive presidents.

Although the Pentagon Papers did not bear on his management of the war, Nixon was uncomfortably aware of his own administration's secrets and public lies, particularly concerning the bombing of Cambodia. In July 1971 top presidential assistant John Ehrlichman assigned Egil "Bud" Krogh, a White House aide, to take charge of an "in-house" project to prevent further leaks of secret information to the media. The personnel Krogh recruited to the anti-leak project, the so-called "plumbers", were soon involved in illegal activities. In September 1971, a team of them broke into the offices of Ellsberg's psychiatrist in a bid to find medical documents that would discredit him. Whether Nixon knew of this plan is unclear, but the episode marked the first fateful steps toward the Watergate scandal that brought about his downfall.

Mid 1971 proved the nadir of Nixon's first term as president. The combination of declining popular support for a war that had by now become identified as his war rather than one he inherited, the furor over the publication of the Pentagon Papers, and mounting economic troubles seemed to put his reelection at risk. The growth of antiwar feeling in the United States had also encouraged North Vietnamese intransigence both at the official peace talks in Paris and in secret negotiations simultaneously being conducted by Kissinger.

Nevertheless, Nixon confounded his critics by scoring two historic diplomatic successes that marked the high point of his presidency.

Detente at high tide, 1971–1973

On 15 July 1971 Nixon surprised the nation, and indeed much of the world, by announcing that he planned to visit China in the following year. US relations with Communist China had been deeply hostile since 1949. Some 56% of Americans still regarded the PRC as the world's most dangerous nation. Nixon himself had been one of its foremost enemies throughout his political career, but he now seized the opportunity to put Sino-American relations on a new footing. Concerned about Soviet military activities along their border, the Chinese had already signaled their desire for rapprochement with the United States. A flurry of diplomatic activity in mid 1971 culminated in a secret visit to Beijing by Kissinger to arrange this.

Nixon had not been under domestic pressure to change course concerning China, so he could claim sole responsibility for taking the initiative. The move encouraged hope at home and abroad that international relations were entering an era of peace and stability. Nixon had emerged as a world statesman. The Republican right apart, there was widespread support for the new policy. In February 1972, not coincidentally just before the start of that year's election campaign, Nixon became the first US president ever to visit China. The trip dominated press headlines and television news coverage, doing him a power of good with voters. But he wanted — and got — more from it than this.

One outcome was the strengthening of the new economic relations that had been opened up between the two countries in 1971, after twenty-two years of US-imposed restrictions. At a time when America's international trade position was under pressure, this was a welcome development. By late 1973 US-China trade had grown from a mere $5 million to $900 million annually, and now exceeded the volume of US-Soviet trade (excepting special grain deals).

Nixon's visit also had important political consequences. It did not produce outright US recognition of the PRC (which finally occurred in 1979), but it laid down the foundations for growing diplomatic and political ties. Both sides agreed to differ over the most contentious issue between them: the Chinese insisted on maintaining their claim to possession of Taiwan, while Nixon declared that the United States would maintain its military presence on this island in support of the

Nationalist Chinese regime of Chiang. Kai-shek ensconced there. However, in the Shanghai communiqué of February 1972, the United States affirmed its interest in a peaceful settlement of the Taiwan issue by the Chinese themselves and promised a progressive reduction of its forces on Taiwan as the tension in the area diminished. From Nixon's perspective this gave the PRC a stake in putting pressure on its fellow communists in Hanoi to negotiate peace in Vietnam, the main source of "tension" in East Asia. In fact Beijing's efforts to this end proved fruitless because of its declining influence with North Vietnam. As the Sino-Soviet split intensified, Hanoi grew closer to Moscow — not for ideological reasons, but out of nationalist fear of Vietnam's historical enemy, China.

Above all else Nixon's China initiative had succeeded in putting pressure on the Soviet Union, whose two greatest foes were now seemingly united against it. The Shanghai communiqué, in a thinly veiled reference to the Soviets, pledged that the United States and the PRC would oppose any nation seeking to establish hegemony in the Asia Pacific region. In fact the mere announcement of Nixon's visit to Beijing had been sufficient to prompt a Soviet invitation for him to visit Moscow in mid 1972. The stage was now set for marked progress in the negotiation of Soviet-American detente.

Arms-control agreement held the key to detente. Nixon inherited the reality that the Soviet Union possessed, in Kissinger's words, "powerful and sophisticated strategic forces approaching, and in some categories exceeding our own in numbers and capability". By mid 1972 the United States had 1054 intercontinental ballistic missiles (ICBMs), 656 submarine launched ballistic missiles (SLBMs), and 450 long-range bombers; Soviet strength in each category was 1607, 740 and 200 respectively. Following the Cuban missile crisis, the Soviets had launched a crash buildup of their nuclear arsenal to ensure that they could not be faced down by American superiority in the future. Given the constraints of the Vietnam War, the Johnson administration could not initiate a counter-buildup to sustain the American lead. Nor could the Nixon administration hope to divert resources to this end as it wound down US commitments in Southeast Asia.

Growing mistrust of presidential warmaking in Vietnam had caused antimilitary attitudes to take hold in Congress. Between 1945 and 1965 the legislature had been much more prone to cut presidential spending proposals in the domestic field rather than in defense. This trend was reversed in the 1970s. The Democrats, who controlled both houses of

Congress, sought to use the savings from the Vietnam "peace dividend" for social programs. Defense expenditure declined as a percentage of total federal spending from 40.8% in fiscal 1970 to 23.3% in fiscal 1978, the lowest level of the post-World War II era. Nixon received clear warning of the new mood in 1969 when Senate approval of funds to continue development of the antiballistic missile (ABM) system was carried by only a single vote. Although the president insisted that this defensive weapon was vital as a bargaining chip for arms control talks, many senators feared that it would accelerate the arms race by encouraging the Soviets to embark on a vast increase of their missile armory in order to overwhelm the ABM.

The Johnson administration had previously secured Moscow's agreement for arms control talks, but called these off following the Soviet invasion of Czechoslovakia in 1968. Impelled by international and domestic concerns, Nixon and Kissinger quickly signaled their willingness to begin negotiations. Progress in the talks was initially slow, because the Soviets wanted them limited to defensive weapons, while the Americans wanted offensive systems included too. Backstairs diplomacy by Kissinger eventually smoothed the way for an agreement that covered both. At the Moscow summit of May 1972 Nixon and Soviet leader Leonid Brezhnev signed the Anti-Ballistic Missile Treaty and the five-year Interim Agreement on the Limitations of Strategic Arms. The former limited both superpowers to two ABM sites each (at which a maximum of one hundred missiles could be deployed). The latter provided that neither side would undertake construction of land-based ICBM launchers after July 1, 1972, while increases in SLBM launchers would be limited to those already under construction. These agreements, collectively labeled SALT-1, sought to ensure that the United States and the Soviets had second-strike capability but that neither had adequate defense against missile attack. It was assumed that the balance of terror established between the superpowers would deter them from a nuclear war which could only result in mutual destruction.

Nixon's rhetoric stressed that "sufficiency" rather than "superiority" was America's new strategic goal, but in reality he conceived detente as an instrument for preserving nuclear supremacy. Despite allowing the Soviets quantitative superiority in missiles, SALT-1 favored the United States whose missiles were superior in quality, accuracy, and warhead capability. At American insistence, SALT-1 did not limit the number of warheads that missiles carried, and therefore did not affect Multiple Independently Targeted Reentry Vehicles (MIRVs). The

United States led the race to develop these technologically advanced weapons, which could give each ICBM up to ten separately-targeted nuclear warheads. Nixon and Kissinger were confident that the MIRVS, when fully deployed, would give the United States a two-to-one lead in deliverable warheads. It was also significant that aircraft and new weapons systems were not covered in SALT-1. Accordingly, the United States could increase its strength by developing the Trident submarine, the MX missile, the B-1 bomber, and the cruise missiles. Far from halting the arms race, SALT-1 helped to accelerate it.

The arms control agreements established the foundations of a new US-Soviet detente. Most Americans welcomed this development, though some continued to harbor traditional suspicions of the Soviets and feared that Nixon had given too much away at Moscow. Arms control experts were also critical of the specific details of SALT-1, particularly the effective concession of quantitative missile superiority to the Soviets, and claimed that better terms could have been achieved through formal negotiation by specialists rather than Kissinger's personal diplomacy. Critics of detente in Congress seized on this charge, but they were too few to block approval of SALT-1. To outflank them, Nixon and Kissinger inevitably oversold the benefits of SALT-1. Over the next few years, political and popular support for the agreement eroded as its limitations in halting the arms race and ensuring American security grew apparent. This in turn resulted in the underestimation of SALT-1's genuine historical significance as the first superpower agreement to control nuclear arms. Whatever its shortcomings in practice, by proving that the Americans and Soviets could negotiate limits to their destructive capabilities, it represented a symbolic break-through in arms control. Moreover, the ABM treaty ensured that both sides had a fundamental interest in preventing nuclear war.

SALT-1 also encouraged hopes of further progress in improving Soviet-American relations. Nixon and Kissinger were convinced that the Moscow summit marked the beginning of a new era in world politics. Their confidence on this score was encouraged by other superpower agreements and negotiations that underlined the relaxation of Cold War tensions in Europe. The thaw had been marked first by the four-power agreement of August 1971 (between the United States, the Soviets, Britain and France) guaranteeing unimpeded movement of people and commodities between West Germany and West Berlin. Two further agreements tied up other loose ends from World War II. In both cases it was the Americans who made concessions. The Berlin

Agreement, providing formal US recognition of East Germany, marked the abandonment of America's postwar policy of seeking a reunited Germany. Talks started in November 1972 eventually resulted in the Helsinki Accords of 1975, which signified the West's acceptance of Soviet regional hegemony by recognizing the boundaries of East European communist states.

Without doubt, however, the main political significance of the Moscow summit so far as Nixon and Kissinger were concerned was that prospects of a negotiated peace in Vietnam had apparently been boosted. In this respect the very fact that the summit took place at all was important. In April 1972 North Vietnam launched a major offensive against the South. With the US presidential election campaign soon to begin, its aim was to repeat the political success of the 1968 Tet offensive and pressurize American withdrawal by proving the ineffectiveness of Vietnamization. Still determined to pursue "peace with honor" as a guarantee of America's global credibility, Nixon responded strongly. The Duck-Hook plan of 1969 was resuscitated in a modified version known as Operation Linebacker. US planes pummelled communist positions and supply-lines in South Vietnam. More significantly, intensive bombing of North Vietnam, including its main cities and ports, was undertaken for the first time since Johnson's decision to suspend air raids over the North in November 1968. Also, to prevent the import of military supplies from the Soviet Union and its allies, mines were planted in six North Vietnamese ports, including Haiphong. Nixon's decision to escalate was taken in the knowledge that it might cause the Soviets to cancel the summit and so destroy the prospects for detente.

In going ahead with the summit, the Kremlin signified that it placed greater value on detente, with its attendant political, strategic and economic benefits for the Soviet Union, than on communist victory in Vietnam. The Chinese, too, made no response to the Linebacker operation. Nixon and Kissinger could therefore claim to have separated North Vietnam from its allies. Linebacker was also a military success. It ground the communist offensive to a halt and provided a further breathing space for Vietnamization. Meanwhile, the outcome of the Moscow summit and the fact that American troop withdrawals continued during the crisis kept antiwar protest in the United States at a low pitch and strengthened Nixon's reelection prospects.

All this did not mean that real victory was at hand for the United States. Far from undermining communist military capability, the 1972 summer campaign had merely intensified the violence of the stalemate.

Paradoxically, the outcome made Nixon more willing to make concessions in pursuit of peace because he was satisfied that Linebacker had preserved America's credibility as a superpower. Through Soviet intermediaries, Kissinger informed Hanoi in mid 1972 that the United States would now accept a peace settlement that permitted North Vietnamese forces to remain in the South after a cease-fire.

Negotiating a final settlement still proved a tortuous process. The fundamental division, as had been the case since negotiations were first started in 1968, was over the future of Vietnam. North Vietnam had always been adamant that the United States should withdraw without seeking guarantees about its future conduct toward the Saigon regime headed by Nguyen Van Thieu. The Americans in turn wanted assurances that after their departure Hanoi would not use force in settling the problems of a divided Vietnam. In October 1972 Kissinger finally agreed a compromise settlement with North Vietnamese diplomats during secret talks at Paris. Hanoi dropped its insistence on the ouster of Thieu; the Americans modified their absolute commitment to his regime by accepting that a tripartite commission composed of Thieu's representatives, neutralists, and communists should organize elections in South Vietnam.

Kissinger's public announcement that peace was at hand proved premature owing to Thieu's reluctance to go along with the deal. Without South Vietnam's approval, of course, Nixon could not claim to have achieved peace with honor. To make matters worse, North Vietnam sought to delay negotiation of a final settlement in the hope that Thieu's intransigence would provoke the newly-elected US Congress to cut off aid to Saigon. A final act therefore had to be played out in order to enhance America's standing in the game of international power politics to which the actual war in Vietnam had long been subservient.

North Vietnam's delaying tactics prompted Nixon to renew the air offensive against it. The heaviest bombing raids of the war were unleashed during the Christmas season of 1972. The B-52s, previously in operation only against communist positions in South Vietnam and Cambodia, attacked every city in the North. For Nixon and Kissinger the bombing was intended not only to bring North Vietnam back to the peace table but also to serve as a warning of how the United States would respond if it tried to break the settlement and overthrow the Saigon regime by force. In the meantime, however, Thieu was also warned that US aid would be cut off unless he accepted peace terms.

The carrot that went with this stick was a secret promise from Nixon that the United States would use force to protect the Saigon regime if it came under future military threat. Almost certainly he had no intention of ever reintroducing American ground troops, but it is equally probably that he was sincere in his willingness to recommit air power if necessary.

The display of American military and political muscle paved the way for a cease-fire agreement on January 23, 1973. The United States had finally negotiated an exit from the longest war in its history, but on terms acknowledging its failure to all intents and purposes to settle the issues for which the war had been fought. South Vietnam's future was left undecided. The process for electing a new government in Saigon was unworkable, making it inevitable that the use of force would continue to be the determining factor. In view of this the peace terms allowed the communists a significant advantage. Although US combat troops were to be withdrawn from South Vietnam within sixty days, North Vietnam was not required to follow suit and only promised to remove its forces from Laos and Cambodia. This was hardly peace with honor. In truth the United States had lost a war for the first time in its history.

For the time being, however, reality was dimmed by the national sense of euphoria that America's long nightmare was over. Opinionmakers in the media generally voiced confidence that the terms negotiated by Nixon and Kissinger were enough to secure South Vietnam's survival. A war-weary public rejoiced, particularly when television captured the highly emotive scenes of the first American POWs arriving at Clark Air Base in the Philippines. His first term crowned by triumph, Nixon looked forward to building a new world order on the foundations of his triangular diplomacy with the Soviets and Chinese during his final years in office. However, the fragile nature of his foreign policy achievement soon became evident.

Detente in decline, 1973–1976

In 1972 detente had boosted Nixon's reelection prospects. Four years later it was seen as a vote-loser and became a non-word in President Gerald Ford's election campaign. The inherent stresses and contradictions of this policy were now plain. Although detente would remain an important concern of Soviet-American relations until 1979, it had suffered serious erosion by 1976. The main causes of this were fundamental differences between the two superpowers as to the meaning of detente, setbacks to US interests in the Third World, and the changed configurations within domestic American politics.

From the American perspective, detente was a means to contain the Soviet Union's growing power by enlisting its cooperation for the management of a new international order that would serve US interests and preserve US world leadership. SALT-1's recognition of Soviet military parity was not complemented by American recognition of Soviet political parity. Nixon and Kissinger never intended detente to be a partnership among equals. Their aim was to persuade the Soviet Union that cooperation with the West was more profitable than confrontation by integrating it into the network of international economic relations. Secondly, they sought Soviet cooperation for the regulation and resolution of crises in the Third World periphery where US power was weakest and most easily eroded. Nixon and Kissinger's first goal may have been practicable, but they were mistaken in assuming that the two superpowers could manage the affairs of developing nations at a time when global power was becoming increasingly fragmented and that the Soviets would want to assist the United States in this task.

By contrast, Russia believed that detente signified a changed world in which America's postwar preeminence was replaced by political as well as military parity between the two superpowers. So far as the developing world was concerned, the Soviet Union now expected the United States to treat it as an equal in regions where both had important interests, notably the Middle East, and to accept that competition between capitalism and socialism was now legitimate even in regions where Soviet interests were not well developed, such as Africa and Latin America. For the Kremlin, the purpose of detente was not to eliminate US-Soviet competition in any part of the world but to prevent it from dangerous escalation. This perspective ensured that superpower rivalry in the Third World increased rather than diminished under detente.

Covert involvement in the military coup that overthrew the elected socialist government of Chile in September 1973 showed that the United States was not willing to tolerate the emergence of regimes friendly to the Soviet Union in its own hemisphere. It also bested the Soviets in a struggle for influence in the Middle East, a region of rapidly growing significance for world affairs, but this success had problematic consequences.

Both superpowers had clients in the Middle East, where the United States aligned with Saudi Arabia and Israel, and the Soviets backed

Egypt and Syria. Yet the region was on the periphery of Nixon and Kissinger's strategic diplomacy until 1973. Israel's security, the principal concern of America's Middle Eastern policy, had seemingly been ensured by the crushing defeat of its Arab neighbors in the Six Day War of 1967. But in reality the conflict had served to increase rather than diminish tensions in the region. Egypt, Syria, and Jordan wanted to recover territory they had lost in this war and to end Israeli occupation of the West Bank of the river Jordan, the homeland of a million Palestinians. These festering regional problems increasingly embroiled the superpowers, bringing them close to direct confrontation.

In a surprise move, President Anwar Sadat summarily broke Egypt's links with the Soviet Union in 1972 and sought better relations with the United States. Sadat hoped to get new economic assistance from the Americans and to enlist their influence in securing a political settlement of Middle Eastern territorial disputes. Nevertheless Egypt's initiative and its warnings about a new war unless Arab land was restored were ignored by Kissinger and Nixon, who deemed the Arabs incapable of a further military challenge to Israel. Such confidence was badly misplaced. After securing a promise of renewed Soviet aid, Egypt joined with Syria to launch a surprise attack on Israel on October 6, 1973 during the Jewish religious holiday of Yom Kippur. Helped by a massive Soviet airlift of military supplies, their armies were initially victorious. The US responded with an even bigger airlift of supplies to the Israelis, whose successful counter-attack drove back the Syrians and encircled the Egyptian army.

Anxious to save Egypt from complete defeat, the Soviets cooperated with the United States in supporting a United Nations cease-fire resolution, but Israel ignored this and sought to starve Sadat's army into surrender. The Kremlin then called for joint military intervention by the superpowers to establish the cease-fire and warned that it would act unilaterally if necessary. Nixon and Kissinger were not prepared to allow the Soviets to become power-brokers in the Middle East. On October 24 Kissinger told them to stay out of the region, and US forces worldwide were moved to a "Stage 3" alert in readiness for possible nuclear confrontation (which would take place at "Stage 5"). The Russians backed down, leaving the stage clear for the United States to mediate a settlement. This task fell to Kissinger, who had recently been promoted to Secretary of State and would henceforth assume the main responsibility for foreign policy because of Nixon's growing preoccupation with the emergent Watergate scandal.

Knowing that the Israelis would not make territorial concessions if they achieved total victory, Kissinger pressured them to accept a cease-fire by threatening that US military supplies would be halted unless the encirclement of Egypt's army was lifted. Nevertheless his efforts to negotiate a permanent peace in the region had limited success. By the end of 1975, Kissinger's shuttle diplomacy between Cairo and Tel Aviv had won Sadat's promise to deal peacefully in future with Israel, who agreed in turn to relinquish some occupied territory. On the other hand Syria remained obdurately hostile to Israel. More seriously, Kissinger's diplomacy could not resolve the issue of Palestinian sovereignty, which now became the principal focus of Arab-Israeli tensions. In 1974 Arab states declared support for the Palestine Liberation Organization, whose goal was to establish an Arab state in Palestine. The Middle East remained an armed camp, and the United States had to ensure Israel's security through providing it with hugely increased supplies of high-tech weaponry.

As the historian Robert Schulzinger commented, US success in establishing preeminence over the Soviet Union in Middle Eastern affairs meant that the "Arab fantasy of an all-powerful America manipulating Israel had finally become a reality". This spelled danger for the United States because of its new vulnerability to Arab oil power. Nixon and Kissinger had assumed that the Arab world was too divided to achieve a coordinated boycott of oil supplies. Under Saudi Arabia's leadership, however, eleven Middle Eastern states agreed in October 1973 to embargo oil exports to nations considered too friendly to Israel. The need to get the embargo lifted lent urgency to Kissinger's diplomacy and his efforts to win concessions from Israel. The Arab oil powers finally relented in May 1974, but not before the Organization of Petroleum Exporting Countries (OPEC) had exploited the West's energy shortage and raised the price of crude oil by three hundred per-cent. The resultant surge in inflation meant that Kissinger's diplomatic triumphs had a hollow ring to them so far as ordinary Americans were concerned.

Relations with Iran provided further evidence of Kissinger's ambiguous achievement in the Middle East. In 1972 Nixon and Shah Mohammed Reza Pahlevi had negotiated an agreement making Iran the principal protector of US interests in the oil-rich Persian Gulf in return for unlimited access to advanced US weaponry (except nuclear arms). This was an important step in the Nixon-Kissinger strategy of reducing America's global commitments while preserving its global interests.

Over the next seven years Iran became the world's biggest customer for US arms, spending in excess of $21 billion. However, the Shah proved himself an undependable ally by leading OPEC into the 1974 oil price increase. Association with his regime also sucked the United States into the vortex of domestic Iranian affairs, with disastrous consequences later on for the Carter administration.

Africa also emerged as a battleground between the superpowers in the detente era. The United States fared less well in this case because it made unwise regional alignments. National Security Study Memorandum 39, a secret review of US interests in Africa ordered by Kissinger in 1970, recommended that the country should aid the new black African nations but prioritize its relations with the white regimes of South Africa and Portugal's colonial possessions. South Africa's position at the tip of the continent was deemed to have immense strategic and economic significance for US world interests, while support for Portugal was dictated by its importance to the NATO security apparatus in Europe. Africa experts within the State Department were aghast that this so-called African policy almost entirely subordinated regional considerations to global concerns. They dubbed it the "Tar-Baby option" that would stick the United States to losing causes in Africa.

Despite US economic aid, Portugal could not crush anticolonial movements in Angola, Mozambique and Guinea, all of which were granted independence in 1974. A Marxist regime soon came to power in Mozambique. Kissinger failed in his efforts to prevent the same thing happening in Angola, where the struggle for independence mutated into a civil war to decide who would rule the new nation. An all-party agreement to hold elections after independence broke down in 1975 when the National Front (FNLA), with secret aid from the Central Intelligence Agency (CIA), attacked the Popular Movement (MPLA), the Marxist organization. Having previously suspended aid to the MPLA, the Soviets quickly restarted support. In this instance it was they who gave their clients superior assistance, and the FNLA was easily defeated. Desperate to prevent a Marxist victory, South Africa then sent troops to Angola in support of a third party, the National Movement for Total Independence (UNITA). This led to counter-intervention by a Soviet surrogate, Cuba, whose despatch of 15,000 troops to assist the MPLA tipped the balance decisively in its favor.

The outcome in Angola was probably Kissinger's greatest disappointment so far as detente was concerned. He had expected the Soviet Union to restrain itself and its allies in Africa in return for the benefits of SALT-1 and increased trade, but the episode clearly revealed the shortcomings of linkage. Since the carrot was not working, the United States resorted to the stick to block further expansion of Soviet influence. Huge shipments of arms were sent to friendly regimes, notably Ethiopia, Kenya, and Zaire, but the Soviets did the same for Uganda and Somalia. The superpowers' activities further destabilized an already volatile continent, whose growing turmoil locked them tighter into a new regional cold war.

Whatever Kissinger's feelings about setbacks in Africa, the principal manifestation of detente's inadequacies in the American public's eyes was in Southeast Asia. Neither North Vietnam nor South Vietnam had observed the 1973 cease-fire for long. After two years of sparring, the communists decided to go for a knockout blow. By now South Vietnam had descended into economic and political chaos, and Hanoi adjudged congressional cutbacks in aid to the Thieu regime as a clear sign that America lacked the will to reenter the war. In March 1975 communist forces launched a major offensive with the anticipation that final victory would require two years of fighting. Instead, the campaign lasted just over a month. Despite their superior fire-power, South Vietnamese forces lacked the will to fight and collapsed rapidly. Their government surrendered on April 30 following the capture of Saigon. Vietnam was finally united under communist rule. Meanwhile, in Cambodia the pro-American regime led by Lon Nol was overthrown by the renewed military offensive of the communist Khmer Rouge. These developments also sealed the fate of Laos, where communists had shared power in a coalition government for two years. In mid 1975 they expelled non-communists from office and took full control of the country.

Apart from local communist forces, the other victor in Southeast Asia was the Soviet Union. Thanks to events in this region, American foreign policymakers could no longer sustain the illusion that detente would induce the Soviets to show restraint in the Third World. North Vietnam's offensive would probably not have succeeded without the huge build-up in Russian military supplies received in 1974. At comparatively little cost to itself, the Soviet Union had supplanted US influence throughout much of Southeast Asia. The most literal evidence of this came when the newly unified Vietnam allowed its Soviet ally to take over strategic naval bases which the Americans had built in South Vietnam in the 1960s.

Domestic developments also undermined the foundations of detente.

Though in all probability doomed to fail because Soviet good intentions had been overestimated, the strategy of linkage never had a fair trial. As conceived by Kissinger, it entailed the coordinated application of pressures and inducements to modify Soviet behavior. Such a policy required a degree of presidential control over US diplomacy that was no longer possible. For three decades following America's entry into World War II Congress had largely deferred to the president in foreign policy. The legislature's pliancy was rooted in the Cold War consensus over the anticommunist aims of US diplomacy, recognition that the executive was better able to devise a consistent foreign policy and manage crises, and the success of containment strategy. However, in the wake of the Vietnam war and Watergate, mistrust of presidential power led Congress to reassert itself in foreign policy. As a result Nixon and Kissinger were unable to insulate the instruments of linkage, the military "sticks" and the economic "carrots", from congressional interference.

Nixon's policy of keeping alive the threat of renewed military intervention in Southeast Asia in order to compel communist obser- vance of the 1973 peace settlement faced an immediate challenge from Congress. US bombing of Cambodia had continued after the cease-fire agreement in Vietnam, partly to aid the Lon Nol regime against the Khmer Rouge but also as a warning to North Vietnam that air raids over its territory might be resumed. In June 1973 Congress voted to cut off funds for the bombing and required the cessation of all military operations in and over Southeast Asia from July 1 onward. Hitherto the feeling that ground forces fighting in Vietnam deserved all-out protection had deterred Congress from restricting presidential war- making, but now it was determined to employ its constitutional power of the purse to extricate the country entirely from the conflict. Speaking for many congressmen in both parties, Senator Norris Cotton (New Hampshire), a conservative Republican, avowed, "As far as I'm con- cerned, I want to get the hell out." Although the House sustained the president's veto of the bill, Nixon found it expedient to recognize the legislature's growing reluctance to support him. A compromise was worked out extending the deadline for the termination of US bombing to August 15.

US military involvement in Southeast Asia ceased after this date. Congress also took action to ensure that it would not be renewed by presidential fiat. With Nixon's authority now disintegrating because of the Watergate scandal, the War Powers Act was passed over his veto in November 1973. It required the president to inform Congress within forty-eight hours of the deployment of US forces to combat areas abroad and to withdraw them within sixty days (provision was made for a thirty day extension if necessary for the safety of US forces) unless Congress endorsed their continued presence. The measure also decreed that in the case of hostilities undertaken without its specific authorization, Congress could require the disengagement of US forces through passage in both its houses of a concurrent resolution that the president had no power to veto. In fact the measure implicitly gave the presidency more direct authority than before to commit forces abroad, and its long-term effectiveness in restricting presidential war-making has been ambivalent. However, it ensured that Gerald Ford could not honor Nixon's secret pledge to protect the Saigon regime by force when the final communist offensive was launched in 1975.

On occasions Congress also thwarted presidential efforts to support friendly regimes with substantial military economic aid as a warning to communists and Marxist insurgents of America's continuing commitments. It voted a 50% cut in economic aid to South Vietnam in 1974 in a bid to pressurize Thieu into negotiating a political settlement with the communists. According to some analysts this action provided the crucial encouragement for the North Vietnamese offensive of the following year. Even when the final crisis came, Congress refused emergency military aid for South Vietnam on grounds that the money would be wasted on a lost cause. To Kissinger's fury, it followed a similar course towards Angola. Revelations of the CIA's secret involvement in this country's internal conflict prompted enactment of the Clark amendment to the 1976 appropriations bill specifically prohibiting US aid to any of the warring factions.

Congressional anxiety to limit US involvement in Third World conflicts was not matched by comparable concern to improve US-Soviet relations. Taking for granted that the relaxation of superpower tensions would be popular, Nixon and Kissinger had done little to build up a domestic constituency for their foreign policy. But detente enjoyed only precarious support and faced growing criticism from quite different sources. Many Republican right-wingers and those Democrats who continued to hold hawkish views on the Cold War were hostile from the start. Another group of critics emerged in the wake of the Yom Kippur war. It was concerned above all else that detente might lull the United States into reducing support for Israel, a fear strengthened by Kissinger's diplomatic maneuvers to save the encircled Egyptian army.

This second group included not only Jewish-Americans but also Demo-cratic and Republican politicians representing constituencies with important Jewish segments. Finally, disillusion with detente gradually spread through the ranks of liberal Democrats, who complained that it was too close in spirit to Cold War foreign policy.

This tripartite coalition mobilized against the trade reform bill of 1973 that gave the Soviets most-favored-nation (MFN) status and generous access to export credits to assist trade with the United States. As a result Congress approved the Jackson-Vanik amendment that made MFN status conditional upon Soviet liberalization of Jewish emigration rights, particularly the removal of the recently imposed "exit tax". In 1974 a further amendment sharply limited Export-Import Banks credits available to Soviet Union. According to historian Thomas McCormick, these actions "gutted the economic content of detente. . . . [and] transformed the meaning of linkage" by making detente dependent on good Soviet behavior at home as well as abroad.

Beyond the Cold War consensus

The Cold War consensus had withered away by the early 1970s, but no broad agreement about the new directions that the country should take in world affairs emerged in its place. Detente widened the ideological splits over the aims and methods of American foreign policy that were initially provoked by Vietnam. Nixon had undertaken bold diplomatic initiatives without waiting for a constituency to develop behind his policies. Instead he anticipated that success abroad would create support at home for detente. Its early triumphs appeared to prove him right, but its later failures prompted widespread criticism. Without doubt, Nixon and Kissinger oversold the benefits of detente when they were basking in the glory of their initial successes and aroused false expectations about its capacity to shape global politics to America's benefit. Detente's indelible association with Nixon personally was also disadvantageous in at least two respects. Its popular and political appeal was diminished by Nixon's disgrace and eventual resignation over the Watergate scandal in August 1974. Moreover, Nixon and Kissinger's insistence on excluding the State Department and Congress from the policymaking process meant that detente had no alternative base of institutional support once the presidency was discredited.

By 1976 the Republican party, which Nixon had neither heeded nor educated with regard to foreign policy, was openly divided over detente. The GOP right was increasingly voicing anti-detente and pro-military views that reflected its traditional anticommunism. Many conservatives now charged that America's military superiority had been bargained away for the sake of detente and called for a renewal of hard-line policies against the Soviets. Articulating their discontent, former California governor Ronald Reagan was nearly successful in wresting the GOP presidential nomination away from Gerald Ford. Under pressure from this challenge, Ford himself had to modify his support for detente, the policy whose name he no longer dared to speak, by claiming to stand for "peace through strength". In addition, the president accepted the inclusion of a "Morality in Foreign Policy" plank in the 1976 Republican party platform that effectively repudiated detente with communism. Bowing to domestic pressures, he also made little effort to break the deadlock that had developed in the new round of arms limitation talks with the Soviets.

Many Democrats were also critical of detente, though for differing reasons. Some, mainly but not exclusively those on the right of the party, continued to support Cold War globalism. However, they were out of touch with the mainstream, as was indicated by the weak showing of the hawkish Senator Henry M. Jackson (Washington) in the 1976 presidential primaries. By contrast, most liberal Democrats applauded the concept of detente but disliked the way it had been carried out in practice. Holding antimilitarist attitudes that were a legacy of Vietnam, they objected to Nixon and Kissinger's tendency to rely on military power to enforce linkage. In addition liberals perceived a moral vacuum within Nixon-Ford-Kissinger policy because it subordinated issues like human rights and Third World aid to preoccupation with superpower affairs. Hence many of them supported congressional measures to make economic detente dependent on the treatment of Soviet Jews. Though presidential candidate Jimmy Carter did not belong to the liberal wing of the party, he shared its concern for a more idealistic foreign policy. And while he was not antimilitarist, he made concessions to the liberals on this score for the sake of party unity. The most notable examples were his acceptance at the 1976 party convention of platform planks supporting a general pardon for Vietnam draft evaders and cuts of 5 to 7 billion dollars in the defense budget.

Trends in partisan opinion indicated the emergence of new divisions between conservative Cold War internationalists and liberal post-Cold War internationalists. In essence, most Republicans and conservative Democrats continued to espouse views associated with the Cold War consensus. By contrast, liberal Democrats and the dwindling band of liberal Republicans remained in favor of an active US role in world affairs, but rejected militarism and interventionism in favor of a more cooperative internationalism that emphasized peace, arms control, environmental protection and Third World aid. These divergent views were also reflected within the broader foreign policy establishment. The influential quarterly journal *Foreign Policy* became the main forum for advocates of liberal internationalism, while *Commentary* served this role for supporters of conservative internationalism. Shortly after the 1976 election the debate between the two sides gathered momentum with the formation of official lobbying groups to promote these differing views. Liberal internationalists organized New Directions, while their conservative counterparts set up the Committee on the Present Danger.

These developments were reflected to some extent by trends in public opinion. Disillusion with failure in Vietnam, detente, and the shortcomings of US democracy as revealed by Watergate caused many Americans to want a retreat from world affairs. According to an opinion survey undertaken by the Harris poll for the Chicago Council on Foreign Relations, only 57% of the public was in favor of an internationalist foreign policy in early 1975, well below the level of support that prevailed in the 1950s and early 1960s. Nevertheless, the decline of internationalism was reversed as memories of Vietnam faded in the 1980s. Of greater long-term significance were the new signs of ideological divergence among the mass public who favored US activism abroad. A third of respondents in the Harris survey held views that could be classified as conservative internationalism, while a quarter identified with the tenets of liberal internationalism.

*   *   *

Nixon and Kissinger had tried and ultimately failed to establish a new foreign policy. They could claim at least four great achievements — they got the United States out of Vietnam, they normalized relations with the PRC, they laid the basis for peaceful coexistence with the Soviet Union, and they negotiated the first ever nuclear arms limitation agreement. In spite of these successes, their record was deeply flawed. Nixon and Kissinger had been unable to save Vietnam from communism, they failed to halt the arms race, and they did not succeed in controlling the global adventurism of the Soviet Union. These shortcomings prevented the development of consensual domestic support for the foreign policy of detente. As a result the question of what role the United States should play in a changing world remained unanswered.

4
Beyond Eden: the Political Economy of Stagflation, 1969–1976

The 1970s proved the most miserable period for the American economy since the Depression decade of the 1930s. The high growth-full employment-low inflation economy of the postwar era gave way to a stagflation-prone economy that suffered simultaneously from stagnation and inflation. The impact on the American psyche was immense. Long-standing assumptions about the promise of American life came into question. Economic woes, commented the pollster Daniel Yankelovich, had turned Americans from a "nation of optimists to a nation of pessimists". In the mid-1970s opinion surveys showed that only 56% of non-college educated young people believed that hard work always paid off, compared with 70% in 1969. By the late 1970s belief in the prospects of economic mobility and rising living standards, the hallmarks of post-war American confidence, had evaporated. One survey discovered that nearly two-thirds of the population now felt that "Americans should get used to the fact that our wealth is limited and most of us are not likely to become better off than we are now".

The inflationary consequences of the Vietnam War had made the first breach in the liberal consensus on political economy. The stagflation of the 1970s finally destroyed it. By the late 1960s the assumptions of the new economics that government could manipulate the economy to achieve a painless trade-off between growth, employment and inflation had been discredited. Nevertheless economic policymakers and the leaders of both political parties remained confident that the economy would go on growing and that unemployment and inflation could be kept within tolerable limits. By the mid 1970s this consensus had disappeared and ideological divisions were emerging over economic policy. Politicians found themselves having to make painful choices about economic priorities. The majority of Democrats hewed to the traditional Keynesian position that keeping unemployment low should be the main goal. By contrast Republicans increasingly argued that low inflation and a reduced public sector were necessary to revitalize the economy.

The ailing economy

In 1970 the United States, with 6% of the world's population, still accounted for about a quarter of the Gross World Product. America's Gross National Product (GNP), standing at $974 billion, dwarfed that of every other country. The Soviet Union, its closest rival, had a GNP of $505 billion, and Japan's stood at only $197 billion. Quite clearly the American economy was far and away the richest and most productive in the entire world. Yet it was equally evident that this colossus was showing signs of vulnerability. The inflation generated by the Vietnam war was the first manifestation of this. Other weaknesses relating to America's changing position in the world economy and declining productivity were also beginning to make themselves felt. The problems of inflation, increased reliance on foreign products, and a reduced rate of domestic investment reinforced each other and generated a vicious circle of decline in the 1970s.

America's share of world trade was little more than 10% in 1970, compared with 25% in 1948, and it had been overtaken by the European Community (EC) as the largest trading entity. The same trend was evident in the specific context of manufactured products. In 1955, US goods accounted for 32% of the overall exports of the world's major capitalist economies; by 1970, their share had fallen to 18%. The decline was particularly manifest in manufactures once synonymous with American industrial might. In 1973 the United States produced only 19.6% of the world's steel, compared with 46.6% in 1950. As recently as 1965 it had been responsible for half of the world's output of motor vehicles, but produced less than a third by 1973.

A declining share of world exports did not necessarily spell trouble for the United States, whose economy was self-supporting to a greater degree than most others. Exports made up some 5% of its national income (compared with around 20% in the cases of Britain and Canada, for example). More serious were the breaches that foreign products were also making in the citadel of the US domestic market itself. The foreign share of the American automobile market, which stood at a mere 4% in 1960, had risen to 17% by 1970 and exceeded one third by 1980. The main challenge came from Japan, whose annual car exports to America shot up from just 26,000 in 1965 to 625,000 by 1973. In consumer electronics, the foreign share of the US market rose even more spectacularly from 4% to 31% during the 1960s. The pattern was similar in clothing, luxury goods and other items. The situation was even worse in the case of strategically important raw materials. By 1973 the United States imported 15.2 million short tons of steel, compared with one million tons in 1950. In 1971 its reliance on iron imports amounted to 46% of domestic production, compared with only 3% in 1939.

More significant than anything else was the growing American dependence on foreign oil. Before World War II the country had been a net exporter of crude petroleum. With the opening of new oil fields, particularly in California, Oklahoma and Texas, America continued to produce more crude oil than any other single country in the postwar era. Its output rose rapidly from 1.2 billion barrels in 1939 to 2.5 billion in 1960 and 3.5 billion in 1970. However, this expansion could not keep pace with the demand for energy to fuel the expanding production of the buoyant postwar economy and to meet the expectations of middle-class Americans to own luxury gas-guzzling cars and air-conditioned homes. By 1970 Americans consumed about 30% of the world's annual energy output. Their daily consumption of oil, which stood at 9.7 million barrels in 1960, had skyrocketed to 16.2 million barrels by 1974. Having become a net importer of oil shortly after World War II, the United States found its reliance on foreign producers growing very rapidly after domestic oil production peaked in 1971. Imports met 38% of America's oil needs by 1974, compared with 24% in 1970 and 19% in 1960.

The relative decline of America's position in the international economy had many causes. The most significant factor was the "economic miracle" achieved by the nations of Western Europe and Japan, who had rebuilt their war-shattered economies with remarkable speed — and with US assistance — after 1945. In reality America's postwar economic hegemony rested on artificial foundations because it had not suffered the massive destruction which the conflict had inflicted on its industrial rivals. Its dominance was bound to decline once these nations reconstructed their economies. Also, industrial modernization in many developing nations meant that by the 1970s American producers found themselves in competition for the first time with rivals in Asia and Latin America who enjoyed the advantage of a low-wage labor force.

Nevertheless, US trade problems were partly self-inflicted. In some respects America was guilty, like Aesop's grasshopper, of frittering away its high summer of economic power and not doing enough to safeguard itself for the future. Business corporations had pursued some short-sighted strategies in their drive for fatter profits. Since the 1950s oil companies had deliberately reduced exploration and development of domestic wells in favor of increased investment in the Middle East, where production costs were lower. Automobile manufacturers concentrated in the 1950s and 1960s on the production of large gas-guzzling cars which yielded higher profits on sales than small cars. They would pay heavily for this policy when the energy crisis of 1973–4 made cheap fuel a thing of the past. Worst of all, America's rate of capital investment in domestic industry fell behind that of its rivals, with dire consequences for its industrial productivity and competitiveness.

US productivity increased at an annual average of 3.3% between 1947 and 1965, but the rate slumped to around 1.5% in 1966–75 and to only 0.2% in 1976–80. By the late 1960s, owing to stronger investment in plant modernization, Japan, West Germany, France, Italy, and even Great Britain were all achieving higher rates of manufacturing output than the United States. Leading the field were the Japanese, whose productivity grew at four times the American rate in the 1970s, thanks to large investments in heavy automation. The benefits were particularly evident in automobile manufacturing. By 1979 Toyota was annually producing fifty cars per production worker, five times the average for the Michigan plants of the three largest American automobile companies.

There were many reasons for the insufficiency of US domestic investment, but two stood out. Firstly, in pursuit of Cold War aims the United States spent far more of its GNP than did its trading competitors on military power, and so had proportionately less to invest in improving its civilian productivity. Secondly, and more significantly, lured by cheap labor, tax incentives, and other investment advantages, American firms increased their overseas manufacturing capacity by over 500% in the 1960s, compared with only 72% for domestic capacity. In total, American firms invested some $100 billion overseas between 1950 and 1974. By 1975 one of every five dollars of US capital investment was going abroad, and domestic investment was no longer keeping pace with GNP.

America's declining competitiveness coincided with the internationalization of its economy, which added to its problems. Its increased integration into the world economy in the 1970s marked a virtual revolution in its international economic relations. In 1970 exports and imports together only comprised 8.3% of GNP, roughly similar to the pre-World War II level. By 1980 their share had more than doubled to 17.4%. It was estimated that more than 70% of American-produced goods were now competing with foreign-made products. US firms had to operate in an environment in which prices were affected by international market forces beyond their control. As a result they tended to become "price takers" rather than "price makers".

The "cost-push" inflationary consequences of America's increasing integration into the world economy were soon apparent. Increased demand from the booming economies of Western Europe and the Far East created worldwide raw material shortages in the early 1970s. The resultant increase in prices particularly hurt US industry, which had become reliant on low-cost imports of these commodities. Even economic sectors in which the United States was a net exporter were vulnerable to this type of international pressure. Crop failures abroad led to increased foreign demand for American agricultural products, leaving inadequate supplies for domestic needs. The result was a cycle of inflation which increased US farm commodity prices by about two-thirds from 1971 through 1974.

The most spectacular example of cost-push inflation resulted from the five-month Arab oil embargo of 1973–4 and the subsequent decision of the Organization of Petroleum Exporting Countries (OPEC) to quadruple their prices in 1974. Many Americans deemed these actions tantamount to an "energy Pearl Harbor". The massive increase in the cost of imported oil produced corresponding price pressures on other energy sources. As Secretary of Commerce Peter G. Peterson quipped, "Popeye is running out of cheap spinach". The effects reverberated throughout the economy, since energy prices were a cardinal element in the production and distribution costs of almost everything. Among other things Americans had to get used to the 60-cent gallon of gasoline, compared with the 1970 price of 30 cents. It should be emphasized, however, that rising energy costs were not the sole nor necessarily the most important cause of US inflation in the 1970s. Lacking their own oil resources, Western Europe and — more particularly — Third World countries suffered far more as a result of OPEC's actions. Nevertheless, the psychological impact of the 1973–4 energy crisis on Americans was immense. They had been rudely awakened to the reality that the United States could no longer control its economic destiny in the way it used to.

The internationalization of the American economy also did much to end the labor-management consensus of the postwar era. For a quarter-century the two sides had been united by a social contract: unionized workers were paid good wages and their prosperity made them an essential part of the market for American manufactures. In response to the first surge of Vietnam-generated inflation, many trade unions had been successful during the late 1960s and early 1970s in winning labor contracts that provided for automatic cost-of-living salary increases pegged to increases in the Consumer Price Index. In turn, businesses sought to insulate themselves from rising wage costs by building inflation escalators into their pricing policy. This arrangement was a rational attempt to insure against the uncertainties of the future but the effect was to aggravate inflation still further, because wage settlements were no longer tied to productivity increases. It also made American wage rates uncompetitive in international terms just as the process of US integration into the world economy gathered pace. Fearful that rising wage levels were now economically unsustainable, corporate management went on to the offensive to weaken the power of organized labor.

This attack took various forms. Corporate leaders stepped up their efforts to block labor's attempts to expand its legal powers. Business lobbyists twice engineered the defeat of a bill to legalize "common situs" picketing, which was sought by hard-pressed construction unions. Many firms relocated plants or built new ones in states which had antiunion right-to-work laws. Illegal firings of workers for union activities more than quadrupled in the 1970s. Management also became more active in fighting unions in representation elections. As a result the union victory rate in these contests, which averaged 58% in the 1960s, fell to 52.7% in the first half of the 1970s and to 48.6% in the second half of the decade. The number of workers organized through National Labor Relations Board elections fell by 43% in the 1970s and the number lost through union "decertification" elections (whereby employees voted whether to get rid of union representation) more than doubled. The organized share of the total civilian workforce had been slipping throughout the postwar era, but the business offensive against the unions did much to accelerate its decline from 25.7% in 1970 to 20.9% in 1980.

The economic problems of the 1970s also affected the lives and aspirations of millions of Americans in other ways. The perpetual improvement in living standards that marked, the postwar decades now ceased. Real median family income, which had doubled between 1947 and 1973, declined by 6% from 1973 to 1980. In 1970 the real gross income of workers was lower than it had been in 1968. It rose again to a postwar peak in 1972 but declined by 2% each year from 1973 through

1981, by when the average worker's spending power was at its lowest level since 1961.

Americans also had to get used to higher levels of unemployment. There had never been full employment in the strictest sense since World War II, but joblessness had rarely strayed above four to five percent for long. In fact, average yearly unemployment was a mere 3.8% during Lyndon Johnson's second term in office, below the four percent level that the new economics accepted as the norm in an effective full-employment economy. However it rose to 5.4% over 1970–4 and to 7% over 1975–79. As a result economic policymakers regularly made upward adjustments in their estimates of the "natural rate" of unemployment. The Ford administration set a target of 5% and the Carter administration raised this to 6% in 1979. In addition to the incremental rise in unemployment, the United States suffered periods of economic recession in 1969–70, 1974–5, and 1979–80. In the second of these unemployment peaked at 9.1%, the highest level since the 1930s. The other two downturns were less severe in comparison, but joblessness still exceeded 7%. Each of these recessions was brought on by the federal government's periodic imposition of restrictive economic measures to throttle inflation.

The effects of unemployment were not felt evenly throughout the country, however. In the Great Recession of 1974–5, for example, the number of states with unemployment above the national average was three times greater in the Northeast and Midwest than in the Sunbelt region of the South and Southwest. This pattern underlined significant changes which had taken place in the regional structure of the American economy since World War II. In 1950 some 66% of manufacturing employment was concentrated in the Northeastern, Middle Atlantic and Great Lakes states; by 1977 their share was only 50% and falling. Corresponding gains had been registered in the Sunbelt states, which were home to relatively new industries, like aerospace, computers, electronics, defense systems, plastics and oil, that had largely been developed since World War II. Cheap energy resources, a good climate, inexpensive real estate, state laws inimical to trade unionism, low state-local taxes, and the construction of a nationwide network of interstate highways had made the region a haven for modern industrial development.

The older industries of the North, like steel and automobiles, were the ones hit by foreign competition, low productivity, and declining rates of investment in the 1970s. Almost the entire overall decline in

US manufacturing between 1970 and 1978 occurred in the North, which lost over 1 million jobs. By contrast, the Sunbelt gained over 300,000 new manufacturing jobs, and new capital spending on its industries was two and a half times greater than on those of the old industrial heartland. Hailed as the harbingers of a new industrial revolution, the Sunbelt's "high-tech" industries were far less labor-intensive than the old "smokestack" industries, so they could not counterbalance job losses in traditional manufacturing.

Paradoxically the partial deindustrialization of the old manufacturing heartland occurred at a time when the number of jobs in the economy as a whole was undergoing a huge expansion. Altogether, 26.5 million new jobs were created in the 1970s, representing a remarkable increase of nearly one-third in total employment. However, about 70% of all new private-sector employment created between 1973 and 1980 was in low-paid retail and service jobs. Displaced factory workers who could not find new manufacturing jobs in the so-called Rustbelt were faced with the alternative of either migrating to the Sunbelt in search of employment or staying put and taking low-paid low-skill jobs, such as gas station attendants, security guards, or fast-food restaurant employees. With exaggerated yet understandable despair, the AFL-CIO lamented that the United States was becoming "a nation of hamburger stands, a country stripped of industrial capacity and meaningful work . . . a service economy . . . a nation of citizens busily buying and selling cheeseburgers and root beer floats".

Service sector jobs were also the best that many of the newer entrants into the labor market could hope for. Between 1965 and 1980 the US workforce grew by some 40%. This phenomenal increase amounted to almost 30 million workers, a number greater than the entire labor force of either France, or Great Britain, or West Germany. It resulted from the entry into the labor market of the postwar "baby-boom generation" and increasing numbers of women. Those who came from low-income backgrounds and lacked educational qualifications tended to find themselves in low-paying jobs. They were also vulnerable to periods of unemployment because the growth of new jobs did not keep pace with the growth of job seekers.

The economic problems of the 1970s were most deeply felt at the intersection of race, gender and class. Freed in the 1960s from some impediments of racism and sexism, blacks and women who were well-qualified and came from economically secure backgrounds were able to achieve economic advancement. But those who lacked these advantages fared badly. The combination of limited economic opportunities and a huge increase in the number of female-headed families resulted in the feminization of poverty in the 1970s. By 1980 two-thirds of all adults officially classified as poor were women. Moreover, while between 35% and 45% of black Americans achieved a middle-class lifestyle in the 1970s, some 30% of blacks experienced decline into deeper poverty. Between 1970 and 1974 the unemployment rate among blacks ran at 9%, more than double the white rate, and among black teenagers it stood at 32%. Worst affected were black women who suffered from the twin disadvantages of race and gender.

In 1974 the economist Robert S. Browne warned, "[W]e're on our way to having a permanent black underclass." This prediction was soon borne out. "The great unmentioned problem in America today", proclaimed Senator Edward Kennedy in 1978, "[is] the growth, rapid and insidious, of a group in our midst, perhaps more dangerous, more bereft of hope, more difficult to confront, than any for which our history has prepared us. It is a group that threatens to become what America has never known — a permanent underclass in our society." Out of about 30 million Americans officially classified as poor in 1980, some 9 million could be categorized as belonging to this underclass. Approximately 70% were nonwhite, 50% came from female-headed households, and some two-thirds were children under eighteen. Those in the underclass experienced virtually permanent unemployment and had to depend for income on welfare, crime, or hustling.

"Nixonomics"

In addition to addressing the problem of America's relative decline in world politics, President Richard Nixon had to face up to its emergent economic weaknesses. According to Council of Economic Advisers (CEA) chairman Herbert Stein, the Nixon administration's efforts to cure the ailing economy marked the "beginning of a transition to more conservative economics". Nixon did not plan a drastic departure from the political economy of his Democratic predecessors. During his final years in office, however, he grew more conservative in response to worsening inflation and trade problems.

Nixon's decision not to bid farewell to Keynes at the outset of his administration was not due to the absence of a credible conservative alternative. Thanks to the University of Chicago economist Milton Friedman, Keynesianism was currently facing the first serious challenge to its intellectual domination within the community of professional economists. A passionate advocate of the free market, private enterprise, and a minimal public sector, Friedman regarded government as the cause of inflation and derided fiscal policy as having almost no value as an instrument of economic management. His insistence that the monetary powers of the Federal Reserve were the essential tool of economic policy established him as the principal critic of the new economics.

From Friedman's monetarist perspective, the deficit budgets that resulted from big government spending and tax cuts could not generate sustainable growth. Deficits had to be financed through increased public borrowing, which only served to "crowd out" from the money markets an equivalent amount of private and business borrowing. In other words the fiscal stimulus was counterbalanced by the contraction of private credit. For Friedman, the sole determinant of demand, at least in the short term, was the money supply (the measure of total currency in circulation and in checkable deposits in banks and other institutions). From this it followed that inflation occurred when the Federal Reserve allowed the growth of the money supply to exceed the growth of productive output. Put another way, if the money stock expanded more rapidly than there were extra goods and services to spend it on, the result would be to bid up prices of the scarcer commodities. In Friedmanite theory, inflation was the greatest threat to the wellbeing of the private economy because it undermined the value of savings and investments and created uncertainty about the future. The only cure was a strong dose of monetary restraint — even at the cost of high unemployment.

Nixon did not believe the patient was sick enough to require such painful medicine. The economic horizon was hardly one of unrelenting gloom in 1969. GNP had been rising steadily for nine years, a trillion-dollar economy was in sight, unemployment was low, and inflation — though worrying — was not out of control. Nixon and his advisers were confident that moderate restraint could choke off inflationary pressures without threatening economic growth, which they expected to continue at an annual rate of around 4%.

Friedman's ideological purity was also out of step with Nixon's pragmatic conservatism. The president certainly had conservative preferences, but he recognized that political reality ruled out any attempt to return to free-market economics. Moreover, he viewed the mixed public and private economic system that had evolved since the New Deal as basically sound. According to the political scientist James

Reichley, for Nixon and his advisers "the economic problem was essentially one of administration: through conservative management, they believed, a mixed system could be made to operate with reasonable efficiency for the public good." As Stein put it, they were "conservative men with liberal ideas". Although the Nixon CEA, unlike the new economists, accepted that monetary policy was the key to stabilizing the economy, it labeled itself "Friedmanesque" rather than "Friedmanite". In other words, it thought that "money mattered" — but not to the exclusion of all else, and it recognized that fiscal policy was also important for economic management.

Political considerations, specifically the need to ensure his reelection, also determined the new president's economic policies. Already a proven vote-winner in the nation's suburbs and small cities, Nixon hoped to build up a new Republican majority by gaining support in the urban North from ethnics and working-class whites. He had no intention of alienating them by prioritizing price stability at the expense of jobs, traditionally the major economic concern of these constituencies. Bitter experience reinforced this determination, since Nixon attributed his defeat by Kennedy in the 1960 presidential race to the pre-election recession brought on by President Eisenhower's anti-inflation policies.

In its earliest incarnation, therefore, "Nixonomics" aspired to reduce inflation without pushing unemployment much above the acceptable level of 4%. It placed its trust in the efficacy of monetary policy, the elixir that the Keynesians had ignored, to slow down the growth of total demand gradually. On the fiscal side, the administration planned to balance the budget through moderate reductions of expenditure, mainly resulting from the rundown of the Vietnam war. Unfortunately for Nixon, the Federal Reserve pursued a more robust policy of monetary restraint than he wanted. By manipulating rediscount rates and reserve requirements, it slowed down the growth of the money supply from 7.2% in 1968 to 0.7% in 1969. Even Milton Friedman criticized this as overkill. With business already in an uncertain mood because of inflation, the Fed's credit crunch plunged the economy into recession in late 1969.

In 1970 unemployment reached 6 percent and the GNP declined (by 3.9%) for the first time since 1958. Some businesses were very hard hit. A major corporation, Penn Central Railroad, went bankrupt, and other giants like Lockheed, Chrysler, TWA, and Pan American experienced severe difficulties in repaying bank loans. Financial markets were thrown into panic. The Dow-Jones average of industrial stocks, which stood at 985 when Nixon took office, fell to 631 in May 1970, the sharpest decline since the 1930s. The recession was historically significant for at least two reasons. The first downturn since 1961, it ended the longest period of uninterrupted economic expansion in American history. Also, contrary to normal trends in periods of growing unemployment, inflation continued to rise. The CPI rose 5.7% in 1970. Americans were experiencing their first taste of stagflation. The Democrats, who did well in the 1970 elections, blamed everything on "Nixonomics", gleefully defined by party chairman Larry O'Brien as meaning "that all the things that should go up — the stock market, corporate profits, real spendable income, productivity — go down, and all the things that should go down — unemployment, prices, interest rates — go up."

Some economists believe that the inflationary momentum of the Vietnam war could have been stemmed had Nixon been willing to incur a deeper and longer recession. However the president would not gamble his reelection prospects on this possibility. This was a perfectly reasonable position to adopt, since leaders in a democracy are supposed to heed the public's preferences. In moving against unemployment, Nixon undoubtedly did what most Americans wanted and saved many of them from being jobless. It is equally true that an opportunity was missed to stifle inflation before the cost-push pressures of 1973–4 compounded the nation's economic problems. As the economist Lester Thurow observed, "We had been paying an economic price for President Johnson's decision to misfinance the Vietnam War, and we were about to start paying the economic price for President Nixon's reelection campaign."

In response to presidential prodding and the stock market decline, the Federal Reserve relaxed monetary policy. Nixon also abandoned fiscal restraint. The budget that he presented for fiscal 1972 had a large projected deficit of $11.6 billion. This was justified as non-inflationary because the proposed expenditures did not exceed the hypothetical level of receipts if the economy were at full-employment. "By spending as if we were at full employment", Nixon told Congress, "we will help to bring about full employment." He was effectively speaking the language of the new economics, but neither Kennedy nor Johnson had so openly embraced the concept of the full-employment budget. Nixon felt compelled to admit to Howard K. Smith of ABC News, "I am now a Keynesian in economics." This was greeted as a Damascene conversion. Smith later remarked that Nixon's statement was akin to "a

Christian crusader saying, 'All things considered, I think Mohammed was right.' " It was nothing of the kind. Whether Nixon had become an actual Keynesian is unlikely. In reality all that he had done was to prioritize a cure for unemployment over inflation. For political reasons Nixon had always accepted this fundamental tenet of the liberal political economy.

Keynesian or not, the change of policy had little effect. Unemployment remained high throughout 1971 and inflationary pressures grew stronger after several unions, most notably the United Steelworkers, won large pay increases. To make matters worse, the United States recorded its first international trade deficit since 1893. This immediately brought about a dollar crisis which spelled the end of America's preeminent position in the postwar international economy.

America had been operating an international balance of payments deficit almost constantly since the early 1950s. At first this had worked to the mutual advantage of the United States and its trading partners. The outflow of US dollars, mainly via military expenditures, foreign aid, and overseas investments, lubricated the postwar international economy. With weak currencies of their own, foreign nations in the process of economic reconstruction were glad to build up their dollar holdings. The Bretton Woods agreement of 1944 had established the dollar as the universal reserve currency, convertible into gold at the fixed rate of $35 per ounce. All other currencies, their values also determined by gold, were freely convertible into dollars. In return for the privileged position accorded the dollar as the fixed norm around which other currencies rotated, the United States promised to redeem all foreign-held dollars in gold whenever required. Founded on the economic dominance of the United States, the international monetary system worked well so long as this dominance lasted and other countries needed dollars. By the late 1960s neither of these conditions held good. The industrial countries of Western Europe and Japan had a glut of dollars far in excess of their reserve needs and increasingly began to convert their surplus dollars into gold.

The merchandize trade deficit of 1971 turned the move to gold into a rush as foreigners dumped their dollars and bought into stronger currencies, notably the West German mark. The problem was that the United States did not have the resources to meet its obligations. Foreign-held dollars totalled some $40 billion, while American gold reserves amounted to $12 billion. Meanwhile, foreign governments were unwilling to negotiate more realistic international exchange rates that would devalue the dollar and thereby make American exports cheaper abroad. This situation called for desperate remedies. The Nixon administration's response was the New Economic Policy (NEP), announced on August 15, 1971.

The NEP, a composite of measures designed to resolve America's domestic and international economic problems, was the second stage of Nixonomics. It included the traditional economic restoratives of tax breaks for business and, less substantially, for individuals, which were to be financed by some reductions in federal expenditure. What made the program "new", however, were the decisions to impose a 90-day wage-price freeze as an anti-inflation measure, to suspend the dollar's convertibility into gold, and to levy a temporary 10% surcharge on dutiable imports. The political impact of these measures was immediately apparent. The wage-price freeze had the same psychological impact as Franklin D. Roosevelt's decision to close the banks in 1933. Nixon's initiative had persuaded the American people that the administration could remedy their economic problems. Such confidence was misplaced. The NEP could not resolve the basic structural problems of the American economy, notably low productivity, inadequate domestic investment, and overdependence on cheap energy.

All seemed to go well at first. By closing the "gold window" the Nixon administration had recognized that the postwar hegemony of the dollar was dead. It now sought to compel other nations to join with the United States in working out a new monetary order that took cognizance of this. As intended, the unilateral termination of the Bretton Woods agreement spread confusion abroad. West Germany and Japan were forced to revalue their currencies, but the stability of the new exchange rates was precarious because of the absence of an effective international mechanism to guarantee them. Some observers claimed that the world monetary system was on the verge of collapse. Eventually western governments were forced to dance to the new American tune. In December 1971 the International Monetary Fund (IMF) meeting in Washington resulted in the Smithsonian Agreement, which restored fixed exchange rates and gold convertibility but accepted devaluation of the dollar and an increase in the price of gold to $38. In addition the United States relinquished the import surcharge in exchange for agreement from other nations, particularly Japan, to reduce their trade barriers and end discrimination against American goods. Nixon called this the "greatest monetary agreement in the history of the world". But all it did was to provide a breathing space for more substantial reforms to be worked out.

The volatile economic conditions of the early 1970s militated against fixed exchange rates. Devaluation did not assist the American trade deficit, rooted as it was in the structural problems of domestic industry and the heavy military costs of defending the free world. Apart from small surpluses in 1973 and 1975, the merchandize trade balance stayed in the red for the remainder of the 1970s. This aggravated inflation because the devalued dollar made imports, particularly of oil, more costly. Inflation in turn led to renewed pressure on the dollar, forcing Nixon to devalue it once again and finally terminate gold convertibility in 1973. Other countries were facing similar problems with their own currencies in the wake of the Arab oil embargo and subsequent oil price increases by OPEC. With monetary stabilization virtually impossible, the western world moved toward a system of floating exchange rates over the next few years. These already existed in practice by the time that they were sanctioned in principle by the IMF in 1976. Although the United States welcomed this development, power within the new system was in different hands. Led by West Germany, the European Community countries agreed to set fixed rates among themselves and let the composite EC currency float against the dollar. From now on global demand rather than political agreement would determine the purchasing power of the dollar in the world market.

The NEP also broke fresh ground in introducing economic controls for the first time in peacetime. This decision represented a personal U-turn of mammoth proportions for Nixon, who had always repudiated controls as incompatible with the free-market. To some extent he was swayed by the economic arguments of Treasury Secretary John B. Connally, who warned that inflation would skyrocket unless drastic action was taken to hold the line against the large pay increases being sought by labor. It is more likely, however, that political considerations once more overrode Nixon's conservative preferences. The introduction of controls allowed the administration to pursue expansionary fiscal and monetary policies without risk of inflationary consequences during the election year of 1972.

The first phase of the program was a ninety-day freeze on wages, prices and rents. In Phase II, which began in November, 1971, wage and price increases were allowed, but federal supervisory councils were established to ensure compliance with mandatory limits. The controls did much to douse inflationary psychology, that is the popular expectation that price rises were inevitable. Only the trade unions expressed strong opposition on the grounds that the controls were unfair to workers whose current wages had already been devalued by inflation. The CPI rose by just 3.4% during the Phase II program. However, long-term price stability was a mirage, because fiscal and monetary policies were overheating the economy and stoking up inflationary demand.

Concerned that the still high unemployment level would affect his reelection, Nixon and his advisers drew up an expansionary budget for fiscal 1973. Owing to the recession, the two previous budgets had accrued deficits of around $23 billion each (which far surpassed projections). The fiscal 1973 budget proposals, sent to Congress in January 1972, continued this trend by projecting a deficit of $25 billion and a 10% increase in expenditure. As Defense Secretary Melvin Laird recalled, "Every effort was made to create an economic boom for the 1972 election." Monetary policy was working to the same end. The Federal Reserve, now chaired by Nixon's ally, Arthur Burns, permitted a substantial increase of over 8% in the money supply during the election year. In these circumstances recession did give way to boom. Unemployment fell to just over 5% and the economy achieved a healthy growth rate of 6.5% in 1972. Americans had a brief and tantalizing reminder of the good times that they had once taken for granted. The bad times returned with a vengeance in 1973. The chain of disasters that overtook the economy was partly traceable to Nixon's original decision to introduce controls, which provided the deceptive security for the excessive stimulation policies of 1972.

The administration reversed its economic course following Nixon's landslide reelection. No longer concerned to manipulate the electoral-economic cycle, it now sought to ensure that economic growth was not accompanied by renewed inflation. Nixonomics entered its third and most conservative stage. Implicit in this new approach was an acceptance that inflation was the nation's primary economic problem, which had to be eliminated even at the cost of high unemployment. Monetary policy was now tightened with a vengeance. Also, expenditure cuts were made in the fiscal 1973 budget which ended with a deficit of only $14 billion. In pursuit of this aim, Nixon impounded funds that Congress had appropriated for social programs. This tactic, deemed unconstitutional by many, helped to deepen the Watergate crisis that eventually brought the president's term in office to a premature end.

Meanwhile, further spending reductions were targeted for fiscal 1974 and succeeding budgets.

Confident that fiscal and monetary restraint would hold inflation in check, the president relaxed the wage-price controls that had operated in tandem with the previous expansionary policies. These had never been popular with Nixon and his advisers, who now persuaded themselves that they would shackle economic growth. In early 1973 the mandatory controls were abruptly replaced by a system of voluntary controls, but these proved utterly ineffective. Inflationary pressures, which mandatory restraint had kept in check, now reappeared and were intensified by the excess demand generated by Nixon's election-year policies. The dike finally burst under the added weight of the cost-push inflation produced by rising oil, raw material, and food prices in 1973–4. A desperate effort to reimpose a sixty-day wage-price freeze in mid 1973 proved futile. The CPI rose 8.8% in 1973 and double-digit inflation followed in 1974. Already reeling from the effects of skyrocketing oil prices, American industry suffered a second blow when the Federal Reserve engineered yet another credit crunch in a desperate bid to control inflation. As a result the economy tipped over into recession in late 1974.

Due in part to domestic and international factors beyond his control and in part to his own misjudgements, Nixon left office with a disastrous economic record. His failure produced many casualties. One of them was the liberal political economy which this pragmatic conservative had inherited and tried to maintain. Nixon's efforts to keep unemployment low had tended to make inflation worse. No benign trade-off between these problems was possible in the economic circumstances of the early 1970s. Political leaders eventually had to face up to the dilemma of prioritizing one at the expense of the other.

Towards the end of its life, the Nixon administration unequivocally focused on controlling inflation and sacrificed the high employment aims of the liberal political economy. The mandatory wage-price controls represented the last hope of balancing these goals. These might have worked had they not been mismanaged by the Nixon administration and had they been given more time. However their failure had immense political significance. Conservatives, both pragmatic and doctrinaire, took it as final proof that economic salvation depended on the restoration of free-market principles which had been superceded by the liberal political economy of the postwar era. This meant a return to what Herbert Stein called "the old-time religion", in other words balanced budgets, the reduction of the public sector, a roll-back of the regulatory state, and lower taxes. The Nixon administration was moving in this direction during its final two years, and the succeeding administration of Gerald R. Ford would maintain the transition towards conservative economics.

The Great Inflation, the Great Recession, and party politics, 1974–1976

In comparison with Richard Nixon, Gerald Ford was both more honest and more conservative. Once lampooned unfairly by Lyndon Johnson as being unable to walk straight and chew gum at the same time, Ford actually possessed greater knowledge of economics than any other incoming president of the modern era. Not only had he once considered becoming a professional economist, but also long service on the Appropriations Committee during his career as a congressman had given him practical expertise in fiscal policy. Whereas Nixon had initially been willing to operate within the liberal consensus on political economy, his successor was disposed to move beyond it. Ford believed that the public sector created by the New Deal and expanded by the Great Society had grown excessively large and was inherently responsible for destabilizing the economy. By the mid 1970s social expenditures exceeded military expenditures and the expansion of government, previously funded by the incremental resources of economic growth, was now being financed from the expansion of the budget deficit in a stagnant economy. The new president and his economic advisers were determined to balance the budget and reduce government. But Ford's economic conservatism proved more gradual than purist, as his response to the Great Recession of 1974–5 showed.

Ford intended the fight against inflation to be the main theme of his administration. In October 1974, two months after taking office, he presented Congress with a package of anti-inflation measures, including a temporary tax surcharge of 5%, substantial reductions in federal spending, and supply-side policies to encourage increased domestic production of energy and food. This program was accompanied by the so-called WIN campaign (Whip Inflation Now) to convince Americans that inflation had to be crushed, a public-relations fiasco best remembered for the president's much-ridiculed exhortation that concerned citizens should wear WIN buttons.

However, the onset of recession in 1974 confronted Ford with the other side of the stagflation coin. Unemployment soared to its highest level since the 1930s, with the automobile, construction, and steel industries being worst hit. Many workers experienced for the first time the economic and emotional difficulties of having to draw and live on unemployment insurance benefits. Meanwhile everyone was having to cope with rising prices. In spite of record postwar unemployment, inflation also remained close to its postwar high at 9% in 1975.

Ford attempted a conservative balancing act that responded to the plight of the unemployed without ignoring inflation. To boost the private economy, the president withdrew his tax surcharge proposal and proposed instead a substantial temporary reduction of corporate and personal taxes. Meanwhile he sought to impose a ceiling on federal spending and a moratorium on new domestic programs (except energy) in order to prevent an expansion of the public sector under cover of the recession. This strategy led to confrontation between the Republican administration and the Democrats, who enjoyed massive majorities in both houses of Congress as a result of the Watergate-affected midterm elections of 1974. True to New Deal traditions, the Democrats attempted to enact their own anti-recession program featuring increased federal expenditure to stimulate the economy and boost jobs. However, most of their legislative proposals fell victim to the president's veto.

Among modern presidents, FDR, Truman and Eisenhower vetoed a far higher number of bills than Ford, but the bulk of their vetoes were cast against relatively insignificant private bills passed at the behest of congressmen seeking immigration privileges, special pensions, or monetary settlements for individual constituents. Only five of Ford's 66 vetoes fell into this category. During his brief tenure of office he undoubtedly vetoed more bills affecting substantive matters than any other president. Thirty-nine of his vetoes affected spending legislation, and only six of these were overridden. Federal expenditure did go up in the recession, of course. Outlays on unemployment insurance and other programs mandated by previous legislation increased automatically. Nevertheless Ford was largely successful in his battle to hold the line against legislation which would have saddled the present budget and future ones with large new obligations. Viewed from this perspective, the record deficits that were incurred during his recession-affected presidency ($45 billion in fiscal 1975 and $66 billion in fiscal 1976) were not quite as bad as they looked.

The battle over anti-recession spending signified a widening partisan gulf over economic policy. Further evidence of the differences among party elites was provided by the Harvard Center for International

Affairs-*Washington Post* survey of county committee chairpersons, members of state committees, and members of national committees, undertaken in 1976. At this juncture inflation had been brought down to about 5% but unemployment was still running high at 7.5%. Asked to rank ten national problems in order of importance, Democratic party officials on average placed unemployment first and inflation second. By contrast the Republicans saw curbing inflation as the first priority and ranked reducing unemployment in sixth place — behind reducing the role of government, maintaining a strong defense, developing energy resources, and reducing crime.

This division spilled over into the 1976 presidential election. The party platforms and the positions adopted by the candidates, Ford and Jimmy Carter, were further apart over the economy than on any other issue. The GOP platform labeled inflation "the number-one destroyer of jobs" and the expansion of the money supply to pay for federal deficit spending as "the number one cause of inflation". Inflation, it avowed, destroyed the incentive to save and invest, and thereby impeded business from engaging in capital formation, the prerequisite for improved productivity and high employment. The Republican prescription for reduced inflation was a strong dose of economy in government. It also envisaged that spending cuts would finance business and personal tax cuts.

By contrast, the Democratic platform contended that full employment was the panacea for US economic problems because the boost it would give to consumption would lead in turn to business expansion, higher profits and greater investment in productivity. The party proclaimed that it was "the right of all adult Americans willing, able and seeking work to have opportunities for useful jobs at living wages". To this end the Democrats promised to enact the Humphrey-Hawkins full-employment bill. This measure required the federal government to undertake every effort to reduce unemployment to 3% within four years. It would have made government — in effect — the employer of last resort. The Democrats also promised tax relief for middle-income groups, but this was to be financed by closing tax loopholes that benefited the rich. Finally, the platform pledge to reintroduce wage and price controls if necessary showed that Democrats were committed to the use of government powers to combat inflation as well as unemployment.

In essence the Republicans adopted a "trickle-down" theory of economic growth in contrast to the "trickle-up" theory of the Democrats.

The 1976 presidential election entailed a contest between an early version of what became known as supply-side economics and what proved to be the final Democratic expression of commitment to the Keynesian precepts of the postwar liberal political economy. In contrast to Nixon, Ford did not attempt to strengthen his reelection prospects by giving the economy an artificial boost. The odds appeared to be against him, because the Democrats traditionally had strong appeal at times of high unemployment and the GOP was still handicapped by the political fall-out from Watergate. Nevertheless Carter's eventual margin of victory was very narrow. Ford's record of success in the battle against inflation nearly carried him to a new term in office. Election polls indicated that a majority of Americans shared his belief that inflation was a more fundamental problem than unemployment. As journalist David Broder observed, "The Republicans won the argument, but lost the election."

In the country at large it was not surprising that business and trade unions held opposite views on the inflation-unemployment dichotomy. According to one business leader, "Recession is like a sore. Inflation is like cancer." Another commented, "It would be better if the recession [of 1974–5] were allowed to weaken more than it will, so that we would have a sense of sobriety." Such views typified the conviction of the corporate elite that an increase in unemployment was necessary to douse inflationary pressures. By contrast, the AFL-CIO leadership avowed, "[T]he goal of full employment should be the top priority". However, many rank-and-file trade unionists did not share this concern. Everyone suffered from high inflation, but only a minority had to put up with unemployment. Politically, it was the fear of unemployment that counted. Thanks to gains previously won by the unions, many workers were protected by seniority rights, job tenure and other safeguards that made them feel reasonably secure about continued employment. Belonging to what scholars have termed the "contract society", they were less concerned about joblessness than about paying the bills out of a paycheck depleted by taxes and inflation. Older workers also tended to worry more about the effect of inflation upon pension funds than about teenage unemployment. As a result Ford did very well in many industrial states where unemployment might have been expected to hurt him badly. He carried Indiana, Michigan and New Jersey, and ran Carter close in Ohio and Pennsylvania.

*   *   *

Between 1960 and 1976 political consensus about the economy had broken down because of the combination of inflation and rising unemployment associated with stagflation. The strong performance of the American economy in the quarter-century after World War II had spared its political leaders from having to prioritize one of these problems at the expense of the other. A Republican president, Richard Nixon, had initially attempted to sustain the liberal political economy in the hope of achieving an acceptable balance between inflation and unemployment, but the economic conditions of the 1970s ruled this out. By the time of his enforced resignation, Nixon was moving beyond the confines of the liberal consensus in economic policy. Ford sustained and accelerated this trend. In the meantime the Democrats, who had began to worry about inflation during the Johnson era, reaffirmed their primary concern for high employment during the Great Recession of 1974–5. By 1976 the two parties were further apart on economic policy than at any time since the 1930s. Nevertheless, Jimmy Carter's narrow election as president hardly constituted a ringing endorsement for the restoration of the liberal political economy. Americans were more worried about inflation than unemployment. Carter would soon face the dilemma of responding to their concern or upholding his party's commitment to restore the full-employment economy.

5

Beyond Roosevelt: Parties, Politics and Domestic Issues, 1969–1976

Domestic issues were as important as international issues and economic problems in shaping political change in the United States between the presidential elections of 1968 and 1976. The period was an important transitional era in American politics, during which some of the foundations of the Reaganite 1980s were laid. Richard Nixon sought to build a new Republican majority by appealing to Democratic voters who had been alienated by the social, racial and cultural changes of the 1960s. Despite failing to achieve its ultimate aim, Nixon's strategy helped to accelerate the decay of the New Deal coalition and hastened the process of political dealignment that had marked the Johnson era. In other words the attachments of many loyal Democratic voters were displaced without, for the most part, new ones being built in their place. Important changes also occurred in the power structures of both parties, benefiting supporters of the so-called "New Politics" in the case of the Democrats and the right in the case of the Republican party. As a result of these developments the New Deal political order had experienced significant erosion by 1976.

Nixon and a new Republican majority

The need to win reelection has shaped every modern president's first-term approach to domestic issues, but this consideration was particularly pressing in Richard Nixon's case. He had been elected with the lowest share of the popular vote (43.4%) of any victorious presidential candidate since Woodrow Wilson in 1912 (41.9%), and he was the first new president since the disputed election of 1876 to win office without his party simultaneously gaining control of the House of Representatives. It was evident that the Republicans had not made the kind of electoral breakthrough in 1968 that the Democrats had made in 1932. Nevertheless, 57% of voters had not supported the Democratic presidential candidate in 1968. Many white southerners, blue-collar workers, and Catholic ethnics had been prised loose from their habitual loyalty to the party of Roosevelt. Nixon's reelection would be ensured if he could convert these groups to Republicanism.

The problem facing Nixon was how to bring together disaffected Democrats and bedrock Republicans into a new political coalition. As the Goldwater debacle of 1964 had shown, there was only minority support in the nation for anti-statist conservatism. The groups whom the Republicans had to win over had vested interests in many federal programs. Their resentments were focused not against public policies associated with the liberal consensus of the postwar decades but against the social and cultural changes associated with the Great Society. Most of the voters who had deserted the Democrats in 1968 were conservative in their belief that they had more to lose than to gain from the social changes of the 1960s, but they wanted the continuation of federal programs that were broadly within the New Deal legacy. Polls suggested that socially conservative blue-collar workers and senior citizens would have backed Nixon in much greater numbers in 1968 but for their fear that a Republican administration would undermine social security, Medicare, and aid to education.

Nixon therefore had to operate within the liberal tradition of Franklin D. Roosevelt while maintaining a critical attitude to the Great Society. According to some commentators, he consciously adopted ideas associated with neoconservatism, an intellectual movement that had emerged in the mid 1960s, to build a new Republican majority. In the view of historian Alonzo Hamby: "The neconservative approach, situated somewhere within the broad center of the political spectrum, was so ideally suited for the purpose that it became the dominant policy tone of his administration." Prominent members of this movement, like Daniel Bell, Irving Kristol, and Daniel P. Moynihan, had been enthusiastic supporters of New Deal liberalism but now condemned Great Society liberalism as wasteful, excessively bureaucratic, too redistributionist, and antimeritocratic. The core ideas of neconservatism harked back to the old liberal consensus. They entailed: acceptance of the welfare state but opposition to social engineering by an intrusive bureaucracy; respect for the economic market; and support for traditional values, social order, and religion against the new cultural influences of the 1960s.

Other commentators offer a different interpretation of Nixon's strategy. In their view it was influenced by the ideas of campaign aide Kevin Phillips, whose book *The Emerging Republican Majority* was widely hailed as the political bible of the Nixon era. According to Phillips, Nixon could build a new majority on the "immense middle-class impetus of Sun Belt and Suburbia". He contended that demographic change spelled doom for the 30-year domination of liberalism, whose political center of gravity was the urban Northeast. Population was shifting out of the old industrial heartland into the Sunbelt states of the South and West. It was also moving on a nationwide basis from city centers to suburbs, that were now homes not only to the affluent but also to millions of blue-collar and lower middle-class Americans. The residents of the Sunbelt and the suburbs, Phillips proclaimed, were the new American masses who had been elevated in the post-industrial era to middle class status and conservatism. They were in revolt against the "caste, policies, and taxation of the mandarins of Establishment liberalism". In other words, the emergent Republican majority would be based on populist animosity against taxes, bureaucracies, federal regulations, judicial activism, and social engineering, all of which were perceived as the instruments of a political establishment that was liberal, upper class and northeastern.

There were obvious similarities between neoconservatism and the populist conservatism advocated by Kevin Phillips. Both reacted against Great Society liberalism rather than New Deal liberalism, against enforced equality, and against sociocultural change. But there were also tensions between them. The neoconservatives were an intellectual elite who had little rapport with the mass public of the Sunbelt and the suburbs. They did not oppose renewed action by government to resolve social problems provided this was undertaken within the confines of the old liberalism. Phillips, who was more attuned to middle America's resentment of social experimentation by the state, contended that the new Republicanism should accept the New Deal edifice but draw the line against further expansion of government activism.

In many respects Nixon's domestic policies can best be understood as a reflection of both neoconservative and populist conservative tendencies. He was ideally suited as president to position himself astride these similar but still different positions. His rise to eminence in postwar American politics had conditioned him to accept the precepts of the liberal consensus, and as the first California-born president he understood the aspirations of the Sunbelt and the suburbs. Nixon signaled his neoconservative sympathies by appointing Daniel Moynihan, a Democrat who had previously served in the Johnson administration, to head the newly-created Urban Affairs Council. Pointing to the example of Benjamin Disraeli, Prime Minister of late-Victorian Britain,

Moynihan persuaded Nixon that "Tory men with liberal policies" were the most effective reformers and could win working-class support for being so. Yet the Nixon administration contained other members, like Attorney-General John Mitchell and Vice-President Spiro Agnew, who favored the strategy blueprinted by Kevin Phillips. For most of his first term Nixon sought a balance between these competing visions for building the new Republican majority.

Domestic policies of the first Nixon administration

Welfare reform exemplified Nixon's neoconservative tendencies. By the late 1960s the Great Society's optimistic assumption that poverty could be eradicated by self-help programs was increasingly untenable. As swelling welfare rolls testified, what the poor needed and wanted most was cash aid. Between 1965 and 1969, despite an overall decline in poverty, recipients of Aid for Families with Dependent Children (AFDC) increased in number by 3.3 million (42%). In contrast to the early 1960s, when only a third of those eligible claimed this assistance, over 90% did so by 1971. In part this expansion took place because bureaucrats who moved into top positions in the Department of Health, Education and Welfare (HEW) during the Johnson and Nixon administrations were committed to maximizing antipoverty assistance. But the main reason, thanks to the tutelage of civil rights activists, the community action agencies fostered by the Great Society, and the National Welfare Rights Organization (NWRO), was the growing belief among the poor that welfare was a right not a privilege. As a result they were increasingly aware of their eligibility for aid and more assertive about claiming it.

Despite these improvements, the welfare system was widely perceived by liberals and conservatives alike as being in a state of crisis. Three-quarters of the AFDC expansion was borne by eight northern states and California, causing concern that it would bankrupt their treasuries. Elsewhere, like other public assistance programs inherited from the New Deal, AFDC's effectiveness as a national welfare program was undermined by inadequate state contributions and wide state-to-state differences in benefit levels and eligibility rules. Meanwhile, conservative critics complained that increased demand for AFDC at a time of low unemployment signified spreading welfare dependency. In August 1969, under Moynihan's influence, Nixon proposed the Family Assistance Plan (FAP) to reorganize welfare. Though not the cure-all remedy that its architects claimed, the strengths of this measure far outweighed its shortcomings. The *New Republic*, the voice of American liberalism, adjudged it "the most substantial welfare reform proposal in the nation's history".

The FAP would have replaced the AFDC program with a national system of income maintenance guaranteeing every poor family with children an annual minimum of $500 for each adult and $300 for each child. States whose current AFDC benefits were above the proposed national minimum had to continue these higher levels by supplementing federal payments. In contrast to AFDC, however, the working poor with children were eligible for aid, provided their income did not exceed specified levels. Also eligible were households in which the father was present (whereas more than half the states currently restricted AFDC to female-headed families). Unemployed heads of families receiving aid were required to register for job training or work if their children were of school age; failure to do so would result in loss of adult benefits. According to some estimates, the program would have made thirteen million additional Americans eligible for welfare, given aid to three times the number of children served by AFDC, and would have raised 60% of the poor above the poverty line. The main benefits would have been felt in the South, the nation's most impoverished region, where the gross income of poor families would have been tripled.

The FAP had widespread support among economists and social policy experts. Some conservative politicians and commentators were also in favor of it, partly because of the work incentive provisions and partly because income maintenance, being far easier to administer than welfare services, promised to reduce the size of the welfare bureaucracy. Moreover, a 1969 Gallup poll indicated that 65% of Americans who were aware of the scheme approved of it, and only 20% disapproved. This did not signify a groundswell of popular support, since other surveys showed that the public continued to regard most welfare recipients as lazy and undeserving. Nevertheless, the FAP's work incentives saved it from being seen as an outright dole, and the inclusion of the working poor, who numbered 10 million and were mostly white, saved it from being viewed as a program disproportionately benefiting blacks.

The bill was passed by the House of Representatives, but an unholy alliance of conservatives and liberals engineered its defeat in the Senate. Right-wing Republicans and conservative pressure groups like the Chamber of Commerce complained that the measure would triple the size of welfare rolls, double welfare costs, and provide inadequate work incentives. Further opposition was voiced by conservative southern Democrats, who feared that the scheme would diminish the supply of cheap labour which helped to attract new business to the South. But the FAP also displeased the NWRO, an organization created in the mid 1960s to speak on behalf of impoverished black ghetto dwellers. It claimed that the income maintenance floor should be raised to $5,500 in order to support a minimum standard of urban living, that the workfare requirements would force the unemployed into taking demeaning, low-paid jobs, and that the needs of childless people, who comprised about 20% of the poor, were being ignored. The NWRO's stand divided liberal Democrats, some of whom regarded the FAP as the only welfare reform that was politically feasible, while others chose to support the demands of the black poor.

As historian James Patterson noted, it was the FAP's misfortune "to run the congressional gauntlet just when social turbulence was rending a one biracial liberal coalition". The episode offered further proof that the New Deal political order was coming under contrary pressures exerted by core Democratic constituencies. It was evident that welfare provision, which many working class whites considered excessively generous, was deemed inadequate by many of the black poor, whose expectations had been aroused but left unfulfilled by the Great Society. Partly due to the resultant divisions in the Democratic party, the most important welfare reform proposed since the New Deal was lost. The opportunity to enact comparable legislation did not arise again in the economically unstable conditions of the 1970s and the conservative climate of the 1980s.

Thwarted in his goal of welfare reform, Nixon settled instead for piecemeal improvements of the social welfare system. The food stamps program, which benefited fewer than one million people when he took office, was substantially expanded in 1970 and assisted 17.1 million Americans by 1975. In contrast to the FAP, this administration measure had support from influential lobbies, notably senior citizens organizations and food producers and retailers. Moreover, conservatives who opposed giving the poor money were willing to give them food. Similar political and cultural considerations underlay the enactment of Supplemental Security Income in 1972, which established a national income floor under benefits to aged, blind, and disabled people, and unified assistance to these formerly separate welfare categories in one program financed and administered entirely by the federal government. Senior citizens were again active in its support, as were state governments anxious to reduce their welfare costs, and conservatives deemed its beneficiaries to be "deserving" in a way that the welfare poor were not. Finally, Social Security benefits were raised by 20% in the election year of 1972, and were indexed by cost-of-living adjustments to keep pace with inflation in 1974.

Largely due to these changes and the expansion of AFDC, federal expenditure on human resource programs exceeded spending on defense in every budget for which the Nixon administration was responsible (fiscal 1970 to 1975), a reversal of the pattern that had prevailed every year from 1945 to 1970. Social program funding underwent a sevenfold increase under Nixon, making him rather than Johnson the last of the big domestic spenders. All this was achieved without the Republican administration arousing the kind of political backlash that had engulfed its Democratic predecessor. Nixon's welfare measures did not transgress traditional values, benefited groups like the aged and sick who suffered less from popular prejudice than black ghetto dwellers and female-headed families, and were not accompanied by grandiose rhetoric that frightened middle Americans into believing that the poor were getting a hand-up at their expense. Moreover, the jewel in the crown of the Nixon welfare state was the liberalization of social insurance programs that benefited groups whom the president hoped to convert to Republicanism.

Nixon also sanctioned a significant expansion in the regulatory powers of the federal government for reasons of political expediency. Organized labor was gratified by the establishment of the Occupational Safety and Health Administration (OSHA) to regulate workplace conditions. Nor was Nixon blind to the growing influence of the consumer movement, which had emerged in the mid 1960s after Ralph Nader's investigations revealed that automobile manufacturers were making unsafe cars. Accordingly, a congressional initiative creating the National Highway Safety Administration received presidential support.

Environmental reform was another unlikely cause championed by the Nixon administration. Public awareness of environmental issues had been growing since the publication in 1962 of Rachel Carson's book *Silent Spring*, which disclosed the harmful effects of pesticides on water quality and wildlife. It was also fueled by environmental disasters, notably the oil spill in the Santa Barbara Channel off California in 1969, and by the emergence of "green" pressure groups such as the Environmental Defense Fund and the National Resources Defense Council. Earth Day, a nationwide series of environmental observance activities held on April 22, 1970, offered umistakeable proof that environmentalism had become part of the national agenda.

The congressional Democrats quickly took up the issue. Under the leadership of Senator Edmund Muskie, they enacted the National Environmental Policy Act of 1969, which set up the Council on Environmental Quality to advise the president and required all federal departments to prepare environmental impact statements on their proposed actions. Conversely, Nixon clashed with environmentalists on a number of issues during his first year in office, but he soon mended fences once he realized the popularity of their cause. In 1970 he created the Environmental Protection Agency to oversee federal guidelines for air pollution, toxic waste, and water quality. The administration also backed enactment of Democratic bills dealing with oil spills, dumping of waste at sea, state regulation of coastal land use, and clean air regulation.

The host of new agencies set up during the first Nixon administration added up to a virtual regulatory revolution. This was a strange record for a president who deemed the federal government to be overly bureaucratic, inefficient and wasteful. Nevertheless, there were votes to be won on the issues of environmental protection, consumer rights and occupational safety, and Nixon was determined that a goodly share of these should go to the Republicans. Paradoxically, the regulatory agencies that he viewed as instruments of partisan gain came under attack in the 1980s from the Republican administration of Ronald Reagan, which saw them as a deadweight on free enterprise.

Pragmatism rather than principle guided Nixon the reformer. Perhaps the sole exception to this rule was the revenue-sharing experiment that was the centerpiece of the New Federalism program. This represented Nixon's main effort to reverse the growth in federal power and make government more responsive to the differing needs of states and localities. The State and Local Assistance Act of 1972 departed from the New Deal principle of giving the states categorical federal grants-in-aid (money for specifically earmarked purposes). Instead, it appropriated $30.2 billion for a five-year general revenue-sharing program that allowed states and localities to spend the money in ways they wanted. In parallel with this, a special revenue-sharing plan consolidated various existing categorical programs in a particular policy area (such as health services or education) into one large block grant, which each state could then use to meet its needs in this field as it saw fit.

Not surprisingly these changes were very popular at state and local level. They boosted support for Nixon in the Sunbelt, where resentment of federal intrusiveness was traditionally strong. But revenue-sharing did not become the foundation for a new consensus about the direction of late twentieth-century federalism. Its concern with the transfer rather than the reduction of government powers left conservatives dissatisfied. In the 1980s the Reagan administration would introduce its own version of New Federalism designed to minimize government at all levels. Revenue-sharing also held little appeal to congressmen in both parties because it did not allow them to channel special aid to their constituencies in the way that categorical grants did. As a result Nixon's reforms made limited headway. Federal expenditure on categorical grants continued to rise rapidly throughout the 1970s. The lack of support for revenue-sharing made it vulnerable to the economy drives of the Carter and Reagan years. The program had been run down by 1981 and was finally terminated in 1986.

Nixon's pragmatism enabled him to support many progressive initiatives that Reagan would seek to reverse a decade later. With regard to racial matters, however, Reagan followed in Nixon's footsteps. Nixon was among the first Republicans to understand that the racial agenda could be manipulated to construct a new GOP majority. In the words of Thomas and Mary Edsall: "Nixon found a message that encompassed the position of the growing majority of white Americans who had come to believe that the denial of basic citizenship rights to blacks was wrong, but who were opposed to the prospect of substantial residential and educational integration imposed by the courts and the federal regulatory bureaucracy through involuntary mechanisms, especially busing".

The desegregation of Southern schools was the first race problem facing Nixon. In spite of the *Brown* decision of 1954, fewer than one in three black children in the South attended mixed schools by 1969. But the pace of school desegregation was about to accelerate. The Johnson administration had fixed final deadlines for the desegregation of many school districts, and Southern ability to circumvent these by implementing freedom-of-choice plans had been negated by the Supreme Court in its 1968 ruling, *Green* v. *New Kent County School Board*. Anxious to build up his support among white southerners who had voted for George Wallace in 1968, Nixon initially attempted to slow down school desegregation. The administration shocked civil rights groups by asking the courts to postpone the date set by the HEW department for the termination of Mississipi's dual school system. In 1969,

however, the Supreme Court ruled in *Alexander* v. *Holmes County Board
of Education* that Mississippi had to integrate its schools at once.
This decision gave a powerful boost to desegregation throughout the
entire South. By the start of the 1971–2 school year only 8% of southern
black children attended all-black public schools. Historians acknowledge that there was more school desegregation under Nixon than any
other president, but most attribute this to the previous actions by the
Johnson administration and to judicial rulings. For example, Stephen
Ambrose asserted that Nixon "had to be hauled kicking and screaming
into desegregation on a meaningful scale, and he did what he did not
because it was right but because he had no choice." This judgement
may be fundamentally accurate, but it downplays Nixon's success in
assuring that school desegregation was achieved without tension and
without requiring the use of federal troops. The Nixon administration's
low-profile approach, which emphasized persuasion rather than coer-
cion, and its strategy of establishing state advisory committees to promote desegregation did much to moderate the white South's resentment
of federal interference in racial matters.

However Nixon's handling of the southern school desegregation
issue exemplified another side of his racial strategy. Many commentators
have observed that he failed to use the symbolic power of the presidency
to disavow racism. Some, like historian and former Johnson administration official Roger Wilkins, even argue that he sent "cultural signals"
which legitimized the innate racism of some Americans. White
southerners tended to blame the courts rather than Nixon for the overthrow of the dual school system. The president signaled his sympathy
for them by attempting to place a southern conservative on the Supreme
Court in 1969, but the Democrat-controlled Senate first refused to
nominate Clement Haynsworth and then turned down G. Harrold
Carswell. A number of factors worked against the former, including
a conflict-of-interest charge and labor's hostility to his appointment,
while the latter was simply deemed inadequate as a judge. Nevertheless
Nixon portrayed the rejection of both nominees as a slap in the face
to the South and publicly accused the Senate of regional discrimination.
Rhetoric of this kind did much to cement the support of white
southerners.

Nixon's stand on another aspect of school desegregation also sent out
clear signals not only to the white South but also to the suburbs and
ethnic communities of the North. Due to demographic factors many
schools throughout the nation were far from being bi-racial. Poverty

and racism kept millions of blacks trapped in inner city ghettoes, while the suburbs were over 95% white. During the Johnson administration the HEW department had established guidelines for the achievement of racial balance in schools through the busing of children from one school district to another. In 1971 the Supreme Court affirmed in *Swann v. Charlotte-Mecklenberg Board of Education* that busing could be ordered by lower courts as a way of promoting integration if other methods failed.

More than any other issue, busing exposed the dichotomy between Americans' belief in racial equality as an abstract principle and their resentment of enforcement mechanisms to make it a reality. One poll found that busing was supported by only 2% of the population. George Wallace's vow to stop it made him the early front-runner for the 1972 Democratic presidential nomination. Determined not to be outbid, Nixon called for legislation to place tighter controls over busing and urged a moratorium on court-ordered busing until this was enacted. The school bus, he told Americans, had become a "symbol of social engineering on the basis of abstractions".

Affirmative action further underlined the divisive nature of the changing civil-rights agenda. By the late 1960s the federal government was moving towards acceptance of the need for racial preference programs to compensate blacks for past disadvantages in the workplace and business. Nixon himself favored this strategy, having always believed that jobs and free enterprise were more effective means of uplifting racial minorities than enforced desegregation. His administration pursued three affirmative action initiatives. Black capitalism received encouragement from the contracting program known as 8a, which set aside fixed percentages of federal contracts for minority-owned businesses. The Office of Minority Business Enterprise was created to assist minority businesses obtain federal contracts. Most controversially, the third program sought to increase black access to well-paid blue-collar jobs in industries such as construction, which had a practice of racial exclusion. This was known as the Philadelphia plan, after the city where the first agreement was made, but 55 plans involving ten cities had been established by 1972.

Put into effect by executive order in 1969, the Philadelphia plan established federal authority to require companies with government contracts to set up "goals and timetables" for minority hiring and promotion. It also set specific "ranges" for minorities holding skilled jobs in industries organized by the craft unions. In 1969, for example, only

0.5% of unionized plumbers and pipefitters in Philadelphia were black. Federal targets required the number to be increased to between 5 and 8% in 1970, and to between 22 and 26% by 1973. The unions immediately denounced the scheme as a racial quota plan. Many white workers regarded it as reverse discrimination. As an unemployed Brooklyn carpenter complained, "Those quotas and Philadelphia plans made us angry. They should create plans to help both sides. Create jobs, but don't take from one to give to the other and create bitterness."

Fearful of white backlash, the National Association for the Advancement of Colored People denounced the Philadelphia plan as a calculated effort by Nixon to break up the alliance between blacks and labor from which "most of the social progress in this country has resulted". But other black organizations endorsed the administration's policy. Northern Democrats were also divided, as was evident when Congress attempted unsuccessfully to kill the scheme in late 1969. Most Democrats with sizeable black constituencies voted to continue the Philadelphia plan, while those representing white working-class communities generally opposed it. By contrast Republican congressmen solidly supported the administration measure by a three-to-one margin.

The Philadelphia plan, whose driving force was Secretary of Labor George P. Shultz, was conceived with the best of intentions. As the controversy surrounding it grew, however, Nixon quickly realized that he could exploit matters for political gain. Enforcement of the program was effectively suspended in the construction industry after building workers and their union leaders demonstrated support for the president's policy in Vietnam. In the 1972 election Nixon even campaigned against racial-preference policies initiated by his own administration. Stoking the fires of blue-collar resentment, he avowed: "When young people apply for jobs . . . and find the door closed because they don't fit into some numerical quota, despite their ability, and they object, I do not think it is right to condemn those young people as insensitive or even racist." Many Republicans would speak in similar terms over the next twenty years, thereby helping to polarize the electorate on racial lines.

Women's rights also forced their way on to the political agenda during Nixon's first term. One reason for this was the rebirth of feminism, a cause largely dormant since the suffragette era of the early twentieth century. The cultural ferment of the 1960s and the successful example of the black civil rights movement prompted many women to question traditional gender identities that entrapped them in the role of homemakers, while men enjoyed the power and status of being bread-winners. The new mood was pioneered by Betty Friedan's critique of domesticity in her best-selling book *The Feminine Mystique*. In 1966 Friedan was also instrumental in the establishment of the National Organization for Women (NOW) to lobby on behalf of women's rights. Its immediate concern was to secure stronger enforcement by the Equal Employment Opportunities Commission (EEOC) of the clause in the Civil Rights Act of 1964 prohibiting employment discrimination on the basis of gender. In addition to picketing EEOC offices throughout the country and filing legal suit against the agency, NOW organized a highly successful one-day nationwide strike by tens of thousands of women to publicize its cause in August 1970.

The feminist movement was the preserve of well-educated, middle-class women, many of whom were part of the 1960s generation. A 1974 survey of the NOW's 40,000 members, for example, revealed that a disproportionate number worked in professional occupations and nearly half were aged under 30, while only 17% were homemakers and only 5% were black. By the early 1970s, however, the majority of women, regardless of background, had grown resentful of their second-class status. According to Gallup opinion surveys, only one in three women considered themselves the victims of discrimination in 1962, but in 1970 half of all women held this opinion and the proportion grew to two-thirds in 1974. More than anything else women complained of being denied equal opportunities to fulfill their potential in the workplace.

Despite being stereotyped as wives and mothers, women constituted 42.6% of the labor force by 1970, compared with 25.8% in 1940. Over this thirty-year period the percentage of married women who worked had doubled and the increase was even greater among working mothers. Initially, most women worked to supplement the family income rather than to forge a career, thereby not challenging traditional gender roles. By the late 1960s, however, as a result of increased expectations, greater educational qualifications, and growing awareness of the feminist message, more and more women looked for career satisfaction, but this proved hard to find. Many employers had prejudiced opinions about women's reliability and usually assigned them to low-grade, low-paid work. Over four-fifth of women workers were in clerical, sales, service, and unskilled manufacturing jobs; fewer than a fifth of them were in unionized jobs. Those women who did break through into better jobs often found that they were paid less than male co-workers. The reality of gender discrimination was underlined by the fact that the ratio of women's earnings to men's earnings declined from 63% in 1945 to 57% in 1973.

Another item on the feminist agenda, abortion rights, also gained widespread support outside the movement. Many women came to agree with feminist arguments that women could not be truly equal until they controlled their own bodies. Each year in the 1960s about 300,000 women became pregnant against their will. Some of these put their lives at risk by seeking illegal abortion from unqualified practitioners. No one can calculate precisely how many women died as a result, but the feminist Robin Morgan estimated that the yearly number was greater than the death rate of American males in Vietnam.

Public policymakers could not ignore the newly expressed concerns of women. In 1971 the Democrat-controlled Congress enacted the Comprehensive Child Development Act authorizing federal funding of day-care centers. Legislation guaranteeing rights of equal pay to federal employees, prohibiting sex discrimination in educational programs receiving federal funds, and extending the powers of the EEOC to prohibit job discrimination based on sex followed in the next year. Also in 1972 the Equal Rights Amendment (ERA) to the Constitution, which had first been introduced in 1923, was finally approved by Congress and sent to the states for ratification. It declared: "Equality of rights under the law shall not be denied by the United States or by any State on account of sex."

Abortion reform also made progress. In 1967 no state allowed abortion except when necessary to save the mother's life. By 1971, led by New York, twelve states permitted termination of pregnancies resulting from rape and incest, as well as those threatening the physical and mental health of the mother. The Supreme Court set national standards for abortion rights in *Roe* v. *Wade* (1973). This ruling decreed that in the first three months of pregnancy, the abortion decision was to be left to the woman and her doctor. To protect the mother's health, states could restrict but not prohibit abortion in the second trimester of pregnancy. Finally, in the last trimester, states could regulate or even prohibit abortions to protect the life of the fetus, except when medical judgement ruled an abortion necessary to preserve the mother's life. The constitutional justification for this decision rested on an earlier judgement, *Griswold* v. *Connecticut* (1965), which ruled that the right of privacy was one of the personal liberties protected by the Bill of Rights and by the Fourteenth Amendment's due-process clause. In striking down a state law criminalizing the use of contraceptive devices, the

Griswold ruling had stipulated that married people had a right to make certain intimate personal choices, including the right to decide whether to engage in sexual intercourse for reproduction or pleasure. The *Roe* decision extended this principle on a qualified basis to a woman's right to decide whether to have an abortion.

Far from reflecting an emergent consensus, the advance in women's rights quickly generated a backlash from traditionalists, both male and female. Anti-abortion and anti-ERA movements came into being. It was perfectly feasible, as many Catholic women exemplified, to support ERA while opposing abortion. By the mid 1970s, however, the anti-ERA and anti-abortion causes developed increasingly close links because both reforms were perceived as a threat to traditional family values. Significantly, both movements drew their strongest support from southern Christian fundamentalists and Catholic ethnics, groups whom Nixon sought to convert to Republicanism.

Although Nixon supported the principle of equal employment opportunities, political calculation and personal conviction made him an opponent of those women's rights that seemingly challenged the sanctity of the family. In addition to voicing personal opposition to abortion, he vetoed the Comprehensive Child Development Act on grounds that federal encouragement of child care arrangements outside the family would "Sovietize" America. As historian Rochelle Gatlin noted, this veto reinforced two traditional attitudes: "first, that the nuclear family is 'natural' and 'private', not an institution amenable to government intervention, and, second, that child-rearing is primarily a mother's responsibility". In making the family a Republican issue, Nixon blazed a trail that Ronald Reagan would later follow.

Nixon also appealed to the cultural conservatism of the Sunbelt, ethnic communities, and habitual Republicans in other ways. His administration sought to portray the Republicans as the party of law and order, patriotism and traditional values, and the Democrats as supporters of sexual permissiveness, pornography, crime, drugs, the counterculture, student radicalism, black militancy, feminism and the dissolution of the family. The enactment in 1969 of the Washington DC crime bill, which contained controversial preventive detention provisions, was part of this campaign. Rhetorical outbursts from Nixon and Vice-President Agnew also fanned silent majority resentments of antiwar protest, lack of patriotism, and drug abuse on college campuses. In similar vein, the president implicitly condoned construction workers who had attacked peace demonstrators in New York City in May 1970 by meeting a week later with 22 "loyal" union leaders, from whom he accepted his own hardhat bearing the inscription "commander-in-chief". Nixon further appealed to patriotic sentiments by advocating leniency for Lieutenant William Calley, whom the army had sentenced to life imprisonment after troops under his command massacred Vietnamese civilians at My Lai in 1968. By contrast, Attorney General Mitchell sought more vigorous prosecution of antiwar activists by the courts, bringing suit against prominent individuals like Philip Berrigan, Daniel Ellsberg and the "Chicago Eight".

Democrats in disarray

While Nixon was attempting to forge a new Republican majority, the Democrats were engaged in new internal disputes of immense consequence for the decline of the New Deal order. A power struggle broke out between the party's traditional leadership and the forces of what journalists labeled the "New Politics". In many respects this developed into a battle between the old liberalism that was rooted in the postwar consensus and the new liberalism that had emerged in the second half of the 1960s.

Organizational power in the national Democratic party was traditionally held by a loose confederation of state and local party leaders, who largely controlled the selection of delegates to the national convention that met every four years to choose a presidential candidate. Delegates attending pre-1972 conventions were socially unrepresentative of American society, being overwhelmingly white, male, middle-aged or older, and of upper-status occupation. Nearly all were party regulars who supported the party year-in and year-out. Many were either party officials or officeholders at congressional, state or local levels. In recognition of close Democratic ties with the trade union movement, labor leaders were also invited to attend the convention, and AFL-CIO chief George Meany expected to be consulted about who the presidential nominee should be. As a result party chieftains and delegates had common priorities to choose a presidential candidate who could win the election, unite the party behind him, and leave it in the best possible condition to fight future elections.

The New Politics challenge to the dominance of traditional party elites was first signaled by the candidacies of Eugene McCarthy and Robert Kennedy in the 1968 presidential primaries. These two men attracted support from a new class of activists whose loyalty was to causes rather than to the Democratic party itself. The formative political experience of many McCarthy and Kennedy campaign participants had been involvement in the civil rights movement, the antiwar movement, the feminist movement, the environmental movement, or the consumer rights movement. In general these new-class Democrats were aged under forty, were college-educated, held well-paid professional or managerial jobs, and were not so overwhelmingly male and white as regular Democratic activists. They were enthusiastic about the social and cultural changes of the 1960s, and the prior participation of many in the civil rights and women's rights movements caused them to perceive equality in terms of result as well as opportunity.

In a bid to restore party unity after the highly divisive contest for the 1968 presidential nomination, the regulars agreed to the establishment of a special Commission on Party Structure and Delegate Selection (known as the McGovern-Fraser Commission). Party chieftains had expected to control these proceedings, but the new-class Democrats quickly gained the upper hand. As a result the commission ended up recommending reforms that radically shifted power within the party. The new rules sought to increase popular participation in the presidential selection process. However they made the Democratic party less rather than more representative and made things more difficult for it to absorb competing factions and mediate differences between them.

The reforms broke the control of state and local party leaders over the presidential nomination process. A quota system was effectively established to ensure that women, blacks, and youth participated as delegates in "reasonable relationship" to each group's presence in a state's population. The closed-party caucus system, hitherto the most common form of delegate selection, was banned. The "blind" primary, which allowed delegates to be elected without stating their candidate preference, and the practice of granting *ex-officio* delegate status to party officials and office-holders were also prohibited. The party was now obliged to use primaries or open conventions to choose delegates committed to a particular presidential candidate. By 1976, 29 states operated Democratic presidential primaries, compared with only 17 in 1968.

The effect of these changes was significant. Women constituted 40% of delegates at the 1972 Democratic presidential convention, non-whites 15%, and the under-thirties 22%, compared with 13%, 5%, and 3% respectively in 1968. Allowing new groups greater access to participation as delegates in the presidential selection process was laudable, but the reforms did nothing to extend similar rights to groups that had loyally supported the Democratic party since Roosevelt's day. In 1972 the delegation from New York, the nation's most unionized state, had only three members who belonged to labor organizations, and Catholic ethnics were generally under-represented in the delegations of every urbanized state.

Most black, women, and young delegates had upper-income, high-status backgrounds. Overall there was a markedly wider gap between the socioeconomic status of convention delegates and of Democratic identifiers in the electorate in 1972 than was previously the case. The gap on policy issues was also wider, with delegates having far more liberal preferences than Democratic identifiers on social, racial, cultural and lifestyle issues. Partly because of their convictions but also, no doubt, because affluence removed them from the front-line of change, new-class Democrats had little understanding of the fears felt by blue-collar and ethnic whites about race-related issues. Moreover, the Democratic officials and office-holders who were close to the concerns of these constituencies had been removed by the new rules from the presidential nominating process.

The proliferation of primaries also served to distance the Democrats from their traditional constituencies. Voter turn-out in primaries was significantly lower and far more class-skewed towards the affluent than in general elections. In 1976, for example, 35% of Democratic voters in the California primary and 32% in the New York primary had annual incomes exceeding $20,000, compared with 23 and 16% respectively in the presidential election. Accordingly, Democrats pursuing the nomination tended to focus their campaign towards this elite constituency which was unrepresentative of the broad-based constituency that had to be won over to achieve victory in the general election.

Nothing exemplified the change within the party better than the decision of the 1972 convention to expel the Cook County delegation that had been handpicked in violation of the new rules by Mayor Richard Daley of Chicago. Since 1932 no big-city political machine had been more important to the success of Democratic presidential candidates than Chicago's. Now, in place of its representatives, was seated a slate of delegates containing the appropriate quotas of blacks, women and youth, but hardly any white ethnics or blue-collars. As the political scientist Byron Shafer observed, "Before reform there was an American party system in which one party, the Republicans, was primarily responsive to white-collar constituencies and in which another, the Democrats, was primarily responsive to blue-collar constituencies.

After reform, there were two parties each responsive to quite different white-collar coalitions, while the old blue-collar majority within the Democratic Party was forced to try to squeeze back into the party once identified predominantly with its needs."

Under the new rules the Democrats chose as their presidential candidate in 1972 the man least capable of defeating Nixon. The early favorite for the nomination, Edmund Muskie, fell away after a poor showing in the New Hampshire primary, where he fell victim to dirty tricks by the Nixon campaign organization. It also became evident that his moderate liberalism had less appeal to traditional Democrats than the conservative populism of George Wallace. The Alabama governor quickly established himself as putative front-runner, performing well in southern states like Florida and industrial states like Michigan and Pennsylvania with a campaign focused against busing and bureaucracy. However, Wallace was shot by a crazed would-be assassin in a Maryland shopping mall on March 15. His wounds left him permanently disabled and removed him from the campaign. By this time Wallace had amassed 3.35 million primary votes but only 323 delegates. In contrast, Senator George McGovern (South Dakota), a leading critic of the Vietnam War, had won 2.2 million votes and 409 delegates, many of them garnered from nonprimary states.

McGovern's support came from new-class Democrats, college students (newly enfranchized after the 26th amendment to the constitution gave the vote to eighteen year-olds in 1971), blacks, and the welfare poor. Though these groups made up a distinct minority of Democratic voters, McGovern had no rival for their support. By contrast, the traditional Democratic constituencies had divided amongst a host of other candidates, including Wallace, Senator Hubert Humphrey (Minnesota), and Senator Henry Jackson (Washington). After Wallace's elimination, only Humphrey posed any threat to McGovern.

The exponents of the old liberalism and new liberalism clashed head-on in a bruising primary in California. McGovern's narrow defeat of Humphrey turned out to be a pyrrhic victory. Humphrey's denunciations of him as the candidate of "acid, amnesty, and abortion" fixed his image in the eyes of socially and culturally conservative voters. The McGovern "demogrant" proposal to give $1,000 to everyone in the country, rich and poor, also came under devastating attack from the Minnesota senator, who warned that it would be financed largely by ordinary taxpayers. Meanwhile, McGovern's intentions to make sweeping cuts of $30 billion in the defense budget aroused concern about jobs among blue-collar workers and the labor unions. Unsurprisingly a poll taken shortly after the California primary found that 40% of Democrats who had voted for Humphrey preferred Nixon to McGovern.

The 1972 election

Once nominated, McGovern found it difficult to broaden his appeal. Polls showed that 31% of voters in the 1972 election regarded him as liberal and 31% thought him radical, political positions respectively shared by only 17% and 1% of the electorate. Although McGovern dropped the "demogrant" proposal and blocked adoption of a pro-abortion plank in the party platform, this made him appear inconsistent and indecisive rather than moderate. More often than not, however, he hewed to the conviction politics that had helped win him the nomination but which proved a weakness in his campaign against Nixon.

McGovern's message that the nation needed more programs to abolish poverty, racism, and inequality fell on unreceptive ears. Fearful that he would drag down the entire ticket, many big-city Democratic organizations, notably the Daley machine, kept their distance from his campaign. Frank Rizzo, Democratic mayor of Philadelphia and a former police chief, openly backed Nixon. A number of southern Democratic governors, led by Jimmy Carter of Georgia, refused to endorse the national ticket because of McGovern's unpopularity in their region. Also, for the first time in its history the AFL-CIO witheld its endorsement from a Democratic presidential candidate. Labor leaders were piqued at their exclusion from the nomination process, and McGovern's savage attacks on the Vietnam war ran counter to the Cold War convictions that most of them still harbored. "He's become an apologist for the Communist world," complained George Meany. Many Democratic voters reached the same conclusion when McGovern compared Nixon to Hitler in his conduct of the Vietnam war. Others came to question the Democratic candidate's patriotism, not only because of his stand on amnesty for Vietnam draft evaders but also because of his promise to "crawl" to Hanoi, if necessary, to obtain the return of American prisoners-of-war.

Faced with such a weak candidate, Nixon did not feel the need to campaign as actively as usual. The speeches that he did make caught the public mood by attacking bureaucracy, busing, social engineering by government, the high cost of welfare, and "the age of permissiveness". Nixon's reward was the largest majority ever given to a

Republican presidential candidate. He took 60.7% of the popular vote, winning 18 million votes more than McGovern and taking the electoral college votes of every state except Massachusetts and the District of Columbia. Almost 40% of habitual Democratic voters backed Nixon. For the first time ever a majority of Catholics voted for a Republican presidential candidate. In a remarkable turnaround 59% of the ethnic vote went to Nixon, whereas 56% had gone to Humphrey four years earlier. Nixon's blue-collar vote ran at 52%, compared to 37% in 1968. His southern support leaped even more dramatically from 38 to 72%.

The presidential vote seemingly indicated that the realignment foreseen by Kevin Phillips was coming true, but Republican success was not replicated at other levels. Congress remained solidly Democratic, with the GOP making a net gain of only eleven seats in the House of Representatives and actually suffering a net loss of two seats in the Senate. The emergence of southern Republicanism was still uncertain, since Nixon's coat-tails only helped to elect two additional GOP senators and three more GOP representatives in Dixie. Meanwhile, the large majority of governorships nationwide remained in Democratic hands.

Something of a "class inversion" had taken place in the Democratic presidential vote. McGovern's support among low, middle, and high socioeconomic (ses) status whites stood at 32%, 26%, and 32% respectively. He held little appeal for working-class and lower-middle-class Americans, but he ran particularly well with affluent, college-educated voters aged under thirty. Of the New Deal coalition only blacks (87%) and Jews (67%) remained loyal to him. On the other hand, at the congressional and gubernatorial levels of the party, where the influence of the New Politics was relatively weak, the Democrats held on to their traditional constituencies. Catholic support for Democratic candidates in House, Senate, and gubernatorial elections ran at 65%, 55% and 60% respectively. The parallel figures were 62%, 53%, and 67% for labor union families, and 69%, 60%, and 59% for white southerners.

The 1972 election did not see a critical voter realignment. At best what had occurred was a partial dealignment. Nixon had been the beneficiary of a negative landslide that signified more the rejection of McGovern than a positive endorsement for him. The low turn-out by only 55.2% of the electorate and the extent of split-ticket voting showed that neither candidate had truly enthused voters. In fact polls showed that only 23% of the electorate were Republican identifiers' 1% down on 1968. Democratic identifiers had also declined from 45% to

40% in this period, but the defectors had become "independents" (who now accounted for 34% of the electorate) rather than Republicans.

The resurgence of the Republican right

Nixon's relationship with the GOP right during his first term had been ambivalent. His interventionist economic policies, expansion of welfare and regulatory government, and the foreign policy of detente had all been difficult for conservative Republicans to swallow. In the 1950s Dwight D. Eisenhower had encountered bitter criticism from the right for far milder transgressions from the paths of Republican orthodoxy. By contrast there was little public dissension within the party during Nixon's first term. John Ashbrook launched a right-wing protest candidacy for the 1972 Republican nomination, but this made little impact and attracted far less attention than Pat Buchanan's challenge to George Bush twenty years later. Confident of being the beneficiaries of the new Republican majority that Nixon was seeking to build, most conservatives remained loyal to him. They viewed the 1972 election as proof that the nation was moving right.

To the Republican right's joy, the president also seemed to interpret his victory as a conservative mandate. Relieved of reelection worries, Nixon rejected Keynesianism and controls in favor large cutbacks in federal spending as an antidote to inflation. His second inaugural address clearly set out limited government-free market themes for his final term. A few weeks later, the administration announced plans to eliminate 112 Great Society programs (including community action) and to reduce funding for others. The new conservative trend affected more than just budgetary and economic matters. Nixon dismissed Reverend Theodore M. Hesburgh, head of the Civil Rights Commission, who had been trenchantly critical of his record on racial affairs. He also vetoed "a bill of rights" for the disabled and rural anti-pollution legislation. Speaking for many Democrats, Congressman Carl D. Perkins (Kentucky) characterized the administration's actions as "an ill-concealed effort to repeal the nineteen-sixties".

Nixon was unable to follow through on his conservative plans because of the Watergate scandal. It was the ultimate irony that Nixon's disgrace and enforced resignation stemmed from his insecurity about being reelected in 1972, even when facing a no-hope opponent like McGovern. The Committee to Reelect the President, Nixon's personal campaign organization, and members of his White House staff became party to illegal political espionage. Whether Nixon personally had prior knowledge of the attempted break-in at Democratic National Committee headquarters at the Watergate office complex in Washington DC on June 17, 1972 is unclear. Nevertheless his involvement in a cover-up of White House complicity in the affair brought about his downfall. After eighteen months of investigations by journalists, judges, Justice Department officials, and Congress, Nixon's guilt became clear and he resigned office on August 9, 1974 to escape impeachment. Adding to Republican discomfiture, Vice-President Agnew had earlier been forced to resign on October 12, 1973 after effectively pleading guilty to charges of bribery and income tax exasion.

The electoral impact of the scandal has occasioned much debate. Some conservative analysts have suggested that 1980 was the election that Watergate postponed. In their view Nixon's second-term policies would have laid the foundations for another Republican landslide in 1976, thereby giving the GOP the kind of conservative mandate won by Reagan four years later. However, Watergate linked the Republicans in the public mind with Nixon's sordid activities. In addition, it paralyzed the presidency, preventing first Nixon and then Gerald Ford from taking strong action against economic and international problems, such as the energy crisis, the recession, and the collapse of South Vietnam, all of which hurt the GOP's political standing. This counterfactual view drew some support from Kevin Phillips, who suggested that Nixon's hand-picked successor in 1976 would have been John Connally not Ronald Reagan. Formerly Democratic governor of Texas but now a committed Nixon supporter who had served as Secretary of the Treasury in 1971–2, Connally was regarded by the president as the man best qualified to continue the job of converting doubting Democrats, particularly his fellow southerners, into Republicans.

Fascinating as these speculations are, the truth is that Watergate happened and it did hurt the Republican party. In mid 1974 the GOP reached its lowest voter-identification level (18%) since the Gallup poll began posing such questions in 1937. Shortly afterwards, thanks to the combined effects of Watergate and the recession, the Republicans went down to one of the worst midterm defeats in their history, suffering a net loss of 49 congressmen, five senators, and four governorships. Two years later they lost the presidency, albeit narrowly, and failed to recapture lost ground in Congress. Despite these setbacks, however, Nixon's disgrace indirectly assisted the advancement of Ronald Reagan and his conservative supporters in the GOP. Watergate ended the prospect of a Nixon-engineered Connally candidacy in 1976, it made the public look kindly on political outsiders with no connection to Washington, and it brought to power an unelected president who had no claim to be renominated for office as of right.

Gerald Ford, the onetime Michigan congressman, was unsuited by background and temperament to carry on the work of building the new Republican majority in the Sunbelt and the suburbs. In spite of his economic conservatism, the new president's moderate views on social issues such as abortion, ERA, and busing meant that he was ill-equipped to speak the language of populist conservatism. According to Kevin Phillips, he represented "the old Northern middle class, high church Republicanism [that was] uncomfortable with Southern preachers and Polish ethnic leaders". Whereas the Nixon-Agnew ticket had teamed together a Sunbelt politician and an ethnic, Ford's nomination of Governor Nelson A. Rockefeller of New York as his vice-president appeared to resurrect the formerly dominant Midwestern-Northeastern axis of the GOP. In promoting the archdeacon of liberal Republicanism, the president angered Sunbelt Republicans whose conservatism was more aggressive and ideological than his own.

Ford's toleration of large deficit budgets and the continuation of detente in the face of communist advances in Southeast Asia fueled conservative ire. Right-wing publicists like Pat Buchanan and the *National Review* publisher William Rusher called for the creation of a new party to contest the 1976 election, but this aroused little enthusiasm. Many prominent conservative Republicans, like Senator Barry Goldwater (Arizona), decided to endorse Ford's renomination for fear that party divisions would ensure a Democratic victory in the forthcoming election. However other right-wingers, conservative intellectuals and publicists, and a host of grass-roots Republican activists united in support of Reagan's challenge for the nomination.

Reagan campaigned on the issues of a balanced budget, law-and-order, and a strong national defense. At first things went badly for him. A narrow defeat at Ford's hands in the New Hampshire primary was followed by clearcut defeat in Florida. Senior citizens, an important force in the Sunshine state, took a dim view of Reagan's ill-conceived statements that social security program costs had to be reduced. Ford also swept home in the urbanized northeastern states. Victory in North Carolina turned things around for Reagan just as it seemed that his campaign would fold. This was followed by other wins in the South, notably in Texas, and in Indiana.

Reagan's comeback was partly due to the fact that his attacks on Ford-Kissinger foreign policy finally hit home. It also benefited from George Wallace's failure to capture the Democratic nomination. After Wallace's defeat by Jimmy Carter in the Democratic primary in Florida, many of his supporters in other states crossed over to vote for Reagan in GOP primaries. Underlying these factors were changes in party rules that worked to Reagan's advantage. To avoid charges that they were a boss-controlled party, the Republicans had followed the Democratic example and increased the importance of primaries in presidential delegate selection. They had also pursued their own brand of affirmative action by apportioning "bonus" delegates to any state, regardless of size, that had voted Republican in recent federal and state elections. The first of these changes weakened the grip of the party leadership on the nomination process and the second increased the Sunbelt's delegate strength at the expense of the northeastern states.

Although Reagan's challenge eventually ended in narrow defeat, he had enhanced his standing within the GOP. His absorption of the Wallace constituency was a significant milestone in the advancement of conservative Republicanism to national power. Moreover, in recognition of his strength within the party, Ford allowed Reagan supporters, led by Senator Jesse Helms (North Carolina), to redraft much of the GOP platform that had been drawn up by White House aides. The new foreign policy planks were critical of detente, the Helsinki Accords, and the proposed Panama Canal "giveaway". On the domestic front, right wing influence was reflected in new platform statements opposing "forced busing" and compulsory national health insurance and supporting constitutional amendments to permit prayers in public schools and to prohibit abortion. About the only concession won by Ford lieutenants was an endorsement of ERA. The vice-presidential nomination also provided a significant indication of the changing balance of power within the GOP. To appease Reagan's supporters, Ford dropped Rockefeller from the ticket and replaced him with Senator Robert Dole (Kansas). It was hardly surprising, therefore, that conservatives regarded the 1976 convention as a turning-point in their drive to gain control of the Republican party.

Return to Roosevelt?

As the Republicans turned right, the party of Roosevelt seemed to be moving back from the New Politics to its New Deal roots. US withdrawal from the Vietnam war in 1973 removed from the political agenda one of the issues that had divided Democrats. Also, the political significance of social issues declined in the recession-hit mid-1970s and economic issues, traditionally a source of Democratic strength, rose to the fore. Sweeping Democratic success in the 1974 midterm elections and Jimmy Carter's election as president two years later seemed to offer hope that the New Deal coalition could be reconstituted. Democratic support among middle and low ses whites ran at 62% and 67% respectively in 1974. Nevertheless the class differences in voting behavior that had underpinned the New Deal party system were no longer salient. The Democrats were supported by 57% of high ses whites, and ran particularly well among voters who were aged under 35, college-educated, and employed in professional or managerial posts. Representing this economically diverse constituency imposed new strains on the congressional wing of the party.

In 1974 the Democrats amassed massive majorities of 291 to 144 seats in the House of Representatives and 60 to 37 seats in the Senate. Further success in the 1976 congressional elections enabled them to hold on to their huge leads, but the Democratic position was not as strong as it seemed. Many of the new congressmen and senators represented traditionally Republican or marginal constituencies with a large percentage of high ses white voters. With an average age of forty, these freshmen had a common generational experience in the 1960s. Most were veterans of grass-roots political organizations and the New Politics rather than the old Democratic party. The content and style of their politics in office became increasingly oriented to developing a base among upper-income and upper-middle-income suburban voters rather than among the working class components of the New Deal coalition. They were liberal on social and international issues, but reflected the concerns of their better-off constituents on taxation, spending and labor issues. In other words the congressional freshman class of 1974 stood outside the New Deal tradition. The man who became its most famous member served notice of this shortly after his election. "We're not a bunch of little Hubert Humphreys," said Senator Gary Hart (Colorado).

The influence of the newcomers was strongest in the House of Representatives, where the freshman classes of 1974 and 1976 together constituted some two-fifths of total Democratic membership. Reflecting post-Watergate disillusion with the political establishment, many of these new congressmen were interested above all else in achieving procedural reforms that diffused power in the House, particularly within the standing committees, from senior members to junior members. This bred an adversarial relationship between the newcomers and the congressional party establishment. Moreover, the institutional changes that the former helped to promote made it more difficult for the latter to engage in the kind of special-interest bargaining that conventionally oiled the enactment of distributional policies. This divergence between the heirs of the New Politics and representatives of the party's traditional constituencies occurred at a particularly unfortunate moment for the congressional Democrats. As Thomas Edsall noted, "For a party struggling to formulate economic policy at a time of severe strain, this combination was a formula for inaction."

Watergate rather than a desire to return to the New Deal past shaped the outcome of the contest for the Democratic presidential nomination in 1976. In a year when it was an asset to be an outsider unconnected to the Washington establishment, the winner was Jimmy Carter, an obscure former governor of Georgia with no experience of national politics. His candidacy also benefited from the recent party reforms which had undermined the power of the established Democratic leadership. Presidential selection procedures had been modified after the 1972 debacle, most notably by replacing the delegate quota system with less rigid affirmative action requirements and abolishing the winner-take-all primary, but the participatory process inaugurated by the McGovern-Fraser reforms had been preserved in its essence. A strong showing in primaries was still essential to win the nomination, making it impossible for party leaders to control candidate selection.

Carter was neither a New Deal Democrat nor a New Politics Democrat, but his ambiguity made him acceptable to both groups. His success in the early primaries took better known Democrats by surprise, allowing him to develop vital momentum before they could organize against him. Hubert Humphrey did not campaign actively for the nomination in the hope that the primary process would not produce a clear winner and that a deadlocked convention would then turn to him. The candidate endorsed by labor and Cold War hawks, Senator Henry Jackson, sought to steamroll his way to the nomination by winning the early primaries in the industrial states, but defeat by Carter in Pennsylvania effectively eliminated him. Carter also ended George Wallace's challenge in the South with victory in the crucial Florida primary. After disposing of Jackson and Wallace, he faced only scattered opposition in the remaining primaries and went on to become the first Democratic presidential nominee from the Deep South since the Civil War.

Though not a Roosevelt Democrat in the fullest sense, Carter's campaign against Ford harked back to New Deal traditions. In contrast to recent elections, the Democratic and Republican candidates were most sharply divided over economic issues rather than social and cultural issues. The major racial issue centered on how far the Supreme Court's 1971 ruling on busing should be enforced. Violent demonstrations had taken place against busing in Louisville in 1975 and in Boston, supposedly the cradle of northern liberalism, in the following year. Recognizing the dangers of stirring further controversy, both candidates opposed mandatory busing. Ford called for a constitutional amendment to forbid it, while Carter's solution emphasized the need to improve the quality of education in black neighborhoods. Both avowed personal opposition to abortion but adopted different positions on the issue. Ford moved somewhat away from the GOP platform in expressing support for a constitutional amendment to allow each state the right to decide the legality of abortion for itself. Carter promised to respect the Supreme Court's *Roe* v. *Wade* decision, but opposed the use of federal funds to pay for abortion.

The outcome was a narrow victory for Carter, who took 50.1% of the vote to Ford's 48.1%. The electoral college margin of 297 to 240 votes was the closest since 1916. Carter owed his victory to two groups above all others. Blacks gave Carter 83% of their votes. Without their support, he could not have swept the South, where he won every state except Virginia. And with the economy in trouble, trade union leaders rediscovered the Democratic loyalties that McGovern's New Politics campaign of 1972 had stifled. Though Carter was not its favorite during the nomination contest, the AFL-CIO made every effort to ensure that organized labor backed him in the presidential election. As a result 61% of the votes of union families went to Carter. This was not as high as expected because a substantial minority of trade unionists were swayed by Republican arguments that inflation was the main economic problem. Nevertheless the votes of organized labor proved crucial to Carter's victory in states such as New York, Ohio, and Pennsylvania. It was significant that the Democratic candidate did not carry a single state in the West, a region where neither the black vote nor the union vote was strong.

Yet any assumption that the 1976 presidential election represented a resurgence of the New Deal coalition was mistaken. Carter's support was different from Roosevelt's in important respects. Roosevelt had carried over 70% of the white southern vote at a time when Dixie's black electorate was negligible. Carter could carry the South because of overwhelming support from blacks enfranchized by the voting rights legislation of 1965. The dealignment of the white South from the national Democratic party was not reversed in 1976. Carter won only 43% of its vote. Also, Catholic support for the Democratic ticket was relatively anaemic at 55%, well down on Roosevelt's heyday. Carter's stand against a constitutional amendment banning abortion, which was criticized by Catholic prelates, and his well-publicized Baptist views limited his appeal to this constituency. As partial compensation, he was backed by 46% of Protestant voters, a high level for a Democrat. In this instance his Baptist creed was an advantage. It appealed to co-religionists in the South and southern migrants settled in other regions.

*　　*　　*

American politics were in an uncertain state as the nation celebrated its bicentenary in 1976. Richard Nixon's hopes of building a new Republican majority had foundered on the rocks of Watergate. The Republicanism that he sought to promote combined acceptance of New Deal tradition with social-issue conservatism. As such it was something of a throwback to the politics of the liberal consensus. However, Nixon's disgrace had opened the way for a challenge by a rejuvenated Republican right which preached the virtues of anti-statist conservatism. The Democrats were also in a state of flux. Rivalry between old and new liberals pulled the party in different directions. Regardless of George McGovern's landslide defeat by Nixon in 1972, his candidacy demonstrated that the dominance of old liberals over the presidential wing of the party had been broken. Two years later the midterm landslide gave representatives of the New Politics an important entree into the congressional wing of the party. The question facing the Democrats in 1976 was whether a new president who belonged to neither faction could keep the party united and resuscitate the New Deal political order.

6

Malaise: the Politics of the Carter Era, 1977–1980

Jimmy Carter took office on a wave of national optimism that a new leader untainted by previous association with national government could redeem America after the traumas of Watergate and Vietnam and restore its wellbeing. Such hopes quickly gave way to disillusion. Renewed economic problems and a series of foreign policy failures in the late 1970s bred a public mood of pessimism and uncertainty. Carter himself spoke of an American malaise, "a crisis of confidence . . . that strikes at the very heart and soul and spirit of our national will". His ability to delineate this crisis was not matched by his ability to resolve it. As a result he was overwhelmingly defeated in his bid for reelection in 1980 by Ronald Reagan.

Carter's presidency has gone down in history as a failure. It was his misfortune to take office at a time of transition in America's economic and global power. In essence the Carter era was one of limits and of relative decline for the United States. Many of the problems of the late 1970s were beyond the power of government to resolve. The historical circumstances were not conducive to successful presidential leadership. Indeed political scientist Erwin Hargrove claims "it is not clear that anyone else could have done as well" as Carter, whose record included some significant achievements. This may be true, but in at least one important respect he contributed to the national mood of uncertainty. Carter did not possess the vision nor the leadership to develop a new consensus about how the United States should function in the age of limits. Moreover, Carter's U-turns in foreign and economic policy saddled his presidency with an image of inconsistency and left the American people confused as to whether his purpose was to break new ground or recreate the past.

From detente to confrontation

Carter became president at a time of intense debate about US foreign policy between liberal internationalists, who advocated so-called "world order politics", and conservative internationalists, who wanted to continue the global struggle against Soviet communism. At first Carter inclined towards a new foreign policy in recognition that the United States had to adapt to a changing world, but setbacks abroad caused him to change course in 1979–80. This inconsistency prevented him from establishing a new role for the country in world affairs. According to the historian Gaddis Smith, Carter "tried consciously and explicitly to discover and apply an effective combination of morality, reason, and power in the conduct of American foreign policy" but ended up sanctioning a "return to militarism". Similarly, the political scientists James A. Nathan and James K. Oliver concluded that in the late 1970s the United States lay suspended "between its cold war past and an interdependent international future of which it had little vision".

Supporters of world order politics envisioned taking the foreign policy of detente to its ultimate logic. They believed that America's future role was to exercise leadership without hegemony in a multipolar world where its limited power would have to be applied selectively. In their view the major problems facing the late twentieth century international community were economic in nature and were too complex for solution by military power. Ideological conflicts between capitalism and communism were no longer considered relevant. Economic issues within the industrialized world and between the West and the Third World were now deemed crucial. Interdependence was seen as the crux of a new world order in which national prosperity would depend on international cooperation and no nation would enjoy economic hegemony. The Soviets were perceived as a power in decline, unable to exert leadership in the interdependent world order because of their economic weakness and incapable of threatening global stability because of their need for western economic assistance.

According to this new school of liberal internationalism, East-West relations would be superceded in significance in future by North-South relations. Detente had already begun the process of economic modernization in the Soviet-bloc countries of Europe. The next step was to aid the Third World's economic development by increasing its access to western capital, technology and markets. Departing from Cold War orthodoxy, world order internationalists regarded peasant revolutions not as signs of spreading communist influence but as a necessary step to remove the semi-feudal oligarchies that hindered the modernization of many underdeveloped countries. They assumed that change-oriented regimes brought to power by such revolutions would eventually turn to the West to improve the material conditions of their people.

The opposite side in the foreign policy debate argued that the new world order could not be built until the United States overcame the global challenge of Soviet communism. According to conservative internationalists, failure in Vietnam did not reflect the limitations of US power but had resulted from America's loss of will to use its power. They were confident that US capacity to wage global containment could be restored through the remilitarization of its foreign policy. To this school of thought, only military power could safeguard against Soviet expansionism, counter against revolution and disorder in the Third World, guarantee the stability of authoritarian regimes that could promote pro-western modernization in developing nations, and ensure that the new economic powers of Western Europe and Japan would continue to look to the United States for political leadership of the West.

The lack of consensus on America's world role was underlined by the wide-ranging nature of the debate. Among Democrats, devotees of the New Politics and those old-style liberals who had turned against the Vietnam war called for a new foreign policy. By contrast, unrepentant Democratic Cold Warriors like Henry Jackson and neoconservative intellectuals like Irving Kristol and Norman Podhoretz were in the conservative internationalist camp. Both these groups were particularly active in the Committee on the Present Danger, which spearheaded criticism of detente. This organization avowed that "the principal threat to our nation, to world peace, and to the cause of human freedom is the Soviet drive for dominance based on unprecedented military buildup." Remilitarization was also a cause dear to the Republican right, and featured strongly in Ronald Reagan's campaigns for the GOP presidential nomination in 1976 and 1980.

A new political force, the Christian right, and a well-established one, the American Legion, were supporters of Cold War internationalism. The AFL-CIO hierarchy was in the same corner, thanks to its strong anticommunist traditions and its desire to protect jobs in defense industries. On the other hand the business community held divergent opinions. Banking and financial institutions, which were anxious to profit from new investment opportunities, and mass production industries, which were keen to transfer some of their operations into countries where labor costs were low, saw world order politics as a means of enhancing capital movement. Conversely, defense corporations and oil companies, both of which were expanding industries with a strong base in the Sunbelt, favored remilitarization. The former had an obvious interest in the restoration of big defense budgets and the latter believed that military power would safeguard US interests in the Middle East against the excesses both of the Soviet Union and the Organization of Petroleum Exporting Companies (OPEC). These divisions existed within the Carter administration itself. Secretary of State Cyrus Vance wanted to extend detente, stabilize the arms race, and improve US relations with developing nations. "There can be no going back", he declared, "to a time when we thought there could be American solutions to every problem." Similar views were held by Andrew Young, onetime civil rights activist and close aide to Martin Luther King, whom Carter appointed ambassador to the United Nations as a demonstration of his commitment to improve relations with black Africa and with the Third World in general. The National Security Adviser Zbigniew Brzezinski, a Columbia University professor, also recognized the reality of economic interdependence but insisted that Soviet strategic power constituted the greatest threat to the stability of the emerging world order. Though Carter hoped to pick and choose from his advisers' ideas, their contending viewpoints were difficult to reconcile and the president's inexperience in foreign affairs made his task even harder. As a result administration policy lacked consistency and coherence.

Carter set out to formulate a new foreign policy. As a member of the Trilateral Commission, a private organization formed by the banker David Rockefeller in 1973 to improve the coordination of economic policy between the United States, Western Europe, and Japan, he had learned the importance of international economic issues before becoming president. More significantly, his religious beliefs and his vision of post-Watergate national redemption required the United States to act as a force for good in the world. Carter identified with the democratic idealism of Thomas Jefferson and Woodrow Wilson rather than the militarism of America's recent past. Accordingly, he viewed the goals of peace, nuclear arms reduction, human rights, self-determination, and international cooperation as paramount. A constructive approach to Third World problems was also part of Carter's agenda. In a speech at the University of Notre Dame in May 1977, he avowed, "Being confident of our own future, we are now free of that inordinate fear of Communism that led us to embrace any dictator who joined us in that fear."

At first the Carter administration gave precedence to these new ideals over the traditional concerns of Soviet-American relations. Congressional Democrats had already begun to pressure for a human rights policy in the mid 1970s. Carter took up the cause, making it part of his crusade for national redemption and using it to restore global respect for American ideals and moral leadership. He established the Bureau of Human Rights in the State Department to monitor the practices of other nations and announced that aid to America's friends would be given or withheld on the basis of their respect for human rights and political liberties. However, it proved difficult to build up a domestic consensus in support of the program. Liberal critics were dissatisfied by the inconsistent application of the policy against Third World dictators, while those hostile to the Soviet Union feared that Carter was overly critical of America's client regimes and not tough enough on communist violations of human rights.

The diplomacy of human rights was pursued most aggressively in Latin America. Argentina, Bolivia, Brazil, Chile, El Salvador, Guatemala, Haiti, Nicaragua and Paraguay, all of whom had appalling records on human rights, suffered cutbacks or cancellations of US economic and military assistance during the late 1970s. Only Brazil and, to a less extent, Argentina modified their behavior as a result. Nevertheless, denied American support, the Somosa regime in Nicaragua was unable to suppress the left-wing Sandinista revolution that overthrew it in 1979. Conservative Republicans vilified the Sandinistas as procommunist, but Carter remained true to the principles enunciated in his Notre Dame speech and persuaded a reluctant Congress to grant economic aid to the new regime.

Elsewhere the needs of US globalism caused Carter to apply the human rights program more selectively. The administration initially attempted to treat African issues on African terms. It adopted a tough stance against South Africa's apartheid system, including banning sale of police and military equipment to the Pretoria regime. Support was also given to Britain's efforts to establish majority rule in its rebel colony of Rhodesia (which, as Zimbabwe, gained legal independence in 1980). A US trade boycott of Uganda indirectly encouraged a Tanzanian-backed rebellion that overthrew the murderous regime of Idi Amin in 1979, but this was a congressional initiative that the administration had reluctantly endorsed. Anti-Soviet imperatives prompted more lenient treatment of other repressive regimes. Zaire and Morocco, for example, continued to receive substantial aid in spite of human rights abuses. Meanwhile, in the Middle East US sales of weaponry to the Shah of

Iran continued unabated, even though his regime held as many as 50,000 political prisoners. Criticism of human rights abuses by Pakistan, the Philippines and South Korea was also muted for fear of destabilizing these strategically significant Asian allies.

By comparison, Carter was actually quite tough with the Soviets, refusing to subordinate the human rights issue in his dealings with the Kremlin and temporarily suspending computer sales in protest at its imprisonment of dissidents in violation of the Helsinki accords of 1975. His stand earned the disapproval of several European allies, notably West Germany and France, who feared that it would undermine detente and disrupt their growing trade with the Soviets. However the Kremlin did make some concessions in order to facilitate agreement on a new arms limitation treaty. Political dissidents began to be offered emigration as an alternative to prison and the permissible level of Jewish emigration was substantially increased.

Carter's concern for national redemption was also exemplified by his courageous decision to complete negotiations begun by the Ford administration for a treaty relinquishing America's permanent lease on the Panama Canal. Panama had been seeking to remove US control since the opening of the canal in 1903. Its quest for national sovereignty had widespread support throughout Latin America. In the United States, by contrast, polls showed that 78% of the public who held an opinion on the issue opposed yielding the canal, which was considered an American possession. With Ronald Reagan making political capital of the issue in his bid for the Republican presidential nomination, President Gerald Ford had shelved negotiations with Panama in 1976. Talks reopened by Carter produced two treaties in 1977. One restored legal jurisdiction over the canal zone to Panama in the year 2000, the other gave the United States permanent rights to defend the neutrality of the waterway.

There followed an intense battle to secure Senate ratification of the treaties, which were unpopular with conservatives in both parties. A Republican critic, Senator Orrin Hatch (Utah), denounced them as "the culmination of a pattern of appeasement and surrender that has cost us so much around the world". Administration supporters retorted that the treaties guaranteed US strategic interests. The conservative movie star John Wayne, a personal friend of the Panamanian president, was enlisted to counter the fulminations of his onetime actor colleague Ronald Reagan. The treaties were finally ratified by one-vote margins. The narrow victory diminished rather than increased Carter's influence in Congress because he had expended so much of his political capital in lobbying to get it. Nevertheless the treaties were the clearest sign of US desire for better relations with Latin America since the good-neighbor policy of the 1930s. In Brzezinski's words, Carter viewed the issue as "the ideal fusion of morality and politics: he was doing something good for peace, responding to the passionate desires of a small nation and yet helping the long range US, national interest."

Carter's greatest foreign policy achievement came in the Middle East. The truce that Kissinger had negotiated between Israel and its Arab neighbors was fragile. By 1978 the region was on the verge of another conflagration. The severity of Israeli retaliation against Palestine Liberation Organization (PLO) attacks, launched from bases in neighboring Lebanon, provoked growing Arab concern. In response Carter sought to propose a joint US-Soviet peace initiative, but neither Prime Minister Menachem Begin of Israel nor President Anwar Sadat of Egypt would deal with the Kremlin. In desperation he invited both leaders for talks in the United States in September 1978. Two weeks of intensive negotiations produced the Camp David accords. Begin pledged to return Sinai to Egypt, which in turn agreed to make a separate peace with Israel and recognize its government. Israel's other Arab neighbors were invited to negotiate similar peace agreements.

Carter and Sadat thought that Israel had also agreed to freeze Jewish settlement of the West Bank and enter negotiations to resolve the status of this area, but Begin later denied that the ambiguously worded accords committed him to such action. Other difficulties arose to hold up a formal treaty. One was finally signed in Washington in March 1979, after Carter undertook a further round of personal diplomacy that included visits to Cairo and Jerusalem. The resultant euphoria bred unrealistic expectations about the prospect of involving other Arab states in the peace process. The issue of a Palestinian homeland, which the treaty did not address, continued to fester as the main cause of instability in the Middle East. In these circumstances the Soviets regained influence in the region and signed a friendship treaty with Syria in 1980. Nevertheless Egypt's removal from any potential Arab military coalition and its realignment with the United States had fundamentally changed the strategic situation in the Middle East and made war between Israel and other Arab states less likely.

While Carter was pursuing the diplomacy of peace, he was also deliberating about weapons of war. At first the administration's defense budgets represented an uneasy compromise between the views of officials who believed that military outlays were too high in an era of limited national resources and those who deemed them inadequate to meet the Soviet threat. Contrary to his election promise, Carter allowed defense spending to rise by some three percent a year, but kept it below the levels projected by the Ford administration. Development of the B-1 supersonic bomber was canceled on grounds of cost-effectiveness. Conversely the MX, an accurate new ICBM with ten warheads and a mobile launching system, received the go-ahead in 1979 to reassure critics of SALT-II that the United States had not surrendered strategic balance.

The tortuous progress towards an arms reduction treaty also testified to Carter's search for compromise between defense doves and hawks. His inheritance from Ford included nearly completed negotiations on SALT II. Critics of detente believed that the United States was giving too much away at the conference table. Their fears were exacerbated when Carter nominated Paul Warnke, a Vance supporter and critic of nuclear overkill capability, to head the Arms Control and Disarmament Agency. After hostile lobbying by the Committee on the Present Danger, Senate approval of Warnke's appointment was only carried by 58 votes to 40. This foretaste of the difficulty of securing a two-thirds majority to ratify an eventual treaty persuaded Carter to appease the hawks. Accordingly, he proposed that SALT II negotiations should be started anew with a broadened scope to include the heaviest missiles, on which the Soviets were mainly reliant. The Soviet leader Leonid Brezhnev countered that the American forward base system (FBS) in central Europe, which put the Soviet heartland within reach of US cruise missiles, should also be placed on the agenda. The resultant deadlock in negotiations was not broken until the Vienna summit in July 1979. By then Brezhnev badly needed an arms deal to relieve pressure on the Soviet economy, while Carter needed a diplomatic success to assist his reelection.

SALT II established parity, upper limits, and technical verification for strategic delivery vehicles. It also restricted the number of Multiple Independently Targeted Reentry Vehicles (MIRVs) and cruise missiles to 1,320 launchers. These were marginally better terms than Carter could have got by following through with the Ford negotiations in 1977. Although the treaty allowed the Soviets to keep 300 missiles and warheads that were much larger than anything possessed by the United States, the limitation on MIRVs negated this advantage. This did not prevent SALT II from being savaged by the Committee on the Present

Danger, GOP conservatives, and Democratic hawks. The treaty's slim prospects of ratification all but disappeared when the Senate Armed Services committee, chaired by Henry Jackson, issued a report that it was "not in the national security interests of the United States".

SALT II's fate became entwined with the death of detente. Had the treaty been agreed in 1977, it would have encountered less opposition than it faced in 1979. International circumstances had changed significantly in the intervening period. By now Carter himself was placing greater emphasis on power than morality and reason in his foreign policy. The transition had occurred in mid 1978 owing to developments in the so-called "arc of crisis", stretching from the horn of Africa to Afghanistan, and to changes in the European security situation. Henceforth the influence of Vance and Young over the president diminished, that of Brzezinski correspondingly increased. Young was eventually dismissed in 1979 for holding secret talks with representatives of the PLO, a body that the United States did not recognize. Vance resigned in 1980 in protest at Carter's use of force to free the Iranian hostages.

In 1978 Soviet-supported coups produced Marxist regimes in Afghanistan and South Yemen. Meanwhile a quarrel between two Soviet clients, Ethiopia and Somalia, resulted in the latter seizing part of the former's territory. The Soviets rushed in 13,000 Cuban troops by airlift to assist Ethiopia, arousing suspicions that a counter-invasion would be launched to establish a more pliant pro-Soviet regime in Somalia. Vance and Young believed, probably correctly, that Soviet actions in Northeast Africa and Southwest Asia were opportunistic responses to local situations. However Carter heeded Brzezinski's geopolitical analysis that the Soviets were engaged in a coordinated effort to expand their influence in strategic locations close to the maritime routes along which oil was transported from the Middle East. The president was persuaded by his national security adviser to play the China card as a counter against further Soviet expansionism within the arc of crisis. Brzezinski visited Beijing in May 1978 to lay the foundations for the normalization of relations with the People's Republic of China. Full diplomatic relations were restored between the two countries on January 1, 1979. Visiting the United States soon afterwards, the Chinese deputy leader Deng Xiaoping issued stern lectures on the need to resist Soviet hegemonism. In response the Kremlin warned that detente could not survive in the face of an overt anti-Soviet alliance between China and the United States.

Nuclear force modernization was another bone of contention

between the superpowers. In 1977–8 the Soviets pressed ahead with the introduction to the European theater of mobile and very precise SS-20 missiles to counter the first-strike capability that the FBS gave NATO. This aroused considerable concern among Western European leaders, who supported detente but held reservations about the nuclear parity agreements that it had fostered. They feared that the United States might back down in the face of Soviet aggression in Europe because it no longer possessed a margin of safety against intercontinental missile attack on American territory. In other words America's allies wondered whether it would risk the destruction of its own cities to defend Europe's.

Anxious to safeguard arms limitation negotiations, Vance and his supporters in the administration were initially able to persuade the president not to commit the United States to counter Soviet modernization with an intermediate-range theatre nuclear force (TNF) of Pershing-II and cruise missiles. To the consternation of European allies, Carter also decided on moral grounds to reverse his decision to develop a neutron bomb, designed to counter a conventional Soviet attack by killing people through radiation but not destroying buildings. But by mid 1978 Brzezinski had convinced him that the TNF was necessary for political reasons to reassure Western Europe at a time of heightening concern about Soviet power and expansionism. The remilitarization of NATO took place in spite of SALT II. In late 1979 the United States began deployment of 108 Pershing IIs and 464 cruise missiles to add to the 7,000 or so tactical nuclear missiles that it already had in Europe.

What finally killed detente was the Soviet Union's invasion of Afghanistan in December 1979 in support of a coup against Hafizullah Amin, whose Marxist regime had proved an undependable client. Amin's failure to quell an Islamic insurgency had impelled him to adopt an increasingly independent line from Moscow in order to widen his domestic support. The Kremlin's move was probably a defensive one to establish a buffer against the spread of Islamic fundamentalism into the Soviet Union's own Central Asian republics, which had sizeable Muslim populations. However Carter viewed the Soviet presence in Afghanistan as a threat to the oil-rich Persian Gulf and responded with a full reassertion of American power.

In early 1980 the president issued the so-called Carter Doctrine, which pronounced that the Persian Gulf region was vital to American security interests and warned that the United States would intervene by force if necessary to prevent it from falling under Soviet control.

To give this credibility, the administration ordered a naval build-up in the Middle East, approved the development of a rapid deployment force to intervene in brush-fire wars in the arc of crisis, and began channeling economic aid and military equipment to the Islamic mujahedeen rebels whose resistance would tie down the Soviet army for some eight years in Afghanistan.

US remilitarization did not focus solely on the Persian Gulf. In his 1980 State of the Union address, Carter avowed that "in a world of major power confrontation . . . we have a new will at home to do what is required to keep us the strongest nation on earth." To restore military superiority, he called for annual increases of 5% in the defense budget into the mid-1980s and sought approval for the largest new weapons program in thirty years. The administration also withdrew SALT II from consideration by the Senate and reintroduced the Selective Service military draft. Shortly afterwards Carter signed Presidential Directive 59, a plan to develop America's capability to fight and win a protracted nuclear war at every level of escalation. Largely drawn up by Brzezinski, this document signified an important shift in US military strategy from the balance of terror and mutual deterrence doctrines that had held sway since the Soviets had achieved nuclear parity. In essence the Carter defense policies of 1980 laid the foundations for the massive military buildup under Reagan.

Carter's strong response to the Soviet invasion of Afghanistan was also prompted indirectly by another development that had weakened the US position in the Persian Gulf. In early 1979, the Shah of Iran, the surrogate for American interests in this region, was driven into exile by a popular uprising. Taken completely by surprise at this turn of events, the Carter administration dithered about whether to intervene to save its ally, but finally decided that the only practical course was to work for the emergence of a moderate government in Tehran. It soon became evident that America could no longer influence developments in Iran. After months of turmoil a fundamentalist Islamic regime led by the Ayatollah Khomeini took power. The new government was deeply hostile to the United States, which it suspected of plotting a coup to restore the Shah. These fears were fueled by Carter's decision to allow the Shah into the United States for cancer treatment. On November 4, 1979, Iranian militants attacked the American embassy in Tehran and took its personnel hostage. The price demanded for their release was the US government's return of the Shah and his treasure to Iran.

Carter steadfastly refused to yield to Iranian demands but the crisis dragged on for 444 days and blighted his final year as president. The hostages were not returned until the day he left office in January 1981. Many Americans failed to understand why Carter did not order the bombing of Iran's oilfields and military installations. In all probability, of course, military action of this kind would have resulted in the execution of the hostages rather than their return. It would also have aroused anti-American feeling throughout the Muslim world. Carter was particularly anxious to avoid this, partly for fear of an Arab boycott of oil supplies to America but also because he hoped to enlist Islamic opposition to the Soviet invasion of Afghanistan. Unable to understand the complex issues involved, Americans grew increasingly critical of the diplomatic maneuvers and coercive economic measures that showed no signs of breaking Iran's will.

Kept in the forefront of popular consciousness by television, the long ordeal of the hostages bred feelings of national impotence and humiliation among the mass public, emotions which the disastrous failure of the military rescue mission ordered by Carter in April 1980 only heightened. With America seemingly in retreat everywhere in the world in 1980, opinion makers and political elites regarded the crisis as symptomatic of the waning of America's global position. "For the first time in its history", commented *Business Week*, "the United States is no longer growing in power and influence among the nations of the world . . . [The] Pax Americana that shaped modern history since World War II is fast disintegrating."

For a time Jimmy Carter had tried, in the words of Gaddis Smith, to make Americans "think as citizens of the world with an obligation towards future generations". By the end of his presidency, however, Cold War internationalism and militarism had been reinvigorated as a result of the Iranian and Afghan crises. The seeds of a new foreign policy had been sown during his first two years in office. But the lack of domestic consensus in support of a new role for the United States in a changing world and enduring fears of the Soviet Union, which were fueled by the Kremlin's short-sighted and uncooperative behavior, impelled Carter to change course. The reassertion of militarism did not save his presidency because it made him appear inconsistent rather than strong. The seemingly endless Iranian hostage crisis also contradicted his claim to have restored American power. Polls held during the 1980 elections showed that four out of five Americans were dissatisfied with Carter's foreign policy record, three out of four believed that Ronald

Reagan would ensure that the United States was respected by other nations, and two out of three believed that he was much more likely than Carter to maintain a strong posture against the Soviets. The public yearned for a new leader who would reestablish America's international power and prestige. Reagan shared this desire to recreate the past. He reassured his fellow citizens, "We have it in our power to begin the world all over again."

The battle against inflation

Carter's economic policy was also criticized for inconsistency. At first he pursued traditional Democratic goals but later moved in different directions. With unemployment running at 7.4% in early 1977, the new administration's initial concern was to get the economy moving out of recession. However economic revival was accompanied by a strengthening of inflationary forces. In response, Carter and his advisers resorted to fine-tuning measures to keep the economy stable but were unable to steer a middle course between the extremes of recession and inflation. In these circumstances they had to decide which problem should be given priority. Carter eventually resolved that "my major economic battle would be against inflation, and I would stay on the side of fiscal prudence, restricted budgets, and lower deficits." As a result he was the first modern Democratic president to place greater emphasis on economic restraint than on the full-employment goals of commercial Keynesianism.

Carter's own views on the economy could not be categorized as uniformly liberal or conservative. Reflecting the more cautious mood of his own times, he did not regard the new economics of the 1960s as a suitable model for economic policy in the 1970s. The new president was a fiscal conservative who regarded large budgetary deficits as a principal source of inflation. On the other hand he came to office determined to pursue the traditional Democratic goal of full employment. The economy had been the principal issue in the 1976 election. Carter owed his victory to the fact that three-quarters of those voters whose primary worry was unemployment had supported him. Once elected he came under immediate pressure from organizations representing core constituencies of the New Deal coalition, notably the AFL-CIO, the National Conference of Mayors, and black groups, all of whom wanted federal action to boost jobs. Carter's economic policy reflected the dichotomy of his liberal and conservative values for most of his presidency. In essence he sought to aid economic recovery and then balance the budget by the end of his first term in office.

In early 1977 the administration devised a two-year package of stimulative measures that increased spending by some $15 billion on urban aid, public works, and training. It also ran up what were regarded at the time as very large budget deficits of $57.9 billion in Fiscal 1977 and $48.8 billion in Fiscal 1978. Only under Ford had the budget gone deeper into the red. White House prompting also induced the Federal Reserve to liberalize monetary policy. The money supply expanded more rapidly in 1977–9 than in any three-year period since 1945. Finally, Carter demonstrated at least symbolic commitment to full employment by supporting the enactment in 1978 of the Humphrey-Hawkins bill. However, he did nothing to protect this measure from drastic congressional amendments that placed primary responsibility for job creation on the private sector and sought to place a brake on federal spending by mandating a reduction in inflation to 3% within five years. As a result the full-employment provisions of the legislation were rendered ineffective in practical terms.

The fiscal and monetary stimuli had immediate effect. Unemployment fell to 5.8% by late 1978, but there was a corresponding increase in inflation to 7.7% in 1978. In spite of the severity of the previous recession, all the signs indicated that inflation would be higher than ever in the new cycle of recovery. By now business, labor, and consumers were all in the grip of an inflationary psychology that bred expectations of wage and price increases. Cost-of-living escalators built into most labor and business contracts had developed a self-generating momentum. Fear of inflation and the availability of investment opportunities abroad continued to deter business from investing in domestic plant modernization. The annual productivity rate of US business, having grown at only 1.4% in 1973–7, actually fell by 0.4% a year from 1977 to 1980. Such trends further reduced the competitiveness of American industry against foreign business. The growth of the money supply and the amount of credit available to consumers also fueled inflationary demand. To make matters worse foreign concern about US economic problems sent the value of the dollar tumbling by some 20% on the international money markets in 1977–8, further pushing up the price of imports.

In late 1978 the Carter administration began to prioritize the problem of inflation over unemployment. Expansion gave way to restraint in fiscal and monetary policies. The fiscal 1980 budget proposals that

Carter sent to Congress in January 1979 sought to reduce domestic program expenditures in real terms. Meanwhile, the Federal Reserve raised domestic interest rates to combat inflation and increased its intervention in foreign exchange markets to prop up the international value of the dollar. Also, though Carter remained true to his election pledge never to introduce mandatory economic controls, the administration did issue voluntary guidelines to labor and business to keep wage increases within 7% and price rises within 6.5%. At this juncture the president and his advisers were convinced that only a moderate change of economic course was necessary. They hoped to keep inflation within single digits without incurring a significant increase in joblessness. However their calculations were upset by a further round of oil price increases in 1979.

The internal turmoil following the Shah of Iran's overthrow in 1979 temporarily disrupted Iranian oil production. As a result the international oil glut which had existed in 1978 quickly gave way to international shortages. Exploiting this situation, OPEC mandated price increases that pushed up the cost of crude oil by over 60%. The United States consequently found itself paying nearly $60 billion for its oil imports in 1979, compared with $40 billion in 1978. Nevertheless the effects of this second oil crisis would have been less severe had Congress responded more promptly to Carter's earlier efforts to develop a national energy policy.

Carter was convinced that America's economic regeneration was entwined with the resolution of its energy problems. One of his first actions as president was the creation of a new cabinet-level Department of Energy to coordinate energy policy. Shortly afterwards he proposed a wide-ranging energy bill designed to halve both the level of oil imports and the growth rate in domestic energy demand by 1985. Its main features were: a tax on gasoline pegged to rise with consumption; a tax on cars with a high fuel consumption; taxation of domestic crude oil at the wellhead to raise domestic prices to world levels; a tax rebate to the public funded from the higher energy taxes; price deregulation for newly discovered natural gas; decontrol of gasoline prices; tax credits for consumers who installed home insulation and for factories that converted to coal use; and support for the development of uranium-fueled nuclear reactors as an alternative energy form.

Carter's energy bill lacked a political constituency because it demanded sacrifices from both consumers and producers. This proved its fundamental weakness. Though enacted by the House of Representatives, the measure was blocked in the Senate by a coalition of Democrats and Republicans from the energy-producing states of the South and West. The oil and gas industries, which wanted higher energy prices without the encumbrance of higher taxes, also mounted a powerful lobby against it. Only by mobilizing popular opinion could the president have overcome this entrenched opposition, but his efforts to convince the public that the energy issue was "the moral equivalent of war" fell flat. Polls showed that half the nation doubted that energy problems were real and viewed them as a hoax perpetrated by the oil companies to boost profits. After battling on for some eighteen months, Carter eventually had to make substantial concessions to secure any kind of legislation. The National Energy Act of 1978 met some of his objectives, but it did not tax gasoline consumption and domestic oil production and it mandated the gradual deregulation of all natural gas prices. Though an important first step in the battle to reverse the growing rate of American energy consumption, this measure was too little and too late to cushion the nation against the economic effects of the oil price increases of 1979.

The only positive consequence of the 1979 crisis was that it convinced Americans that energy problems were real. The familiar sight of long lines of cars waiting outside gas stations and the temporary use of alternate day gasoline rationing in some states dispelled old illusions that energy was plentiful. Capitalizing on the new mood, Carter ordered the decontrol of domestic oil prices in late 1979, and in 1980 he persuaded Congress to enact a "windfall profits" tax on domestic oil production and subsidies for synthetic fuel production. Nevertheless the new energy consensus was a limited one. Thanks to intensive lobbying by the oil companies, Congress rejected Carter's efforts to impose an import fee that would discourage reliance on foreign oil. The battle ended with a presidential veto being overridden, the first time in 28 years that this had happened when the same party was in control of Congress and the White House.

Spiralling oil prices helped to drive inflation up to an annual rate of 11.3% in 1979. The administration's voluntary guidelines on wage and price increases were too weak to hold back the tide. The dollar came under renewed pressure on the world's financial markets and a full-scale currency crisis loomed. Public concern about rising prices reached new peaks. In these circumstances Carter decided that moderate measures were insufficient to combat inflation. In late 1979 he decided to induce a short recession, which he hoped would choke off inflation and still allow time for economic recovery to take place before the 1980 presidential election. This policy had little success in economic terms and proved politically disastrous for the president. In the words of political economist Douglas Hibbs, Carter's strategy was "a textbook example of how not to run the economy to win reelection."

With Carter's approval, Federal Reserve chairman Paul Volcker switched the emphasis of monetary policy to control of the money supply. This monetarist formula was a much more potent means of slowing down the economy than interest rate manipulation. Despite the steady rise in interest rates to around 10% in 1979, high inflation meant that the real cost of borrowing remained relatively low. The Federal Reserve's refusal to accommodate shifts in money demand made interest rates much more volatile. They rose rapidly to unprecedented levels, reaching a peak of 20% in mid 1980. Consumer borrowing was also squeezed in other ways. Easy availability of cheap credit had encouraged ever greater reliance on credit cards. The number of Master Charge cardholders, for example, jumped from 32 million in 1974 to 57 million in 1979. This trend was abruptly halted after the Federal Reserve was empowered to impose restrictions on credit card usage. These measures plunged the economy into recession and the unemployment rate rose to nearly 8% in mid 1980.

The contraction came too late to exert significant downward pressure on prices before the election. The annual rate of inflation rose to 13% in 1980. This was the first occasion that the United States had experienced double-digit inflation in consecutive years since World War I. Dearer energy costs were working their way into the general structure of wages and prices. The OPEC price shocks were not the sole reason for this. It was unfortunate for Carter that congressional delay in enacting his energy program meant that deregulation of domestic oil and natural gas prices also began to push up the price of energy in 1980. Meanwhile, the new conservatism of administration economic policy did little to boost the confidence of financial markets, as was revealed by the sharp decline of bond prices in early 1980. Wall Street harbored strong doubts that a Democratic president could maintain long-term commitment to economic restraint in view of the needs of his party's mass constituency.

Owing to the persistence of inflation, however, Carter broke with Democratic traditions by refusing to take action to get the nation out of the 1980 recession. To all intents and purposes he abandoned the device of the "full employment budget" used by the Democratic administrations of the 1960s and maintained by the Republican administrations of the 1970s. Although the Federal Reserve relaxed monetary policy in the second half of 1980, Carter maintained a conservative course in fiscal policy. He became increasingly convinced that the large budget deficits he was operating were fueling inflation. His principled insistence on taking action to correct this helped to bring about his election defeat. In fact there was little evidence of a strong causal relationship between the budget and inflation. In fiscal 1979, for example, the real budget deficit of $27.7 billion converted into a "full-employment deficit" of only $2.4 billion, which was hardly enough to create double-digit inflation in a $2.4 trillion economy. Other factors, notably oil price increases and cost-of-living labor contracts, had far greater effect.

Carter's dogmatic insistence that deficits were inflationary had important political consequences. Domestic expenditures were clawed back in the budgets of fiscal 1979, 1980 and 1981 in an effort to curb the deficit. As a result discretionary spending on domestic programs increased by less than one per cent in real terms over the course of Carter's presidency. The cutbacks were particularly severe in the fiscal 1981 budget because of the need to compensate for military spending increases. The main effect fell on welfare, healthcare and jobs programs that particularly benefited low-income groups with whom the Democrats had traditionally identified. Carter also reduced federal aid to the states and cities. This caused considerable divisions within the party, with old-style liberals demanding firmer action to aid the poor and unemployed. The dispute was a major factor in prompting Senator Edward Kennedy to run for the Democratic presidential nomination in 1980. Carter's determination to reduce the deficit also induced him to rule out pre-election tax cuts that might have boosted recovery and reestablished his hold on wavering Democratic voters.

The return on such heavy investment of political capital to reduce the deficit was negligible. No matter what action Carter took, the deficit was bound to increase during a recession when tax revenues automatically declined and federal outlays on unemployment insurance automatically increased. The budget ended up in the red by $59.6 billion in fiscal 1980, double the deficit level originally anticipated, and by $57.9 billion in the following year. Calculated on a "full-employment" basis, the imbalances only amounted to $18 billion and $800 million respectively, but Carter had long ceased to defend public expenditures in these terms.

Carter's stern warnings about the inflationary effects of deficit budgets rested on questionable economic assumptions. They also discredited his party's conventional instrument of governmental activism. Since the days of the New Deal the Democrats had been the party of big government and big spending. Democratic presidents from Roosevelt through to Johnson had promoted this image as a positive one. Carter set himself against this tradition. During his tenure of office the idea that the budget should be used for social purposes had given way to the notion that the economy should shape the budget. This meant, in the words of historian James Savage, that any "budget proposal that added a single dollar to the deficit instantly lost legitimacy on the grounds, supplied by the Democrats themselves, that it helped cripple the economy. . . .[and] all deficit spending became identified as a primary source of inflation or high interest rates."

Carter's deeds and words in the field of budgetary policy added grist to Ronald Reagan's attacks on big government profligacy and the evils of deficits. Nevertheless it was the state of the economy rather than of the nation's finances that was the uppermost issue for voters in the 1980 presidential election. One in three voters identified inflation as their main concern, and one in ten worried primarily about unemployment. Ordinarily this would have worked to the advantage of the Democrats. The notion that they were the party that cared about economic problems had been the main rallying point of the New Deal coalition since the 1930s. In 1980, however, 67% of voters whose main issue-concern was inflation and 51% whose main issue concern was unemployment backed Reagan. During the televised debate between the presidential candidates, Reagan urged Americans, "Ask yourself, are you better off than you were four years ago?" The majority of voters did not feel that they were and expressed their economic frustrations through the ballot.

In some respects Carter may be judged to have been unlucky. Unemployment had fallen significantly during his first two years in office. Thereafter, moderately restrictive economic policies might have kept inflation within acceptable levels had it not been for the 1979 oil price shocks. The president's consequent decision to prioritize the reduction of double-digit inflation was in line with the policy preferences of the public. This was even true of groups within the New Deal coalition.

Surveys showed that low-income groups, blue collar workers, and Democratic identifiers in general were far more worried about inflation than unemployment in 1978–9. Although the level of concern about inflation underwent some decline among all three of these groups with the onset of the 1980 recession, only low-income groups showed a renewed inclination to prioritize unemployment. Regardless of the difficult circumstances, however, Carter's response to the crisis of 1979–80 was ineffective in both economic and political terms. Had the president been truer to Democratic traditions, he would not necessarily have been more successful in handling the economic aspects of the crisis but at least he could have defended the political legitimacy of liberal economic activism. Instead, his actions and rhetoric weakened the credibility of what his party had long stood for, and the failure of his policies to curb inflation meant that he was unable to provide the Democrats with a viable new political economy.

The economic problems of 1979–80 made a deep impact on the American people's morale. One poll revealed that 62% of Americans felt that their nation had entered an era of enduring shortages, and a 1980 Gallup poll recorded that 55% believed that "next year will be worst than this year". As a result Jimmy Carter was fated to become for the Republicans the kind of political symbol that Herbert Hoover had once been for Democrats. For the next decade GOP leaders would continually remind Americans of how bad things had been under the previous Democratic administration (rather as Prime Minister Margaret Thatcher and the Conservatives kept alive the British public's memory of the so-called "Winter of Discontent" of 1978–9 under a Labour government). In essence, the last vestiges of the liberal political economy had been swept away by the economic crisis of 1979–80 and Ronald Reagan had been provided with the opportunity to promise bold action that would replace the economics of misery with the economics of joy.

The end of the New Deal order

Political and economic developments in the Carter era led to the final collapse of the New Deal order. Its demise became entwined with the decline of the presidency itself. From Franklin D. Roosevelt to Lyndon B. Johnson strong presidents had played an essential role in defining and achieving the Democratic party's legislative aims. It was difficult for Carter to sustain this tradition because of the new institutional context in which the presidency operated in the late 1970s. All modern Democratic presidents had encountered opposition from Congress and from sections of their own party, of course, but Carter's problems were unprecedented. A series of earlier presidential misjudgements, most notably the undeclared war in Vietnam and the Watergate scandal, led Congress to reassert its political and constitutional authority in the mid 1970s. Carter inherited a legislature that was resistant to presidential leadership and determined to uphold its status as a coequal branch of government.

Meanwhile the congressional power structure grew more diffuse. Until the 1970s Congress was dominated by an oligarchy of standing committee chairmen, whose powers rested on the prerogatives of seniority. Procedural reforms introduced in the mid 1970s diminished their influence and enhanced the importance of subcommittees at the expense of standing committees. In 1976 there were 151 subcommittees in the House and 140 in the Senate, compared respectively with 22 and 15 standing committees. Subcommittee chairmen became highly influential political actors within the narrow policy area under their jurisdiction. This dispersion of power made executive leadership all the more difficult because the president now had to deal directly with an increasing number of congressmen to win support for his policies.

The growing importance of congressional subcommittees coincided with and facilitated the increasing involvement of interest and issue groups in the legislative process. The vast expansion in the scope of federal activities since the mid 1960s meant that far more groups, representing virtually all sectors of society and the economy, stood to gain or lose from public policy than was the case in the past. The 1970s consequently saw a widespread mobilization by pressure groups to influence government. By 1981 there were 5,662 lobbyists registered with Congress, compared with only 365 in 1961. The vast majority of pressure groups had narrow legislative interests. Their activities in the political arena ran counter to the modern president's need to simplify complex issues in order to develop broad-based support for his program in Congress.

The decline of party solidarity which resulted from changes in electoral politics added to presidential problems. The extent of split-ticket voting since 1968 indicated that voters were becoming less partisan. As a result congressmen seeking reelection tended to highlight their personal qualities and their service to their constituents rather than their party record. Their growing reliance on television campaigning further emphasized personality over party. It also increased the cost of congressional elections, which rose more than twice as fast as the rate of inflation between 1966 and 1980. Party treasuries could not keep pace with this. Candidates had to rely on their own ability to raise funds. Contributions solicited from individuals through computerized mail shots quickly became the main source of funds. Also important were contributions from political action committees (PACs), which business corporations, trade unions and other interests groups had been allowed to set up to channel funds to political candidates under terms laid out by the 1974 amendment to Federal Election Campaign Act. These organizations rapidly increased in number from 608 in 1974 to 3,479 in 1982. By 1980 only 6% of House election funds and 9% of Senate election funds came from the parties. In these circumstances Democratic congressmen grew more independent and less responsive to the leadership of a Democratic president.

All these developments made congressional politics more atomized and therefore more unpredictable. A former Johnson aide commented: "In 1965, there were maybe ten or twelve people you needed to corral in the House and Senate. Without these people you were in for a tough time. Now, I'd put that figure upwards of one hundred. Believe it, there are so many people who have a shot at derailing a bill that the President has to double his effort for even routine decisions." It was now extremely difficult, some said impossible, for a president to build lasting coalitions in support of his program. A few years after berating the dangers of the "imperial presidency", many commentators were speaking of the "imperilled presidency" or the "no-win presidency" in the late 1970s.

Carter's difficulties with Congress were also compounded by his approach to presidential leadership. Too much can be made of his inexperience in national politics and his lack of political skills to explain this. The problems stemmed more from his self-image as a "trustee president". Owing to his religious beliefs, his strong sense of morality, and his status as an outsider in relation to the political establishment, Carter regarded himself as a steward who represented the public rather than party or pressure group needs. As a result he had an uneasy relationship with interest groups important to his party. Pork-barrel politics were anathema to him. His plan to eliminate nineteen water projects from his first budget, though only partly followed through, hurt the Democratic party in the West. Carter's conviction that his policies embodied the public good and were the right answers to the nation's problems also made him reluctant to engage in the political horse-trading necessary to secure their enactment.

All this ran counter to the politics of persuasion, bargaining, manipulation, and legislative compromise that previous presidents had used to win the cooperation of Congress. During his final two years in office Carter did show more willingness to play by the conventional rules of Washington politics. Overall, however, he was more concerned with doing what was moral than what was political. This approach won some victories, such as Panama Canal treaty ratification, but failed to secure passage of many domestic policy measures. It also aroused the resentment of powerful congressmen, most notably Senator Russell Long (Louisiana), Democratic chairman of the Senate Finance Committee, who did much to delay and dilute the administration's energy legislation and to defeat its tax, healthcare and welfare reform proposals.

Great though the difficulties of presidential government were, America's economic problems had far more impact on the decline of the New Deal political order in the late 1970s. Some commentators claim that Jimmy Carter's presidency lacked the kind of unifying theme and sense of direction that characterized previous Democratic administrations. It is true that he never developed a popular slogan to label his political program, thereby breaking a Democratic tradition that ran from Woodrow Wilson's New Freedom to Johnson's Great Society. Nevertheless, it can be argued that Carter's policies derived a distinctive coherence from being a response to curtailed economic growth. According to Erwin Hargrove, the domestic theme of his administration was "consolidation and curtailment with equity". In contrast to the expansionary agenda of Great Society liberalism, Carter's concerns were budget balancing, tax and welfare reform, energy conservation, environmental protection, civil service reform, and deregulation.

Arthur Schlesinger Jr, the intellectual doyen of postwar American liberalism, labeled Carter the most conservative Democratic president since Grover Cleveland in the 1890s. This judgement says more about the antipathy that many old-style liberals felt for Carter than about his political views. Carter was neither liberal nor conservative in the traditional sense of those terms. The political values that inspired him were not those of New Deal liberalism but of late nineteenth-century southern Populism, which sought to help the poor, the uneducated, the unemployed, and minorities within the financial limits of good government. Accordingly, Carter saw himself as "a fiscal conservative but quite liberal on such issues as civil rights, environmental quality,

and helping people overcome handicaps to lead fruitful lives".
Economy, efficiency, and equity were the guiding principles of many
of Carter's domestic initiatives. His major welfare measure, the Program for Better Jobs and Income, paralleled the Nixon administration's
Family Assistance Plan. The aim was comprehensive reform of the
welfare system to create more efficient administration and provide more
effective assistance to the needy at reduced expense. This entailed cutting benefits for a large number of recipients while extending coverage
to more people and boosting work incentives for the poor. The measure
was not enacted, in part because Carter did not fight hard enough for
it, but mainly because it met the kind of opposition that Nixon's proposal had aroused from conservatives who wanted greater emphasis on
"workfare" and liberals who wanted more generous cash assistance to
the needy. Carter also prioritized cost-effectiveness in his approach to
healthcare, seeking a hospital cost-containment bill that would curb the
increasingly expensive demands of the Medicare and Medicaid programs
on the public purse. A powerful lobby mounted by medical interests
helped to defeat this bill.

Not all Carter's domestic proposals were defeated, of course. Despite
their dilution, the 1978 and 1980 energy bills were significant achievements. There were also major successes in environmental policy,
including passage of a strip-mining control bill and the establishment
of the Arctic National Wilderness Reserve protecting 100 million acres
of Alaska from development and oil drilling. Carter's desire for
economy did not deter his approval of a $1.6 billion "superfund" to
clean up chemical waste sites following the environmental catastrophe
that overtook the community of Love Canal, New York, in 1978. In
other respects, however, the administration sought to reverse the
growth of the regulatory state. By the late 1970s federal regulation of
the marketplace was seen as a drag on the efficiency and competitiveness
of American industry and a cause of high consumer prices. The
deregulation of air routes and fares in 1978 fostered greater competition
among airlines, and similar measures benefited the trucking and railroad
industries in 1980. Carter initiatives also opened the way for the eventual deregulation of the banking and communications industries. Other
achievements in the field of government reform included the creation
of new Cabinet-level departments responsible for energy policy and
education, and the most significant civil service reform of recent times,
which sought to reward bureaucrats for effective performance and make
them more responsive to oversight by administration officials.

Concerns for economy and equity shaped Carter's efforts to assist low-paid and unemployed workers within the limits of fiscal conservatism. His administration promoted a massive public works program to boost economic recovery in 1977, raised the minimum wage requirement, and enacted the first-ever national youth employment law. Moreover, Carter supported the 1980 "bailout" of the Chrysler Corporation, which faced bankruptcy because of increased competition from foreign automobiles. Chrysler received federal loan guarantees of $1.5 billion conditional on it obtaining wage reductions from employees, concessions from banks, and state and local aid.

Similar considerations influenced Carter's civil rights agenda. He did not spend money on new antipoverty initiatives that might have strengthened the economic foundations of racial equality, but he used his executive powers to assist racial minorities in other ways. His administration had a better record than any of its predecessors in appointing blacks and women to top positions in government, the civil service and the judiciary. The Justice Department was also active in support of legal test cases to promote school desegregation and affirmative action. Blacks were initially disappointed with the results. In 1978 the Supreme Court ruled in *Regents of the University of California* v. *Bakke* that explicit quotas setting aside a fixed number of positions for blacks and other minorities were not a legitimate means of pursuing affirmative action. But this position was modified in two later rulings, *Kaiser Aluminum and Chemical Corporation* v. *Weber* (1979) and *Fullilove* v. *Klutznick* (1980), both of which endorsed the use of quotas to benefit minorities. The *Fullilove* decision also ruled that Congress had authority to enact racially preferential remedial measures as a means of overcoming societal discrimination. As a result, constitutional historian Herman Belz has concluded, "affirmative action was greatly strengthened during the Carter Administration".

Carter's record on women's rights was more ambiguous. His response to the Houston Program, a wide-ranging manifesto adopted by the National Women's Conference in 1977, was hesitant at best. Though he declared support for the Equal Rights Amendment, the anti-ERA movement had gained sufficient momentum to stall the ratification process three states short of the required number. Meanwhile, administration efforts to amend the Equal Employment Opportunity Act of 1964 to extend employment disability benefits to include pregnancy went down to defeat. On other issues Carter found himself at odds with feminists. Anti-inflationary imperatives prevented him from supporting their demands for federal aid for child-care centers and other social programs. His moral reservations about abortion made him sympathetic to congressional initiatives that limited its availability. The Hyde amendment of 1976, which prohibited use of Medicaid funds to finance abortions for welfare recipients, was upheld by the Supreme Court in the following year. Encouraged by this, Congress added further amendments in 1978 to forbid federal funding of abortions for military personnel and their dependents and to permit employee health insurance programs to cancel abortion coverage. Relations between Carter and the women's movement reached a low point in 1979 when he fired Bella Abzug, one of his feminist critics, from her post as head of the President's National Advisory Committee for Women.

Carter's presidency marked an important stage in the political debate about what the Democratic party should stand for in the late twentieth century. His policies added up to an effort to reorient the Democratic agenda away from its free-spending liberal past to a cost-conscious centrism that combined fiscal prudence with social concern. He failed because too many Democrats disagreed with his message and because he was too much of an outsider to succeed at the task of party leadership, particularly in the difficult circumstances of the times. Nevertheless Carter's new agenda struck a chord with some Democrats who came to be labeled "neoliberals". In this sense his presidency coincided with and facilitated the evolution of the New Politics liberalism of the early 1970s into the neoliberalism of the 1980s.

A new generation of Democrats who were graduates of the New Politics had gained elective office in the mid 1970s and would achieve prominence in the 1980s. It included Senators Gary Hart (Colorado) and Paul Tsongas (Massachusetts), Representatives Christopher Dodd (Connecticut), James Florio (New Jersey), and Tim Wirth (Colorado), and Governor Michael Dukakis (Massachusetts). These Democrats retained the foreign policy and social liberalism of their New Politics past but shifted to the right on budgetary issues in the late 1970s. This was partly a response to the economic climate, and partly because many of them depended on the support of middle-class suburban constituencies that had libertarian social views and were antimilitarist but had no interest in the big-spending, high-taxing, pro-labor policies espoused by more traditional Democrats. Like Carter, these younger Democrats did not believe that traditional policies would solve contemporary economic problems. Gary Hart, for example, opined that the nation was "weary of the old New Deal approach". The neoliberals had no doubts that inflation was the number one economic problem and were willing to make difficult policy choices in order to deal with it. Typifying this view, Tim Wirth avowed in 1980 that to win the battle against inflation and achieve economic renewal "it is imperative to balance the budget".

To a generation of older Democrats, there was a fundamental contradiction between fiscal conservatism and social liberalism. In their eyes Jimmy Carter's tendency to subordinate the latter to the former violated the spirit of New Deal liberalism. His right-turn on the economy in 1979–80 drove many of them into open rebellion in support of Edward Kennedy's candidacy for the Democratic presidential nomination. The Kennedy campaign was firmly rooted in New Deal-Great Society traditions. Its overriding theme was that government could resolve society's problems provided that it had the will and the leadership to do so. In an echo of Roosevelt's famous words that the "only thing we have to fear is fear itself", Kennedy said, "The only thing that paralyzes us today is the myth that we cannot move." Pronouncing unemployment the main economic problem, he demanded Keynesian measures and a massive public works program to cure it. His solution for inflation was mandatory wage and price controls rather than fiscal and monetary restraint. Kennedy also called for a renewed attack on poverty and the introduction of a comprehensive system of national health insurance.

Though early opinion polls showed him well ahead, Kennedy's challenge ended in failure. The difficulties of wresting the nomination from an incumbent president who had control of the party organization were formidable. This was underlined by the two-to-one lead that Carter achieved in delegates chosen by states using the convention or caucus system of delegate selection, whereas his popular vote margin in primary states was much narrower (52.7% to 38%). Foreign policy and personality factors also hurt the challenger. The revival of the Cold War following the Soviet invasion of Afghanistan generated a patriotic national mood that helped Carter and worked against Kennedy, who was a critic of renewed militarism. At first the president also benefited from the Iranian hostage crisis, which he used as an excuse to avoid formal campaigning. This strategy and the publicity for his initial efforts to secure the hostages' release enhanced his presidential image. Meanwhile, Kennedy's ill-judged call for the extradition of the Shah to Iran aroused doubts about his integrity and precipitated a rapid decline in his poll ratings. Above all else, the Massachusetts senator could never overcome the widespread feeling that he was morally unsuited to be president. On this score the Chappaquiddick affair of 1969 was an albatross round his neck. The public had strong memories of his failure to report the automobile accident that resulted in the death of his female passenger.

Kennedy had suffered a personal rather than a political defeat. Carter's victory did not mean that the Democratic party had moved away from its New Deal-Great Society traditions to embrace a modern centrism. This became evident at the 1980 party convention, which turned into a celebration of Roosevelt and his legacy. Kennedy's electrifying speech in praise of the New Deal transformed proceedings. Sensing the mood of the delegates, Carter's lieutenants surrendered to the senator's demands for the inclusion of numerous liberal planks in the Democratic platform, most notably a $12 billion program to boost jobs. In contrast to the Republican convention of 1976, which revealed the emergent power of the GOP right, the Democratic convention four years later did not indicate the ascendancy of new forces in the party of Roosevelt.

Carter's belated nod to his party's traditions could not save him from crushing defeat in the general election. Ronald Reagan carried all but six states, winning an electoral college majority of 489 votes to 49. His margin of victory in popular vote terms was also impressive. Reagan took 50.8% of the vote, Carter 41%, and third-party candidate John B. Anderson 6.6%. The New Deal coalition unraveled at the seams. One in three voters who backed Carter in 1976 switched to Reagan in 1980. Carter was supported by only 36% of white voters, 42% of Catholic voters, 46% of blue-collar voters, 48% of union-household voters, 45% of Jewish voters, and 44% of southern voters. He had the backing of only 50% of low-income voters (under $10,000 annual family income), and failed to gain a plurality among any other income group. Blacks, 85% of whom voted Democrat, were the only New Deal constituency to remain loyal. Republican success at presidential level was replicated at congressional level. A gain of 12 seats made the GOP the majority party in the Senate for the first time since 1954. It also won 33 extra seats in the House of Representatives, cutting the Democratic majority there from 117 to 51. The GOP showing was similarly impressive at state level and included a net gain of four governorships.

The result was a personal repudiation of Carter rather than a positive endorsement of Reagan. Widespread dissatisfaction with his economic and foreign policy in 1979–80 had sent Carter's Gallup approval rating crashing to the lowest level recorded for any president. An election exit poll found that 38% of voters backing Reagan did so principally because they wanted a change of leadership, while only 11% cited admiration for his conservatism as their main reason for voting for him. Only a half of those voting for either Carter or Reagan did so primarily because they liked the candidate. The favorability ratings received by both candidates in Gallup polls during October 1980 were the lowest since records began. Public unease with the choice on offer had encouraged an independent candidacy by John Anderson, a centrist Republican. Votes cast for Anderson exceeded the margin of difference between Carter and Reagan in thirteen states, helping to create the latter's lopsided electoral college majority.

Not until the last days of the campaign did Reagan forge ahead in the opinion polls. The crucial factor appeared to be his success during the televised presidential debate in portraying himself as a moderate on domestic and foreign policy. The groundswell of anti-Carter sentiment rather than any pro-Reagan mood did much to drag down the rest of the Democratic ticket. Among the losers were five prominent liberal senators, Birch Bayh (Indiana), Frank Church (Idaho), John Culver (Iowa), George McGovern (South Dakota), and Gaylord Nelson (Wisconsin).

The most startling fact about the 1980 presidential election was the extent of nonvoting. Only 52.6% of eligible voters cast their ballots. Reagan won with the backing of a mere 28% of the potential electorate. Polls of nonvoters' candidate preference suggested that Carter would have won had turnout been very high. Blue-collar workers, the low-paid, those with the least amount of formal education, minorities, and the poor made up some four-fifth of nonvoters. Reagan held no appeal for them, but on the basis of his policy record and his vision of what the Democratic party stood for, neither did Jimmy Carter. As William Leuchtenburg observed, "[M]uch of Carter's difficulty on Election Day came from being so little in the image of FDR that millions in the Roosevelt coalition . . . did not go to the polls". The president and his party paid the price for his adoption of economic policies that excluded the interests of the Democrats' natural constituency.

Conservatives, on the other hand, regarded the outcome of the 1980 election as the culmination of a rightward trend in popular opinion that had initially been signalled by the "tax revolt" of the late 1970s. In 1978 California voters approved Proposition 13, a ballot initiative to limit local property taxes and reduce property assessments on which they were based. The movement quickly spread, winning victories in states as politically diverse as Massachusetts, Washington, Maine, Idaho, and Nevada, but encountering defeats in Colorado, Michigan and Oregon. The "revolt" tended to be strongest in the suburbs, where spiralling property values in the inflationary 1970s had driven up property assessments.

Paralleling this development was a growing outcry against the burden of federal taxes. Many middle-income Americans had become victims of tax bracket-creep as a result of inflation. Between 1960 and 1979 the median family income grew from $5,620 to $19,684 (in current dollar terms, unadjusted to inflation). However federal tax-brackets remained tied to the dollar levels of the 1950s, so Americans earning an average wage in the late 1970s found themselves paying marginal tax rates set for what had once been a high income. By 1978, according to one opinion survey, 69% of families felt they had reached breaking point on taxes. Nevertheless, polls also pointed to the absence of widespread support for federal income tax cuts at the expense of domestic program reductions.

In spite of the tax revolt and Reagan's election as president, conservative optimism that the nation had turned to the right was misplaced. Poll evidence offered little support for this view. The aggregate of surveys held in the preelection month suggested that only 25% of Americans considered themselves conservative, compared with 18% perceiving themselves as liberal and 55% as moderate. National Opinion Research Centre (NORC) data for 1980 showed that large majorities of Americans supported increases or no changes in the levels of federal spending in virtually all major domestic policy areas, particularly environmental protection, the cities, healthcare, and education. This does not gainsay the fact that many Americans regarded government as wasteful and inefficient, were dismayed by the incapacity of their leaders to resolve the nation's economic and international problems, and regarded federal bureaucrats as insensitive and dictatorial. Pollster Daniel Yankelovich's findings concluded that in the course of "a single generation Americans have grown disillusioned about the relation of the individual American to his government". By 1980 only 29% of the public believed that government would "do what is right most of the time", compared with 56% a decade earlier, and the proportion of people believing that government officials were "smart people who know what they are doing" fell from 69% to 29% over the same period. Nevertheless such feelings indicated that what Americans wanted was better government rather than less government.

On some issues, of course, conservative trends that had emerged earlier were manifest. This was particularly true of race, even though the issue never appeared on the surface of the 1980 campaign. The defection of lower middle-class white Democratic identifiers to the GOP was due primarily to economic problems, but racial matters helped to make many voters more volatile. Busing, affirmative action programs, and resentment of black welfare dependency fueled their discontent. Reagan responded to these concerns more subtly than Barry Goldwater in 1964 and George Wallace in 1968. He proclaimed support for equal opportunities for all citizens, thereby endorsing the principle of racial equality but implicitly questioning the legitimacy of affirmative action programs that practiced so-called reverse discrimination in favor of racial minorities and women. He promised to reverse judicial activism by appointing judges who held a restrained view of the Constitution. Also, some of Reagan's attacks on welfare used race-laden images, notably his allegations concerning a Chicago "welfare queen" with "eighty names, thirty addresses, twelve Social Security cards" whose "tax-free income alone is over $150,000". This woman was never identified but it was universally assumed that she was black. Significantly, 66% of voters in 1980 (compared with 40% in 1976) believed that the Republican party was not likely to help minorities.

Polls revealed a significant inconsistency in popular attitudes towards federal aid for minorities in 1980. According to the NORC, three out of four Americans believed that government spending to improve the conditions of blacks should be maintained or increased. Its findings also showed that a majority of the public only supported expenditure cutbacks in one area of domestic policy. This was welfare, on which blacks were disproportionately reliant. In 1980, blacks constituted 11.7% of the total population but 43% of AFDC recipients, 34.4% of subsidized housing recipients, and 35.1% of food stamp recipients. Popular disaffection with welfare signified that the difficulties of holding together the biracial Democratic voter coalition had intensified in the economic conditions of the 1970s. The tax-paying constituents of the Democratic party felt increasing hostility to its non-taxpaying, poor constituents, many of them black. To make things worse, while over one in four black families lived in poverty, the black middle class was growing and its success reinforced old stereotypes held by many whites that the black poor were only so because they chose to be.

Nevertheless, the extent of negative voting against Jimmy Carter pointed not to political realignment but the continuation of electoral dealignment. Many analysts expressed concern that this trend signified the existence of a new party system in which two narrow-based coalitions were polarized against each other and the bulk of the electorate was dealigned, free to redefine its partisan loyalty every four years in elections that were in reality presidential referenda. Without strong parties, the difficulties of establishing a stable consensus on public policy were immense. As Everett Ladd observed, "[W]hat was indicated most clearly was a new order where each presidential election is disconnected from the partisan past, a highly volatile referendum of the public record of the previous four years." By contrast, old-style Democrats like Edward Kennedy saw the outcome as proof that their party had to reassert its liberal traditions, while "new politics" Democrats like Gary Hart and Paul Tsongas interpreted it as evidence that the party had to modernize its ideas and develop a new, more realistic liberalism. The problem for the Democrats, of course, was that they were no longer the moving force within the party system. It was the GOP that was now in a position to mold a new political agenda.

*   *   *

In the opinion of many Americans, the 1970s had been the most dismal decade in the nation's history, worse even that the 1930s. During this period the United States had suffered its first defeat in war, had undergone a decline in its international power, had witnessed the disgrace of the presidency, and had experienced economic decline. The Carter years saw the intensification of many of the nation's problems and a growing uncertainty about the future. America's sense of purpose seemed to have evaporated.

At a ceremony to honor John F. Kennedy, the president who had best symbolized the vigor and optimism of postwar America, President Carter observed, "The world of 1980 is as different from what it was in 1960 as the world of 1960 was from 1940. . . . We have a keener appreciation of limits now, the limits of government, limits on the use of military power abroad, the limits of manipulation without harm to ourselves [of] a delicate environment. . . . And we face centrifugal forces in our society and in our political system — forces of regionalism, forces of ethnicity, of narrow economic interest, of single issue politics — [that] are testing the resiliency of American pluralism and of our ability to govern." Carter's acceptance of these limits and his efforts to govern within them helped to make him a one-term president. His successor saw the world differently and believed that the United States could go forward to the past. Ronald Reagan promised the restoration of global hegemony, economic regeneration, and minimal government. These would be the issues that shaped American politics in the 1980s.

7

True Believers: Conservatives and the Conservative Agenda of the 1980s

When Ronald Reagan became president, few seasoned observers of the Washington scene anticipated that he would have a profound impact on American politics and public policy. It was widely believed that he was little more than a media-friendly politician who would have even less success than his predecessor in coping with the substantive and managerial problems of modern presidential government. By the time that he left office, however, he was widely regarded as the most significant president of the postwar era.

Reagan aimed to establish conservatism as the dominant force in American politics. This was not a lone crusade. The new president had the backing of a new conservative movement that had emerged in the 1970s. As his domestic policy adviser Martin Anderson acknowledged, "[T]he Reagan Revolution is not completely, or even mostly, due to Ronald Reagan. He was an extremely important contributor to the intellectual and political movement that swept him to the presidency in 1980. He gave that movement focus and leadership. But Reagan did not give it life." In addition to examining Reagan's ideology, this chapter discusses the groups whose ideas shaped the new conservatism and the extent to which the Republican party became a vehicle for these views. It also analyzes Reagan's political agenda during his first year in office.

Reagan

Ronald Reagan made his name as a media personality, first in radio, then in films, and finally in television. Not only was he a late entrant into the profession of politics, he was also a late convert to conservatism and indeed to Republicanism. In his autobiography he described himself during his early days in Hollywood in the 1930s and 1940s as a "very emotional New Dealer" and a "near hopeless hemophilic liberal" who voted Democrat in every presidential election from 1932 to 1948. His political transformation began when liberals failed to share his concern about supposed communist infiltration of Hollywood during the Cold War era. Also important was his growing resentment against high marginal tax rates which reduced his earnings at the peak of his Hollywood stardom. By the early 1960s Reagan had become an archconservative who believed that the welfare state undermined fundamental American values and that the graduated income tax had been invented by Karl Marx. He finally registered as a Republican in 1962. Two years later he gained political fame by appearing on national television to laud the presidential candidacy of Barry Goldwater. Presentational skills honed during his media career enabled Reagan to present Goldwater's ideas in a far more appealing and less threatening manner than the candidate himself could do. Boosted by this success, Reagan ran for governor of California in 1966 and won a landslide victory against the Democratic incumbent.

There was no revolution in state government during Reagan's two terms as governor. Facing a Democrat-controlled legislature, he recognized the need for compromise and consensus in order to govern effectively. The state budget nearly doubled during his period in office and taxes went up to pay for this. Reagan also signed a pro-choice abortion bill, an action that he later repented, and voiced support for the Equal Rights Amendment (ERA), which he later recanted. His greatest achievement was a welfare reform measure that tightened eligibility requirements for public assistance but paid more generous benefits to recipients of aid. Nevertheless Reagan continued to speak out for conservative values and established himself as the darling of the right-wing of the national Republican party by 1968. He would remain the nation's preeminent conservative for the next twenty years.

Reagan's route to national power was long and arduous. Many observers believed that his defeat for the Republican presidential nomination in 1976 marked the end of his career, but he soon bounced back. According to Arthur Schlesinger Jr, "Reagan is the triumph of a man who earnestly believed in something. . . . [He] is proof of the power of conviction politics." Though he abandoned some of his extreme views, such as the Marxist origins of income tax, he remained deeply committed to a set of conservative ideas throughout his political career. He believed that: government should be constrained; high taxes were a disincentive to individual effort, which was the essence of wealth creation; welfare made individuals dependent on the state; traditional moral values had made America great and had to be preserved; and, finally, communism was an evil that the United States had to resist everywhere.

Reagan's credo was radical, simple, and optimistic. It was radical in the sense that he was the first major American politician of the postwar era, Barry Goldwater apart, who sought to reverse the post-New Deal course of domestic policy. It was a simple philosophy, rooted largely in his personal values and experience rather than in intellectual abstractions. The fact that high marginal tax rates had actually discouraged him from making movies was proof to Reagan that taxes were a disincentive to individual effort. Similarly, his experience with communists in Hollywood convinced him that communism was bent on world domination and that its leaders were ready to lie and cheat in pursuit of this aim. Optimism that America would triumph over the adversities of the 1970s was also an essential part of Reagan's credo. As the journalist Lawrence Barrett observed, "His was a thoroughly American vision, derived from his own, and his country's, robust youth."

Reagan was the most ideological president of modern times. At another time and in the person of another president this might have been a disadvantage, but it turned out to be one of his greatest strengths. Only a president with Reagan's ideological certainty could have interpreted the outcome of the 1980 election as a clearcut mandate for conservatism. Moreover, however simplistic his views were, they gave his administration a clear sense of direction. After the uncertainty of the 1970s, Americans appreciated the upbeat and confident approach of a new president who knew where he wanted to lead them. In conjunction with the media skills that he possessed, Reagan's ideological commitment also helped to make him a consummate spokesman for conservative ideas because he was so convinced of their truth.

Reagan's dedication to conservative ideas also shaped his style of presidential leadership. It was principles rather than details of government policy that interested him. As he remarked in his memoirs, "I don't believe a chief executive should supervise every detail of what goes on in his organization. The chief executive should set broad policy and general ground rules, tell people what he or she wants them to do, then let them do it." This hands-off approach ensured that Reagan would not be seen as power hungry, an image that had damaged Lyndon Johnson and Richard Nixon. It also saved him from getting bogged down in costly political battles over policy details, as had happened to

Jimmy Carter. On the other hand his leadership style delegated considerable responsibility for policy formulation to subordinates, who
sometimes appeared to act outside his control. The Iran-Contra scandal
eventually underlined the dangers of this.

The two twentieth-century presidents whom Reagan most admired
were Calvin Coolidge and Franklin D. Roosevelt. At first sight they
do not make an appropriate pairing, but the choice was not entirely
illogical. Reagan idealized the economic prosperity and minimal
government of the Coolidge era in the mid 1920s. Despite his eventual
disillusionment with the New Deal, he admired Roosevelt for giving
Americans hope at a time of despair and for using the powers of the
presidency to redirect the nation's political life. In essence Reagan knew
that his hopes of reestablishing a public philosophy akin to that of
Coolidge's time rested on his ability to emulate Roosevelt's leadership.
In contrast to "silent Cal", who was something of a "do-nothing" president, Reagan had to be an activist to achieve conservative ends. As the
political scientist James Wilson noted, "Today, an administration cannot be conservative by doing little, it can only be conservative by doing
a great deal."

The revived right

In 1964 Barry Goldwater's conservatism was so far outside the political
mainstream that most Americans thought him a cranky extremist. In
1980, espousing ideas that were fundamentally similar to Goldwater's,
Ronald Reagan was widely regarded as serious and credible. In large
part this was because conservatism had achieved intellectual respectability in the 1970s. The right, which had been a reactive force in
American politics for so long, had been transformed into an innovative
force during this decade. Stagflation had undermined the credibility of
New Deal-style welfare Keynesianism, and liberalism had no new ideas
to offer in its place. In these circumstances conservatism rediscovered
its intellectual vigor and exerted increasing influence on political debate.
The right was not a monolithic entity. A number of groups spearheaded
its revival. These did not see eye to eye on every issue and often had
different priorities, but the outpouring of their ideas gave respectability
to Reagan's rhetoric and helped to shape the policies that his administration would follow.

The neoconservatives who had emerged in the late 1960s were
at the forefront of conservatism's intellectual renaissance. They were

prolific publicists whose writings did much to redefine some of the
central assumptions of American public policy. The journals *Public
Interest*, edited by Irving Kristol, and *Commentary*, edited by Norman
Podhoretz, gave them a regular forum, and these were supplemented
by a huge output of books, articles, and newspaper columns. The
neoconservatives remained on the fringes of the modern right. Their
animus was against Great Society liberalism rather than the more
limited liberalism of the New Deal, which they continued to believe
in. Nevertheless, as former liberals disillusioned with the path taken
by the Democrats in the 1960s, neoconservatives became powerful
legitimizers of Reaganism. For their own part the neoconservatives
saw Reagan not as a traditional conservative but as the usurper of
abandoned Democratic traditions. Commenting on Reaganomics, for
example, Benjamin Wattenberg declared, "It's growth economics.
That's New Deal economics. That's Democratic economics. That
ain't Republican economics."

The neoconservatives lent weight to Reaganite skepticism about the
ability of government to solve society's problems. They insisted that
the unanticipated outcomes of social programs were always more
important and usually less welcome than the expected results. From this
perspective an expanded welfare state could never end poverty because
it would make the poor dependent on government aid and incapable
of improving themselves. Neoconservatives also championed family
values. In their eyes the family, the church and the neighborhood had
a vital role to play in ensuring that society had a shared code of morals.
Great Society programs and Supreme Court decisions of the 1960s and
early 1970s were deemed to have weakened these institutions, with
negative consequences in areas such as crime, drugs, indiscipline in
schools, and the decline of the work ethic. Finally, neoconservatives
were highly vocal critics of detente because they regarded the Cold War
as a conflict between rival ideologies that could never coexist together.
Appalled by the post-Vietnam retreat from globalism, they proclaimed
that the United States had to reassert its faith in the traditional values
of democracy and liberty, place itself at the head of free world once
again, and renew the ideological struggle with communism.

Big business was also instrumental in the conservative revival. The
rapprochement that the pro-growth policies of the Kennedy-Johnson
administrations had forged between the New Deal coalition and the
traditionally Republican labor-intensive industries came to an end in the
1970s. The anxiety of firms in this sector to hold down wages and

preserve profit margins in the face of inflation led to a breakdown of the industrial relations consensus between management and labor. The stagnant economy also spelled trouble for businesses that depended on federal contracts, notably those within the military-industrial complex. In the quarter-century following World War II it had been possible to finance the expansion of the warfare state and the welfare state from the incremental revenues generated by economic growth. However, the budgetary constraints of the 1970s required government to prioritize the nation's needs more stringently. Defense corporations consequently developed a less benign attitude towards social programs that made rival claims on scarce federal resources. Meanwhile, many of the capital-intensive industries that had supported the Democrats since the 1930s, notably oil, petrochemicals, and pharmaceutical businesses, realigned with the right in the 1970s. Resentment that the expansion of the regulatory state had resulted in increased production costs was one reason for this. Another factor was the concern shared by big businesses of every kind that corporate tax levels disadvantaged them in the increasingly competitive international market.

Big business mobilized its resources to become an extremely active and influential interest group in the 1970s. By 1980 some 15,000 business lobbyists were operating in Washington, compared to just 8,000 in 1974. Corporate political action committees (PACs) also grew in number from 80 in 1974 to 1,496 in 1982, accounting for 49% of the expansion in the total numbers of PACs during this period. They donated far more money than other types of PACs to election campaigns, favoring Republican congressional candidates over Democrats by almost a two-to-one ratio from 1978 to 1982. In 1978 big business used its political muscle to-engineer the defeat of the Carter administration's bill to legalize common situs picketing by labor. In the same year it persuaded Congress to set aside Carter's proposal to eliminate business tax loopholes and to enact instead a regressive measure that reduced the capital gains tax and provided a one-off tax reduction for upper-income earners while raising social security taxes. This measure, the product of a Democrat-controlled Congress, entailed a reversal of post-New Deal tax policy and foreshadowed the Reagan tax cut of 1981.

In addition, big business helped to promote the entry of conservative ideas into the political agenda. According to William Simon, a New York financier and former Treasury Secretary in the Ford administration, it set out to fund "books, books, and more books. . . .[by] scholars, social scientists, writers, and journalists who understand the relationship between political and economic liberty". Most of the money was given to conservative research institutes or "think-tanks", which generated new ideas and policy proposals, communicated these to political elites and policymakers, and provided informed personnel to staff the Reagan administration. Although the lion's share of publicity for these activities went to Sunbelt entrepreneurs like Joseph Coors, the main sources of funding were the old elites of the big business establishment such as banker Richard Mellon Scaife and the John M. Olin Fund.

Some of the think-tanks were new creations. The Heritage Foundation, founded in 1973, helped to develop supply-side economic ideas and the concept of the Strategic Defense Initiative. Reagan administration members associated with this body included Secretary of the Interior James G. Watt and Secretary of Education William Bennett. The Committee on the Present Danger, founded in 1976, quickly established itself as the foremost advocate of increased military strength to combat Soviet power. Among its members, Richard Allen became Reagan's National Security Adviser, and Paul Nitze and Richard Perle were given top posts in the field of arms control negotiations. Meanwhile, older bodies raised their profile with the aid of new money. The most notable was the American Enterprise Institute, which influenced policy debates concerning regulation and the role of the private sector. It provided more personnel for the Reagan administration than any other think-tank, including UN ambassador Jeane Kirkpatrick and Council of Economic Advisers (CEA) chairman Murray Weidenbaum. Also important were the National Bureau of Economic Research, which specialized in tax policy and whose director Martin Feldstein became CEA chairman in 1982, and the Hoover Institution on War, Revolution, and Peace, whose interests were wide-ranging and whose fellows included Martin Anderson.

The conservative revival also gained support from within the community of academic economists. In the 1950s and 1960s Keynesianism ruled the roost in the economics departments of most universities. Milton Friedman and his University of Chicago colleagues were the main exception to this trend. Their advocacy of free-market ideas gained increased credibility in the economic circumstances of the 1970s. In essence, they believed that social as well as economic problems were best resolved through the instrument of the market rather than the state. Government programs were counterproductive in the opinion of free-marketeers. George Stigler, a Nobel laureate in 1982, earned a reputation as the father of the deregulation movement because of his trenchant charges that federal regulations, however well-intentioned, made US business uncompetitive, thereby helping to cause inflation and unemployment. Others charged that minimum wage legislation destroyed low-paid jobs, and that public housing was of poor standard and should be replaced by cash grants to enable tenants to rent decent private accommodation. Friedman, who received the Nobel Prize in 1976 and was president of the American Economics Association in 1977, continued to be the brightest star in the free-market firmament. He had a regular column in *Newsweek*, and in 1980, with the aid of $500,000 from the Heritage Foundation and other business grants, he was able to propagate his views in his own ten-part television series, "Free to Choose".

Friedman was most famously associated with the idea that inflation was determined by the money supply. In the late 1970s, however, a new conservative economic theory challenged the assumptions of monetarism as well as Keynesianism. Though originally conceived by Chicago professor Robert Mundell, supply-side doctrine was mainly developed and popularized by University of Southern California professor Arthur Laffer and *Wall Street Journal* columnist Jude Wanniski. It was based on the assumption that individuals respond to one fundamental incentive — the financial return on their labor and efforts. In Wanniski's words, supply-side theory "is a distinctly different approach from the monetarist who sees everything as depending on the proper amount of money printed by the Federal Reserve, or from the neo-Keynesian who sees everything as depending on demand management by the government. Both of these 'macroscopic' theories are inherently managerial in nature. Mundell and Laffer go back to the older style of economic thought in which the incentives and motivations of the individual producer and consumer and merchant are made the keystone of economic policy." For supply-siders, America's economic problems were largely attributable to the fact that taxes were too high. People were deterred from working harder and saving more of their money for investment purposes because too large a proportion of the gains they could make would be taken away by government. As a result productivity and investment suffered and inflation was encouraged.

The "Laffer curve", the supply-siders' riposte to the "Phillips curve" beloved by Keynesians, sought to display that above a certain point tax rates produced diminishing revenues because entrepreneurial activity was discouraged. Laffer and Wanniski went so far as to claim that tax cuts would actually generate more revenues than current rates produced. Other supply-siders made the more guarded prediction that lower taxes would not produce a marked decline in revenues from current levels. Whatever their expectations on this score, the majority of supply-siders did not emphasize the need for balanced budgets. To Paul Craig Roberts, who became Assistant Treasury Secretary for Economic Policy in 1981, the budget deficit was "a residual of the economy's performance. . . .[and] would gradually be eliminated by economic growth". Supply-siders also believed that tax reduction was a better safeguard than monetary restraint against demand-led inflation. In their view lowering taxes would boost output and increase the supply of products, thereby countering the problem of too much money chasing too few goods. Supply-side doctrine similarly disputed the Carter administration's insistence that balanced budgets were necessary to combat inflation. It held that deficits were only inflationary if public borrowing had to be financed through an increase in the money supply.

Federal regulation of industry and public welfare programs also came under the attack of some supporters of the new doctrine. Dave Stockman whose appointment as director of the Office of Management and Budget (OMB) made him the highest-serving supply-sider in the Reagan administration, claimed: "[O]ur capitalist economy's natural capacity to expand and generate new wealth and societal welfare was being badly hobbled by the sweeping anti-supply and incentive-destroying policies of the modern state." From his perspective the Reagan Revolution was to be in essence a supply-side revolution: "Its vision of the good society rested on the strength and productive potential of free men in free markets. It sought to encourage the unfettered production of capitalist wealth and the expansion of private welfare that automatically attends it. It envisioned a land the opposite to the coast-to-coast patchwork of dependencies, shelters, protections, and redistributions that the nation's politicians had brokered over decades".

In addition to elite groups of intellectuals, academics, and businessmen, organizations with populist characteristics played a part in the conservative revival. The so-called New Right was a loose movement of conservative organizations which developed independently of the political parties in the 1970s. Its most influential figures and groups were: Richard Viguerie, director of the fundraising organization RAVCO; Terry Dolan of the National Conservative Political Action Committee (NICPAC); Howard Phillips of the Conservative Caucus; and Paul Weyrich of the Committee for the Survival of a Free Congress.

The movement also embraced many single-issue organizations, such as Life Amendment Political Action Committee, a militant anti-abortion group, and Eagle Forum, the anti-ERA group headed by Phyllis Schlafly.

The New Right held free-market views on economic policy and advocated anticommunist foreign policy, but its most distinctive contribution to the conservative agenda was its emphasis on social and moral issues. According to Weyrich, "the very essence of the new right is a morally based conservatism . . . our view is not based on economics but in a religious view". The movement vented its spleen against the sociocultural legacy of the 1960s and the public policies associated with this, particularly abortion, ERA, busing, gay rights, and judicial decisions affecting school prayer, sexual freedom, and pornography. It believed that the most basic values and institutions of American society — the family, the church, sexual morality, and patriotism — were under threat from a liberal elite in government and the judiciary. The range of New Right concerns was subsumed under the banner of family issues. This was exemplified by a letter sent to millions of homes by one conservative group warning that "the children in your neighborhood are in danger. How would you feel if tomorrow your child . . . was taught by a practising homosexual . . . was bused twenty to thirty miles away to school every morning . . . was forced to attend classes in a school where all religion is banned? If you think this could never happen . . . you are in for a shock!"

The New Right's significance owed less to the intellectual quality of its ideas than to its means of propagating them. Many conservative activists had drawn the lesson from Goldwater's defeat in 1964 that having the correct values and policies was useless without the power to sell them to the electorate. The neoconservatives, think-tanks, free-marketeers and supply-siders were intent on persuading political elites to adopt their policy ideas. By contrast, the New Right sought to cultivate grass-roots support. Being more directly relevant to the lives of ordinary people, social issues were seen by New Right leaders as the best means of popularizing the conservative cause.

Direct mail became the New Right's bridgehead to the mass public. This method of communication enabled it to bypass the liberal media, send conservative ideas into peoples' homes, and raise political funds from millions of small contributors. Richard Viguerie, whose organization sent out about 100 million letters a year by the late 1970s, pioneered this form of political action. Others quickly followed suit, building up their own mailing lists and sharing them with like-minded organizations. A single issue strategy was most commonly employed. Computerized analysis of responses to mail shots enabled New Right organizations to discover the issue on which an individual felt most strongly. They used that issue to get the person politically active and then sought to educate him or her about the conservative position on other issues.

By 1980 New Right direct mail reached about 10% of the population. Less than a quarter of the funds raised in this way went into the campaign coffers of conservative candidates at election times. The rest went to pay for the costs of the mailing operations. But the New Right was successful in the broader purpose of activating voter resentment in support of social conservatism. According to some surveys, recipients of its communications had nearly twice as high a turn-out rate as the national average in congressional elections. This committed minority could exert considerable influence at a time when fewer and fewer Americans were bothering to vote. In 1980 Paul Weyrich admitted: "I don't want everyone to vote. Our leverage in the election quite candidly goes up as the voting population goes down. We have no responsibility, moral or otherwise, to turn out our opposition."

The New Right supplemented these tactics by targeting negative advertising against prominent liberals. It took credit for the defeat of liberal Democrats like Senators Dick Clark (Iowa) and Thomas McIntyre (New Hampshire) in 1978 and for liberal losses in the 1980 senatorial elections. Such claims were exaggerated. The major Democratic losses in 1978 were sustained in normally conservative states and those in 1980 owed more to Jimmy Carter's unpopularity than any other factor. In fact Dan Quayle, who narrowly defeated New Right target, Senator Birch Bayh, in Indiana, complained that the movement's negative campaigning gave it a bully-boy image that created a backlash of public sympathy for its intended victims. But no one could deny that the New Right had established itself as a serious force in American politics.

Family issues also brought a new Christian right into the political arena. Many Americans found religious certainty appealing in an age of national uncertainty. As a result Protestant fundamentalist churches, which view the Bible as God-given truth, became the fastest-growing religious organizations in the 1970s. They had over 10 million members by 1980 and their influence extended into the wider evangelical movement that claimed the allegiance of at least 30 million Americans.

Fundamentalist church leaders had traditionally eschewed politics for fear of being tainted by secularism, but they now chose to act out of concern that America was in the grip of an unprecedented crisis. In their eyes America's decline in the 1970s was God's judgement on its abandonment of traditional moral values.

Like the political New Right, the new Christian right regarded the legacy of the 1960s as the root of all evil. Its leaders denounced abortion as murder, feminism as a threat to the family, homosexuality and its toleration as sinful, prohibition of school prayer as a challenge to God's authority, and sexual permissiveness as morally corrupt. Their message was accompanied by secondary themes lauding free enterprise as Christian in spirit and excoriating communism as godless. Convinced that its cause was the only true one, the religious right regarded those who disagreed with it as morally wicked. Jerry Falwell, its most important figure, proclaimed: "The godless minority of treacherous individuals must now realize they do not represent the majority. They must be made to see that moral Americans will no longer permit them to destroy our country with their godless, liberal philosophies."

Encouraged by New Right leaders, notably Viguerie and Weyrich, Falwell established the Moral Majority in 1979 to crusade against moral decline. His original intention to enlist support from all denominations, including Catholics and Jews, was never fully realized, but within two years his organization claimed a membership of 4 million, predominantly among Protestant fundamentalists. In 1980 a Gallup poll indicated that only 8% of Americans approved of Moral Majority aims, but these represented a hefty block of potential voters, particularly in the South. Other religious organizations founded for political purposes included Religious Roundtable, which ran political seminars for fundamentalist preachers, Christian Voice, which kept records on the votes cast by all congressmen, and Christian Freedom Foundation, which specialized in promoting free-market economics to its fundamentalist constituents.

Also important were the activities of television preachers. Thanks to new developments in cable television, they had a massive potential audience of 30 million in total by the late 1970s, though regular viewers of their programs were far smaller in number, of course. The best-known were Jim Bakker, James Robison, Pat Robertson, and Falwell himself. Falwell's "Old Time Gospel Hour", a mix of hymns, preaching and political invective, was broadcast by 225 television stations and had a regular audience of 1.4 million, the largest of any religious program.

Robertson, a Southern Baptist preacher, founded the Christian Broadcasting Network that had access to 1,800 cable channels by 1979. He gave new meaning to the adage that the medium was the message in claiming that God had told him, "Pat, I want you to have an RCA transmitter."

It would be inaccurate to suggest that the loose-knit conservative movement which had emerged by 1980 and what became known as Reaganism had identical agendas. Reagan had his own priorities, based on his own strongly-held convictions, and was not personally committed to supporting all the wide-ranging aims of the various conservative groups. The economic and foreign policy elements of the conservative agenda were far closer to his interests than were the family-issue concerns of the New Right and the new Christian right. Even when Reagan appeared to embrace a conservative doctrine, he often shrank from its full implications. This was particularly the case with supply-side economics. Nevertheless the existence of a new conservative agenda was important in itself. It helped to legitimize Reaganism and facilitated the transformation in the terms of political debate that took place in the 1980s.

The Republican party

The intellectual revival of conservatism was the work of groups operating outside rather than within the Republican party. Some right-wingers despaired that the GOP could ever become a genuine conservative party. The New Right in particular viewed it as rooted in the politics of pragmatism and consensus, too willing to adopt a "me-too" attitude towards liberal Democratic policies for the sake of electoral advantage. Richard Viguerie avowed in 1976: "The Republican Party is like a disabled tank on the bridge impeding the troops from crossing to the other side. You've got to take that tank and throw it in the river." Many like-minded right-wingers hoped that a new conservative party party might emerge in place of the GOP. In 1976 Viguerie himself threw his weight behind the American Independence Party, even seeking its vice-presidential nomination. However its poor showing forced the New Right and other conservative groups to pin their hopes for the future on the Republican party. By 1980 they felt grounds for optimism that the GOP was at last willing to launch a real assault against big government and liberal public policy.

The Republican party was more conservative in 1980 than it had been during the Nixon era or even in 1976. A number of factors accounted for this. The failure of government to resolve US economic problems in the 1970s was the most important. Inflation, columnist George Will observed, was the great "conservatizing agent". Republicans of all hues became more willing to endorse free markets and low taxes as the formula for economic salvation. Regional factors also played a part. The growing number of Republican candidates elected in the conservative states of the Sunbelt and the Rocky Mountain West moved the GOP's ideological center of gravity rightward. The activities of the corporate PACs, the New Right, and the new Christian right similarly influenced the conservatism of the Republican party in the electoral arena. Finally, the GOP's confidence that the nation was itself turning right fortified its own move in this direction.

The field of candidates for the 1980 presidential nomination, dominated as it was by conservatives, provided the best indication of the Republican party's new position. Reagan's victory did not represent the triumph of the right over other factions, as Goldwater's had done in 1964. He won the nomination because he was considered the most electable conservative. In fact he was not the first choice of the New Right, which felt that Congressman Philip Crane (Illinois) was a stronger advocate of social and moral conservatism. Reagan's main rival was George Bush of Texas, whose support for energy deregulation, smaller government, and big defense spending placed him safely with the conservative mainstream of the party. Detail rather than principle separated the leading contenders on tax policy. Bush, who famously described Reagan's proposals as "voodoo economics", was himself in favor of smaller-scale though still substantial tax cuts. Only in his opposition to a constitutional ban on abortion and support for the ERA did Bush differ from Reagan. The gap between them was small enough for the victor to give his rival the vice-presidential slot on the Republican ticket. The price for this was Bush's public endorsement of the party platform that rejected abortion, ERA, and busing. So complete was the conservative triumph that Congressman John Anderson (Illinois), the only representative among the Republican nomination candidates of the moderate-liberal traditions associated with Thomas Dewey and Nelson Rockefeller, quit the party to run for the presidency as an independent.

The Republican party in Congress had also changed by 1980. Just before the elections of that year Reagan met with 285 Republican congressional candidates to issue the Capitol Compact. This general statement of party intent avowed Republican unity in support of less government, less welfare, less taxes, and more defense. Absent from the list was a commitment to social conservatism, on which Republican consensus was lacking. Many congressional Republicans were already committed to parts of Reagan's program before he became president. They had signaled their stand on national security through strong and voiciferous opposition to SALT II. More significantly, perhaps, many of them had already endorsed supply-side economics. In 1977 Congressman Jack Kemp (New York) and Senator William Roth (Delaware) had jointly introduced a bill to cut marginal tax rates by thirty percent over a three-year period. Though the Republican leadership in the House and Senate was lukewarm to the proposal, it won widespread support from the younger generation of Republicans who had entered Congress in the 1970s. The measure eventually formed the nucleus of Reagan's economic program in 1981.

Reagan took office at a time when nearly half the Republicans in the House of Representatives were new members who had first been elected in 1978 or 1980. Compared with many senior Republican congressmen, who had developed a "minority complex" during their long years in opposition, the newcomers had a very strong sense that the political tide was turning in favor of conservatism. They were confident that the "Reagan Revolution" would transform the GOP into the majority party in the House in the near future. Conservative influence was even stronger in the Senate. According to one estimate of factional strength in the upper house, there were 12 moderate-liberal Republicans, 12 mainstream or centrist Republicans, and 29 right-wing Republicans in 1981, compared with 13, 10, and 15 respectively in 1975. The mainstream group was also far closer to the right-wingers on economic and defense issues than in the past. The liberal faction, which had enjoyed considerable influence in the 1960s and early 1970s, was now isolated. Election defeats suffered by three of its most prominent members, Edward Brooke (Massachusetts) and Clifford Case (New Jersey) in 1978 and Jacob Javits (New York) in 1980, further weakened its position. Both Case and Javits had failed to win renomination battles against conservative Republicans who received strong support from the New Right.

The growth of the Republican right was entwined with a regional transfer of power within the GOP from the north and midwest to the west, southwest, and south. Kevin Phillips' prediction of a Sunbelt-dominated conservative-oriented Republican party enjoying presidential and congressional preeminence seemed on the verge of coming true in 1980. Insofar as representation in Congress was concerned, Republicanism in the northeast, mid-Atlantic, and urban Midwest, the bastions of the liberal wing of the party, had been in steady decline since the mid 1960s. Conversely, Republican strength grew significantly in the Plains states, the Rocky Mountains, and the Sunbelt states of the Southwest, areas where the right wing of the party was powerful. The GOP's success in establishing itself as a significant force in the South for the first time in the twentieth century also worked to conservative advantage.

In 1961 the Republicans held only six southern seats in the House of Representatives and one in the Senate. John Tower's victory in a special election that year to fill the Texas seat vacated by Lyndon Johnson made him the South's first GOP senator since Reconstruction. By 1977 Republican numbers were still modest, standing at 29 in the House and six in the Senate. The next four years saw substantial advances. By 1981 the GOP held 40 Southern seats in the House (compared with 68 for the Democrats) and 11 in the Senate (equal with the Democrats). A number of factors contributed to this development. Middle- and upper-income suburbanites, whose numbers had burgeoned in the 1970s as the post-World War II economic modernization of the South reached a peak, identified with conservative Republican attacks on high taxes and big government. Meanwhile, the Democratic loyalties of small town and rural whites had been weakened by racial issues in the 1960s, and this process continued in the 1970s as a result of the politicization of Protestant fundamentalism.

Despite the growing influence of the Sunbelt, the Republican party's support for the social agenda of the New Right and the new Christian right was less than wholehearted. Many mainstream Republicans like Jack Kemp and Senator Howard Baker (Tennessee) had little sympathy for sociocultural conservatism. The GOP right was itself divided over New Right aims. The strongest supporters of this cause tended to be Sunbelt and Rocky Mountain Republicans who had entered office in the 1970s. In the Senate, Orrin Hatch (Utah), Paul Laxalt (Nevada) and, in particular, Jesse Helms (North Carolina) were the most prominent advocates of family issues. However, members of what could be termed the "old" Republican right were concerned that the New Right agenda called for an unwarrantable intrusion by the state into the private lives of citizens. Barry Goldwater declared in 1981: "I have spent quite a number of years carrying the flag of the 'old conservatism' and I can say with conviction that the religious issues of . . . [New Right and Christian right] groups have little or nothing to do with conservative or liberal politics."

The ideological cohesion of the GOP, at least of its mainstream and right-wing factions, was strongest on the issues of taxation and public spending. Even on these matters its unity should not be exaggerated. Pragmatism continued to vie with principle in the political universe of mainstream Republicans. Many of them may have believed that the conservative moment had arrived in 1980 but their political solidarity in support of Reagan would soon come under challenge from the institutional factors — notably subcommittee government, the power of private lobbies, and candidate-centered elections — that had done much to fragment the congressional Democrats in the late 1970s. Much depended on Reagan's leadership if the Reagan Revolution was to triumph over these obstacles. The new president took office with one great advantage. His landslide victory over an incumbent president and the attendant Republican advances at congressional level induced his party to regard him as the Roosevelt of the right. The loyalty of many within it to the conservative causes that he espoused would rest on whether the electoral benefits of Reaganism for the GOP matched those of FDR's New Deal for the Democrats.

The political agenda of Reaganism

Reagan's first year in office was the most important and, at least in political terms, the most successful of his presidency. Seasoned political observers compared his performance with Roosevelt's in 1933 and Johnson's in 1964. By the end of 1981 Reagan had established the political course that his administration would follow, defined his priorities, and made an important start in the task of translating conservative ideas into actual policies.

Reagan knew that the success of his administration would depend largely on how effectively he dealt with the nation's economic problems. The president and his advisers decided to capitalize on the political momentum gained from his election victory by moving quickly to enact his economic program. In his inaugural address on January 20, 1981 Reagan proclaimed: "In the present crisis, government is not the solution to our problems; government is the problem . . . in the days ahead I will propose removing the roadblocks that have slowed our economy and reduced productivity. . . . It is time to reawaken this industrial giant, to get government back within its means, and to lighten our punitive tax burden. And these will be our first priorities, and on these principles there will be no compromise. . . .'

The economic strategy that became known as "Reaganomics" was unveiled in detail a month later when the president announced his Program for Economic Recovery in his first State of the Union address. It drew on the entire range of conservative economic solutions propounded in the late 1970s. The main elements were: a large tax cut, based on the Kemp-Roth formula, to stimulate economic activity; monetary restraint to control inflation; net cuts in federal expenditure to reduce government and achieve a balanced budget by the end of Reagan's first term in office; and extensive deregulation of the economy. Reagan intended that each component of the program should be acted upon simultaneously in order to ensure a comprehensive approach to resolving the nation's economic problems.

According to Martin Anderson, the broad outlines of Reaganomics were set out in a policy memorandum which Reagan and his campaign team had approved in August 1979, seventeen months before he took office. Owing to the political need to act quickly, however, the new administration put together the specific details of its economic program in great haste and failed to reconcile the diverse priorities of the conservative economic ideas on which it was based. Growth-oriented supply-side tax cuts sat uneasily alongside monetary restraint designed to curb inflation. Reagan's promise to balance the budget was also out of step with his promises to cut taxes and his plans for a massive and immediate increase in defense spending. These contradictions would have immense consequences for the US economy and the budget in the years to come.

The Program for Economic Recovery was a typical product of bureaucratic politics in being a compromise between the conflicting views of various groups in the Reagan administration. Supply-siders within the Treasury, notably Paul Craig Roberts and Norman Ture, wanted economy-boosting tax cuts worth around $300 billion over three years. The bulk of this was to come from across-the-board cuts in income taxes, with the rest coming from reductions in corporate taxes, capital gains taxes, and investment income taxes. This would be the largest income tax cut in US history (dwarfing the previous largest reduction of $22.5 billion in 1975). It would also benefit all income groups instead of being targeted, as was normally the case with tax legislation, towards the bottom end of the scale. To this end, the highest marginal tax rate would be cut from 70% to 50%. Roberts and Ture professed confidence that the expansionary effects of tax reduction would generate an increased supply of federal revenue that would soon bring the budget into balance.

Other economic policymakers were more pessimistic about the impact of tax cuts. Monetarists in the Treasury like Beryl Sprinkel wanted tight money supply to ensure that economic growth did not fuel inflation. Meanwhile, Dave Stockman argued that it was essential to link tax cuts with spending cuts in order to balance the budget. Unless the deficit was wiped out, he warned, the public and private sectors would have to compete for credit resources that would become increasingly scarce as monetary restraint took effect. The result would be higher interest rates that would lead to renewed recession rather than recovery. With no time available for protracted debate, a compromise was reached that gave the three groups what they wanted in spite of their contradictory concerns.

The administration's economic policymakers assumed that the tax cuts would give the economy a quick boost and that monetary restraint would then work to ensure that recovery did not bring inflation in its wake. This expectation that tax reduction would be the quickest-acting part of the program turned out to be mistaken, with the result that the balanced-budget objectives of the Reagan administration were seriously undermined. Stockman anticipated that the tax cuts would result in a net loss of $100 billion in federal revenues over three years (in other words that two-thirds of the $300 billion giveaway would be made up by the increased revenues produced by economic growth). Net spending reductions would be necessary to make up this balance. The assumption that Congress would accept cuts of this magnitude was debatable at best. However, Stockman's calculations rested on the even more questionable premise that the economy would grow by 5% a year from fiscal 1982 to 1984 to generate $200 billion in extra revenue.

The problems of Reaganomics were compounded by modifications that had to be made to get the administration's initial budgetary proposals approved by Congress. In the Senate a number of conservative Republicans shared the concern voiced by many Democrats about the effects of the tax cuts on the deficit. In order to overcome this opposition, the president reluctantly agreed to reduce the proposed 30% reduction in income taxes to 25% over three years, to operate a cut of just 5% in the first year of the program, to delay its implementation until October instead of June 1981, and to trim business allowances. Accordingly, the initial tax cuts were smaller in scope and were introduced later than the supply-siders had anticipated. As a result the economy felt the depressing effects of the monetary element of Reaganomics prior to the stimulative effects of its fiscal measures.

The administration had to make further concessions to get the tax cut through the Democrat-controlled House of Representatives. Egged on by tax lobbyists who highlighted the effects of tax bracket creep, Reagan and the Democrats outbid each other to deal with this problem and win favor with middle-class voters. As a result the Economic Recovery Tax Act of 1981 permanently insured taxpayers against the effects of inflation by providing automatic cost-of-living adjustments in personal exemptions from 1985 onwards. This had the long-term effect of reducing federal revenues by far more than the administration had planned.

The battle for spending cuts was even tougher. In the presidential campaign Reagan had avowed that budgetary savings could be achieved largely by reducing waste and inefficiency in public programs rather than through actual program reductions. Soon after the election, however, Stockman convinced him of the need for drastic cuts in the budgets inherited from the Carter administration if he was to make good on his promise to balance the budget by the end of his first term. Defense program expansion and the social insurance programs were exempted from retrenchment on the president's orders. This ensured that the economies would disproportionately affect discretionary programs, notably means-tested public assistance for the poor (Aid for Families with Dependent Children, food stamps, child nutrition, and Medicaid) and annually-funded grants to state and local governments.

Stockman managed to come up with savings totaling $9 billion in Fiscal 1981 and $40 billion in fiscal 1982, but warned that further reductions would be necessary. Reagan's first budget had to be sent to Congress before the administration could decide where future savings should be made. As a result it contained what became known as the "magic asterisk" commitment to make reductions totaling $74 billion in fiscal 1983–4 without specifying which programs would be affected. The difficulties that would be encountered in achieving future economies were foreshadowed by the problems of getting the first round of cuts through the House of Representatives. The president had to make several concessions, notably on sugar price supports and fuel subsidies, to win the votes of conservative southern Democrats. In the end Congress approved cuts totaling $34 billion. This was a substantial retrenchment but was well short of the level needed for eventual budget-balancing.

By the end of 1981, however, the political success of the administration's program was more apparent than its economic shortcomings. As Democratic Speaker Tip O'Neill noted, Reagan had "pushed through the greatest increase in defense spending in American history together with the greatest cutbacks in domestic programs and the largest tax cuts the country has ever seen". This was a remarkable achievement in view of the presidency's relative impotence in the 1970s.

Reagan showed a sure political touch in dealing with the legislature. On Stockman's advice, he insisted on employing a reconciliation strategy, an unprecedented tactic but permissible under the terms of the 1974 Budget and Impoundment Act, to secure spending reductions. Congress was required to vote on the complete package of cuts before its committees deliberated on specific economies. This procedure established tight guidelines for budget policymaking that constrained the normal process of congressional bargaining and negotiation over appropriations. Reagan made full use of his communication skills to win popular support for his economic program. By mid-March 1981, one reporter commented: "The consensus in the country has reached Washington. Reagan has a momentum on his side." Their morale shattered by the recent election, the Democrats seemed frightened of standing up to him. It was Speaker O'Neill's conviction, one of his advisers commented, that the party should "recognize the cataclysmic nature of the 1980 election results. The American public wanted this new president to be given a chance to try out his programs. We weren't going to come across as being obstructionists."

In addition to establishing a new economic policy, Reagan restored anticommunism as the core element of US national security policy. In his first presidential press conference, he avowed that Soviet leaders "reserve unto themselves the right to commit any crime, to lie, to cheat" in pursuit of the communist aim of world domination. Reagan regarded the Soviets as a malevolent power responsible for all the unrest in the world. This view received its most famous expression in 1983 when he told a gathering of Christian fundamentalists that the Soviet Union was "an evil empire" and "the focus for evil in the modern world". Accordingly, Reagan was convinced that efforts to achieve diplomatic accommodation with the Soviets, such as Nixon, Ford, and Carter had sought, were misguided and bound to end in failure. To him the only sure way of controlling Soviet behavior in world affairs was through a build-up of American military power.

A sense of crisis lent urgency to the militarist agenda of the Reagan administration. Conservative internationalists were increasingly concerned about a "window of vulnerability". According to this theory, the Soviet Union had been allowed to establish nuclear superiority in the era of detente, and was therefore likely to engage in ambitious military adventures, possibly even in Western Europe, in the belief that the United States could not retaliate adequately. To negate this danger and restore America's assertiveness in world affairs, Reagan had called for a policy of "peace through strength" during the 1980 campaign. He would sound this theme throughout his presidency. It was premised on the conviction that only a strong and self-confident United States could resist the Soviet challenge to world peace. "Peace through strength is not a slogan," Reagan avowed in 1984, "it's a fact of life — and we will not return to the days of hand-wringing, defeatism, decline and despair."

Fears about the window of vulnerability were based on grossly inflated estimates of Soviet capability. But it was true that America's military budget had declined in real terms by 36% between 1968 and 1978, while the Soviet Union's had increased by some 30% over the same period. Carter had reversed this trend in his final two years in office, when defense outlays rose by almost 5% in total and plans were laid for a massive military expansion in the first half of the 1980s. Reagan intended to spend even more. He agreed with Secretary of Defense Caspar Weinberger that the level of national security expenditures should be determined by the existence of the Soviet threat rather than by the concerns of a balanced budget. The same message was being trumpeted by the influential Committee on the Present Danger, several of whose members had been appointed to important positions in Weinberger's department. Reagan's first budget proposed an immediate increase in defense spending from $280 billion to $304 billion. It also projected total expenditure of $1.5 trillion from fiscal 1982 to fiscal 1986. This figure represented an average annual increase of 10% and was some $400 billion higher than Carter had planned. Reagan got most of what he wanted, with the result that he presided over the largest defense build-up in America's peacetime history.

Much of the defense budget expansion went to fund the strategic modernization program that NATO members had approved in 1979. The extra money paid for increased capability in intercontinetal and submarine-launched ballistic missiles and strategic bombers. Nevertheless there was a paradox at the heart of Reagan's policy on nuclear weapons. His deep distrust of the Soviets meant that he had no faith in arms control agreements. He also believed that the two SALT agreements of the 1970s had inhibited the regeneration of American military power. On the other hand, in Martin Anderson's words, Reagan was "morally appalled at the doctrine of mutually assured destruction (MAD) that had been our national nuclear weapons defense policy for some twenty years." Probably by 1976, and certainly by 1980, he had become convinced that deterrence policy was inherently flawed, because the only alternatives for the United States in the event of a Soviet strike would be nuclear retaliation or surrender.

Few members of his administration shared this concern but as top aide Donald Regan later acknowledged, Reagan assumed the presidency with a personal commitment to "the idea of one day sitting down with the leader of the USSR and banning weapons of mass destruction from the planet". In November 1981 he took the first step toward this end by proposing the "zero-zero" option that required the United States and the Soviets to eliminate their entire intermediate land-based missile armories. This was a declaration of intent. Reagan did not expect the Soviets to come to the negotiating table until America proceeded with its defense build-up and showed itself willing to enter a competitive arms race that it was certain to win because of its technological and economic superiority.

The defense expansion also funded big increases in conventional forces. This signaled a return to Cold War globalism. The Reagan administration sought to reestablish the role that the United States had played in the Third World before the Vietnam debacle. To this end measures were taken to attract better quality recruits into the armed forces, especially the marines, and a huge naval expansion was planned with the aim of creating a 600-ship navy based on about 15 aircraft-carrier battle groups. Money was also poured into the development of Rapid Deployment Forces that increased America's capability to win low-intensity conflicts in developing nations. These programs represented, in the words of two leading analysts, "a strategic reorientation of the US military establishment, and a renewed commitment to employ force [against] . . . Third World revolutionary movements and governments".

The Reagan Doctrine was another manifestation of the new commitment to Third World activism. Though not formally enunciated until 1985, its principles were present in the Reagan administration's foreign policy from the beginning. They represented a fusion of the president's ideological values and the ideas of neoconservative intellectuals. The foreign policy of detente, neoconservatives complained, had failed to draw a moral distinction between the United States and the Soviet Union, due to its emphasis on pragmatism and realism at the expense of idealism in superpower relations. The neoconservatives insisted that America had to resume its moral and ideological struggle against world communism. Reagan was of the same opinion. In 1980 he proclaimed: "We in this country, in this generation, are, by destiny rather than choice, the watchmen on the walls of world freedom."

The Reagan Doctrine aimed to restore moral idealism to US foreign policy in a number of ways. An ideological offensive was launched to publicize the superiority of western democratic values over those of communism. This battle of ideas included the creation of Radio Marti to broadcast to Cuba, increased funding for Radio Free Europe and Radio Liberty, and increased activity by the United States Information Agency. More significantly, the Reagan Doctrine also mandated the provision of military economic aid to rebel groups attempting to overthrow Third World governments that were aligned with the Soviet Union. In this respect it implied that a roll-back strategy had superceded the containment strategy of the Truman Doctrine insofar as developing nations were concerned. Reagan proclaimed in his second inaugural address in 1985, "Our mission is to defend freedom and democracy . . . we must not break faith with those who are risking their lives — on every continent, from Afghanistan to Nicaragua — to defy Soviet-supported aggression and secure rights which have been ours from birth. . . . Support for freedom fighters is self-defense."

Such pronouncements made it necessary to justify US support for noncommunist regimes which had appalling human rights records. The rationalization for this was provided by Jeane Kirkpatrick in a 1979 essay that brought her to Reagan's attention and led to her appointment as US ambassador to the United Nations. Kirkpatrick drew a distinction between totalitarian regimes, which were communist and inherently antidemocratic, and authoritarian regimes, which suppressed political freedoms but had the potential to evolve into democratic systems because their economies were capitalistic and their leaders were pro-American. Accordingly, the Reagan Doctrine had a much more limited concept of human rights than the Carter administration. It tolerated authoritarian regimes provided they made some effort to advance basic political freedoms, such as allowing the right to vote.

Family issues were the third element in the agenda of Reaganism. In March 1981 the president declared: "We do not have a separate social agenda, a separate economic agenda, a separate foreign agenda. We have one agenda. Just as surely as we seek to put our financial house in order and rebuild our nation's defenses, so too we seek to protect the unborn, to end the manipulation of schoolchildren by utopian planners and permit the acknowledgment of a Supreme Being in our classrooms." Rhetoric and reality were far apart in this instance. Family issues held a low priority for Reagan, who was much more concerned about the dead-hand of Big Government on the nation's economy than on its moral values. Also, aware as he was that many of the economic libertarians among his supporters had little sympathy for New Right's aims, he had no intention of alienating them for the sake of a group that had not initially committed itself to his candidacy in 1980. Reagan did symbolically endorse social agenda initiatives by conservative Republican congressmen early in his presidency, but he provided neither the leadership nor the support necessary to give their proposals hope of being enacted. Only when family issues were entwined with fiscal retrenchment did he truly commit himself to this cause. Reagan's first budget proposed huge funding reductions for three family planning programs. Congress mandated a 23% cut for the most important of these, the Title X provision of the Public Health Act of 1970, but left the other two intact.

In spite of the president's half-hearted approach, others within the administration were sowing the seeds which ensured that family issues would eventually have a more important role in the political agenda of Reaganism. With the exception of the Kennedy-Johnson era, when it had steadfastly identified with the civil rights movement, the Justice Department adopted a more politicized view of courts, judges, and law during the Reagan years than at any other time in the postwar era. Departmental recruiting policy targeted young, conservative-minded attorneys who had a sense of being in the vanguard of a new legal movement. The newcomers identified with a free-market analysis of regulatory law and with New Right positions on family issues and civil rights. An aggressive litigation strategy was pursued in support of this agenda, particularly in cases that provided opportunities to challenge liberal Supreme Court rulings on criminal justice, abortion, affirmative action, busing, and school prayer. Most significantly, the Reagan Justice Department paid close attention to judicial selection because it was more keenly aware than previous Republican administrations that judges made law and that law was an instrument for political control and change.

Paradoxically Reagan's first Supreme Court nominee, Sandra Day O'Connor, was chosen for symbolic rather than ideological reasons to fulfill his campaign promise to appoint the first woman justice. She was a disappointment to Justice Department right-wingers, who deemed her insufficiently committed to the new judicial conservatism, but appointments to lower federal courts gave them more cause for satisfaction. There had been a substantial expansion of the federal bench in the late 1970s to take account of rising caseloads, with the result that about forty vacancies occurred each year during Reagan's first term. From 1981 onwards the Justice Department carefully screened prospective nominees to ensure their ideological soundness. This strategy did not bring about an immediate judicial counter-revolution but it did lay the foundations for the evolution of a conservative ideology on the federal bench. Supreme Court nominees were also subjected to this rigorous screening process in Reagan's second term.

Another important element of Reaganism was its concern to restore national morale after the tribulations of the 1970s. In 1981 Reagan avowed: "What I'd really like to do is to go down in history as the president who made Americans believe in themselves again." This was not empty rhetoric. Reagan was firmly convinced that the resolution of the economic crisis facing the nation was dependent on the renewal of national will. "I felt we were going to solve our problem," he explained in his memoirs, "because we had a secret weapon in the battle: our factory workers, our farmers, our entrepreneurs, and the others among us who I believed would prove once again that the American people were gifted with and propelled by a spirit unique in the world, a spirit tenaciously devoted to solving our problems and bettering our lives, the lives of our children, and our country — and if these forces could be liberated from the restraints imposed on them by government, they'd pull the country out of its tailspin."

Reagan sought to uplift the nation through his deeds and words. His courageous conduct after being shot by a would-be assassin, his tough stand against the strike by air traffic controllers, and his triumph in winning congressional approval of his economic program established his image as a bold and decisive leader during his first year in office. He also made effective use of the presidential bully pulpit. Whereas Carter had told Americans about the complexity of the problems they faced, Reagan reassured them that everything would turn out right in the end because of the nation's greatness. "We have economic problems at home and we live in a troubled and violent world," he declared in a 1981 speech, "but there is a moral fibre running through our people that makes us more than strong enough to face the tests ahead." The process of regeneration took time. The nation's sense of wellbeing faltered again with the onset of recession in late 1981. But Reagan's persistence in presenting an upbeat account of America's prospects eventually paid off. National morale recovered during the second half of 1983, boosted by the economy's improved performance and the successful US invasion of Grenada, and rode high until the exposure of the Irangate scandal in late 1986. The sense that "America's back" was one of the most distinctive features of the middle years of the Reagan presidency.

*   *   *

Ronald Reagan had assumed office as president with the intention of enacting bold policies that drew on the wide-ranging ideas of the revived conservative movement. He forged an impressive record during his first year in office. Substantial tax cuts were approved by Congress, the domestic budget was cut, and military spending was scheduled to increase massively. The terms of political debate had also been transformed. For nearly fifty years politicians had defined their position on domestic issues in relationship to the New Deal and its Fair Deal-New Frontier-Great Society extensions. More recently their foreign policy deliberations had focused on the question of how the United States should adjust to its post-Vietnam international decline. By the end of 1981 the domestic and international agendas of Reaganism dominated political discourse. But this list of achievements did not yet add up to a Reagan Revolution. The new president had delivered the American political system a short, sharp shock, and had started to move the country in a new direction. It remained to be seen how well Reagan could build on these promising beginnings during his remaining years in office.

8
Incomplete Revolution: Politics and Policy in the Reagan Era, 1981–1988

It is ironic in view of his reputation as the Great Communicator that Ronald Reagan never coined a popular label for his political program. The term "Reagan Revolution" was the invention of others. Journalists began making common use of this convenient alliteration in 1981 to convey the significance of Reagan's early achievements. The label stuck and has become the historical symbol for America's political experience in the 1980s. Reagan himself was reluctant to use the term as the hallmark of his policies. In his farewell address in 1988, he commented, "They called it the Reagan Revolution, and I'll accept that, but for me it always seemed like the Great Rediscovery: a rediscovery of our values and common sense." Reagan's coyness may have reflected his realization that his presidency would be judged a failure if measured by the yardstick of whether it had brought about a political revolution.

The "Reagan Revolution" may have transformed the terms of political debate but its impact in terms of actual policy was more limited. This can be illustrated by measuring Reagan's achievements in relation to the aims that he set for his administration. These were: the restoration of America's economic wellbeing by means of tax cuts and free-market policies; a marked reduction in the size and domestic responsibilities of federal government; the roll-back of the social legacy of the 1960s; and the reassertion of America's power in the global struggle with communism. The limitations of the "Reagan Revolution" were also manifest in another important respect. The Democratic party's attainment of majority status in the 1930s ensured its ability to sustain and extend the New Deal legacy for the next thirty years. In view of this, the GOP's inability to make a comparable breakthrough in the 1980s must be examined.

"Reaganomics"

When Ronald Reagan took office inflation was still in double-digits and unemployment was running at over 7%. Eight years later the misery index made for happier reading. Inflation stood at 4% and unemployment was down to 5.6%, its lowest level since the early 1970s. The cycle of stagflation that had troubled the US economy from the late 1960s until the early 1980s had come to an end. Judged on this basis Reaganomics appears to have been a success. Nevertheless its record was deeply flawed in other respects. Reagan's successes had been achieved at the cost of seriously aggravating structural problems within the economy. By 1988 the United States had to cope with the consequences of spiraling budget and trade deficits. Equally worrying were the serious deficiencies in the nation's economic infrastructure. Finally, despite Reagan's promises of renewed prosperity, the maldistribution of wealth in American society increased rather than decreased while he was in office.

The runaway budget deficits of the Reagan era were inextricably linked with the fundamental miscalculation at the heart of the Program for Economic Recovery (PER) that had been launched in the *annus mirabilis* of 1981. The administration had been excessively optimistic in believing that it could tame inflation and generate growth without an intervening period of rising unemployment. In late 1981 the economy entered what proved to be the most serious recession since the 1930s. The Federal Reserve authorities were responsible for the severity of the contraction. Some downturn would have been inevitable even if the comparatively mild degree of monetary restraint envisaged by the PER had been implemented. However, during Reagan's first eighteen months in office the rate of growth in the money supply fell far below the target rates anticipated by the president's economic advisers.

Acting on its own initiative, the Federal Reserve, under the leadership of Paul Volcker, chose to pursue a monetarist strategy of draconian proportions. Money supply growth had been accelerated in the second half of 1980 to assist Jimmy Carter's reelection. In 1981 Volcker abruptly reversed direction to seek a drastic cure for inflation before the advent of a new electoral-economic cycle. The result was to drive up interest rates and restrict the available supply of credit. This strong dose of monetarist castor oil forced inflation down from an annual rate of over 10% in 1981 to 4% in 1982. But unemployment rose in the meantime towards a postwar peak of 10.7%. Worst hit were the industries that were directly sensitive to interest rate fluctuations, notably automobiles, farm machinery, and construction, and the supply industries that depended on their orders, particularly steel.

The recession made nonsense of the administration's fiscal calculations and its hope to balance the budget by the end of Reagan's first term. Instead of being reduced to the target figure of $45 billion, the deficit leaped to $128 billion in fiscal 1982 and rose again to $208 billion in the following year. Cyclical factors, namely increased outlays on unemployment benefits and related entitlement programs and the depressing impact of the recession on tax receipts, were primarily responsible for this. By mid-1983 the economy was on the mend, due mainly to the Federal Reserve's relaxation of monetary policy but also in part to the compensatory effect of the huge deficits operated by an administration that professed to have turned its back on Keynesianism. Yet the gap between budget outlays and receipts remained immense. The deficit fell to $185 billion in fiscal 1984, but rose again to $212 billion in fiscal 1985 and to $221 billion in fiscal 1986.

Reagan had indeed wrought a revolution in federal finances, though not the one he intended. The United States had only operated eight balanced budgets in the years from 1945 to 1981, but deficits had been relatively moderate and usually constituted less than 2% of Gross National Product (GNP). Moreover, every postwar administration — with the exception of Gerald Ford's — had been able to reduce the deficit during periods of economic recovery after recession, and the hypothetical full-employment budget had often been in surplus. Under Reagan the budget imbalance widened as the economy recovered from recession. As a result the country consistently operated what economists termed a "structural deficit", which annually averaged 4.5% of GNP from fiscal 1984 to 1988.

There were a number of reasons why economic recovery failed to bring the budget back onto the course plotted by the administration. The knock-on effect of the revenue miscalculations caused by the recession was immense. Revenue loss resulting from the 1981 tax cuts was also greater than the administration had anticipated because of amendments made to win congressional support for the measure, particularly the automatic cost-of-living adjustments that came into effect in fiscal 1985. The Office of Management and Budget estimated that the supply-side tax cuts had reduced federal receipts by $963 billion over the fiscal 1982–7 period; the Congressional Budget Office put the figure even higher at $1,041 billion.

Administration spending estimates proved to be very inaccurate too.

Congressional Democrats, particularly in the House of Representatives, fought doggedly to limit domestic expenditure reductions during the recession. Their party's strong showing in the 1982 midterm elections encouraged them to persist in the battle against retrenchment and caused many GOP congressmen to doubt the political wisdom of cutting back on programs that served important voter constituencies. As a result, domestic spending reductions were nowhere near adequate to counterbalance the expansion of the defense budget. Meanwhile, Reagan's first-term deficits sent the national debt ballooning from $914 billion in fiscal 1980 to $1.7 trillion in fiscal 1985 and to $2.6 trillion by fiscal 1988.

The spiraling budget deficit was directly linked to the growing trade deficit because of its impact on interest rates, capital flows, and currency exchange rates. In 1982 the United States was still the world's largest creditor nation; by 1986 it had become the world's largest debtor nation. America's low savings ratio prevented the budget deficit being financed entirely out of domestic resources. Accordingly the country became dependent on overseas investors to help fund its debt. Despite low inflation, interest rates had to be kept at a relatively high level for much of Reagan's presidency to attract foreign creditors. As a result there were huge inflows of capital from abroad in the 1980s, particularly from Japan and Western Europe. Net investment by foreigners in the United States amounted to only $95 billion between 1945 and 1980. During the Reagan era it totaled over $600 billion. This development was accompanied by increased international demand for US dollars, which consequently rose in value by some 80% against the basket of 11 major currencies between late 1979 and early 1985. The strong dollar made many US goods and services uncompetitive by pricing them out of both foreign and domestic markets. This produced a series of record trade deficits.

The American trade deficit, which stood at around $25 billion when Reagan entered office, had skyrocketed to $170 billion by 1986. Japanese banks and other foreign financial institutions were therefore able to buy US government securities with the profits made by their country's manufacturers in selling goods to the United States. There was a supreme irony in all this. As Benjamin Ginsberg and Martin Shafter noted, "Americans, in their capacity as voters, demonstrated in 1984 that they opposed increased taxation as a means of financing the federal government's expenditures, as consumers they willingly — indeed, enthusiastically — handed over billions of dollars that were used for this purpose when they purchased Japanese goods."

In 1985-6 administration officials became worried that the

combination of tight credit and a strong dollar posed a threat to sustained economic growth. The emergence of protectionist sentiment among Democratic congressmen representing the northern manufacturing areas worst hit by the inflow of cheap imports also caused concern. Accordingly, monetary policy was eased and the dollar was effectively devalued during Reagan's second term. The trade gap consequently narrowed in 1987–8. But the country was now vulnerable to a "dollar strike", a mass withdrawal of funds by foreigners if the value of their American investments was undermined by interest rate reductions and a further weakening of the dollar. To guard against this the Reagan administration negotiated the Louvre accord of 1987 with America's G-7 partners (the group of seven leading industrial nations) to stabilize their currencies and prevent the dollar going into free-fall in the international money markets. However the near-breakdown of this agreement heightened concern about the dollar and sparked off the Wall Street stock market crash of October 19, 1987, when $500 billion was wiped off the value of securities in a single day. Though investor confidence was quickly restored, the crash underlined the structural problems of the Reagan economy.

The only way to end the harmful binge of public borrowing was by restoring order to federal finances, a solution that proved beyond the capability of the Reagan administration. In 1982 some officials, like OMB director Dave Stockman and White House chief of staff James Baker, had recommended deferring the final tranches of supply-side tax cuts and the next round of defense increases in order to prevent the deficit getting out of control, but Reagan would not budge on these issues. Accordingly, the second budget which the administration sent to Congress, that for fiscal 1983, contained a Deficit Reduction Plan proposing expenditure cuts of $238 billion over the next three years, mainly in discretionary domestic programs. This had no chance of enactment and was nothing more than political posturing by Reagan. Instead of seeking a workable compromise, he continued to press the scheme after it had been summarily rejected by Congress. This was a strategy calculated to serve Reagan's political interests rather than to resolve the nation's fiscal problems. It enabled him to protect the sacred cows of Reaganomics and blame the legislature, particularly its Democratic members, for the budgetary consequences. In these circumstances the main responsibility for dealing with the deficit passed from the presidency to Congress.

The partisanship that characterized congressional action on the budget in 1981 quickly gave way to bipartisan cooperation in the face of the astronomical deficit. In 1982 the GOP-controlled Senate threatened to delay the second instalment of supply-side tax cuts to compel Reagan's acceptance of a budget package that included tax increases and cuts in both defense ($22 billion) and discretionary domestic program expenditures ($30 billion). The most significant outcome of this congressional initiative was the Tax Equity and Fiscal Responsibility Act of 1982, which increased some business taxes but left intact the supply-side cuts in personal taxation. These measures could not prevent the first $200 billion budget deficit in US history in fiscal 1983, but without them the imbalance would have exceeded $300 billion. Continuing to lead on the fiscal front, Congress raised energy taxes in 1983 and levied a further increase in business taxes in 1984. It also accepted a proposal put forward by a presidential commission to raise social security taxes in 1983.

In 1985 Congress produced what many hoped would be the definitive solution for the nation's fiscal problems. The so-called Gramm-Rudman-Hollings (G-R-H) plan was enacted with bipartisan support as the Balanced Budget and Emergency Deficit Control Act of 1985. This established a schedule for reducing the annual deficit by $36 billion in each budget from fiscal 1986 onward in order to achieve a balanced budget in fiscal 1991. Exceptions were only permitted in the event of war or recession. If the reductions were not made through the conventional budget process, the measure mandated automatic spending cuts drawn in relatively equal proportions from defense and domestic programs.

Initial optimism about G-R-H quickly gave way to disillusion. The administration and Congress did cooperate in bringing down the deficit to $155 billion by fiscal 1988, but this was well above the originally mandated target of $108 billion. The G-R-H timetable was torpedoed by the administration's tendency to make inflated revenue estimates on the basis of over-optimistic predictions of economic growth and by the willingness of Congress to connive in this practice. Everybody was thereby spared from having to make the expenditure reductions that were necessary. Partisan calculation also played a part. As the 1988 elections approached, both Democrats and Republicans showed little enthusiasm for politically risky retrenchment. In late 1987 congressmen reached an agreement that effectively removed budget issues from the legislative agenda until the election of a new administration.

Reaganomics bequeathed a visible legacy of failure in the shape of the budget and trade deficits, but even its successes had an illusory quality. The decline in the inflation rate was the most important economic achievement of the 1980s. Nevertheless it is worth keeping in mind that the 1983–8 average yearly inflation rate of 3.3% only looked impressive in comparison to the 1970s. This scale of inflation had been considered unacceptable in the twenty years following World War II. Moreover, the decline in inflation was due far more to the monetary policies of the Federal Reserve and the strong dollar than to the calculated effects of Reaganomics. Reagan was also fortunate in not having to cope with the kind of supply shocks that had affected vital sectors of the economy in the 1970s. Owing to the existence of an international oil glut from 1982 onwards, the Organization of Petroleum Exporting Countries was compelled to behave in a more restrained fashion than in the past. Low food and commodity prices on the international market similarly helped to reduce US inflation.

There is no evidence to suggest that the 1981 tax cuts performed the economic miracles that Reagan and the supply-siders had predicted. The economy enjoyed a boom in the mid-1980s but the overall US growth rate from 1981 to 1988 was virtually the same as the average rate for OECD (Organization of Economic Cooperation and Development) countries. The picture was somewhat bleaker when the cyclical effects of recession and recovery were factored out. Labor productivity growth improved in comparison with the abysmal trends of the late 1970s but only averaged 1.4% in the 1980s. Supply-side tax cuts were also intended to boost savings and investment ahead of consumption. In fact the net savings rate in relation to personal disposable income fell from 7.8% in 1979 to 2% in 1987. Business-fixed investment did grow significantly in the mid-1980s but this was from a very low base in the 1981–2 recession. The real improvement was no greater than in previous cyclical upswings, and the strongest gains occurred in industries that were not major beneficiaries of ERTA incentives, notably computers and motor vehicles. Moreover, the investment boom, such as it was, proved short-lasting and slacked off during Reagan's second term.

A case can be made that Reaganomics actually impaired productivity in some respects. The proportion of GNP devoted to the military went up from around 5% to 6.5% in the Reagan era. No other G-7 nation came close to matching this. Japan spent about 1% of its GNP on arms and West Germany less than 4%. The US defense build-up of the 1980s engaged about 30% of the country's scientific personnel into military-related research and development that had no significant spinoffs for civilian technology. As economist Robert Lekachman observed, Reagan's militarism "siphons off to the least efficient sector of the economy talented scientists, engineers and technicians who in luckier Japan improve efficiency and quality in industries which, in world markets, have demonstrated their capacity to defeat American rivals."

An even more harmful consequence of Reaganomics was what some analysts labeled the "third deficit" — the growing deficiency of the services financed by public capital. In 1989, 327 economists, including six Nobel laureates, signed a letter to Congress warning that current living standards could not be maintained without an expansion of public capital. The infrastructure of the economy was badly weakened by Reagan's domestic expenditure cutbacks, particularly those affecting discretionary programs and grants to state and local government. By 1990 the United States was spending (in constant dollar terms) less than half what it spent in the 1960s on roads, other transport facilities, and water and sewage systems. According to the Department of Transportation, the wretched condition of the nation's highways imposed a burden of 722 million hours of vehicle delay in 1985 and a huge toll in wasted gas; by 2005 the loss will have risen to 3.9 billion hours unless corrective action were undertaken. Investment in new buildings and equipment as well as in new social programs was also needed to deal with a failing school system, rundown inner cities, and violent drug-filled ghettoes. Dire as these social problems were in human terms, they also blighted economic productivity by preventing individuals from maximizing their talents and fulfilling their potential.

Reaganomics also skewed its benefits to the better-off groups in society in the belief that this was the most efficient means of boosting investment and production to generate jobs and prosperity for all Americans. "A rising tide lifts all boats" was one of Reagan's favorite maxims. In this sense Reaganomics had much in common with the "trickle-down" economics practised by Calvin Coolidge's administration. The strategy worked no better in the 1980s than in the 1920s. There was an unprecedented shift towards income inequality during the Reagan years. Per capita income rose at an annual average of about 1.7% in the 1980s (compared with nearly 3% between 1948 to 1973), but the actual distribution of income gain was very narrow. Between 1977 and 1988 the average income of the top decile (tenth) of American families went up by 16% in real terms. The next highest decile registered a gain of 1%. The other eight deciles all experienced a fall in average income. The lowest decile came off worst with an average decline of 14.8%, followed by the second lowest decile with 8%. In terms of the distribution of family income, the highest quintile (fifth) saw its share of national income go up from 41.6% in 1980 to 44% in 1988, but every other quintile registered a loss.

Reaganomics failed to resolve the underlying causes of the maldistribution of wealth in US society. The decline in industrial jobs progressed throughout the 1980s, thanks to the intimate connexion between the trade deficit and the budget deficit and to the slow advancement of productivity. Meanwhile American corporations increasingly shifted their routine manufacturing operations into low-wage third world countries. By 1990 manufacturing occupied 17.3% of the nonagricultural labor force, compared with 22.4% a decade earlier (and 31% in 1960). Displaced workers and new entrants into the job market were consequently thrust into lower-paying jobs in the service sector. According to a Senate Budget Committee report, 50.4% of the nearly 15 million new jobs created between 1979 and 1987 paid an annual wage beneath the poverty level ($11,610 in 1987), compared to 37.7% that paid "middle" level wages ($11,611 to $49,443) and 11.9% that paid high wages (above $46,444). Many of the new jobs in the service sector were in the retail trade, where the weekly wage averaged 44% of weekly earnings in manufacturing in 1989 (compared with 69% in 1950).

Previous administrations had been unable to resolve these problems, of course, but Reagan's policies made them worse. The tax structure put in place in the 1980s had a regressive effect on income inequality. While the supply-side tax cuts disproportionately benefited higher income groups, the social security tax increase of 1983 dented workers' incomes. Taxpayers in the top income decile experienced an average decline of 6.4% in their effective federal tax rate (the composite of all federal taxes) between 1977 and 1988, while those in the lowest income decile suffered a 20% increase. Meanwhile, cutbacks in social program expenditure by the Reagan administration contributed to the reversal of a two-decade long decline of poverty. In 1987 13.6% of Americans were poor, compared with 11.8% a decade earlier. Even more shocking was the rise of the "hyper-poor", who had to survive on cash income amounting to less than half the official poverty level. By 1989 one of every twenty Americans, that is 12 million people (35% of them black, 61% of them members of female-headed families, and 41% of them children), fell into this category. This represented a 45% increase since 1979.

The merits of Reaganomics remain the subject of dispute. According to Martin Anderson, chronicler of the Reagan Revolution, "It was the greatest economic expansion in American history. Wealth poured from the factories of the United States, and Americans got richer and richer. During the five years from November 1982 to November 1987 more wealth and services were produced than in any like period in history. . . . By then we were producing 65 percent a year more than when Jimmy Carter left office in January 1981. The US economy is now an economic colossus of such size and scope that we have no effective way to describe its power and reach." By contrast Keynesian economist James Tobin complained, "The awful truth is that Reaganomics was a fraud from the beginning. The moral of its failures and of its legacies is that a nation pays a heavy price when it entrusts its government and economy to simplistic ideologues." The evidence suggests that this pessimistic assessment is closer to the truth. The conservative elixir may have helped to reduce inflation but it left the structural foundations of the American economy in a weakened condition. Although Reagan left office proclaiming that his economic mission had been accomplished, many Americans would soon have cause to believe that Reaganomics had been a siren song.

Reducing the colossus of government

Intimately linked with the tax-cutting agenda of Reaganomics was a determined effort to reduce the scope and size of the federal government. One of the core elements of conservative doctrine in the 1980s was the conviction that the public sector economy had to be reduced and the free market enhanced. Reagan's need to make budget savings to compensate for his defense increases also ensured that domestic programs would feel the swing of his axe. His administration's efforts to reduce government focused on three areas: the welfare state; federal-state responsibilities; and deregulation. Though its actions hardly added up to a revolution, they constituted the most significant reversal of the role of government in US society since the advent of the New Deal.

According to Richard Polenberg, the Reagan administration was intent on turning "the welfare state clock back, not to 1929 or even 1939, but to 1959". The social insurance programs that were descended from the New Deal did not face the kind of assault launched against the public assistance programs that had mushroomed in the 1960s. There were obvious reasons for this. Conservatives had fewer ideological reservations about the contributory social programs than about welfare, which they associated with waste, dependency, and laziness. Social security also benefited client groups who packed a big electoral punch. Senior citizens made up just over one tenth of the population but they constituted a third of regular voters in congressional elections. Welfare, by contrast, served politically weak and incohate constituencies, notably members of female-headed families and impoverished minorities. Federal obligation to maintain the social insurance programs, including cost-of-living adjustments (COLAs), was prescribed by law. On the other hand the Reagan administration had greater scope to reduce the public assistance programs by means of discretionary budget cuts and administrative changes, such as lowering benefit levels and tightening eligibility criteria.

The political obstacles to social security reduction soon became apparent. Reagan entered office at a time when this program was facing a financial crisis. Thanks to increased life expectancy, the number of beneficiaries was increasing without a corresponding increase in contributors, and the real value of incoming revenues had been hard hit by inflation. Heritage Foundation scholars and free-marketeers like Milton Friedman called for radical surgery to put social security on an actuarially sound basis by scaling back payouts and making participation voluntary. Reagan's introduction of a benefit reduction package in May 1981 suggested that he intended to proceed with fundamental reform of the program, but this initiative was unanimously rejected by a vote of 96–0 in the Republican-controlled Senate. A bipartisan compromise was eventually worked out in 1983 to increase social security taxes, delay the next-scheduled COLA, and gradually raise the retirement age from the current 65 to 67 early in the twenty-first century. As a result of these relatively modest changes, the social security fund was running a healthy annual surplus of $20 billion by 1987. The program was evidently secure in the long term against right-wing assault by the time that Reagan left office.

In contrast, the means-tested public assistance programs took heavy cuts in Reagan's first budget. Some of these reductions were partially reversed in the recession budget that followed, but overall spending on welfare was lower in real terms when Reagan left office than it had been in 1980. It became more difficult to qualify for welfare because of eligibility changes imposed in the Omnibus Budget and Reconciliation Act (OBRA) of 1981. This measure also marked a significant shift in federal welfare policy by empowering states to introduce discretionary work requirements in return for distributing benefits. By 1987

42 states operated some form of work-welfare programs, though most of these were work-incentive and job-search schemes. This development was consolidated by the Family Support Act of 1988, commonly regarded as the most important welfare reform since the Social Security Act of 1935.

Support for work-welfare, or "workfare", formed the basis of a new welfare consensus in the 1980s. Reagan-era conservatives deemed it the only solution to the problem of welfare dependency. This viewpoint was expressed most influentially by Charles Murray's book *Losing Ground*, a trenchant critique of the liberal social policies of the 1960s. For Murray, the Great Society's sins were manifold: it had broken down the psychological barriers that kept people off welfare rolls; it had made welfare a right that could not be rescinded for bad behavior; it had made unemployment more profitable for the ghetto poor than work; and its educational programs had failed to instill middle-class values in the young black poor. Above all, Murray blamed welfare for the rising tide of illegitimacy, one of the prime causes of black poverty. By 1980 one out of every three black children was born to a teenage mother, 57% of all black births took place outside marriage (compared with 25% in 1965), and 47% of all black families were female-headed (the 1965 figure was also 25%). Murray divined a causal relationship between these statistics and the welfare expansion of the 1960s. He accused the Great Society of transforming AFDC, which the New Deal had created to aid worthy widows, into a program that enabled irresponsible teenagers to bear illegitimate children at the taxpayers' expense.

Few Democrats accepted Murray's thesis, but many recognized welfare dependency as a problem and called for a new approach to poverty. Whereas unreconstructed liberals like Governor Mario Cuomo of New York and Jesse Jackson continued to speak of compassion as the basic principle of welfare policy, others in the party voiced support for notions of civic liberalism. Originally associated with neoconservatives like Lawrence Mead, this idea gained credence with neoliberals and with moderate Democrats within the Democratic Leadership Council. Civic liberalism perceived an obligation on the part of the poor to take some responsibility for self-improvement in terms of work and family obligations. Its advocates regarded workfare as a means to provide welfare recipients with work or training skills to facilitate their transition into full-time employment in the expanding labor market of the 1980s. This contrasted with the Reagan administration's rationale that workfare would discourage people from seeking welfare.

The state workfare programs constituted the genesis of federal welfare reform. In 1987 the National Governors Association executive committee, chaired by Governor Bill Clinton of Arkansas, issued a major policy report entitled "Job-Oriented Welfare Reform". Many of its recommendations were incorporated into a workfare bill devised by Senator Patrick Moynihan, the New York Democrat who had attempted to replace AFDC with the Family Assistance Plan some twenty years earlier as President Richard Nixon's domestic policy adviser. This measure, which became the Family Support Act, attempted to strike a balance between security and incentives for the poor. It required adult welfare recipients, whether members of two-parent families or single mothers with children aged three or more, to seek self-sufficiency or lose their benefits. In return, the federal government would fund comprehensive educational and training programs by the states, job placements, and transitional child care and medical assistance benefits until welfare recipients were self-sufficient. It would also compel absent fathers to support children by having payments deducted from their paychecks or benefits.

This legislation had widespread Republican support for several reasons. It upheld the values of family, individual responsibility, and work; it relied on the creative energies of the states rather than the federal government to uplift the poor; and it consolidated the diverse work-welfare practices that currently existed in most states. Democrats, meanwhile, approved of the training, child care, and healthcare provisions, though they were divided over the issue of whether participation in the workfare programs should be mandatory. Nevertheless the passage of the bill marked a new direction in public welfare policy to resist passive poverty and require the nonworking poor to uphold mainstream values of individual responsibility and endeavor. According to political scientist Gillian Peele, the Family Support Act reflected a "conservative view of the conditions under which welfare should be given and . . . a conception of citizenship that was based on the idea of the obligations of citizenship rather than its rights".

Welfare reform partially compensated Reagan for the earlier failure of the most radical element of his proposals to restructure American federalism. He came to office determined to devolve certain federal responsibilities to the states, particularly welfare, and to make the states use their own resources to fund these. Reagan's purpose was twofold: to bring government closer to the people and reduce domestic federal expenditure. In 1981 the administration created two advisory bodies, the Presidential Advisory Committee on Federalism and the Coordinating Task Force on Federalism, both chaired by Senator Paul Laxalt. These were responsible for devising a blueprint for the "new federalism", a rearrangement of intergovernmental functions and finances. Had Reagan succeeded in implementing this, the effect would have been to reduce federal involvement in domestic policy to what it had been before the 1960s and even to pre-New Deal levels in some aspects of welfare provision.

In 1982 Reagan unveiled an ambitious plan to swap welfare responsibilities between the federal and state governments in programs that both currently cooperated in funding. He recommended that the states should assume full responsibility for food stamps and AFDC within the next ten years and in turn hand over complete control of Medicaid to national government. This proposal got nowhere because it was seen as an abdication of vital federal responsibility. Congressional Democrats and many Republicans feared that some states, particularly the poorer ones and those in the conservative Sunbelt, would simply allow the welfare programs to wither away. The National Governors Association and local government organizations also voiced opposition. They doubted the capacity of the states to undertake complete funding of food stamps and AFDC without politically unpopular increases in state taxes.

Reagan was more successful in other aspects of his program. Thanks mainly to the budget cuts achieved during his first two years in office, federal grants-in-aid to the states fell by 25% and federal monies declined as a proportion of state revenues by 22% between 1978 and 1988. The Omnibus Budget and Reconciliation Act of 1981 terminated sixty federal grants-in-aid programs and reduced funding for others. More significantly, it consolidated 77 categorical grant programs into nine block grant programs, primarily in the areas of public health, education, social services, community development, and vocational training. This merger gave the states far more discretion as to how they would spend federal aid than was the case with categorical grants, but it also enabled the Reagan administration to make substantial reductions (often by as much as 25%) in federal assistance. However the block grant program only represented about one-fifth of federal grants-in-aid. Following the 1982 midterm elections, Congress dug its heels in to resist further significant consolidation. The main success of the new federalism after its halcyon days of 1981–2 was the termination in 1986 of Richard Nixon's revenue-sharing program, which had never been popular with Congress.

Reagan's new federalism had important consequences in spite of its legislative setbacks. Federal aid to the states declined dramatically from $117 billion in fiscal 1981, Carter's last year in office, to $101.7 billion in fiscal 1982. Although it registered slow but steady growth once more from fiscal 1983 onwards, outlays had only risen to around $110 billion by fiscal 1988. In other words Reagan succeeded in halting the incremental growth in federal aid to the states that had persisted since the early 1960s. Reduced federal involvement in domestic policy also hindered progress towards achieving uniform national standards for public services.

The federal retreat compelled new activism by many states. The 1985 report of the US Advisory Commission on Intergovernmental Relations noted that state governments, so long in the shadow of Washington, had become "transformed in every facet of their structure and operations". Many states tried to replace lost grant revenues by raising state taxes and some sought to renew programs axed by Reagan. However, the depressing impact of economic recession on tax revenues curtailed state activism in the early 1990s. In 1991, 39 of the 50 states had to freeze or reduce welfare payments, and many states had to make cuts in basic services. This experience suggests that the states are bound to encounter difficulties in maintaining stable provision of programs and services so long as they are denied the level of federal support that existed in the 1960s and 1970s.

In addition to reducing the welfare state and restoring governmental responsibility to the states, the Reagan administration was intent on rolling back the regulatory state. In many senses the significance of deregulation for the Reagan Revolution was comparable with that of privatisation for Thatcherism in Britain. In the free-market credo of the Reagan era, federal regulations were a drag on the productivity and competitivess of the American economy, were costly for government to administer, and pushed up prices for goods and services (costing consumers $103 billion or $500 per person in 1979, according to CEA chairman Murray Weidenbaum). The Reagan administration sought to speed up the momentum of economic deregulation initiated by Carter and to extend the deregulatory process into the social sphere.

The relaxation of antitrust enforcement constituted the most significant advance in economic deregulation in the 1980s. Corporate mergers and monopolies, once regarded as a threat to free competition and consumer rights, were now seen as an often necessary development to strengthen the market power of American firms in the highly technological and increasingly internationalized modern economy. The new policy was signaled by the administration's decision in 1982 to drop a thirteen-year pending lawsuit against IBM. In 1983 the Federal Trade Commission approved a joint marketing and production venture between the world largest and third largest automobile manufacturers (General Motors and Toyota), and in the following year the Justice Department's Antitrust Division approved the merger of the third and fourth largest American steel companies (Republic and LTV). Almost the only major exception to this trend was the decision to break up the Bell Telephone monopoly on telecommunications, which was taken in order to encourage the entry of other firms into a business sphere essential for national economic growth.

The Reagan administration advanced the process of deregulation started by Carter in the domestic aviation, railroad, energy, and financial services industries, and itself initiated deregulation in some areas, notably intercity busing, television and radio broadcasting, and computer-based services. Nevertheless, the trend of deregulation slowed during the second term. One of the particular targets of the free-marketeers was repeal of the Glass-Steagall Banking Act of 1933, which required the separation of commercial and investment banking to prevent speculative abuses and extended Federal Reserve regulatory power over credit. However the stock market crash of October 1987 undermined the case for rescinding this legislation. Signs that the savings-and-loans industry was in deep trouble also strengthened doubts about the wisdom of further deregulation of financial services.

Another of Reagan's aims was to reverse the process of social regulation initiated by Nixon and strengthened by Carter. The Occupational Safety and Health Administration's (OSHA) powers were significantly curtailed. Its field inspectors were now required to act more as "consultants" than "cops" in an effort to boost cooperation between the agency and business. Meanwhile, overall cuts of some 50% in the Environmental Protection Agency's (EPA) budget served to weaken its regulatory capability. Reagan also appointed personnel to top regulatory positions who were unsympathetic to the goals of regulation. OSHA's new chief was Thomas Auchter, president of a Florida construction company that had amassed forty-eight OSHA violations since 1972. Appointees in the environmental field were unabashed free-marketeers. Secretary of the Interior James Watt, whose department was responsible for the nation's natural resources, likened environmentalists to Nazis in one public statement, and declared that his objective was to to "mine more, drill more, cut more timber, to use our resources rather than keep them locked up". One of his first actions was to open up sections of coastal waters to rapid exploitation of oil and natural gas. Similarly, EPA chief Anne Gorusch Burford delayed implementing a ground-water protection program and weakened enforcement of the Clean Air Act.

In spite of these developments, social deregulation lost momentum by the end of Reagan's first term. The controversial Watt and Gorusch generated a backlash against their policies. Both were forced to resign office in 1983, the former for ill-judged public remarks and the latter for mishandling the superfund for cleaning up toxic waste. Meanwhile, congressional supporters of social regulation in both parties rallied to prevent the Reagan administration from making a single significant change in existing legislation dealing with either occupational safety or environmental control. Indeed, by the end of Reagan's presidency the tide appeared to be turning in favor of re-regulation. This was particularly the case regarding environmental protection, which became an important issue in the 1988 election. President George Bush responded to the concern felt by many Americans that deregulation had harmed the environment by appointing William Reilly, who was strongly linked with conservationist groups, as EPA director.

On balance the Reagan administration was more successful in halting the incremental expansion of government rather than in reducing the size of government. In itself this was a significant achievement in view of the political trends that had held sway during the previous half-century. Nonetheless, Reagan's record did not live up to his promises. With regard to social welfare, federal-state relations, and deregulation, early progress towards conservative objectives was quickly followed by loss of momentum. The only significant achievement in any of these three fields during the second term was the enactment of the Family Support Act, which was not an administration initiative. After initial retrenchment, spending on welfare provision and grants-in-aid to the states began to creep upward once again. Despite the relaxation of regulatory requirements, relatively few regulations were rescinded and the actual number of federal rules was greater at the end of the Reagan presidency than at the beginning.

Race and gender issues

The Reagan Revolution also challenged the social legacy of the 1960s. Its main targets were affirmative action and abortion rights. As a result race and gender issues had a central role in the political controversies of the 1980s.

Racial-preference affirmative action was already under strong attack from conservatives by the time Reagan became president. Critics charged that the program had been expanded far beyond its original scope by administrative fiat and judicial decisions and now made whites victims of "reverse discrimination". In essence they complained that the aim of anti-discrimination policy had changed from equality of opportunity (the idea that each person is guaranteed the same chance to get ahead in life) to equality of result (the concept that government must ensure that socio-economic equality is actually achieved). The 1971 Supreme Court decision, *Griggs* v. *Duke's Power Company*, which adopted disparate impact analysis as a means of determining discrimination, was a particular source of grievance. This judgement was seen as legitimizing the use of numerical goals or quotas to ensure racial balance in an employer's work force or a university's student body without regard for individual merit. To conservatives, such practices not only were unfair to many whites but also hurt American business at a time of serious competitive pressures from abroad. A quota-oriented workforce, they claimed, was not as productive as one selected on ability, and the resultant effects on job growth harmed US workers of all races. In this respect the attack on quotas was part of the conservative critique of the regulatory state.

Dispute also raged over the economic benefits of affirmative action for black Americans. Supporters of the program emphasized that it had increased minority access to jobs, while critics charged that it had done little to improve average minority earnings. There was evidence to support both sides. While the percentage of black males employed in professional and managerial positions doubled between 1965 and 1980, the gap between the average income of black and white males did not close any faster during this period than in the 1945–65 period. Research suggested that affirmative action mainly benefited blacks and other non-whites who had already achieved a high level of education and training but had little impact on unskilled blacks trapped in the underclass. The result was a growing disparity in income within the black community itself. Between 1969 and 1984 there were marked increases in the proportion of black males earning over $30,000 a year and those earning less than $10,000 (measured in constant 1984 dollars).

Critics of affirmative action found a ready champion in Ronald Reagan, who was determined to change the racial-preference policies pursued by the federal government since the late 1960s. In the 1980 election campaign he had avowed: "We must not allow the noble concept of equal opportunity to be distorted into federal guidelines or quotas which require race, ethnicity or sex — rather than ability and qualifications — to be the principal factor in hiring or education." Reagan's first line of attack was through the budget. In 1981–2 affirmative action agencies suffered heavy funding reductions, which inevitably limited their operations. For example, the Office of Federal Contract Compliance Programs budget was cut by one-third and its enforcement staff reduced by a half. But Reagan had limited success in actually changing affirmative action policy, partly because the courts continued to uphold its legitimacy and partly because support for the program was deeply entrenched in sections of the federal bureaucracy. The fact that big business did not press for change was also significant. Affirmative action practices had become part of the corporate culture. In 1984, 88% of the 197 firms that responded to a Fortune 500 survey indicated that they would maintain these even if not legally required to do so.

The Justice Department spearheaded the Reaganite drive against affirmative action. Its civil rights division narrowed its agenda to deal only with specific victims of past discrimination and withdrew support for the use of quotas or any numerical formulas designed, in the words of Assistant Attorney-General William Bradford Reynolds, "to provide to non-victims of discrimination preferential treatment based on race, sex, national origin or religion". Departmental briefs and oral arguments sought to persuade the courts to reject racial-preference programs. This strategy met with little success, but every opportunity was taken to interpret the few judicial rulings unfavorable to affirmative action in the widest possible manner. The most notable example involved the 1984 Supreme Court decision, *Firefighters Local Union No. 1794* v. *Stoots.* This adjudged that Title VII of the 1964 Civil Rights Act did not legitimize an affirmative action promotion plan which set aside the job seniority of white male workers in order to remedy past patterns of discrimination. Though this ruling was couched in narrow terms specific to the case at issue, Reynolds argued that it enabled lower courts to withdraw support for racial-preference programs of any kind.

No federal judge accepted this interpretation, but the Justice Department continued to press its views.

Other federal agencies did not join in the attack on affirmative action to the same extent. To the disappointment of civil rights groups, the Equal Employment Opportunities Commission (EEOC) changed its focus from class action enforcement, involving large numbers of racial groups in single discrimination suits, to discrimination suits filed by individuals. However, EEOC chief Clarence Thomas, a black conservative, was critical of Justice Department efforts to eliminate quotas. He regarded the use of numerical data as a useful standard for assuring compliance with Title VII and succeeded in improving the use of statistics to monitor the federal government's own record in hiring and promoting minorities. The United States Employment Service of the Department of Labor took a similar line in administering the General Aptitude Test Battery, which state employment agencies use as a skills test to screen some twenty million job applicants annually before referring them to private employers. It also endorsed the practice of race-norming as a reliable predictor of job performance. This allowed adjustment of test scores on the basis of race, so that blacks and Hispanics could be scaled up to compensate for the fact that they generally scored lower than whites and Asian-Americans.

The most serious intra-administration dispute over affirmative action ended in defeat for its critics. In 1985 Attorney-General Edwin Meese attempted to persuade Reagan to rewrite the executive order issued twenty years earlier by Lyndon Johnson to combat job discrimination by federal contractors. A strong counter-attack was mounted by Secretary of Labor William E. Brock. Civil rights lobbyists were also up in arms, and a large number of congressmen from both parties, including the majority of senators, signaled their opposition. The Justice Department eventually backed off and the order was never rewritten. Affirmative action received a further boost from the Supreme Court. Justice Department hopes that the *Stoots* decision of 1984 signaled a judicial assault on racial-preference programs were doomed to disappointment. In its 1986 decision, *Local 28 Sheet Metal Workers* v. *EEOC*, the Supreme Court upheld a district court remedial order under Title VII for the first time. This was followed in 1987 by *Johnson* v. *Transportation Agency Santa Clara County*, which upheld a voluntary affirmative action plan against charges of reverse discrimination and ruled that racial and gender preferences were legitimate if intended to overcome under-representation rather than remedy past discrimination.

The limited success of Reagan's assault on affirmative action was also good news for some women. The program had been instrumental in increasing job access for women but, as was the case regarding minorities, the main beneficiaries were educated, middle-class women working in professional and managerial fields. By 1981, women constituted 38.5% of accountants, 37% of bank officials, and 35% of college teachers, compared with 25%, 17.5%, and 28% respectively in 1970. By contrast, gains were slight in craft and skilled work, where men continued to hold very disproportionate shares of the better-paid jobs. The Equal Rights Amendment (ERA), which might have produced significant improvements for women in blue-collar occupations, was still three states short of approval when the time allowed for ratification ran out on July 1, 1982.

The defeat of the ERA encouraged conservative hopes of a successful challenge against abortion rights. Reagan's early expressions of support for legislative efforts to criminalize abortion and for a proposed constitutional amendment to ban it were largely symbolic and ineffective. From 1983 onwards, however, the Justice Department stepped up efforts to reverse judicial precedent regarding abortion. It made little impression on the Supreme Court, which reaffirmed the right of abortion in two important judgements, *Akron* v. *Akron Center for Reproductive Health* (1983) and *Thornburgh* v. *American College of Obstetricians and Gynecologists* (1986).

But supporters of abortion and affirmative action could not afford to be complacent about the continuation of judicial support. By the time Reagan left office 344 out of the total of 712 district court and Appeals Court judges were his appointees. No president had previously nominated so many judges, and only Franklin D. Roosevelt had nominated a higher proportion. Even more significantly, the Supreme Court's political complexion had changed as a result of three conservative appointments that Reagan made in his second term. The retirement of Warren Burger in 1986 opened the way for the promotion of William Rehnquist to Chief Justice. Thirty-three senators, all but two of them Democrats, voted against his appointment on the grounds that he was too extreme. This was the largest vote hitherto cast against a Supreme Court nominee who won confirmation. In 1987 the Democrats, now the majority party, were able to defeat the nomination of Robert W. Bork, an archconservative who questioned the constitutionality of abortion and affirmative action. But two other conservatives, Antonin Scalia and Anthony Kennedy, who prudently avoided confrontation in their confirmation hearings, were routinely approved. As a result Reagan bequeathed his successor a Supreme Court containing a clearcut conservative majority for the first time since the 1930s.

Reagan and the world

Fiscal and economic issues were Reagan's dominant concerns during the first two years of his administration. International affairs rose in priority from early 1983 onwards. The Reagan Revolution in foreign policy had two basic aims: peace through strength and the roll-back of communism in the Third World. By the time he left office Reagan was far closer to fulfilling these aims than his domestic objectives.

The peace-through-strength approach to foreign policy established in 1981 was sustained throughout Reagan's first term. Alongside the huge build-up of American military power, Reagan continued to dangle the prospect of arms reduction before the Soviet leaders. In 1982 he followed up his "zero option" proposal to remove all intermediate nuclear weapons from Europe with a call for both powers to make drastic cuts in their strategic weapons arsenals. Reagan did not expect serious negotiations on either proposal until the Soviets were cowed by the size of America's military expansion. Of more immediate significance was his promise, made in 1983, to abide by the terms of the unratified SALT II treaty so long as the Soviets showed equal restraint. However these overtures were overshadowed by Reagan's surprise announcement in a televised address in March 1983 about plans to develop the Strategic Defense Initiative (SDI). This was to be a space-based defensive shield providing the United States with high-tech protection against missile attack. Dubbed Star Wars by its critics, SDI had an estimated cost of $1 trillion, making it the most expensive weapons development program in history, and would take until the end of the century to develop.

The SDI proposal, devised in secret by a small group of presidential advisers, embodied Reagan's concern to restore America's security to the level enjoyed in the 1940s, before the Soviets had possessed nuclear weaponry. It provoked furore at home and abroad. The Democrats questioned its cost and practicality. They also charged that it would destroy progress towards arms reduction, since the Soviets were thought unlikely to give up any of their missiles if SDI threatened the effectiveness of those that remained. Architects of Cold War policy in previous Democratic administrations, such as George Kennan and

Robert McNamara, warned that the proposal would spark off a new arms race because it undermined the balance of terror on which current arms policy was based. Meanwhile, NATO allies expressed concern that SDI could not protect Western Europe and might fuel a new wave of American isolationism in the future because it afforded security against outside attack. SDI also did much to sour superpower relations in the mid 1980s. The Kremlin was aghast that its recently won status of nuclear parity in offensive weaponry would soon be endangered by the increased defensive capability that SDI would give the United States. Soviet leader Yuri Andropov warned, "Engaging in this is not just irresponsible, it is insane. . . . Washington's actions are putting the entire world in jeopardy."

Reagan's activism in the Third World also encountered problems. El Salvador provided a test case of his determination to support authoritarian regimes against left-wing uprisings. US military economic aid to the Salvadorean government, which stood at $9.5 million in 1979, was stepped up on condition that democratic elections were held. However American officials had to nullify the results of the 1982 elections because of the activities of right-wing military factions and the "death squads" allied with them. American aid flowed more freely after the US-supervised 1984 elections resulted in the victory of an acceptable conservative, José Napoleón Duarte, and rose to $578 million in 1986. This was not enough to put down the rebellion. By 1988 Duarte had lost control of large parts of the country, and land reform, which might have won popular support for his regime, had effectively failed because so many officials and peasants who attempted to carry it out had been killed by right-wing death squads.

The ideological rationale of Reagan's support for undemocratic right-wing regimes, namely Jeane Kirkpatrick's distinction between authoritarian and totalitarian regimes, proved to be unworkable. It tied the United States to repressive governments that lacked popular support. Nowhere was this better demonstrated than in the cases of the Marcos regime in the Philippines and the Duvalier regime in Haiti. Reagan attempted to shore up both governments, but eventually abandoned them after the State Department advised that US interests in these countries would be better served by the development of more representative and stable regimes. In the meantime he showed himself willing to do business with totalitarian regimes. Practical superpower politics required the United States to maintain good relations with the People's Republic of China. In 1981 Beijing warned that it would downgrade those relations if the Reagan administration went ahead with its proposed sale of the FX fighter plane to Taiwan. Not only was the sale canceled, but the United States also announced that it would gradually reduce all arms sales to Taiwan.

Reagan showed greater consistency in supporting rebel groups — freedom fighters as the Reagan Doctrine designated them — who were attempting to overthrow pro-Soviet regimes in the Third World. Under its new director William Casey, the Central Intelligence Agency (CIA) was given wide latitude to channel money, guns and supplies to insurgent forces in Afghanistan, Angola, Cambodia, Chad, Ethiopia, Nicaragua, and Sudan. The most disappointing outcome was in Angola, where civil war had raged since 1975 between the Marxist regime and the pro-western forces of Jonas Savimbi. In 1985 Reagan finally persuaded Congress to lift the Clark amendment prohibiting US involvement in the conflict, but the Angolan government strengthened its domestic position by cooperating with western oil companies and welcoming western investment. Meanwhile, popular support for Savimbi remained low because his main source of aid was the white South African government.

American policy enjoyed far greater success in Afghanistan. Through the gateway of Pakistan, the CIA provided the mujahedeen Muslim guerillas fighting the Soviet-backed regime in Kabul with huge quantities of weapons. US aid rose steadily in the early 1980s, doubled to $400 million in 1985, and exceeded $500 million the following year. From 1986 onwards it included a shoulder-fired anti-helicopter missile known as the Stinger, which proved remarkably effective in mujahedeen hands and probably played a critical part in the eventual Soviet decision to quit Afghanistan in 1988.

The resumption of the global struggle against communism also required the United States to demonstrate that it had rid itself of the so-called Vietnam syndrome, the fear of military involvement abroad. This provoked some dissension within the administration. The armed services chiefs were leery of involvement in another unpopular war that might breed anti-military resentments at home. Accordingly, Secretary of Defense Caspar Weinberger insisted that the use of force should be the last resort. But Reagan sided with his Secretary of State George Shultz, an advocate of selective military interventionism. The president declared: "Military force, either direct or indirect, must remain an available part of America's foreign policy . . . we will not return to the days of defeatism, decline, and despair."

The administration's first military venture was the despatch of US marines as part of an international peace-keeping force to war-torn Lebanon in 1982. This only served to increase the problems of the troubled Middle East. Their mission ill-defined, US forces were sucked into the local conflict and increasingly appeared to side with the Christian Lebanese, backed by Israel, against the Muslim Lebanese and the Palestine Liberation Organization, backed by Syria. Disaster overtook them in October 1983, when a suicide bomb attack demolished a marine barracks and killed 241 servicemen. Reagan proclaimed that America's global credibility required him to keep US forces in Lebanon, but they were withdrawn a few months later having signally failed in their impossible task of bringing peace to the country. In reality Reagan had suffered a defeat in Lebanon as great as Carter had experienced in Iran. This failure did not harm him at home because it was overshadowed by a military success elsewhere. In October 1983 the United States invaded the tiny Caribbean island of Grenada in order to overthrow an apparently pro-Cuban regime that had recently seized power through a coup and to rescue resident American students who were thought to be in danger from it.

There were no further military actions until Reagan's second term. In 1986 US planes bombed Libya in retaliation for its alleged support for recent terrorist attacks on American citizens. Early the following year the United States began a protracted naval action to protect the movement of Kuwaiti oil tankers in the Persian Gulf. This was prompted by concern that Iran, which had been at war with Iraq since 1980, might retaliate against Kuwait for giving financial aid to its enemy. Once involved in the conflict, the United States experienced difficulty in limiting the scope of its intervention. There were clashes between American and Iranian forces, and Iran stepped up missile and mine attacks on Gulf shipping. In response Reagan extended US protection to all neutral vessels in mid 1988.

On balance it can be argued that Reagan's military actions produced limited benefits. Only Grenada was an unqualified success. Lebanon was a disaster. The Libyan bombing did not stop terrorism, and Syria was later found to have been behind the atrocities that provoked the raid. The Gulf naval intervention took longer than anyone estimated and eventually involved 41 US warships, at a cost of over $10 million a day, instead of the nine vessels originally planned. Moreover, many critics charged that the seaway would have remained open to Kuwaiti and other neutral ships without this US commitment, since Iran had never actually threatened to close it and lacked the naval strength to do so.

In the 1984 election the president used Grenada as a metaphor for his campaign theme that America had regained its vigor and confidence under his leadership. Nevertheless his landslide victory owed far more to economic issues than to foreign policy. It did not signify the restoration of the kind of Cold War consensus that had existed before the Vietnam war. Whether Reagan ever seriously believed that it was possible to recreate this is unclear. What is not in doubt is that his anticommunist policy was subject at times to the constraining influence of public opinion and Congress. In this respect his experience was more similar to presidents who had held office since 1968 than to those of the postwar era.

Opinion polls showed that popular support for increased defense spending, which in 1980 reached levels unsurpassed since the onset of the Korean war, had actually peaked by the time Reagan took office. It remained strong during the first year of his presidency but subsided from mid 1982 onwards, in part because the administration's accelerated defense program allayed fears about Soviet superiority and in part because of increasing concern about the deficit. From early 1984 through to the end of Reagan's presidency, polls consistently showed that some 40% of the public believed defense spending was too high, while less than 21% believed the opposite. In similar vein, support for the notion that America should "get tough" with the Soviets dropped from a peak of 74% in January 1980 to 40% in May 1982. By 1988, 59% of Americans believed that economic competitors were a greater threat than military adversaries to US national security.

Moreover, the president's trenchantly anti-Soviet rhetoric and careless speculation by Alexander Haig, Reagan's first Secretary of State, about the possible use of tactical nuclear weapons aroused concern about the administration's stand on nuclear weaponry. Support consequently grew for the nuclear freeze campaign, which sprang from the Massachusetts referendum for a bilateral moratorium on nuclear weapons acquisition. This developed into the most significant citizens' movement on foreign policy since Vietnam. In 1982 nearly 2 million people signed a freeze petition and half a million attended a massive rally in Central Park, New York. In 1983 polls suggested that 86% of Americans supported a freeze on nuclear weapons. Sensitive to this mood, the House of Representatives enacted a resolution requiring the president to negotiate a mutual halt to the arms race, conditional on both sides also agreeing to arms reductions, but the measure died in the Republican-controlled Senate.

Americans remained suspicious of military entanglements abroad. Popular opinion influenced Reagan's decision to remove American forces from Lebanon. The public was also deeply hostile to direct military intervention in Central America, despite persistent warnings from the president about the menace of communism in America's backyard. From 1981 through 1983 Gallup polls showed that more than two-thirds of those who were aware of the situation in El Salvador felt that it "could turn into a situation like Vietnam". Polls told a similar story about US involvement in Nicaragua from 1983 to 1985. Admittedly, barely more than 50% of Americans knew which sides their government was backing in these countries, but at the very least the poll findings ruled out any possibility that Reagan might sanction direct military involvement in Central America.

Reagan also encountered problems in winning congressional support for his national security policy. Though Congress gave him most of the defense budget increases that he wanted, concern about the deficit induced it to trim his requests by an average of 6% a year from 1982 through 1984. Notwithstanding Reagan's landslide reelection, the battle over defense spending grew more intense following the enactment of the Gramm-Rudman-Hollings deficit-reduction measure in 1985. Reagan's defense requests incurred average cuts of around 12% during his second term. Owing to the impact of earlier spending authorizations, however, the actual level of defense expenditure did not fall until the final year of his presidency. Congress also tended to spread cuts so widely that the effects on separate programs within the defense budget was minimal. The one exception to this was the MX missile, the replacement for the ageing Minuteman III ICBM missiles, which incurred major cutbacks because of congressional doubts about its cost and effectiveness.

Congress did not challenge Reagan's military forays, due in large part to the political difficulties of enforcing the War Powers Act. The president's action was accommodated on the one occasion that this legislation was invoked. The initial 90-day commitment of US marines to Lebanon was given an extraordinary 540-day extension in 1983. Congress proved similarly willing to back Reagan's support for authoritarian regimes, except in two instances. The administration's abandonment of the Marcos regime in the Philippines in 1986 was partly a response to congressional pressure. In the same year Congress overrode Reagan's veto in enacting tough economic sanctions against South Africa. This measure undermined the administration's policy of "constructive engagement" to induce the white South African government, an ally in the struggle to rid Angola of Marxism, to modify its apartheid policy through friendly persuasion rather than pressure.

Only over Nicaragua did Congress pose a significant challenge to the Reagan Doctrine. Revelations that Reagan had authorized covert aid to Contra forces fighting against the Sandinista regime prompted congressional enactment of the Boland Amendment in late 1982. This prohibited the United States from giving aid for the purpose of overthrowing Nicaragua's government, but it did not preclude assisting the Contras for other reasons, such as to put pressure on the Sandinistas to make democratic reforms. This loophole enabled the administration to continue its policy of covert aid, but revelations of CIA involvement in the mining of Nicaraguan harbors provoked another furore. A second Boland Amendment, enacted in 1984, banned all kinds of US government support for any military operations in Nicaragua. Reagan's determination to aid the Contras in spite of this prohibition brought about the greatest crisis of his presidency.

Following his reelection Reagan intensified his efforts to win backing for his Nicaraguan policy. This became his most important foreign policy concern outside the immediate realm of superpower relations. Making full use of the presidential bully pulpit, Reagan won increasing public support for his aims and finally persuaded Congress to appropriate $100 million in humanitarian and military aid for the Contras in late 1986. In effect the Boland amendment had been overturned, but the administration had been too impatient to await this outcome. A year earlier it had become involved in a bizarre and illegal arms-for-hostages scheme in pursuit of its aims in both Central America and the Middle East.

Iranian-backed terrorists had seized several American hostages in the Middle East in protest at US sympathy with Iraq in the Iran-Iraq war. Reagan had sworn to take a tough line against terrorists, particularly when running for president against Jimmy Carter, and the United States had been seeking to impose an international arms embargo against Iran since breaking off official links with it in late 1979. Nevertheless, against the advice of George Shultz and Caspar Weinberger, the president sanctioned a secret operation to sell arms to Iran in 1985–6 in the hope of obtaining the release of the US hostages. In parallel with this and apparently without Reagan's knowledge, CIA director William

Casey devised a covert scheme to furnish military supplies to the Contras. This operation was funded from the proceeds of the arms sales and from money that Colonel Oliver North, a National Security Council (NSC) staff member, had raised in private contributions from conservative Americans and foreigners in order to get round the prohibition on government aid to the Contras.

The Iran-Contra affair became public knowledge in November 1986. Unlike Nixon, Reagan escaped the threat of impeachment because the officials involved in the scandal testified that he had no specific knowledge of their activities. Of course this exposed him to the accusation that he was out of touch with the secret foreign policy activities of the CIA and NSC. The congressional committee report on the affair accused the administration of "confusion and disarray at the highest levels of government, evasive dishonesty and inordinate secrecy, deception and disdain for the law", and indicted the president for abdicating his "moral and legal responsibility to take care that the laws be faithfully executed". The scandal crippled Reagan's crusade to free Nicaragua from the Sandinistas and undermined his reputation for strong leadership. With his Gallup approval rating going into free-fall, many pundits were convinced that he was condemned to sit out the rest of his term as an impotent lame-duck.

Foreign policy, which had nearly undone Reagan, also proved his salvation. His assumption that the Soviets could not bear the cost of sustaining the arms race turned out to be correct. The Russian economy had come to the point of collapse by the mid-1980s. A new Soviet leader, Mikhail Gorbachev, who came to power in 1985, was determined to rescue his country from its plight and undertake a fundamental restructuring of its economy and society. The need to cut Soviet military costs impelled him to negotiate arms reduction with the United States and seek relaxation of Cold War tensions.

Gorbachev resumed the arms talks from which the Soviets had walked out in 1983 in protest at Reagan's insistence on continuing to deploy Pershing and Cruise missiles in Western Europe. He also held two summit meetings with Reagan. At Reykjavik in 1986 the two leaders came close to an historic accord to eliminate all US and Soviet nuclear weapons, until Reagan balked at Gorbachev's insistence that this should be tied to a ban on testing and development of SDI. In early 1987, however, the Soviets dropped the idea of linkage and accepted a "double-zero option", the elimination of all medium-range and short-range missiles, and rigorous verification standards. This was the basis for the Intermediate Nuclear Force Treaty, signed in Washington in December 1987, the first-ever agreement that actually reduced nuclear arsenals as opposed to limiting their growth. It left untouched long-range missiles, submarine-launched missiles, and bomber-borne nuclear weapons, but it was an important beginning.

Gorbachev also signaled a Soviet retreat in Africa and Asia. In 1987 he told the XXVII Communist Party Congress that Third World countries had to build socialism mainly through their own efforts. This policy was given concrete expression by the announcement in May 1988 that Soviet troops would be withdrawn from Afghanistan. Six months later the United States and the Soviets announced support for a UN peace settlement for Angola. This was a particularly significant development because it marked an unprecedented collaboration between the superpowers in a regional conflict where they had backed different sides. Peace also came to the Persian Gulf. A UN-negotiated ceasefire ended the Iran-Iraq war in August 1988, thereby relieving the United States responsibility for the protection of shipping in the region.

Reagan left office basking in the successful conclusion of his foreign policy. To some extent he owed this to luck and to events beyond his control. Without Gorbachev's recognition that the Soviet economy was in grave trouble and his determination to do something about it, there would almost certainly not have been much progress on arms control. The quiet diplomacy of the United Nations, an organization that had received little support from Reagan, was largely responsible for the regional peace settlements of 1988. But the tough-guy approach that Reagan had adopted to the Soviets throughout his presidency was at least partly responsible for and was vindicated by the developments of 1987-8.

In assessing Reagan's legacy, Stephen Ambrose observed: "Not in half a century had a president handed over to his successor a foreign policy in better shape". He also noted that there was another side to the coin. Reagan's refusal to pay the financial cost of bringing the United States to the verge of Cold War victory had saddled America with a massive burden of debt that could inhibit its capacity for world leadership in the future. Another historian, Paul Kennedy, suggested that late-twentieth-century America was experiencing "imperial over-stretch". Like other great powers in the past, its economic vitality had been sapped by the ever expanding costs of military power. Other scholars took a more optimistic view of America's future, and the publication of Kennedy's best-selling book *The Rise and Decline of the*

Great Powers provoked a lively debate as to whether the United States was on the verge of a decline similar to Britain's after World War I.

Only future historians will be able to decide whether Reagan's successes strengthened the foundations for America's world leadership or destroyed them. What can be questioned with greater certainty at the present time is the relevance of Reagan's foreign policy, based as it was on anticommunism and military power, for the United States in the 1990s and beyond. As the Reagan presidency drew to an end a high-ranking Soviet spokesman, Georgi Arbatov, told American officials, "[W]e are going to do something terrible to you — we are going to deprive you of an enemy." The post-Cold War world would pose new challenges that only a new foreign policy could address.

Parties, elections, and voters in the Reagan era

The Republicans won the three presidential elections of the Reagan era with ease. After George Bush's victory in 1988, the political scientist Everett Ladd commented, "The New Deal era now seems as remote as the age of McKinley". Few commentators disagreed with this assessment. But it was also evident that the Reagan era had not witnessed the kind of critical realignment necessary to transform the GOP into the majority party. In fact the Republicans were electorally weaker at the end of this period than they were at the beginning. By 1989 they held fewer seats in Congress and controlled fewer governorships and state legislatures than in 1981. It is important to explain why realignment did not occur and to assess the significance of the Reagan era with regard to the post-1968 development of the US party system.

In a sense the Reagan Revolution and indeed Ronald Reagan himself were ill-suited to be agents of party realignment. On this score comparisons with the New Deal and Franklin D. Roosevelt are instructive. The realignment in the 1930s owed much to the impact of the Great Depression, but the politics of the Reagan era were not shaped by a traumatic event of comparable significance. Furthermore, the New Deal was ideally suited to the purposes of electoral coalition-building since it appealed to the particularist interests of different groups of voters. The new programs that it created brought direct economic benefits to a variety of constituencies and welded these together to form a new majority. By contrast the Reagan Revolution, based as it was on an antistatist philosophy, aimed to minimize government rather than to use its powers to undertake a right-wing version of the New Deal's interest group liberalism. As a result the impact of Reagan's policies on the partisan loyalties of voters was inevitably narrower and shallower than Roosevelt's.

Nor did Reagan compare as party leader with Roosevelt. In many ways he kept his presidency distinct from the Republican Party and did little to secure its future. The 1984 election exemplified this. The journalist Sidney Blumenthal commented, "Reagan did not campaign as a Republican and forwarded no positive reason why anyone should become one. . . ." Instead of seeking a mandate for second-term policies, Reagan turned the election into a referendum on his first-term administration. This did little to convince voters that more Republicans were needed in Congress to help the president over the next four years. He also blurred the lines of partisanship by identifying with Democratic heroes like FDR, Harry Truman and John Kennedy. This allowed him to appeal to Democratic identifiers to endorse his leadership without asking them to convert to Republicanism. One in four of them backed him, but these "Reagan Democrats" remained loyal to the Democratic congressional ticket and about half of them supported the Democratic presidential ticket in 1988 when Reagan was no longer a candidate. And to the dismay of GOP leaders, Reagan focused his energies in the last days of the 1984 campaign on Minnesota (the only state he lost) in the hope of winning an unprecedented fifty-state sweep, instead of visiting marginal congressional constituencies in other states which Republican challengers might have won with his support.

This is not to deny that the Republican party made important advances in the Reagan era. Most heartening was the increase of Republican identifiers from 24% of the electorate in 1980 to 34% in 1989, compared with the decline in Democratic identification from 41% to 38%. There was substantial increase in support for the GOP from three groups in particular — upper-income Americans, white fundamentalist Christians, and white southerners — though this was far more evident at presidential level than at congressional and state levels. This dichotomy was especially marked in the case of the South. Reagan carried every southern state except Georgia in 1980 and won them all in 1984, a feat repeated by Bush four years later. By 1989, however, the GOP held only seven of the South's seats in the Senate and 39 of its seats in the House, compared with 11 and 40 respectively in 1981. It controlled five southern governorships, a gain of one over 1981, but only in two states, Florida and Tennessee, did the GOP constitute more than a third of the membership of both houses of the legislature.

Even at presidential level the political significance of Republican gains was ambiguous. In 1984 Reagan won the second largest electoral college majority in American history (525 to 13) and the fifth largest popular vote majority (58.7% to 40.5%). Yet, in contrast to 1980, few thought of this victory as a mandate for conservatism, owing to the personal nature of Reagan's campaign. Many voters, including some who disagreed with him on specific issues, backed the president on account of his leadership record rather than his policies. They credited him with ending the indecision and drift associated with the Carter presidency. Linked with this was a remarkable transformation in the national mood. During the 1982–3 recession opinion polls recorded a deep sense of popular pessimism about the future, such as had existed in the late 1970s. Economic recovery and the patriotic pride fostered by the invasion of Grenada induced renewed optimism. From late 1983 until the the Iran-Contra revelations in late 1986 the American mood was upbeat and confident. The high point came with the Los Angeles Olympic Games of 1984 when the crop of gold medals harvested by US athletes nourished the feel-good factor. Reagan's 1984 campaign, with its highly effective "It's morning again in America" commercials, succeeded in making the president the personification of this new mood.

The bedrock of American optimism and the substantive foundation of Reagan's electoral success was the popular perception that the economy was doing much better than in the 1970s. According to Gallup's analysis, voters who supported Reagan in 1984 cited his economic policies as their main reason for choosing him". One election exit poll indicated that 49% of voters felt they were better off financially than four years ago and that 84% of these backed Reagan. Among the 31% of voters who were in the same financial shape as in 1980, 56% backed the president. Only a fifth of voters felt they were worse off, and 85% of these voted Democrat.

Of course, economic wellbeing was a changeable factor that could hurt as well as help the Republicans. In 1982 the recession had put the brakes on the promising advances that the GOP had made in Congress two years earlier. The midterm loss of 24 seats in the House of Representatives ended whatever prospect the party had of gaining control of this body during the Reagan era. The economy was later an important factor in the 1986 elections which resulted in the GOP's loss of majority status in the Senate. The Republicans did badly in those parts of the country where the Reagan economic miracle had proved short-lived or shallow, notably the old manufacturing heartland and the agricultural regions. Fueled by the mounting budget and trade deficits, popular uncertainty about the fundamental wellbeing of the economy persisted for the remainder of Reagan's presidency. In the 1988 election, 60% of voters expected the economy to stay the same, 26% expected it to get worse, and only 14% were hopeful of it improving. However the failure of the Democratic presidential candidate Michael Dukakis to define his economic agenda early in the campaign allowed George Bush to convince the public that the economy would be safer in his hands.

Bush won the 1988 election with a popular vote margin of 54% to 46% and by 426 votes to 112 in the electoral college. This emphatic victory was not such a clearcut vote of approval for the Reagan legacy as it appeared. With Reagan no longer a candidate, the election was more a referendum on his policies than his leadership. There was a marked division of opinion on this score. According to the *New York Times*-CBS exit polls, 36% of voters wanted continuation of Reagan's policies and 35% wanted to change direction. With these groups cancelling each other out, Bush won because he had more support than Dukakis from Americans who were not voting retrospectively on the Reagan administration. Poll evidence indicated lack of support for the ideological underpinnings of Reaganism. In 1988 33% of voters regarded themselves as conservatives, 18% as liberals and 45% as moderates. These proportions were relatively unchanged since 1980. Whatever else he had achieved, Reagan had not forged a conservative consensus in American politics.

Had such a conservative consensus existed it would have been marked by popular support for the antigovernment philosophy of Reaganism. Popular confidence in government institutions had plummeted during the "malaise crisis" of the final Carter years. Reagan's hopes of turning this into a rebellion against government were thwarted in part by his own political success. The era of good feelings in the middle years of his presidency revitalized Americans' confidence that their government could cope with the nation's problems. Improved attitudes towards government also reflected diminished resentment about the federal tax burden following the 1981 tax cuts. Nevertheless it was significant that Americans did not support federal expenditure reductions to curb the massive budget deficits that the tax cuts had helped to create.

The nation's view of public spending in the late 1980s was remarkably similar to what it had been on the eve of Reagan's election in 1980. In a November 1987 poll, 75% of respondents favored a balanced-budget amendment to the Constitution, but 60% were unwilling for government to economize by providing fewer services in areas like health and education and 73% opposed reductions in social security COLAs. Nor was there strong support for the roll-back of the regulatory state. Two-thirds of respondents to a 1986 poll supported the view that government had to ensure a high level of environmental protection regardless of cost.

In essence elements of the old liberal consensus endured in the 1980s. At the same time the conservative influence of cross-cutting issues that had shattered the New Deal party system in the late 1960s and 1970s persisted and intensified. This was mainly evident with regard to taxation, race, and national values, all of which became tightly entwined in the political symbolism of Reagan-era conservatism.

Reagan had established a distributional tax policy skewed sharply towards the affluent through a political strategy that capitalized on the dissatisfaction of the working and middle classes. The 1981 tax cut and the 1986 tax code reform eroded the progressivity of the income tax structure and did much to redistribute wealth away from the poor and towards the rich. Yet these measures were broadly popular because they afforded some income tax relief for the majority of working Americans. Anyone proposing to reverse Reagan's policy was as good as committing political suicide. The honest avowal by Walter Mondale, the 1984 Democratic presidential candidate, that tax increases were necessary to balance the budget contributed to his overwhelming defeat. Afterwards he commented ruefully, "I taught a whole generation of politicians how to handle the tax issue: to not mention it." Four years later federal finances were still deep in the red but opinion surveys consistently recorded that some three out of five Americans opposed tax increases. George Bush's famous campaign statement — "Read my lips, no new taxes" — was the basis of the clearest policy mandate that emerged from the 1988 presidential election.

Democratic efforts to challenge GOP tax policies as unfair ran into the problem that many white voters had come to associate "fairness" with "fairness to minorities". Reagan's tax cuts and his publicly-expressed skepticism about affirmative action struck a chord with many groups who felt deserted by the Democrats. A study commissioned by the Democratic National Committee following the 1984 election made this clear. Based on a poll of 5,000 voters, it found a pervasive belief among white urban ethnics and white southern moderates that "the Democratic Party has not stood with them as they moved from the working class to the middle class. They have a whole set of middle-class economic problems today, and their party is not helping them. Instead it is helping the blacks, Hispanics and the poor. They feel betrayed." These groups deemed themselves threatened by a lazy, immoral and underserving underclass "that absorbs their taxes and even locks them out of a job, in the case of affirmative action." They now viewed the Democrats as "the giveaway party. Giveaway means too much middle-class money going to blacks and the poor."

These attitudes were reflected in the racial polarization of the electorate. In 1984 only 35% of white voters supported Mondale, compared with 89% of black voters. In 1988 40% of whites and 86% of blacks backed Dukakis. A new politics of race flowered in the 1980s from the seeds planted by the middle American revolt of the late 1960s. With the civil rights revolution over two decades old, the majority of white Americans believed that the struggle for racial justice had been accomplished and no longer deemed themselves responsible for the condition of those blacks who now failed to progress through their own efforts. Increasingly the social pathology of the ghetto, manifested by violence, joblessness, welfare dependence, drug abuse, illegitimacy and family disintegration, were seen as endemic to the black underclass rather than the result of continuing inequality. By contrast the majority of blacks, supported in the main by white liberals, felt that government should continue to accept some responsibility for their condition because the economic, social, and cultural effects of more than three centuries of racism could not be wiped out in a single generation.

The race issue in turn was an integral element in the political conflict over values that reached a new peak in the 1980s. For over two decades the Democrats had championed social policies that embodied the values of the 1960s in their emphasis on the right of the individual to be free from oppression, unjust confinement, discrimination, and intolerant authority. This association came under far more vigorous assault from Reagan and Bush than anything attempted by Nixon in his efforts to mobilize the resentments of middle America. Through his policies and rhetoric, particularly in the 1984 campaign, Reagan helped to reestablish the political ascendancy of traditional values that emphasized the obligations of the individual to family, country, the work ethic, sexual restraint, the authority of the law, and a stable social order. In 1988 values were a major issue for George Bush, who ran the most vitriolic and negative campaign by any major party presidential candidate in modern times.

Bush identified himself with the Pledge of Allegiance, the flag, a strong national defense, and the protection of decent citizens against criminal elements. In conjunction with this, a series of Bush television commercials sought to portray Dukakis as soft on patriotism and law and order. The intensity of the attack did much to wipe out the Democrat's early lead in the polls. Voters were told that he supported defense cuts which would weaken America and that, as Governor of Massachusetts, he had vetoed a law requiring students to pledge the oath of allegiance to the flag. The TV spots were even more hard-hitting on the issue of crime. Dukakis' affiliation with the American Civil Liberties Union, his opposition to the death penalty, and his approval of a Massachusetts program authorizing weekend furloughs for prisoners convicted of violent crimes were all highlighted. The most notorious commercial made the black felon Willie Horton into a household name. It publicized the case of this convicted murderer who had absconded while on furlough from a Massachusetts prison and later resurfaced to commit acts of violence and rape in Maryland. As Thomas and Mary Edsall observed, " 'Crime' became a shorthand signal, to crucial numbers of white voters, of broader issues of social disorder, tapping powerful ideas about authority, status, morality, self-control and race." The Willie Horton ad, in particular, confirmed white stereotypes about the criminality of the black underclass and the threat it posed when coddled by permissive liberalism.

The days were seemingly long gone when the kind of "bottom-up", biracial coalition of low-income and lower-middle-class voters mobilized by Franklin D. Roosevelt could ensure Democratic control of the White House. Reagan and Bush had dominated the presidential elections of the 1980s with the support a "top-down" voter coalition. This new majority was predominantly composed of affluent and middle-income white Americans. Though the Democrats retained the loyalties of the less well-off, the solidarity of this constituency was fragmented by divisions between the working class and the poor. In 1988 Dukakis only gained a 50–49% edge among voters with a family income of between $12,500 and $25,000, who comprised 20% of the participating electorate. Mondale had done even worse in 1984, losing this group by a 57–42% margin. The Democrats kept the support of the majority of trade union households, winning 53% of this vote in 1984 and 57% in 1988. These were significantly smaller proportions than they expected to win in the heyday of the New Deal party system, and the size of the union constituency had itself shrunk as a result of demographic change and deindustrialization. Adding to their woes, nonvoting affected the Democrats far more than the Republicans. Only half of the electorate cast ballots in 1988. As usual turn-out was lowest among racial minorities, low-income groups, and the poor.

For the Democrats to recapture the White House, they had to do one of two things: reenergize the New Deal coalition or build a new coalition. The debate over which option to take shaped the contest for the Democratic presidential nomination in 1984. The Reverend Jesse Jackson, a black civil rights activist and former protégé of Martin Luther King, sought to fashion a "rainbow coalition" that attracted the dispossessed of all races — poor whites, Latinos, Native Americans, Asian-Americans, and blacks. It was his conviction that the Democrats could only defeat Reagan by moving to the left in order to activate the millions of disaffected nonvoters. Lack of money, poor organization, taints of anti-semitism, and the opposition of the party leadership hampered Jackson's campaign, and he had little success in winning support from groups other than blacks. Nevertheless he succeeded in establishing himself as a significant force in national politics and gained recognition for the aspirations of black Americans to shape the politics of the Democratic Party.

By contrast, Senator Gary Hart, the doyen of neoliberals, presented himself as the representative of a new leadership generation in a bid to appeal to middle-class voters, particularly those aged under 35. Eschewing identification with the Democratic party's New Deal traditions, he ran on a platform that combined economic conservatism and social liberalism. Despite a strong start, including victory in the New Hampshire primary, his campaign faded because of financial and organizational problems and voters' concern that he was more style than substance.

The nomination eventually went to Walter Mondale, who succeeded in gaining support from groups identified with the "old" and "new" liberalism. A protégé of Hubert Humphrey, a supporter of New Deal/Great Society programs as Minnesota senator in the 1960s and 1970s, and formerly vice-president in the Carter administration, he was ideally suited to appeal to such diverse constituencies as the AFL-CIO, the National Education Association, civil rights groups, and the National Organization for Women. Hoping to capitalize on the so-called "gender gap" — the relatively low level of support for Reagan among female voters — he chose Congresswoman Geraldine Ferraro (New York) as his running mate. This was the first time that a woman had been selected to run on a major party's national ticket. However, Mondale's strategy backfired in the general election because it made him vulnerable to Reagan's charges that he was the captive of special interest groups and that his call to raise taxes reflected his need to finance government programs demanded by these constituencies. His crushing defeat signified the end of an era for his party. Mondale was the last Democratic presidential candidate whose political lineage could be traced to the New Deal.

In 1988 Hart's renewed challenge for the Democratic nomination was destroyed by his sexual indiscretions. Jesse Jackson also entered the race and ran a campaign with broader appeal to whites than he had achieved in 1984. He hammered away at Reaganite policies that had spread unemployment among factory workers and hurt small farmers, and highlighted the danger of drugs, an issue of considerable middle-class concern. The most charismatic of the Democratic candidates, Jackson won nearly 7 million votes and eventually finished second behind Michael Dukakis. Several factors prevented him from winning the nomination. Many voters considered him too left-wing, and party leaders believed that only a centrist candidate could woo back the Reagan Democrats. Racial concerns also prevented Jackson from forging an interracial alliance behind class grievances. Though he took 12% of the white vote overall (and did considerably better in some states, such as Michigan), many white Democrats were unwilling to support a black candidate. Jackson ran best in the South, due to the support of its large black electorate, but a stop-Jackson movement developed in many northern states in favor of Dukakis. Jackson's earlier references to New York as "Hymietown" and his pro-Palestinian sympathies in the Middle East also hurt his standing with Jewish-Americans in the crucial New York primary.

Dukakis, who came out of the neoliberal stable, had shown sufficient activism as Massachusetts governor to keep the liberal wing of the party happy. His main claim to fame was his involvement with the "high tech" economic miracle that had renewed the state economy in the 1980s. Dukakis presented himself as a technocrat who could do for the nation what he had done for Massachusetts. In the primary contests he ran particularly well with middle-class and suburban voters. These became the target groups of the Dukakis strategy in the general election. For this reason he chose Senator Lloyd Bentsen (Texas) as his running mate instead of Jackson, and his lieutenants blocked the Jackson camp's proposal at the Democratic convention that tax increases for upper-income groups should be written into the platform. In his nomination acceptance speech Dukakis avowed that the election would be about competence not ideology. Ironically, he went on to run the most inept presidential campaign of modern times and allowed Bush to portray him as a liberal.

Dukakis' failure to launch a vigorous counterattack to reestablish his identity as a moderate proved disastrous. Although he won a slim majority of 50–49% among moderate voters, who comprised the largest segment of the electorate, he needed to do far better with this group to counterbalance the fact that conservative voters, among whom Bush had a huge lead, were almost twice as numerous as liberal voters. Despite the outcome, the election of 1988 suggested that the Democrats' best hope in the future was a centrist strategy that would gain the support of middle-income voters and moderates. They would have come far closer to winning in 1988 with a candidate better able than Dukakis to pursue it.

The Democrats' failures at presidential level in the 1980s contrasted with their congressional successes. In 1984, 192 Democrats won reelection to the House of Representatives in districts that gave a majority to Reagan in the presidential election. Two years later the Democrats recaptured control of the Senate by winning Republican-held seats in Alabama, Florida, Georgia, Maryland, Nevada, North Carolina, North Dakota, South Dakota, and Washington, states that Reagan had swept in 1984 and which (except Washington) would go strongly for Bush in 1988. These results perpetuated the period of divided party control of national government that had existed since 1968, the Carter era excepted. Divided government was nothing new in American politics, but the length of time it lasted in this instance was unusual. Moreover, previous periods of divided government were almost always the result of midterm loss of unified party control. In recent times, by contrast, midterm elections merely continued the pattern of divided government established at general elections.

Divided government constrained the Reagan Revolution. Congress only supported Reagan's position on 61.8% of votes from 1981 through 1988. This was the lowest figure for any postwar president except Gerald Ford. Although House Democrats surrendered rather lamely to Reagan in 1981, largely out of fear of voter reaction if they obstructed a popular president perceived to possess a mandate, they grew progressively bolder from 1982 onwards. Even the so-called Boll Weevils, the group of about fifty conservative southern Democrats who backed the president on key votes in 1981–2, kept their distance from him after the 1982 midterm elections.

Democratic electoral success also affected Republican congressional politics. From 1983 onwards mainstream Republicans, the largest GOP faction in both House and Senate, became increasingly unwilling to back presidential demands for massive cutbacks of government programs for fear of encountering an electoral backlash. In Reagan's second term, bipartisan congressional agreement about the need for defense cuts and tax increases to reduce the deficit often put GOP legislative leaders at odds with the president. On average only 64% of Republicans in the House of Representatives backed the president's position in votes from 1981 through 1988. This was the lowest level of party support enjoyed by any postwar president. The Senate figure of 74% was more impressive, but this was only comparable with what Carter, Nixon and Kennedy had achieved, and was well below the top presidential score of 80% gained by Eisenhower.

The question remains: why was Republican dominance of presidential elections not replicated at congressional level in the 1980s? Some analysts claim that the Democrats were the beneficiaries of the incumbency factor. Sitting congressmen have the advantage of name recognition, get much bigger financial contributions from Political Action Committees than do challengers, and can build up a personal vote that transcends partisan and ideological considerations by performing services for their constituents. Other commentators suggest that America is still fundamentally a Democratic country. They regard Republican success at presidential level as the exception in a political system which the Democrats continue to dominate at congressional, state, and local levels. Both of these explanations are incomplete and insufficient. The incumbency factor certainly benefits the Democrats but it does not explain why they have tended since 1968 to be significantly more successful than Republicans in open congressional seats where neither candidate is an incumbent. The "Democratic dominance" argument does not take into account the fact that divided government became increasingly prevalent at state level too in the 1980s. Accordingly, a third explanation has recently gained support: divided government existed in the 1980s because Americans wanted it.

In the view of political scientist Gerald Pomper, "Divided government is the result of a divided American political mind." This explanation is a fitting epitaph for Reagan-era politics. There was no majority party in American politics in the 1980s. Voter dealignment persisted and realignment did not occur because neither party had enough appeal to build a new coalition that would give it full control of government.

Republicans dominated the presidency, the institution responsible for economic policy and national security, because voters considered them more likely to maintain economic prosperity, low taxes, and strong defense. The Democrats were successful in Congress, the body responsible for the distribution of government funds and programs, because they were more trusted to protect public policies that benefited ordinary people and to represent the particularist needs of different groups in American society. In other words, even though Reagan was the most conservative president in half a century, the fundamental characteristic of American politics in the Reagan era was ideological ambiguity.

*   *   *

The redirection of public purpose which Reagan's first-year legislative successes appeared to herald did not come to fruition during his time in office. If Reagan is to be adjudged the most significant president since Franklin D. Roosevelt, the case must rest on his success in halting the momentum of big government rather than in reversing it. Much of the ideological coherence of his presidency had faded by 1988, as was evidenced by swelling budget deficits, the upward curve of domestic expenditure, and the slowing down of the deregulatory revolution. Moreover, the divided government that characterized American politics in the 1980s showed that Reagan's conservatism had failed to win the hearts of the American people in the way that Roosevelt's liberalism had in the 1930s. The high-water mark of conservatism had passed by the time that Reagan left office. The conservative symbolism of his presidency remained strong to the end, but in substantive terms the conservative legacy that he bequeathed largely consisted of low taxes, the promise of continuing prosperity based on incentive-oriented economic policies, and global anticommunism. The durability of this legacy would soon be tested in the new political environment of the 1990s.

9
The Morning After: the Politics of the Bush Era, 1989–1992

Ronald Reagan's "It's morning again in America" election advertisements had perfectly articulated the feel-good national mood of 1984. At the time few Americans heeded critics who warned that the nation was bingeing on a diet of low taxes, high defense spending, and debt, and was doing little to safeguard its position in an increasingly competitive international economy. But the United States had to acknowledge the truth of these jeremiads during George Bush's presidency. America experienced a grey morning-after feeling in the early 1990s, when it faced up to the costs of the 1980s. In spite of foreign policy triumphs, the Bush era was overshadowed by worsening fiscal problems, growing controversy over racial and gender issues, and the end of the Reagan economic boom.

New world order

The world changed more rapidly during the first three years of the Bush presidency than at any time since 1945. With the Cold War ended, communist regimes were replaced by freely-elected regimes in the former Soviet satellites of Eastern Europe, Germany was unified, the Soviet Union ceased to exist and was replaced by a host of non-communist national republics loosely organized together within the Commonwealth of Independent States. The United States was left as the solitary global superpower and its success in organizing and leading a multilateral military coalition during the Gulf war of 1991 — the first international crisis of the post-Cold War era — encouraged hopes that it could shape a new world order.

In 1991 the United States went to war to liberate Kuwait from invasion and annexation by Iraq. At stake in the conflict, President Bush said, was "a big idea — a new world order where diverse nations are drawn together in common cause to achieve the universal aspirations of mankind: peace and security, freedom and the rule of law." But confidence about America's role in developing a new world order soon gave way to doubt. Recession and budget problems imposed constraints on US ability and will to exercise international leadership. It was evident that in contrast to the Cold War, when the perception of external threats shaped American diplomacy, political and economic dynamics at home would largely define foreign policy in the new era.

The rapid collapse of communism took Bush by surprise. Orthodox Cold War assumptions had defined his view of the world when he took office. Despite the recent improvement in relations with the Soviet Union, the president and his advisers were not entirely convinced that superpower cordiality would last. They were especially concerned at the possibility that confrontation would resume if Mikhail Gorbachev, whose domestic position was known to be insecure, was overthrown by Kremlin hardliners. As Secretary of State James Baker commented, "The jury is still out on whether the process of [Soviet] reform will succeed. While there is every reason to look to the future, it would be a serious mistake to assume that continued progress is assured."

The pace of change in Eastern Europe over the next twelve months only reinforced the Bush administration's sense of caution. Conservative internationalists within the foreign policy establishment were also uncertain what to do now that Cold War victory was at last on hand. Paul Nitze, one of the founding fathers of containment policy in the late 1940s, commented in 1990: "Events are going on right now with results that cannot be foreseen. We know things are going to be different, but we are not certain how much better. So maybe we should keep our powder dry." However much it had helped to create the circumstances in which the demise of communism in the Soviet satellites became possible, the United States was a passive observer of the momentous events of 1989. It did nothing to promote the actual process by which democracy movements rose up to topple communist regimes. The Bush administration was also deaf to calls for a new Marshall Plan to facilitate the transition from communism to democracy and capitalism in Eastern Europe.

US foreign aid continued to be targeted at traditional objectives. Pakistan was given $588 million to help make southwest Asia safe from communism, even though the last Soviet troops had departed from Afghanistan. Israel and Egypt together received $6 billion (some 37% of the total US foreign aid budget) to ensure their security in the still troubled Middle East. Generous aid also flowed into the tiny republics of Central America as part of the US crusade against Marxism in the region. The Sandinistas finally fell from power in Nicaragua in 1990, but this was the result of free elections which the military activities of the US backed Contras nearly prevented from going ahead. Significantly, Bush's strongest foreign policy initiative in 1989 was concerned not with Europe but with wielding the "big stick" in America's backyard. In December a division-sized US force invaded Panama to oust dictator Manuel Noriega and bring him back to face drug-trafficking charges in an American court.

Events in the Middle East brought the United States back to the center of the world stage. Geopolitical considerations concerning oil ensured that Iraq's annexation of the oil-rich emirate of Kuwait in August 1990 had global significance. It was widely feared that the next target of Saddam Hussein's ambitions would be Saudi Arabia itself. There seemed a real danger that the Iraqi dictator might gain control over something like 40% of world oil supplies, thereby acquiring veto power over global economic growth. Nevertheless America's response to the crisis was framed in terms of international idealism rather than economic self-interest. Bush frequently compared Saddam with Hitler and likened the significance of the Kuwait crisis to that of the Czechoslovakia-Munich crisis of 1938. The obligation to protect national sovereignty and stop naked aggression by one state against another became his battle-cry.

Undertaking the largest US military deployment since Vietnam, the Bush administration rushed planes and 200,000 troops to Saudi Arabia and established a formidable naval presence in the Persian Gulf. In addition it organized an international coalition against Saddam Hussein. In August 1990 United Nations Security Council Resolution (UNSCR) 661, calling on member states to join in a mandatory trade embargo against Iraq, was given unanimous approval. Three months later, in response to Saddam's continued defiance, UNSCR 678 authorized UN military action against Iraq unless it evacuated Kuwait by January 15, 1991. More than twenty-five countries sent forces of varying size to the Persian Gulf to back this up. The US-led coalition launched its military offensive the day after the UN ultimatum expired. Massive aerial bombing did much to destroy the Iraqi military's will to fight. As a result the coalition ground offensive that began in mid February brought about the liberation of Kuwait by the end of the month.

Popular backing for US military involvement in the Gulf seemed to indicate that the Vietnam syndrome had finally been laid to rest. More than 70% of the public approved Bush's decision to deploy ground forces in Saudi Arabia, a level of support that remained constant as the crisis escalated into war. Americans realized that Saddam's actions posed a clear danger to their own economic wellbeing. Moreover, Bush's presentation of the crisis as the defense of Kuwait against Iraqi aggression skilfully entwined self-interest with the kind of principled idealism that Woodrow Wilson, Franklin D. Roosevelt and Harry Truman had invoked to rally the nation to arms in the past. The president's decision to internationalize the opposition to Saddam also paid dividends at home, as well as abroad. UN support did much to legitimize Bush's policy in the eyes of the American public. Equally important in consolidating domestic support was the willingness of Saudi Arabia and Kuwait (and later West Germany and Japan) to defray part of America's military costs.

International support for US military action also enabled Bush to outmaneuver Democratic critics who charged that economic sanctions against Iraq should be the principal instrument for compelling its withdrawal from Kuwait. Congress was not seriously consulted about the initial deployment of US ground forces. Bush did take care to obtain formal authorization for the possible use of force against Iraq. The passage of UNSCR 678 made it difficult for Congress to deny him this, but four-fifths of Democratic senators and two-thirds of Democratic congressmen still voted nay. The Democrats might have become the rallying point for popular disenchantment with the war had it developed into a long and costly conflict. But rapid military victory, at the total cost of only 376 American lives, left Bush politically triumphant.

America's role in the Gulf war bred optimism about its capacity for world leadership into the twenty-first century. Some analysts claimed that the conflict marked the beginning of a post-Cold War Pax Americana whereby the rest of the world would accept a benign US hegemony. In their view the collapse of Soviet power left the United States in a position of global dominance unparalleled in the history of the modern state system. Charles Krauthammer drew a contrast between speedy victory in the Persian Gulf and the long stalemate in the Korean war: "In the 1950s our adversaries had strategic depth. They had the whole Communist world behind them. . . . The enemies we do encounter today, like Saddam, have to face us on their own. Because of that, they don't stand a chance."

Other commentators doubted the prospects for a unipolar world system because US military power was still constrained by economic limits. Instead, the Gulf war offered them hope that America could build a new world order by acting as sheriff of a global posse, rather than as lone policeman. According to this school of thought, America's political role in the crisis was as important as its military one. It believed that American leadership in getting the UN to denounce the annexation of Kuwait as aggression was crucial, because Saddam might otherwise have gotten away with defining his actions as the postcolonial recovery of a former province and appealing for Arab unity against the pro-Israeli United States. In the words of Joseph Nye, the crisis demonstrated that "the United States is still the largest possessor of both 'hard' power — the ability to command others, usually through the use of tangible resources such as military and economic might — and 'soft' power — the ability to coopt rather than command, to get others to want what you want. . . .and if the largest power [in the international system] does not lead in organizing collective action, no one will."

With domestic approval ratings higher than any president had enjoyed since 1945 and America's international prestige at a post-Vietnam high, George Bush seemingly had the opportunity to begin building the new world order. But the limited initiatives taken toward this end produced disappointing results. Bush and James Baker seized the chance to push for face-to-face negotiations between Arabs and Israelis. Although talks eventually got under way in 1992 after the United States strongarmed Israel into allowing the presence of a Palestinian delegation, the issue of Jewish settlements in the occupied West Bank territories hindered progress towards a regional peace agreement. Bush also unveiled an ambitious plan for reducing nuclear armaments, which became the basis for a new Russian-American agreement in the final weeks of his presidency. However, corollary proposals to curb the international proliferation of nuclear, chemical, and biological weapons made little impact, and Bush did not launch a diplomatic offensive to win support for them.

Meanwhile, the failure of the August 1991 coup against Gorbachev spelled the end of the Soviet Union as a communist state. A democratic regime, headed by Boris Yeltsin, sought to establish itself in Russia in the face of grave economic problems. The Bush administration answered its calls for financial aid mainly with words of encouragement, a response that former president Richard Nixon denounced as "penny ante . . . pathetically inadequate". Many other commentators echoed this view. There was bewilderment that the United States, having spent so much on winning the Cold War, was neglecting to consolidate victory by its reluctance to make comparatively modest outlays on assistance to the impoverished former communist nations of Europe.

To some extent America's hesitant stance in the wake of its Gulf war victory reflected Bush's own uncertainty. By his own admission the president was uncomfortable with what he called the "vision thing" and was more adept at handling the day-to-day operations of international affairs. He never issued what might be called a Bush Doctrine to establish new foreign policy aims in the way that Truman, Nixon and Reagan had done. Insofar as he had a vision of what the new world order should be, it was a narrow one, concerned above all with order, stability, and national sovereignty. This was reflected by his administration's initial preference for the preservation of Yugoslavia over the independence claims of its constituent republics, its tepid reaction to the demands of the Baltic states and Soviet republics for independence from the Soviet Union, and its haste in restoring normal relations with the Chinese communist regime after the massacre of student democracy protesters in Tiananmen Square in June 1989.

This concern for order was demonstrated most clearly by the way the Gulf war was ended. Seeking a speedy resolution of the conflict, Bush issued a public statement on February 15 urging the Iraqi people to force their leader to step aside. His words were intended to encourage anti-Saddam elements in the ruling Baath party to overthrow him. But he only succeeded in prompting rebellions by dissident Kurds and Shiites, who sought independence from Iraq. These insurgents were left to face Saddam's wrath once Kuwait was liberated. Neither the United States nor the Gulf Arab states favored the dismemberment of Iraq, which they wanted to preserve as a regional counter to Iran, and several coalition members, notably Turkey and Syria, were fearful that a Kurdish victory in Iraq would encourage independence demands from their own Kurdish minorities.

The international community stood by as Saddam crushed the rebellions with bloody brutality and wholesale massacres of civilians. Hundreds of thousands of Kurds and Shiites fled to the border regions of Turkey and Iran respectively. The horrific conditions they endured in makeshift refugee camps finally induced the world to act. America and its allies mounted a huge relief effort and deployed military forces to establish safe havens for the Kurds inside northern Iraq. They also secured approval of UNSCR 688, which asserted that humanitarian organizations had the right of immediate access to Iraqi citizens who were victims of repression within Iraq itself. This resolution broke new ground. The United Nations had taken a hesitant step toward redefining its interests and obligations to take account not only of what happened between nations but also of what happened inside them.

The inglorious aftermath of the Gulf war raised fundamental questions about the nature of a new world order. In the recent past, differing positions on the anticommunist priorities of American foreign policy had largely defined the debate between conservative internationalists and liberal internationalists. In the post-Cold War era conservative internationalism and liberal internationalism began to take on new meanings that related to differing perspectives on what kind of new world order the United States should help to build.

In one of his few major addresses on the subject in April 1991, Bush outlined a conservative vision of the new world order. The goals he defined were "peaceful settlements of disputes, solidarity against aggression, reduced and controlled arsenals, and just treatment of all peoples". The vague final reference to justice was significant. No mention was made of values that had been traditionally invoked by his predecessors to justify intervention abroad: self-determination (Woodrow Wilson), freedom (FDR, Truman, and Kennedy), human rights (Carter), democracy and the democratic revolution (Reagan). Bush's priorities lay elsewhere. "The Cold War's end didn't deliver us into an era of perpetual peace", he warned. ". . . . The quest for the new world order is, in part, a challenge to keep the dangers of disorder at bay."

By contrast, the liberal vision of world order accepted that America also had a responsibility to participate in collective action with its UN allies to ensure the good behavior of foreign governments toward their peoples. In other words democracy, self-determination and human rights were deemed to be as important, if not more so, as order and stability. This message found ready support in some, though not all, sections of the Democratic party, including its presidential candidate Bill Clinton. Though foreign policy was not a major issue in the 1992 election campaign, Clinton's public statements advocated a tougher approach towards communist China for its suppression of the democracy movement, greater economic aid for the establishment of democracy in Eastern Europe, and the formation of a Democracy Corps that would send American volunteers abroad in similar vein to John Kennedy's Peace Corps. He gave clear expression to post-Cold War liberal internationalist ideals: "I believe it is time for America to lead a global alliance for democracy as united and steadfast as the global alliance that defeated communism."

The difference between the conservative and liberal visions of world order was not absolute, of course. The assistance given to Saddam's domestic enemies, however belated, indicated that Bush recognized the need at times to place the rights of peoples above those of governments. He also demonstrated humanitarian concern by sending US troops to famine-hit Somalia in late 1992 as part of a UN operation to protect international relief aid from attacks by rival warlords. Correspondingly, liberal internationalists realized that unqualified support for national self-determination in a world where less than 10% of nation-states were ethnically homogeneous would create international disorder. Both sides also saw that the United States would have to resolve its domestic problems before it could devote itself to building the new world order, whatever shape this would take.

By the end of 1991 the afterglow of the Gulf victory had been overshadowed by a deep and enduring recession. Bush came under attack for paying too much attention to foreign policy and too little to domestic affairs. Democrat Harris Wofford scored an upset victory in Pennsylvania's special senatorial election with a campaign theme of "taking care of our own". Congress quickly responded to the public mood. A bipartisan alliance killed the annual foreign aid bill, and the proposal by Les Aspin (Wisconsin), Democratic chairman of the House Armed Services committee, to divert $1 billion from defense spending to help in the establishment of a consumer economy in the former Soviet Union was quashed. Only after CIA warnings of impending chaos in Russia was a stripped-down version of the Aspin plan approved. A number of presidential aspirants also based their campaigns on nationalist themes. Bush faced a challenge for the Republican presidential nomination from Pat Buchanan, a conservative journalist and former Nixon aide, who advocated that the United States should stay out of foreign wars, eliminate foreign aid, bring home all its troops stationed abroad, and treat Japan and Western Europe as economic predators. On the Democratic side, Senator Tom Harkin (Iowa) and Jerry Brown, former governor of California, urged economic protectionism to safeguard American jobs.

Yet "America First" themes did not play well with voters in the presidential primaries. After a faltering start, Bush overcame Buchanan with relative ease, and the Democratic contest developed into a battle between two liberal internationalists, Governor Bill Clinton of Arkansas and Paul Tsongas, the former Massachusetts senator. Economic problems had not turned Americans overnight into isolationists. The Gallup poll, which regularly asks Americans whether they want their country to be active in world affairs, recorded a 71% affirmative response in late 1991, the highest in 26 years. Other polls found that strong opposition to America acting as world policeman (75%) was more than counterbalanced by strong support (79%) for US involvement in UN military action against an aggressive dictator if diplomacy and economic sanctions proved ineffective.

Lack of support for isolationism did not alter the fact that most Americans felt an urgent need to focus on domestic issues. Significantly, the public's international priorities in the post-Cold War era were primarily economic in nature. According to a Chicago Council on Foreign Relations survey, undertaken at the end of 1991, Americans believed that the most important aims of US foreign policy should be: first, saving American jobs; second, protecting the interests of American workers abroad; and third, securing adequate supplies of energy. Defending allies, preventing the spread of nuclear weapons, and advancing human rights were seen as less important. Helping to spread democracy to other nations came last on a list of fifteen priorities. These economic concerns indicated that popular support for world order internationalism, whether the conservative or liberal version, was fragile. It was evident that America had to put right its domestic problems if it was to play a constructive role in world affairs. "Unless the nation embarks upon a comprehensive program of domestic renewal," warned David Gergen, the editor of *United States News and World Report*, "the United States within a few years could become so deeply immired in its own troubles that its politics will turn even more embittered, xenophobic and inward."

Economic malaise

The patriotic euphoria that followed the Gulf war reminded some observers of the feel-good national mood of the mid-1980s. But this soon gave way to a sense of malaise reminiscent of the pessimism of the Carter era. The sources of this discontent were economic. Americans grew increasingly frustrated with their government's inability to deal with the spiraling budget deficit and a prolonged recession. Recent success abroad only served to heighten disenchantment with domestic failure.

The massive budget deficit created by the failed experiment of Reaganomics cast a pall over the Bush era. Domestic renewal required the replenishment of the public sector that had fallen into disrepair in the 1980s. To become more competitive in world terms, the United

States had to strengthen the infrastructure of its economy. It needed a modernized transport system, a better education system, a better trained workforce, the revitalization of inner cities, and a reduction in poverty. All this would cost money, but the deficit problem stymied funding for new programs. To make matters worse, the national debt stood at $3.2 trillion in 1990, compared with $0.9 trillion in 1980. Debt service as a percentage of the federal budget stood at 14%, compared with 9% in 1980. In fiscal 1993 the $215 billion cost of debt service was equivalent to two-thirds of the projected deficit and was the third largest item in the budget. The growth of the national debt resulted in the diversion of ever more resources from domestic needs into the hands of rich foreigners who purchased bonds issued by the US government to fund its borrowing. The restoration of fiscal integrity was therefore a necessary prerequisite for the renewal of the American economy.

Bush was well aware of all this, but his ill-judged pledge of "no new taxes", made when he was behind in the 1988 campaign, hung round his neck like a fiscal albatross. The president's initial determination to keep this promise denied him the most effective means to boost federal revenues and balance the budget. Bush's stand on taxes also made the Democrat-controlled Congress equally determined to ensure that the burden of budget-balancing should not fall on spending programs. There was little scope for retrenchment anyway. Over 90% of federal expenditure was committed to so-called uncontrollable programs, whose funding was mandatory rather than discretionary. As a result Bush's hopes of balancing the budget relied entirely on the economy achieving sufficiently high growth to generate the necessary additional revenues at current tax rates. The man who had once denounced Reagan's fiscal plans as voodoo economics now found himself practicing his own brand of voodoo budgeting. The cost of the savings-and-loan bail out (which ran at $81 billion in fiscal 1991), rising interest payments on the national debt (which passed the $4 trillion mark in fiscal 1992), and — above all — the depressing effect of recession on revenues made nonsense of Bush's fiscal calculations. The budget deficit rose from $152 billion in fiscal 1989 to a record $318 billion in fiscal 1992, instead of falling to $64 billion as projected by revised Gramm-Rudman-Hollings targets that the administration had agreed with Congress. To make matters worse, projections estimated that it would surpass $325 billion in fiscal 1993.

Disturbed by gloomy economic forecasts, Bush did try in 1990 to work out a budget compromise with Congress to keep the deficit from skyrocketing, but this proved ineffective. The White House and Democratic legislative leaders were deadlocked for several months over the inclusion of selective tax increases in a new fiscal package. In September the president was eventually forced to accept an increase in the top rate of income tax, higher excise taxes on gasoline, heating oil, cigarettes and beer, and savings of $60 billion over five years in Medicare costs that would come from raising premium charges and lowering payments to doctors and hospitals. In return the Democratic leaders agreed to some spending cuts and a capital gains tax cut. However this compromise fell foul of Republican and Democratic backbenchers in the House of Representatives, which rejected the enabling legislation. Democratic critics charged that the increase in Medicare premiums and indirect taxes would disproportionately affect people in the lower half of income distribution, while right-wing GOP congressmen vehemently protested about Bush's betrayal of his election pledge on taxes. Further administration concessions helped to produce a second budget compromise which was eventually enacted as the Omnibus Budget Reconciliation Act of 1990. The most significant change from the original proposals placed the main burden of the Medicare economies on doctors, hospitals and better-off beneficiaries.

The final stages of the budget imbroglio occurred at the very moment that Bush's popularity was at record levels because of his handling of the Gulf crisis. The fact that the US president experienced greater difficulty in marshaling a domestic coalition in support of a new fiscal program than in organizing an international coalition against Iraq was a sad comment on the political intractability of America's budget problems. In reality the White House and Democratic leaders in Congress had expended considerable political capital to secure an agreement that fell far short of what needed to be done. Both sides had avoided making the kind of painful choices about tax increases and spending cuts that were necessary to restore fiscal integrity. At best the 1990 compromise might have brought about a reduction of the deficit, not its elimination. In other words, the national debt would have continued to grow at a slightly slower pace. Even this modest goal was thwarted by a persistent recession that upset the revenue calculations on which spending projections were based.

The economy had slipped into recession in mid 1990. White House predictions that the decline would be shallow and short appeared to be borne out by promising economic indicators in the spring of 1991. In fact recovery proved very sluggish, and at one juncture — in the winter months of 1991–2 — there were fears that the country was on the verge of a double-dip recession. The causes of the decline were rooted in the structural problems of the American economy, which Reaganomics had done little to address and in some respects had aggravated.

The recession of the early 1990s was not typical of the business cycle recessions that have punctuated American economic history since World War II. Every recession from that of 1957–8 to that of 1981–2 was triggered by the tightening of monetary policy to curb inflationary pressures. In the run-up to the Bush-era recession, however, monetary policy was benign and inflation had been low for most of the previous decade. The root cause of rising unemployment was the difficulty experienced by many US corporations in facing increasingly fierce competition from abroad. Many firms had started to slash their payrolls in the late 1980s in a bid to make themselves leaner, fitter, and more competitive. Some of the businesses whose names were synonymous with the twentieth-century success of American capitalism were affected. Pan Am, once the world's premier airline, could not save itself from going out of business. IBM, which had pioneered the business systems revolution, underwent a painful restructuring involving the loss of many jobs. And General Motors, the world's largest automobile manufacturer, announced a four-year plan to cut 74,000 jobs after incurring a $7 billion loss on its North American operations in 1991. According to one gloomy analysis, by the end of 1992 fewer than 25% of US corporations had completed the necessary downscaling of their workforces in order to remain competitive in global terms.

Other problems compounded America's economic woes. The construction industry was in a slump, because a binge of overbuilding in the 1980s had glutted city skylines with empty office buildings. Los Angeles, for example, had a 24% office vacancy rate in 1991. The collapse of the savings and loans industry also had a depressing economic effect. So did the ending of the Cold War. Cutbacks in military spending had an immediate impact on California, where 72,000 jobs were lost in the aerospace and high-tech defense industries in 1990–1. One survey estimated that 900,000 defense industry jobs could be lost nationwide by 1996. Finally, the recession generated a vicious circle in relationship to the burden of debt that many Americans had accumulated in the Reagan boom years. Finding difficulty in repaying their loans in the economic circumstances of the early 1990s, corporations cut back on payrolls and consumers cut back on purchases, all of which aggravated recessionary trends.

The psychological effects of the recession were also immense. Unemployment, which peaked at 9%, was less severe than in the 1981–2 recession and the 1974–5 recession. Yet the impact on the national psyche was much greater than either of these previous declines. No doubt the sense of malaise bred by the recession was augmented by the loss of national purpose that accompanied the ending of the Cold War. One poll taken in April 1992 found that four-fifths of respondents were of the belief that the country was seriously on the wrong track, the highest level since 1973. Other surveys indicated that consumer confidence was at its lowest level in 17 years.

Throughout the 1980s Americans had grown accustomed to hearing doom-laden warnings that the economy was structurally weak. They were able to brush these aside because the underlying problems had not yet had an impact on the lives of most of them. It was almost as if they comforted themselves with the question, "If things are so bad, how come they are so good?" In fact things had not been so good. A crucial measurement of economic wellbeing was whether the real income of the average worker was rising. According to the economist Wallace C. Peterson, the United States has been in the grip of a "silent depression" for two decades because the real standard of living of single-income families has not risen since 1972. Only by having two incomes, instead of one, have most families enjoyed rising living standards over the last twenty years, and even two-income families have found a growing proportion of their wealth swallowed up by higher charges for housing, healthcare, and education. The recession brought home to many Americans, including those in the middle class, the reality of their precarious economic position. It made many families fearful about the future. Worries about job security grew, accompanied by concern about whether they could afford adequate health insurance, a good education for their children, and other necessities. Sensitive to this pessimistic mood, Federal Reserve chairman Alan Greenspan told a congressional committee in December 1991, "There is a deep-seated concern out there that I must say to you I haven't seen in my lifetime."

Surveys showed that pessimism had risen more sharply among the affluent than among lower-income groups. This reflected the fact that the middle classes were feeling the pinch of recession as never before. In 1992 white-collar workers constituted 36% of the unemployed, compared with 22% in the 1982 recession. Moreover, they were losing jobs in functional divisions of corporate middle management, such as accountancy, control, and planning, that looked like being lost permanently in the drive to make US business competitive. "We've never been in a situation quite like this," commented Janet Norwood, former US Commissioner of Labor Statistics, "It used to be that when we had a recession, everyone would wait to be rehired. But the psychology now is that many of these jobs are not going to come back."

The baby-boom generation, who had been born during the high summer of American economic strength in the postwar decades and had grown up to be the yuppies of the 1980s, had become the insecure middle classes of the 1990s. Daniel Yankelovich, one of the most perceptive analysts of shifts in the nation's mood, observed, "No group in the population was taken by surprise quite as much as the giant baby-boom cohort. The majority of affluent, well-educated baby-boomers had taken for granted, as if it were a law of nature, that the equity in their homes would increase every year, that jobs were secure, that incomes would rise steadily and inexorably, and that the smart sophisticated way to manage money was to leverage debt. Now this group, like almost every other group in the population except older affluent suburbanites, has been thrown badly of balance. Its assumptions for living are in disarray."

Race, rights, and riots

Coinciding with the economic problems of the early 1990s were disputes relating to racial issues that added to the nation's mood of uncertainty and exacerbated the divisions within it. Racial problems had bubbled under the surface of Reagan's America. They emerged in full force during the Bush era, culminating in the worst race riot since the 1960s.

What triggered the renewal of racial controversy was the apparent emergence of the constitutional counter-revolution which conservatives had been anticipating since the end of the Warren Court era. Thanks to appointments made by Presidents Reagan and Nixon, Bush was the first postwar Republican president to take office with a ready-made conservative majority on the Supreme Court. The last vestiges of Warren-era liberalism within this body disappeared with the retirement of Associate Justices William Brennan (in 1990) and Thurgood Marshall (in 1991). Their replacement by David Souter and Clarence Thomas solidified conservative preeminence on Chief Justice William Rehnquist's Supreme Court.

The conservative orientation of the Rehnquist Court was underlined by its stance on affirmative action. Seven rulings issued in 1989 all made it harder to prove job discrimination and easier to challenge affirmative action programs. These judgements, denounced by civil rights organizations as the "civil rights massacre of 1989" were: *City of Richmond* v. *J. A. Croson Company, Wards Cove Packing Co.* v. *Atonio, Martin* v. *Wilks, Patterson* v. *McLean Credit Union, Price Waterhouse* v. *Hopkins, Lorance* v. *AT&T Technologies*, and *Independent Federation of Flight Attendants* v. *Zipes.* The most significant of these was the *Wards Cove* case, which effectively overturned the landmark 1971 decision, *Griggs* v. *Duke Power Company.* According to the latter, the existence of discriminatory employment practice could be established through "disparate impact" statistical evidence showing that personnel practice had an adverse affect on minorities, even if there was no proof that an employer intended to discriminate. It required employers to prove that tests or other means of selecting employees that had a discriminatory impact were justified by what was termed "business necessity". By contrast *Wards Cove* shifted the burden of proof on to the plaintiff, who now had to demonstrate, instance by instance, that a particular employment practice was discriminatory. Statistics showing even dramatic racial (and gender) imbalance in job categories were no longer enough to prove employer discrimination.

Democratic congressional leaders decided to seek new legislation to counter the impart of the 1989 rulings. The result was the Civil Rights Act of 1990, which shifted the burden of justifying employment practices back to the employer and enabled employee-plaintiffs to establish that a practice had disparate impact without pinpointing the specific cause of the discrimination. It also allowed women and religious minorities who had established employer discrimination against them to be awarded substantial damages by the courts, a right that existing law only conferred on racial minorities. Bush himself favored some legislative redress against the *Wards Cove* judgement, but he chose to veto the Democratic measure. Though quotas were not at issue in the Civil Rights Act, the president claimed that it would result in businesses adopting strict hiring and promotion quotas for racial minorities and women in order to avoid costly discrimination suits.

The bill was reintroduced with some modifications in 1991 but the prospects of enactment seemed slim. In the 1990 midterm elections the victory of right-wing Republican Jesse Helms over Harvey Gantt, a black Democrat, in a close-fought senatorial election in North Carolina was widely attributed to his use of a racially-loaded television advertising campaign against affirmative action. This convinced GOP strategists that the issue could help the party with blue-collar voters and white southerners in the 1992 presidential election. As a result some Democrats, particularly moderates from the South and West, began to question the political wisdom of taking a strong stand on affirmative action. Meanwhile the business community, which had opposed the 1990 legislation, took an even stronger line against the new bill. Its supportive attitude towards affirmative action during the Reagan boom years had been supplanted by fears that a return to the pre-1989 situation would increase the likelihood of costly lawsuits at a time when many firms were engaged in corporate restructuring.

In spite of these difficulties, the second bill did become law after a year-long battle. A crucial role in the passage of the legislation was played by moderate Republican senators, led by John Danforth (Missouri), who feared that a hard-line GOP stand against affirmative action would hurt their standing among socially liberal suburban voters, especially women. They were able to win concessions in the terms of the bill to make it acceptable to Bush. The changes restricted the practice of "race norming", placed ceilings on damages that women plaintiffs could claim, and enabled the conservative-dominated courts to decide what constituted "business necessity". Meanwhile, the danger that opposition to affirmative action might associate the GOP with racism was highlighted when David Duke, a former Ku Klux Klansman and American Nazi party activist, won the Republican gubernatorial nomination in Louisiana. Though eventually defeated by his Democratic opponent, Edwin Edwards, Duke embarrassed the national Republican party by the crude racist appeal of his attacks on affirmative action and welfare. Bush himself was well aware that a second veto would appear to link him with Duke. He eventually signed the bill but signified his reservations through an accompanying statement that interpreted the civil rights it protected in a narrow fashion.

The maneuvering to enact the bill underlined the ambiguous nature of its political significance. It was the most important civil rights legislation since the mid 1960s, but its passage was no occasion for national rejoicing. The affirmative action legislation of 1991 was not underpinned by the kind of consensus that had existed outside the white South in support of the civil rights measures of 1964–5. The real significance of the Civil Rights Act of 1991 was that it ensured the preservation of the legacy of the civil rights revolution of the 1960s. It did not mark a major advance in civil rights, for its main purpose was to restore rights which racial minorities and women had enjoyed from 1971 to 1989.

The new legislation did little to lift the morale of the majority of the nation's 30 million black citizens. While white America coped with a recession, black America was in the midst of a far deeper crisis. The economic plight of blacks had been peripheral to the nation's political agenda throughout the 1980s. The recession did nothing to change this. It was significant that the principal election issues of 1992 — jobs, economic growth, healthcare, education, and crime — were perceived as "white" issues, even though blacks suffered far greater problems on each score.

Black unemployment ran at 12.1%, compared to the national rate of 7.1%. In 1990, the national poverty rate was 13.5%; for blacks it was 31.9%. In numerical terms there had been a 49% increase in the number of blacks living in poverty during the 1980s. Some blacks enjoyed real affluence, of course. One in seven black families had incomes exceeding $50,000 in 1989, and black college-educated married couples earned 93% of the family income of comparable white couples. Nevertheless, black males with college degrees were three times more likely to be unemployed than their white counterparts. Overall, the economic gap between blacks and whites was becoming wider. In 1990, the average annual income of blacks was only 56% that of whites, compared with 63% in 1975.

Black life expectancy was significantly lower than that of whites. In 1989, the death rate among 25 to 34-year-olds for blacks was 280 per 100,000, compared to 118 for whites. Blacks suffered far higher rates of coronary and lung disease, alcohol and drug dependency, and AIDS than whites. To make matters worse, a disproportionate number of the 35 million Americans who lacked any health insurance cover were black. On the education front, black college entrance levels rose in the 1980s, but several studies indicated that black children did less well at school than whites and Asian-Americans. Finally, blacks were caught up in a vicious circle of violent crime — they were far more likely than whites to be both victims and perpetrators of violence. In 1991 about one in four black males aged between 20 and 29 was either behind bars, or on probation, or on parole, and blacks made up 40% of prisoners on Death Row awaiting execution.

The sore of racial division became an open wound on April 30, 1992. On this day a Los Angeles suburban jury delivered a not guilty verdict on four white policemen, who stood accused of the vicious beating of an unarmed black citizen, Rodney King, in March 1991. This outcome flew in the face of the evidence, which included a videotape film of the incident shot by an amateur cameraman. Many blacks saw the verdict as epitomizing the disregard of the white suburbs for the plight of inner city ghettoes and as proof that the politico-legal system held the rights of blacks more cheaply than those of whites. Their rage spilled over into four days of violence, rioting and looting in south central Los Angeles. President Bush had to send in the army to restore order. The rioting left 47 people dead and 2,100 injured and resulted in over 9,000 people being arrested. The cost of the damage done to some 5,000 buildings was put at $500 million.

An uneasy peace was quickly restored to Los Angeles, and the rioting did not spread to other cities. Nevertheless, the nation's leaders could not agree on what should be done to prevent further disturbances. The Reverend Jesse Jackson, the last figure with a national voice still arguing for a resurrection of the Great Society, called for a domestic Marshall Plan. "We need a plan," he told a press conference, "There is a plan to rebuild eastern Europe, there is a plan to help Russia, but we have no plan to rebuild the cities of America." But the budget deficit stymied availability of new funds for such a project, even if the political will existed to implement it.

Moderate opinion, represented by the Democratic presidential candidate Bill Clinton and the Republican Jack Kemp, Secretary of Housing and Urban Development in the Bush administration, appeared to favor an entrepreneurial approach to the cities. Both talked of "empowerment" of the poor by the creation of inner city enterprise zones and tax-free havens to encourage jobs and investment. Yet new investment in the ghettoes was seemingly the last thing on the minds of white-owned banks and of black entrepreneurs who had long since fled to the suburbs. Though Bush himself promised cash aid to the city, the amounts on offer were nowhere enough to meet even the immediate needs of Los Angeles. Moreover, his national television address on the riots suggested that he was more interested in establishing his credentials as the guardian of law and order in the forthcoming election than in dealing with the underlying causes of the violence. "This is not about civil rights," Bush said, "but the brutality of the mob, pure and simple." In similar vein, Vice-President Dan Quayle attributed the rioting to the breakdown of family values and the high incidence of single-parent families in the Los Angeles ghetto.

Rise up, women

The Bush era also saw the intensification of political controversy over gender issues. The passage of the Civil Rights Act of 1991, and the Supreme Court judgements that preceded this, naturally affected women's interests as much as those of racial minorities. At the same time, women's rights organizations and pro-choice groups were increasingly concerned by judicial decisions that appeared to narrow the right of abortion established by the *Roe* v. *Wade* judgement of 1973.

The first judicial challenge to *Roe* centered on arguments that it had removed from the states their legitimate interest in protecting life before birth. A Justice Department brief, filed by the outgoing Reagan administration after the 1988 election (to avoid offending pro-choice Republican voters), contended that the Supreme Court had usurped the states' responsibility to evaluate competing ethical and scientific factors involved in abortion. The Rehnquist Court addressed this issue in *Webster* v. *Reproductive Health Services* (1989). The majority opinion upheld the constitutionality of a new Missouri state law that banned use of public clinics or hospitals for abortion, except for women whose lives were endangered by their pregnancy. Although this judgement had little immediate impact on the availability of abortions, which were mostly performed in private clinics in Missouri and other states, it represented a substantial modification of *Roe* v *Wade*. The Supreme Court had now recognized the principle that the states could restrict the availability of abortion, even though they could not ban it outright.

Webster shifted the focus of attention in the abortion controversy to the states. Hitherto pro-choice forces had largely relied on the federal courts to protect abortion. By contrast right-to-life forces had been active in state politics since *Roe* and had succeeded in electing anti-abortion state legislators in numbers disproportionate to the support that existed for their cause. The National Abortion Rights Action League (NARAL) undertook a major lobbying campaign to redress the balance. It warned, "To politicians who oppose choice, we say . . . 'Take our rights, lose your jobs.' " The effect on the states was significant. By 1993, according to NARAL, 50 of the 99 state legislative bodies supported keeping abortion legal and 31 opposed it, compared with 24 and 55 respectively in 1989. In addition, 31 state governors were pro-choice, compared with 16 four years earlier. But pro-choice success was only partial, for 82 of the state legislative bodies are currently in favor of imposing some restriction on abortion rights. This is broadly in line with public opinion. In 1993, according to a national Gallup poll, 32% of adults felt that abortion should be legal under any circumstance, 13% took the opposite view, and 51% believed that it should be legal under certain circumstances.

The Supreme Court returned to center stage in the abortion controversy when a case relating to a new Pennsylvania anti-abortion law, *Planned Parenthood of Southeastern Pennsylvania* v. *Casey*, came before it in 1992. A bloc of four justices (Rehnquist, Antonin Scalia, Byron White, and Thomas) saw this as an opportunity to overturn *Roe*. Conversely, two justices (Harry Blackmun and John Paul Stevens) wanted to reaffirm *Roe* unequivocally, and three Reagan-Bush appointees (Sandra Day O'Connor, Anthony Kennedy, and Souter) upheld the central principle of this decision, while supporting aspects of the Pennsylvania law. The *Casey* judgement, written by O'Connor, replaced the trimester framework of the *Roe* decision with a ruling that states could regulate abortion but could not place an "undue burden" on the woman's right to terminate her pregnancy before viability. This right, O'Connor wrote, "is a rule of law and a component of liberty we cannot renounce." Also in contrast to *Roe*, which emphasized medical and social matters in justifying abortion, the *Casey* judgement placed the question of women's ability to control their reproductive lives in the context of modern doctrines of equality.

To anti-abortion groups, like the National Right to Life Committee, the opinion was a stronger affirmation of abortion rights than *Roe*. Chief Justice Rehnquist was more sanguine, claiming that the plurality opinion was a retreat from the substance of *Roe*, which "continues to exist, but only in the way a storefront on a Western movie set exists: a mere facade to give the illusion of reality." Many pro-choice groups took the same view, fearing that restrictive interpretations of what constituted "undue burden" on the right of abortion would severely limit the woman's right to choose. They also complained that the *Casey* judgement, like *Webster*, had effectively put women into two classes: those who lived in states where abortion was widely available on the terms defined by *Roe*, and out-of-staters who could afford the travel and accommodation costs to obtain abortion in these places; and those — mainly the young, the poor, and the rural — who were economically entrapped in states with restrictive abortion laws. To redress this situation, pro-choice supporters called for a freedom-of-choice federal law that would restore abortion rights that existed prior to the *Webster* decision.

Women were in the forefront of the pro-choice movement, of course, and some like Phyllis Schlaffly were active on the opposite side. But the legislative bodies and the courts that had the power to decide how much control women had over their bodies were dominated by men. For many women the nomination of federal judge Clarence Thomas, a black conservative and former head of the Equal Employment Opportunities Commission, as Supreme Court justice became a symbol of the incapacity of American government to properly represent their interests. During confirmation hearings by the Senate Judiciary Committee in the fall of 1991, Thomas resolutely refused to state his position on abortion, claiming he had never thought about the *Roe* judgement. The controversy intensified when the law professor Anita Hill, who claimed to have been the victim of sexual harassment by Thomas, was subjected to hostile interrogation by Republican members of the all-male committee. The treatment of Hill epitomized the relative powerlessness of women, and Thomas's subsequent confirmation by the Senate (albeit by the closest margin of approval given to a successful Supreme Court nominee) seemed to indicate that her charges were either not believed or deemed unimportant.

The related issues of abortion rights and the Thomas hearings did much to crystallize a new activism by women in electoral politics. "If we are ever going to make a change on any of our issues — reproductive freedom, health, violence, workplace reform — we've got to change the faces", said the National Organization for Women president, Patricia Hill, "If there was any object lesson out of Clarence Thomas-Anita Hill, it was that we cannot rely on anybody else to represent us. We have to be there to represent ourselves. And it's got to be now." Feminist groups who had long squabbled over legislative priorities united in promoting women candidates to run in the 1992 elections. Women's professional groups, once largely apolitical, became active in the same cause. Meanwhile, Republican women, long overshadowed by Democrat-dominated groups, set up their own organizations to promote GOP women candidates, and Republicans for Choice, a largely female group, became more vociferous in challenging the influence of right-to-life advocates within the party.

A record 119 women, 81 Democrats and 38 Republicans, eventually ran for Senate or House seats (including non-voting delegates), compared with 60 in 1988. Women also won in unprecedented numbers in 1992, boosting the number of women senator from two to six and women representatives from 30 to 47. California became the first state to elect two women senators, Barbara Boxer and Diane Feinstein, both Democrats. Illinois elected the first black woman senator, Carol Mosely Braun, whose victory in the Democratic primary over incumbent Alan Dixon did much to set off the political challenge of women nationwide. Many observers felt that the 1992 elections had broken the last barriers against women candidates and had laid the basis for more to win office at national and state level in the future. As Stephen Hess of the Brookings Institution observed, "The year of the woman was not just a slogan."

Mandate for change?

The relatively high number of female candidates for congressional office was not the only unusual feature of the 1992 elections. Bill Clinton's triumph over George Bush was only the second time since 1964 that the Democrats had succeeded in winning the presidency. The scale of this victory was less than overwhelming. Thanks to the intervention of independent candidate Ross Perot, Clinton received just 43 percent of the popular vote, some three percent less than Michael Dukakis in 1988 and the third smallest winning share in twentieth-century presidential elections. Despite this, Clinton's victory was significant for at least two reasons. Firstly, he showed signs of developing a new Democratic agenda that reflected the concerns of a new political coalition. And, secondly, he was elected on a frank platform of revitalized government that rejected the anti-statist ideals of Reaganism.

The race for the 1992 Democratic presidential nomination indicated that the party's political center of gravity was moving away from its New Deal-Great Society past. Mario Cuomo and Jesse Jackson, the most eminent liberals, were deterred by Bush's post-Gulf war popularity from declaring their candidacies. The same was true of other senior Democrats with centrist views, notably Senator Albert Gore (Tennessee), Congressman Richard Gephard (Missouri), and Senator Sam Nunn (Georgia). Among those who did throw their hat into the ring, only Tom Harkin unambiguously identified himself as a traditional liberal, and he soon dropped out of the race because of poor results in the early primaries. The rest of the field comprised of moderates who wanted to modernize the Democratic party's image in order to appeal to middle class constituencies. With the exception of 1976, each contest for the Democratic presidential nomination since 1968 had developed into a race between candidates representing different wings of the party, but the 1992 election became a struggle between two candidates — Bill Clinton and Paul Tsongas — whose political positions were broadly similar.

Tsongas, who had first been elected to Congress in the post-Watergate midterm elections of 1974, was an articulate neoliberal. He combined a strong attack on Bush's approach to civil rights and women's rights with an appeal to Democrats to understand that they had to embrace business and economic growth to prevent the United States from falling further behind in international economic competition. This had much in common with the themes previously developed by Gary Hart and Michael Dukakis in their campaigns for the Democratic presidential nomination in 1984 and 1988 respectively.

Clinton, too, spoke the language of neoliberalism, though with some southern variations in the dialect. His first bid for office was an unsuccessful run for Congress in 1974, the formative year in the electoral emergence of neoliberals. Thereafter he focused his energies on winning state office in Arkansas, becoming governor at age 32 in 1978 and winning five further terms (interrupted by a single defeat in 1980). Clinton gained an entree into national politics largely through his role on the Democratic Leadership Council (DLC), an organization formed in 1985 to promote the influence of moderates from the South and West within the party.

Though the DLC was disdained by left-wing Democrats, the political differences between it and the likes of Jesse Jackson were far smaller than had been the case between liberal Democrats and conservative Southerners in the postwar era. The old generation of states rights Democrats had largely passed from the political scene in the 1970s. The DLC represented a new generation of southern Democratic leadership which accepted the legacy of the civil rights revolution and whose position within the mainstream of the party enabled its members to bid for national office, which old-style southern Democrats had no serious prospect of winning. Led initially by Sam Nunn and Governor Charles Robb of Virginia, it wanted to de-McGovernize the Democratic agenda, in other words to move the party away from foreign policy liberalism and tax-and-spend domestic policies. However, Clinton, who rose quickly within DLC ranks to become its chairman, argued that it should not get bogged down in a conservative versus liberal debate, but should seek to become the voice of modernity and new ideas within the party. The ending of the Cold War and the onset of economic problems lent weight to his call for a fresh agenda.

Clinton's triumph over Tsongas was partly due to superior campaign organization and finance and greater personal charisma. Paradoxically, it also owed something to the support he won from the remnants of the New Deal political coalition. Although Tsongas outpolled him among suburban middle-class voters in the early primaries, Clinton did consistently well among the aged, blacks, and labor voters. In essence he won the nomination by combining the votes of the South (where the absence of a black candidate benefited him) and the cities. Nevertheless, Clinton was well aware that he had to widen his appeal to other groups if he was to be elected president. It was evident that he had to choose between a suburban strategy or a southern strategy to expand his base. The latter would have enabled Clinton to capitalize on his regional identity, but it was ruled out because the Republicans appeared to have established an unassailable hold over the southern states in the two previous presidential elections. A suburban strategy seemed more promising. It enabled Clinton to focus on areas where Dukakis had run relatively well in 1988, to exploit middle class concerns about the recession, and to capitalize on the fact that the 1992 election would be the first in American history in which the majority of votes would be cast by suburban dwellers.

The 1990 census showed that the demographic trends of the second half of the twentieth century were reaching culmination. Nearly a half of the nation now lived in suburbs, compared to a third in 1960. Seventy years earlier another historically significant census, that of 1920, was the first to record that a majority of Americans were urban dwellers. The New Deal coalition had come into existence shortly afterwards to represent the urban nation. Some analysts claimed that the Democrats could build a new coalition in the 1990s, this time to represent the suburban nation.

Suburban society was not homogeneous, of course, but two large groups within it were regarded as particularly suitable for targeting by a Democratic candidate able to promote a new party image. The analyst William Schneider labelled one group the " 'new collar' Baby Boomers", who were in their thirties and forties, were relatively affluent and well educated, and tended to be fiscally conservative and socially liberal in their political outlook. According to Schneider, "They are independent by heritage and anti-establishment by inclination. They don't like racial politics. They are pro-choice on abortion. And they feel betrayed by George Bush on the economy." The second group were moderate-income whites who had graduated from being the middle Americans of the 1960s to the Reagan Democrats of the 1980s. Pollster Stanley Greenberg, a member of the Clinton campaign team, had conducted detailed surveys of what he called the "working middle class" in a Detroit suburb during the 1980s. According to him, these voters were more progressive on economic issues than on social issues, but evinced concern that the Democratic party had lost contact with mainstream groups and values. Above all they felt that it had neglected their interests in order to expand government programs that benefited racial minorities and welfare recipients.

Clinton's message in the campaign against Bush was pitched squarely at these two groups. "The forgotten middle class", as he called them, became as crucial to the political imagery of the 1992 election as blue-collar workers had been to Democratic presidential campaigns during the heyday of the New Deal party system. Determined to avoid being tarred by the Republicans as a tax-and-spend liberal, Clinton promised that he would only raise taxes on upper-income families earning over $200,000 a year. When addressing expenditure issues, he tended to speak not of government spending but of government investment to boost jobs and to improve infrastructure, education, health care provision, and the welfare system. Clinton pledged to remold government to make it less bureaucratic and more entrepreneurial, in essence to make the state an investor in human capital rather than a guarantor of dependency-creating, incentive-destroying assistance. This "people-based economics" as he called it, enabled him to associate the Democrats with the values of work, personal responsibility, family and community, which were dear to baby-boomer suburbanites and the working middle class. Nor was this mere rhetorical flourish, for it conveyed the substance of his long-term economic strategy.

Clinton ran for office at a time when pro-Democratic elements had recaptured the intellectual initiative in the debate over economic policy. In the face of the recession, it was progressive economists like Robert Reich and Ira Magaziner and the Progressive Policy Institute, a think-tank linked to the DLC, who were the fount of new ideas. Clinton's economic proposals reflected their influence. The Democratic candidate avowed that the cure for the American economy did not lie in the quick-fix macroeconomics of fiscal or monetary policy. In a world of intense global competition, he believed that the US government could best promote higher living standards by focusing on the factors of production that are fixed, namely the workforce and infrastructure. Economic and social policies were therefore interwoven in the Clinton agenda. He was the first successful presidential candidate in American history to tell voters that the country was falling behind its economic competitors because government was failing to provide services which other leading nations took for granted.

Though Clinton stopped short of proposing a formal industrial policy, it was evident that he intended government to have a positive and constructive role, rather than a minimal one, in fostering economic renewal. He pledged massive federal investment in communications and public plant to compensate for the fact that the United States had devoted a smaller share of national wealth to infrastructure than any leading industrial nation in the 1980s. A concern to improve US competitiveness also underlay his education proposals. In a global economy that has become a seamless web for capital, a well-educated and highly trained workforce is an advantage for attracting foreign investment in new industrial development. The Democratic manifesto contained proposals for a national apprentice program modeled on what Germany currently possesses. It also outlined a plan to give every young person the right to a post-high school education by the establishment of a national trust fund to make student loans, that would be repayable from future salaries or through community service. This has parallels with the GI Bill of Rights of 1944, which did much to finance education for the generation of managers and professionals who administered US capitalism during its halcyon postwar period.

Healthcare reform to control the costs of medical service provision and establish a basic universal health insurance system was another prominent feature of Clinton's agenda. If enacted, it would benefit not only the 35 million low-income Americans who currently have no health insurance, but would also ease the financial burdens on corporate America. The country currently spends more of its national output on healthcare than any of the 23 other members of the Organization for Economic Cooperation and Development (nearly 15% in 1989, compared with the OECD average of less than 10%). The private sector also finances about 60% of US healthcare expenditures, compared with the average of 20% in other OECD countries. Employer-based private health insurance schemes, a fringe benefit that became widespread in the 1940s and 1950s, carry much of this burden. The costs inevitably reduced the capital that American companies had available for investment in productivity improvements, with consequent damage to the country's international competitiveness. All other G-7 nations spend proportionately less than the United States on healthcare, but their governments manage to fund a healthcare system that offers universal coverage.

Clinton's approach to welfare issues was also well-suited to his suburban strategy. As Arkansas governor he had firmly established his credentials as a leading advocate and practitioner of workfare policy, which required welfare recipients to develop a sense of personal responsibility for self-improvement. Not only had he been instrumental in promoting the Family Support Act of 1988, he had also established a state workfare program that provided welfare benefits, educational opportunities, training and childcare for a two-year period, after which recipients were obliged to get jobs or undertake community service. Clinton's campaign rhetoric suggested that as president he would seek further reform of federal welfare provision based on the Arkansas model. He frequently spoke of wanting to transform the welfare system, promising a "new covenant [that] will say to people on welfare: We're going to provide the training and education and health care you need, but if you can work, you've got to go to work, because you can no longer stay on welfare forever." This emphasis on obligation and opportunity as well as security for welfare recipients had something in common with the War on Poverty's original intention to equip the poor with the values and the skills to operate effectively in the labor market. But Clinton never explained why his policy should prove more successful in the difficult economic climate of the 1990s than Lyndon Johnson's had in the prosperous 1960s.

In contrast to the fresh agenda offered by Clinton, George Bush seemed devoid of new ideas and unable to offer Americans hope of a better future. In fact — despite being pilloried as a foreign policy president — Bush had a creditable list of domestic achievements. In his efforts to grapple with the damaging fiscal legacy of Reaganomics, he had accepted the second-largest tax increase in US history in 1990. Bush's social policy was more generous than his predecessor's. During his stewardship, federal spending on elementary schooling had risen from $8.5 billion to $14 billion, the preschool program had been boosted, federal spending on child nutrition had risen steadily, Medicaid spending had doubled, and more resources had been put into crime prevention and inner city renewal. Nor had Bush reneged on those worst hit by the recession. The number of food stamp recipients increased by 37% between 1989 and 1992, and unemployment insurance coverage had been extended in response to the economic downturn.

Nevertheless, the recession blighted Bush's term in office. The Republicans had dominated the presidency in the 1980s because voters had more confidence in them than the Democrats to manage the economy. This confidence evaporated in the early 1990s. Bush's claims that things were not so bad as Clinton made them out to be fell on deaf ears, even though unemployment was lower than in most other OECD countries in 1992 and there were distinctive signs of economic upturn in the last quarter of the year. Foreign policy, the Republican banner issue in the recent past, also became entwined with economic problems. Polls taken during the campaign showed that public opinion, as had been the case since late 1991, still regarded the safeguarding of US jobs and economic interests as the nation's international priority. Bush was insufficiently sensitive to the popular mood. His references to world affairs in the campaign tended to emphasize his record as a conflict manager in bringing the Cold War to successful resolution and winning the Gulf war. Clinton, by contrast, highlighted the need for domestic renewal as a precondition for the country continuing to play a strong role in world affairs. In this way he skilfully synthesized domestic and international concerns into the single issue of economic renewal, much as John Kennedy's pledge to get the country moving again had done in the 1960 election campaign.

In a desperate bid to focus popular attention away from the economy (and to mend fences with conservative Republicans who disdained his tax increases), the president sought to emphasize his social-issue conservatism and portray Clinton as a legatee of the cultural changes of the 1960s. Vice-President Quayle went on the attack to portray the Democrats as hostile to family values, while Pat Buchanan and televangelist Pat Robertson, now heading an organization called the Christian Coalition, were given prominent roles in the GOP convention at Houston. The Republican platform reaffirmed the core values of the 1980s. As one journalist commented, "Instead of a battle plan to hold the middle, the [platform] drafters composed a bugle call to their most ardent constituency, the shock troops on the right." These tactics failed to weaken the electoral primacy of economic issues, and only succeeded in alienating moderate Republican voters, particularly pro-choice women.

To add to Bush's problems, Clinton was not the only challenger that he faced in the election. A maverick Texan billionaire, Ross Perot, launched what proved to be the most significant challenge for the presidency by an independent in modern times. His candidacy benefited from two great advantages. One was that he was not a professional politician. With popular esteem for politics and politicians at an all-time low because of gridlock government and the recession, the Texan delivered an alluring message — that America needed the no-nonsense approach of a corporate chief executive in the White House to make things work in Washington. His other advantage was his personal fortune, though he was entirely successful in projecting himself not as a rich businessman but as a patriot with the nation's interests at heart. Perot spent some $60 million on television advertisements and half-hour "info-mercials" on national television. At midyear he was neck-and-neck with Clinton and Bush in the polls, but he pulled out of the campaign in July, making bizarre and unsubstantiated allegations of Republican dirty tricks against his family. After re-entering the race in early October, he performed well in the presidential debates without ever threatening the kind of breakthrough that had once seemed possible.

Perot did not carry a single state in the electoral college, but his popular vote tally of 19% was the highest by an independent candidate since Theodore Roosevelt won 27% in 1912. His presence activated unusual popular enthusiasm in the campaign, reflected by the increased voter turn-out (54%, compared with 50% in 1988). Perot drew an almost equal number of votes away from both Bush and Clinton. Exit polls suggested that had he not been on the ballot, 38% of his support would have gone to Clinton, 37% to Bush, and 6% to minor candidates (while 15% would not have voted at all). Nevertheless, Perot hurt Bush more than Clinton. He articulated the need for change that the Democratic candidate also advocated. He attacked Bush far more than Clinton, ensuring that the former effectively had to fight against two opponents. His main areas of strength were the South and the West, traditionally Republican bastions. Finally, Perot's big issues were the deficit and the burgeoning national debt, which focused attention on the plight of the economy, Bush's big vote-loser. As his campaign developed, the Texan also began to speak in Clintonian terms, though with less precision, of the need to tackle issues like infrastructure, education, and healthcare in pursuit of economic renewal.

Judgements about the political significance of the 1992 vote for president must necessarily be made with caution. The election of a Democratic president reflected dissatisfaction with the economy rather than a popular demand for renewed governmental activism. One exit poll found that 55% of voters preferred government that cost less while providing fewer services, and only 36% wanted government that provided more services while costing more in taxes. Similarly, 69% of respondents in a pre-inauguration poll agreed that the federal government created more problems than it solved. The end of the era of divided government was not accompanied by a surge in Democratic party identification. The two parties remained closely matched in voter identication for most of 1992, with the Democrats holding a lead of just 3% on election day. Like every Democratic presidential candidate from 1968 onward, Clinton failed to win a plurality of white voters. According to most exit polls, Bush had a one-to-two percent lead with this constituency, a far narrower margin than Republicans usually enjoyed because of Perot's intervention. The racial polarization of the electorate remained strong, with 82% of blacks voting for Clinton.

But there were encouraging signs for the Democrats. The working middle class appeared to be coming back to the fold. Clinton won 56% of Democratic identifiers who had backed Ronald Reagan in 1984 and 23% of all voters who supported Bush in 1988. His centrist strategy was also vindicated by the distribution of ideological voting. Self-described conservatives and liberals split about exactly the same for Bush and Clinton respectively, but moderates gave Clinton 48% of their votes, compared with 31% for Bush and 21% for Perot. Clinton gained 44% of the suburban vote, 52% of the urban vote, and 43% of the rural/small town vote (compared with Bush's figures of 36%, 32%, and 38% respectively). His lead in the suburbs proved particularly important in his good showing in the Midwest, a crucial battleground in 1992. Exit polls also suggested that suburban voters were less divided along income lines than urban or rural voters. In the cities and countryside Clinton won huge leads among low-income and lower middle-income voters, but did less well among the affluent. In suburbia, by contrast, voters with incomes over $50,000 were just as likely to support him as those with moderate incomes.

Clinton's support comprised of three main elements: the remnants of the New Deal coalition (trade union families, the aged, and racial minorities); the Reagan Democrats; and the suburbs. To forge a new coalition, he must win over voters from the last two groups who went to Perot in 1992. The independent candidate won the backing of 21% of Reagan Democrats and 20% of voters who supported Bush in 1988. He also took 20% of the suburban vote. The task facing Clinton is reminiscent of Richard Nixon's need to win over voters that had backed George Wallace in 1968. The bridge between Nixon and the Wallaceites was sociocultural conservatism. Clinton's prospects of winning over Perot supporters would appear to depend on what progress he makes in dealing with budget problems and the structural deficiencies of the American economy, issues which formed the core of the independent's campaign agenda.

* * *

George Bush was the last Cold War president. In 1992 Americans elected Bill Clinton to become their first post-Cold War president. Bush's successes in foreign policy could not compensate for his evident inability to deal with problems besetting the American economy. Though he was not to blame for these problems, which were not susceptible to quick-fix solutions, his failure to address the issue of economic renewal conveyed the impression that his administration and the Republican party had run out of ideas and could not respond to the new challenges of post-Cold War America. Like Franklin D. Roosevelt in 1932, Clinton owed his election as president more to the economic failures of the incumbent administration than to the appeal of his own agenda. Unlike Roosevelt, he is a "new" Democrat, rather than a "New Deal" Democrat. Nevertheless, he took office at a time when the US economy was facing a crisis as great in some respects as that of the 1930s. It is likely, therefore, that his success as president, as well as his place in American political history, will depend on whether he emulates Roosevelt in enabling US capitalism to work better than it had been able to do with the party of business, the Republicans, in power.

Conclusion: Beyond the Liberal Consensus

A liberal consensus on the role of government in the economy and society and about US involvement in world affairs implanted coherence to American politics in the two decades after World War II. Since 1965, however, the American polity had been characterized by division, fragmentation, and lack of coherent political direction. Conservatism made a political comeback, but its impact and its support were not sufficient to establish a new consensus.

America's postwar consensus broke down in a different manner to Britain's. The political scientist Dennis Kavanagh has attributed the decline of consensus in Britain to the interrelationship of three factors — ideas, people and circumstances. The ideas of a British new right were initially formulated in the 1940s and 1950s when the postwar consensus was at its peak, they gained the support of influential figures within the Conservative party in the late 1960s and early 1970s when this consensus began to fray, and they became the basis of public policy after economic failures discredited Keynesianism and paved the way for the election of the Thatcher administration in 1979. Ideas, people, and circumstances were also linked together in the conservative revival of the 1970s and 1980s in the United States. However, America's liberal consensus had broken down because of its inherent contradictions long before the right posed its challenge to postwar orthodoxy.

The Vietnam war generated the first serious fissures in the postwar consensus by raising questions about the limits of American power. In response, detente was conceived as a new way to pursue globalism by cheaper means, but diplomatic failures eroded its domestic support. By 1976 internationalist opinion among the nation's political leaders and the foreign policy establishment was no longer monolithic in support of anticommunist priorities. Those who could now be labeled conservative internationalists continued to support the verities of global containment and anticommunism. In contrast, liberal internationalists wanted to move beyond Cold War concerns to address

271

peace, disarmament, human rights, foreign aid, and the resolution of international economic problems.

In domestic policy it was the new directions taken by liberalism rather doubts about established programs that undermined consensus. The Great Society's efforts to assist racial minorities identified liberalism with equality of result rather than mere equality of opportunity. This laid the basis for redistributionist policies like affirmative action which sought to ensure that economic and social equality were actually achieved. The Great Society was also imbued with a new belief that welfare was a right because the poor were helpless victims who could not function in the modern economic system without government assistance. The new liberalism made the Democrats vulnerable to charges of being a tax-and-spend party who squandered the wealth created by ordinary hard-working people on dependence-creating welfare and aid programs that were inherently unfair. New political divisions emerged between those who wished to build on the Great Society and those who sought to roll it back. In this respect there was a marked difference between the modern Republican right and the Thatcherite right in Britain. Whereas the latter sought to eradicate many public policies that grew out of Britain's postwar consensus, the former implicitly accepted much of the New Deal legacy and directed its resentment against the public policy of the 1960s.

The cultural ferment of the 1960s created further divisions. Sociomoral debate had not rippled the surface of postwar politics owing to the primacy of traditional mores and gender roles. All this changed in the latter part of the 1960s and early 1970s with the emergence of new social issues. Pressure groups, political parties, and the courts became involved in conflicts over rights and values. Liberalism became associated with modern secular values, notably equal rights for women, the right of abortion and, eventually, gay rights. Meanwhile conservatism took up the defense of traditional values under the pro-family banner.

The final blows to the liberal consensus were dealt by the economic problems of the 1970s. Postwar political debate had been conducted within the context of expanding economic opportunities. Politicians did not face harsh choices about whether to prioritize low inflation or low unemployment. However the failure of Keynesian policy to cure stagflation undermined economic policy consensus. Blaming America's decline on overtaxation, overspending, and overregulation by government, the Republicans insisted on prioritizing a cure for inflation over unemployment and encouraging private wealth creation. This led ultimately to the free-market, supply-side doctrines of the Reagan era. Only in the context of economic policy, therefore, did the Republicans openly challenge the assumptions of the postwar liberal consensus. In the meantime the Democrats clung uncertainly and inconsistently to the remnants of Keynesian economic doctrine.

Economic decline more than anything accounted for the shift rightward of the Republican party. Without this development, the GOP might have become rooted in the middle-way politics pursued by Richard Nixon to build a new majority. Ronald Reagan's election in 1980 marked the triumph of a new Republican right that was far more astute than its Goldwaterite predecessor in promoting its message, had a new regional base in the Sunbelt, and had intellectual legitimacy thanks to the outpouring of new conservative economic ideas in the 1970s. With Reagan's victory the Republicans ceased to be the "me too" party that they had been in the postwar era. They now stood for the restoration of the free-market economy, the roll-back of the state (at least to its pre-1965 shape), family values, and the resumption of the global struggle against communism.

The breakdown of the liberal consensus also compelled internal debate among the Democrats but the outcome was complex and ambiguous. Three groups sought to shape the party's outlook, though none established dominance. These were liberals who identified with low-income constituents, the neoliberals who largely represented the suburbs, and moderates from the South and West who formed the Democratic Leadership Council. The first group advocated domestic policies that followed New Deal-Great Society traditions and a post-Cold War foreign policy. Neoliberals also embraced liberal internationalism but sought to redirect the party's domestic priorities from welfare Keynesianism to policies that enhanced economic competitiveness. The DLC held similar views to the neoliberals on domestic policy but disagreed with their antimilitarist foreign policy. In spite of their disagreements, these Democratic factions were united in one belief that defined their fundamental difference with Reaganism. Though wanting to employ the powers of the state in different ways, they regarded government as a positive instrument of public purpose.

The downfall of the liberal consensus was marked by the decline of the New Deal political coalition and the Democrats' loss of majority status. But the kind of critical realignment necessary to establish a new Republican majority party did not occur. GOP success at presidential level was paralleled by continuing Democratic success at congressional level. With the exception of 1981, divided government posed an insuperable impediment to the achievement of the Reagan Revolution. Nothing resembling a new conservative consensus emerged in the 1980s. Less than one in three Americans characterized their views as conservative. Voters expressed preference for Republican economic and foreign policies by electing Ronald Reagan and George Bush president. Yet doubts about Republican stewardship of public services were reflected by their willingness to keep the Democrats in control of the House of Representatives (and to restore them to power in the Senate in 1986). In short, a strong case can be made that divided party control of government in the Reagan-Bush era reflected a divided American political mind.

During the second half of the 1980s polls indicated that a majority of Americans were in favor of divided government, but its disadvantages were revealed in the early 1990s. The political symbol of the Bush era was gridlock government. Cold War victory changed the context of American politics and prefaced intensified concern with domestic issues. But two polarized political parties, one controlling the presidency and the other the Congress, appeared incapable of effective common action to tackle worsening budgetary, economic and social problems. In these circumstances public approval of divided government underwent marked decline. Americans signaled this change of heart in 1992 by restoring single party control of government for only the second time since 1968, but this did not signify popular acceptance of Bill Clinton's new Democratic agenda.

Clinton claimed to offer a different approach from both tax-and-spend liberalism and minimal-government conservatism. His New Covenant program entailed respect for market forces while also placing emphasis on social solidarity. Clinton's issues — jobs, education, healthcare, and welfare — had figured strongly in the presidential campaigns of Harry Truman, John Kennedy and Lyndon Johnson, but now they were part of a fresh agenda. Clinton had to address the problems of economic decline, while these earlier Democratic presidents sought only to compensate for the flaws and omissions of US capitalism at the height of its power. In essence Clintonomics is a Democratic version of supply-side economics, which prioritizes private and public investment to make the economy more productive and more competitive to the benefit of all Americans.

Clinton's program struck a chord among left-liberal forces throughout the world. President Mario Soares of Portugal, the grand old man of European social democracy, declared: "This is the first coherent blueprint for the future of liberal politics, and it should not be allowed to fail." After its "tax-and-spend image" sent it down to a fourth successive electoral defeat in 1992, the British Labour party began to remodel its policies along Clintonian lines. Reformers in such diverse countries as Italy, Russia and Japan proclaimed Clinton their inspiration. However, Clinton's efforts to convert ideas into actual policy ran into considerable problems at home.

Clinton's domestic position was inevitably weakened by the fact that he was a minority president lacking a clearcut electoral mandate. He also inherited an office that had shown only sporadic ability over the last twenty years to provide strong domestic leadership. Whereas Clinton's campaign had focused clearly on economic issues, he predictably found it difficult to keep the same degree of control over the political agenda as president. The new administration was soon embroiled in damaging controversies over the gays-in-the-armed-forces issue, Cabinet appointments, and foreign policy. More seriously, the programs outlined by Clinton in his campaign required domestic spending to be substantially increased over the next four years, but he found on taking office that the budget crisis was far more serious than he had anticipated. In contrast to his optimistic campaign statements, the new president began to talk of sharing the pain of tax increases to build a better tomorrow. This encouraged Republicans and many Democrats to oppose his proposals in Congress. A jobs stimulus package was defeated and watered-down deficit-reduction proposals were only approved by the narrowest of margins in spite of assiduous presidential lobbying.

Nevertheless, Clinton has recorded important achievements during his first year in office. A $500-billion four-year deficit reduction plan made up of spending cuts and tax increases has been enacted. Clinton has also made progress on his infrastructure-improvement agenda. Legislation providing government loans for college education that are repayable through community service has been approved. A health reform plan, devised by a task force under Hillary Clinton's leadership, has been unveiled. And a five-year plan for a leaner, more mobile and more cost-effective United States military equipped to deal with the regional challenges of the post-Cold War era has been drawn up by the Pentagon.

Clinton's first-year difficulties indicate the continued absence of consensus in American politics. The divisions that have fragmented the US polity since the mid-1960s are still evident in the mid-1900s. Clinton must overcome these in order to establish a new agenda of economic renewal and convince Americans that government is not just part of the problem, but part of the solution. His success or failure in this task will have immense implications for America's capacity to enhance its competitiveness in the new global economy and to provide international leadership into the twenty-first century.

Select Bibliography

The seminal analysis of the liberal consensus is Godfrey Hodgson, *In Our Time: America from World War II to Nixon*, New York: Macmillan, 1977. For comparison with Britain, see Dennis Kavanagh, *Thatcherism and British Politics: The End of Consensus?*, 2nd edn, Oxford University Press, 1990.

There are a number of very good surveys of American history from the 1940s through to the 1980s. Most useful for this study were: William Chafe, *The Unfinished Journey: America since World War II*, 2nd edn, New York: Oxford University Press, 1991; William E. Leuchtenburg, *A Troubled Feast: American Society Since 1945*, 2nd edn, Boston: Little, Brown, 1983; Frederick Siegal, *Troubled Journey: From Pearl Harbor to Reagan*, New York: Hill & Wang, 1984; and Michael Barone, *Our Country: From Roosevelt to Reagan*, New York: Free Press, 1990.

The Cold War consensus and its decline are surveyed by: Stephen Ambrose, *Rise to Globalism: American Foreign Policy since 1938*, 6th edn, New York: Viking, 1991; Thomas J. McCormick, *America's Half-Century: U.S. Foreign Policy in the Cold War*, Baltimore: Johns Hopkins University Press, 1989; Walter LaFeber, *The American Age*, New York: Norton: 1989; and Charles Kegley and Eugene Wittkopf, *American Foreign Policy: Pattern and Process*, 4th edn, New York: St Martin's Press, 1991.

For the rise and decline of liberal economic doctrines, see: Nicolas Spulber, *Managing the American Economy from Roosevelt to Reagan*, Bloomington: Indiana University Press, 1989; Herbert Stein, *Presidential Economics*, New York: Simon & Schuster, 1985; and James Savage, *Balanced Budgets and American Politics*, Ithaca: Cornell University Press, 1987.

Steve Fraser and Gary Gerstle (eds), *The Rise and Fall of the New Deal Political Order, 1930–1980*, Princeton University Press, 1989 (particularly the essays by Alan Brinkley, Ira Katznelson, and Jonathan Rieder), and Alonzo L. Hamby, *Liberalism and its Challengers: FDR to Bush*, 2nd edn, New York: Oxford University Press, 1992, are excellent on political developments. For a provocative left-wing view of postwar politics and economics, see Thomas Ferguson and Joel Rogers, *Right Turn: The Decline of the Democrats and the Future of American Politics*, New York: Hill & Wang, 1986. The best study of the political impact of racial issues since 1965 is Thomas Byrne Edsall with Mary D. Edsall, *Chain Reaction: The Impact of Race, Rights and Taxes on American Politics*, New York: Norton, 1992.

Indispensable for the 1960s is Allen J. Matusow, *The Unraveling of America:*

A History of Liberalism in the 1960s, New York: Harper & Row, 1984. For sound scholarly assessments of the Johnson administration, see Paul Conkin, *Big Daddy from the Pedernales*, Boston: Twayne, 1986, and Vaughn D. Bornet, *The Presidency of Lyndon B. Johnson*, Lawrence: University Press of Kansas, 1983. The best survey of the Vietnam war remains George Herring, *America's Longest War: The United States and Vietnam, 1950–1975*, New York: John Wiley, 1970. Also good are: Gary Hess, *Vietnam and the United States*, Boston: Twayne, 1990; James Olson and Randy Roberts, *Where the Dominoes Fell: America and Vietnam, 1945 to 1990*, New York: St Martin's Press, 1991; Larry Berman's books, *Planning a Tragedy: The Americanization of the War in Vietnam*, New York: Norton, 1982, and *Lyndon Johnson's War: The Road to Stalemate in Vietnam*, New York: Norton, 1989; and Anthony Campagna, *The Economic Consequences of the Vietnam War*, New York: Praeger, 1991.

The rise of the new economics is enthusiastically charted by Walter Heller, *New Dimensions of Political Economy*, New York: Norton, 1967, but James Tobin offers a more sober reflexion in *The New Economics A Decade Older*, Princeton University Press, 1974. Robert A. Divine (ed.), *Exploring the Johnson Years*, vol. 1, Austin: University of Texas Press, 1981 is a good collection of essays on Great Society programs. For a critical assessment of antipoverty policy, see Daniel P. Moynihan, *Maximum Feasible Misunderstanding: Community Action in the War on Poverty*, New York: Free Press, 1969, and James T. Patterson, *America's Struggle Against Poverty, 1900–1980*, Cambridge, MA: Harvard University Press, 1981. More favorable is John E. Schwarz, *America's Hidden Success: A Reassessment of Public Policy from Kennedy to Reagan*, rev. edn, New York: Norton, 1988.

For racial issues in the Johnson and Nixon years, see: Hugh D. Graham, *Civil Rights and the Presidency: Race and Gender in American Politics, 1960–1972*, New York: Oxford University Press, 1992; and Steven Lawson, *Running for Freedom: Civil Rights and Black Politics in America since 1941*, Philadelphia: Temple University Press, 1991. Sociocultural divisions are explored by Richard Scammon and Ben Wattenberg, *The Real Majority*, New York: Coward-McCann, 1970, and Patricia Cayo Sexton and Brendan Sexton, *Blue Collars and Hard Hats*, New York: Random House, 1971.

Though self-serving, Richard Nixon, *RN: The Memoirs of Richard Nixon*, New York: Grossett & Dunlap, 1978, and Henry Kissinger, *White House Years* and *Years of Upheaval*, Boston: Little, Brown, 1979 and 1982, are essential sources for early 1970s foreign policy. They need to be complemented by the best available biographical studies: Stephen E. Ambrose, *Nixon: Volume 2 — The Triumph of a Politician, 1962–72*, New York: Simon & Schuster, 1989; Harvey Starr, *Henry Kissinger: Perceptions of International Politics*, Lexington: University Press of Kentucky, 1984; and Robert D. Schulzinger, *Henry Kissinger: Doctor of Diplomacy*, New York: Oxford University Press, 1989. The best studies of detente are: John L. Gaddis, *Strategies of Containment:*

A Critical Appraisal of Postwar American National Security Policy, New York: Oxford University Press, 1982; Robert Litwack, *Detente and the Nixon Doctrine: American Foreign Policy and the Pursuit of Stability*, Cambridge University Press, 1984; Raymond L. Garthoff, *Detente and Confrontation: American-Soviet Relations from Nixon to Reagan*, Washington, DC: Brookings Institution, 1985; and Fred Halliday, *The Making of the Second Cold War*, London: Verso, 1983. For the breakdown of foreign policy consensus, see: Michael Mandelbaum and William Schneider, "The New Internationalisms" in Kenneth Oye, Donald Rothchild, and Robert Lieber (ed.), *Eagle Entangled: US Foreign Policy in a Complex World*, New York: Longmans, 1979; and Ole Holsti and James Rosenau, *American Leadership in World Affairs: Vietnam and the Breakdown of Consensus*, Boston: Allen & Unwin, 1984.

Lester Thurow, *The Zero-Sum Society: Distribution and the Possibilities of Economic Change*, New York: Basic Books, 1980, and Samuel Bowles, David M. Gordon, and Thomas E. Weisskopf, *Beyond the Waste Land: A Democratic Alternative to Economic Decline*, London: Verso, 1984, are good on the 1970s economy. Business response to economic decline is outlined in Leonard Silk and David Vogel, *Ethics and Profits: The Crisis of Confidence in American Business*, New York: Simon & Schuster, 1976, and Thomas Byrne Edsall, *The New Politics of Inequality*, New York: Norton, 1984. Labor's experience is also covered by Edsall's book and by Barry Bluestone and Bennett Harrison, *The Deindustrialization of America*, New York: Basic Books, 1982. For the underclass, see William J. Wilson, *The Declining Significance of Race: Blacks and Changing American Institutions*, University of Chicago Press, 1980.

The changing political context of economic policymaking in the Nixon, Ford, and Carter years is discussed by: Fred Hirsch and John C. Goldthorpe (eds), *The Political Economy of Inflation*, Cambridge MA: Harvard University Press, 1978; Alan S. Blinder, *Economic Policy and the Great Stagflation*, New York: Academic Press, 1979; Richard Barnet, *The Lean Years: Politics in the Age of Scarcity*, New York: Simon & Schuster, 1980; David Calleo, *The Imperious Economy*, Cambridge, MA: Harvard University Press, 1982; and Douglas A. Hibbs, Jr, *The American Political Economy: Macroeconomics and Electoral Politics*, Cambridge, MA: Harvard University Press, 1987.

Peter N. Carroll, *It Seemed Like Nothing Happened: America in the 1970s*, Brunswick, NJ: Rutgers University Press, 1990 is an interesting overview of the 1970s. A. James Reichley, *Conservatives in an Age of Change: The Nixon-Ford Administrations*, Washington, DC: Brookings Institution, 1981, is excellent on domestic policy. Nixon's welfare reform is analyzed by Edward Berkowitz, *America's Welfare State from Roosevelt to Reagan*, Baltimore: Johns Hopkins University Press, 1991. Stephen Ambrose's biography of Nixon, cited above, Tom Wicker, *One of Us: Richard Nixon and the American Dream*, New York: Random House, and Gerald Ford, *A Time to Heal*, New York: Harper & Row, 1979, are very good on domestic issues during the Republican administrations. For racial and gender issues, see: Herman Belz, *Equality Transformed: A Quarter-Century of Affirmative Action*, New Brunswick, NJ: Transaction Books, 1991; Rochelle Gatlin, *American Women since 1945*, Basingstoke: Macmillan, 1987, and Susan Hartmann, *From Margin to Mainstream: American Women and Politics since 1960*, New York: Knopf, 1989.

Byron Shafer, *The Quiet Revolution: The Struggle for the Democratic Party and Post-Reform Politics*, New York: Russell Sage Foundation, 1983; and William Schneider, "JFK's children: the class of '74", *Atlantic Monthly*, March 1989, pp. 35–58, analyze the emergence of "new class" Democrats. David Reinhard, *The Republican Right since 1945*, Lexington: University Press of Kentucky, 1983, Christopher Bailey, *The Republican Party in the US Senate, 1974–1984: Party Change and Institutional Development*, Manchester University Press, 1988, and Nicol Rae, *The Rise and Decline of the Liberal Republicans: From 1952 to the Present*, New York: Oxford University Press, 1989, are good on developments within the GOP during the 1970s. For changes in voting behavior, see: Everett C. Ladd with Charles Hadley, *Transformations of the American Party System: Political Coalitions from the New Deal to the 1970s*, New York: Norton, 1975; James L. Sundquist, *Dynamics of the Party System: Alignment and Realignment of Political Parties in the United States*, rev. edn, Washington, DC: Brookings Institution, 1983; and Gerald Pomper (ed.), *The Election of 1976: Reports and Interpretations*, New York: Longman, 1977.

The most valuable assessments of the Carter presidency are Burton I. Kaufman, *The Presidency of James Earl Carter*, Lawrence: University Press of Kansas, 1993; John Dumbrell, *The Carter Presidency: A Re-evaluation*, Manchester University Press, 1993; Erwin C. Hargrove, *Jimmy Carter as President: Leadership and the Politics of the Public Good*, Baton Rouge: Louisiana State University Press, 1988; and M. Glenn Abernathy, Dilys M. Hill, and Phil Williams (eds), *The Carter Years: The President and Policymaking*, London: Pinter, 1984. Jimmy Carter, *Keeping Faith: Memoirs of a President*, Boston: Houghton Mifflin, 1982, is also an indispensable source.

Essential on Carter's foreign policy is Gaddis Smith, *Morality, Reason and Power: American Diplomacy in the Carter Years*, New York: Hill & Wang, 1986. Also useful are Cyrus R. Vance, *Hard Choices: Critical Years in America's Foreign Policy*, New York: Simon & Schuster, 1983, and Zbigniew Brzezinski, *Power and Principle: Memoirs of the National Security Adviser, 1977–1981*, New York: Farrar, Straus, Giroux, 1983. The lack of foreign policy consensus in the Carter era is examined by Richard Melanson, *Reconstructing Consensus: American Foreign Policy since the Vietnam War*, New York: St Martin's Press, 1991.

William E. Leuchtenburg, *In the Shadow of FDR: From Harry Truman to Ronald Reagan*, Ithaca: Cornell University Press, 1985 illustrates Carter's ambiguity towards New Deal traditions, while Joseph Califano, *Governing America: An Insider's Report from the White House and Cabinet*, New York:

Simon & Schuster, 1981 compares Carter's domestic record unfavorably with Lyndon Johnson's. Everett C. Ladd, *Where have All the Voters Gone? The Fracturing of America's Political Parties*, 2nd edn, New York: Norton, 1982, is an illuminating analysis of public opinion in the Carter era. For assessments of Carter's election defeat, see: Austin Ranney (ed.), *The American Elections of 1980*, Washington DC: AEI Press, 1981; Gerald Pomper (ed.), *The Election of 1980*, Chatham, NJ: Chatham House, 1981; and Thomas Ferguson and Joel Rogers (eds), *The Hidden Election: Politics and Economics in the 1980 Campaign*, New York: Pantheon, 1981.

Reagan's memoirs, *Where's the Rest of Me?*, New York: Dutton, 1965, and *An American Life*, London: Hutchinson, 1990, offer insights into his ideology. These should be supplemented with Martin Anderson, *Revolution*, New York: Harcourt Brace Jovanovich, 1988; David Mervin, *Ronald Reagan and the American Presidency*, London: Longman, 1990; and Lawrence Barrett, *Gambling with History: Reagan in the White House*, London: Penguin Books, 1984. Sidney Blumenthal, *The Rise of the Counter-Establishment*, New York: Times Books, 1986 is splendid on the new conservatism. Also very good are: George Nash, *The Conservative Intellectual Movement in America*, New York: Basic Books, 1979; Gillian Peele, *Revival and Reaction: The Right in Contemporary America*, New York: Oxford University Press, 1984; and Steve Bruce, *The Rise and Fall of the New Christian Right: Conservative Protestant Politics in America 1978–1988*, Oxford: Clarendon Press, 1988. For comparison of British and American conservatism, see Desmond King, *The New Right: Politics, Markets and Citizenship*, Basingstoke: Macmillan, 1987.

Hitherto the only study of the Reagan presidency by a historian is Michael Schaller, *Reckoning with Reagan: America and its President in the 1980s*, New York: Oxford University Press, 1992. However, several essay collections by political scientists cover virtually every facet of 1980s politics and policy. Joseph Hogan (ed.), *The Reagan Years: The Record in Presidential Leadership*, Manchester University Press, 1990, and Dilys Hill, Raymond Moore, and Phil Williams (eds), *The Reagan Presidency: An Incomplete Revolution*, Basingstoke: Macmillan, 1990, are Anglo-American collaborations, both containing particularly valuable essays by Joseph Hogan on Reaganomics. See too: B. B. Kymlicka and Jean Matthews (eds), *The Reagan Revolution?*, Chicago: Dorsey Press, 1988; Charles O. Jones (ed.), *The Reagan Legacy: Promise and Performance*, Chatham, NJ: Chatham House, 1988; and Larry Berman (ed.), *Looking Back on the Reagan Years*, Baltimore: Johns Hopkins University Press, 1990. Important memoirs of the Reagan administration include: David Stockman, *The Triumph of Politics*, London: Bodley Head, 1986; Paul Craig Roberts, *The Supply-Side Revolution: An Insider's Account of Policymaking in Washington*, Cambridge, MA: Harvard University Press, 1984; and Donald Regan, *For the Record: From Wall Street to Washington*, New York: Harcourt Brace Jovanovich, 1988.

On foreign policy in the 1980s, see: Coral Bell, *The Reagan Paradox: American Foreign Policy in the 1980s*, London: Edward Arnold, 1989; William G. Hyland (ed.), *The Reagan Foreign Policy*, New York: New American Library, 1987; and Kenneth Oye, Donald Rothchild, and Robert Lieber (eds), *Eagle Resurgent: The Reagan Era in American Foreign Policy*, Boston: Little, Brown, 1987. For contrasting views of America's twenty-first-century international prospects, consult Paul Kennedy, *The Rise and Fall of the Great Powers: Economic Change and Military Conflict from 1500 to 2000*, New York: Random House, 1988, and Joseph S. Nye, *Bound to Lead: The Changing Nature of American Power*, New York: Basic Books, 1990.

Michael Boskin, *Reagan and the Economy: The Successes, Failures and the Unfinished Agenda*, San Francisco: Institute of Contemporary Studies, 1987, and Paul Craig Roberts and colleagues, *Reaganomics and After*, London: Institute of Economic Affairs, 1989, are sympathetic to Reagan's economic goals. For very critical perspectives, see Robert Lekachman, *Visions and Nightmares: America After Reagan*, New York: Macmillan, 1987; Benjamin Friedman, *Day of Reckoning: The Consequences of American Economic Policy Under Reagan and After*, New York: Random House, 1988; and Wallace C. Peterson, "The Silent Depression", *Challenge*, July–Aug., 1991 pp. 29–34.

New approaches to welfare are discussed in two influential books: Charles Murray, *Losing Ground: American Social Policy, 1950–1980*, New York: Basic Books, 1984, and Lawrence Mead, *Beyond Entitlement: The Social Obligation of Citizenship*, New York: Free Press, 1985. Good coverage of the Reagan-era elections is provided in Michael Nelson (ed.), *The Elections of 1984*, Washington DC: Congressional Quarterly Press, 1985, and Gerald Pomper (ed.), *The Elections of 1988*, Chatham, NJ: Chatham House, 1989. Steven M. Gillon, *The Democrats' Dilemma: Walter F. Mondale and the Liberal Legacy*, New York: Columbia University Press, 1992, is a good analysis of Democratic problems.

For useful introductions to the politics of the Bush era, see: Richard Rose, *George Bush as a Post-Modern President*, Glasgow: Center for the Study of Public Policy, 1991; and Gillian Peele, Christopher Bailey and Bruce Cain (eds), *Developments in American Politics*, Basingstoke: Macmillan, 1992. Interesting contributions to the post-Cold War foreign policy debate include: Charles Krauthammer, "The Lonely Superpower", *The New Republic*, July 29, 1991, pp. 23–7; David Gergen, "America's Missed Opportunities", *Foreign Affairs*, XX (Jan. 1992), 3–19; Strobe Talbott, "Post-Victory Blues", *ibid.*, 53–69; Joseph S. Nye, "What New World Order?", *ibid.*, XX1 (March 1992), pp. 83–96; and Graham T. Allison and Gregory F. Teverton (eds), *Rethinking American Security: Beyond Cold War to New World Order*, New York: Norton, 1992. Economic insecurities are assessed in Daniel Yankelovich, "Foreign Policy after the Election", *Foreign Affairs*, XXI (March 1992), pp. 1–12.

For the present, newspaper and magazine articles are the main source for most economic and domestic issues in Bush era. But for useful scholarly assessments of racial and gender issues see: Mary H. Cooper, "Racial Quotas", *Congressional Quarterly Researcher*, May 17, 1991, pp. 279–95; and Michael X. Delli Carpini and Esther R. Fuchs, "The Year of the Woman?: Candidates, Voters and the 1992 Elections", *Political Science Quarterly*, 108 (Jan 1993), pp. 29–57. Good assessments of electoral strategies and voting trends in 1992 are provided by: William Schneider, "The Suburban Century Begins", *The Atlantic Monthly* (July 1992), pp. 33–44; Everett Carl Ladd, "The 1992 Vote for President Clinton: Another Brittle Mandate", *Political Science Quarterly*, 108 (Jan 1993), pp. 1–28; and Gerald Pomper (ed.), *The Elections of 1992* Chatham, NJ: Chatham House, 1993. Ross Perot outlines his program in *United We Stand: How We Can Take Back Our Country*, New York: Hyperion, 1992. Robert B. Reich, *The Work of Nations: Preparing Ourselves for 21st-Century Capitalism*, New York: Simon & Schuster, 1993, exemplifies the new thinking of "Clintonomics".

INDEX

abortion: 122–3, 163; Supreme Court decisions on, 122, 218, 258–9
Abzug, Bella, 163
Acheson, Dean, 26, 34
Afghanistan, 146, 147, 149, 164, 194, 221, 227, 241
Agnew, Spiro, 55, 112, 123, 131, 132
Aid to Families with Dependent Children (AFDC): 20, 43, 112, 113, 115, 168, 190, 209, 210, 211; *see also* welfare
Akron v. *Akron Center for Reproductive Health* (1983), 218
Alexander v. *Holmes County Board of Education* (1969), 118
Allen, Richard, 177
Ambrose, Stephen, 23, 65, 118, 227
American Enterprise Institute, 177
American Independence Party, 55, 183
Amin, Hafizullah, 146
Amin, Idi, 142
Anderson, John B., 165, 166, 184
Anderson, Martin, 171, 177, 188, 207
Andropov, Yuri, 220
Angola, 80, 83, 221, 224, 227
Arbatov, Georgi, 228
Argentina, 140
arms control: 24–5, 244; and SALT-1, 71–3; and SALT-2, 144–6, 147, 148, 219; in 1980s, 192–3, 219, 223–4, 226–7
Ashbrook, John, 130
Aspin, Les, 247
Auchter, Thomas, 213

Baker, James, 202, 241, 244
Bakker, Jim, 182
Barrett, Lawrence, 173
Bayh, Birch, 166, 181
Begin, Menachem, 144
Bell, Daniel, 110

Belz, Herman, 162
Bennett, William, 177
Bentsen, Lloyd, 236
Berkowitz, Edward, 20
Berlin Agreement, 73–4
Berrigan, Philip, 124
black Americans: and civil rights protest, 19; and Democratic party, 16, 57, 136, 165, 233, 235; economic conditions of, 6, 47, 95, 168, 206, 215–16, 256; and ghetto riots, 49, 256–7; *see also* Civil Rights
Blackmun, Harry, 259
Boland Amendment, 225
Bork, Robert, 218
Boxer, Barbara, 261
Braun, Carol Mosely, 261
Brazil, 142
Brennan, William, 253
Bretton Woods Agreement, 99, 100–1
Brezhnev, Leonid, 145
Brinkley, Alan, 8
Britain, politics in, 2–3, 157, 212, 271, 272, 273–4
Brock, William, 217
Broder, David, 107
Brooke, Edward, 185
Brown, Jerry, 247
Brown v. *Topeka Board of Education* (1954), 19, 117
Browne, Robert S., 95
Brzezinski, Zbigniew, 141, 144, 146, 148
Buchanan, Pat, 130, 132, 247, 267
Budget: 10, 23; in Bush era, 249–50; in Carter era: 151, 154–6; and defense, 5, 23, 72, 148, 192, 224; and Nixon–Ford administrations, 98, 102, 105; in Reagan era, 188–91, 200–1, 202–3, 208–9; Vietnam War and, 37–9
Burger, Warren, 218
Burns, Arthur, 102

Bush, President George: 184, 214, 253,
257, 274; and civil rights, 254–5; and
1988 election, 228, 229, 233–4; and
1992 election, 261, 263, 264, 266–7,
268–70; and foreign policy, 240–6,
247; and taxes, 184, 232, 249–50, 266
business, 4–5, 15, 97, 212–3, 251; and
affirmative action, 216, 255; conservatism of in 1970s, 107, 175–7; foreign
policy views of, 67, 140–1; relations
with labor, 91–2
Business Week, 149
Byrd, Harry, 19

Calley, William, 124
Cambodia, 65, 66–8, 76, 81, 82, 221
Camp David Accords, 144–5
Carson, Rachel, 115
Carswell, G. Harrold, 118
Carter, President Jimmy: 128, 133, 174,
213, 222, 225, 230, 231, 238; domestic
program of, 161–3; and economic
policy, 106, 150–7; and 1976 election,
135–7; and 1980 election, 164–5; and
foreign policy, 85, 138–9, 141–50, 191,
192, 246; political values of, 160–1; and
problems of presidential government,
157–60
Case, Clifford, 185
Casey, William, 221, 225–6
Central Intelligence Agency (CIA), 22,
69, 83, 221, 225–6, 247
Chad, 221
Chicago Eight, 124
Chile, 77
Christian Broadcasting Network, 183
Christian Coalition, 287
Christian Freedom Foundation, 182
Christian Voice, 182
Church, Frank, 180
City of Richmond v. *J.A. Croson Company*
(1989), 254
civil rights: 16, 17, 19; and affirmative
action, 119, 215–7; and Civil Rights
Act of 1991, 254–6; and school
desegregation, 10, 117–18, 119–20;
and Philadelphia plan, 119–20; *see also*
Black Americans

Clark, Dick, 181
Clifford, Clark, 34
Clinton, President Bill: 210, 246, 247,
257; and 1992 election, 264–6, 267,
268–70, 274; as president, 275–6
Clinton, Hillary, 275
Cold War: 5; and domestic consensus,
20–6, 34–5, 223; end of, 227–8, 240–1;
post-Vietnam divisions over, 85–6,
139–40, 271–2; *see also* detente
Colson, Charles, 69
Commentary, 86, 175
Committee on the Present Danger, 86,
140, 145–6, 177
Committee for the Survival of a Free
Congress, 179
Community Action Program, 63
Comprehensive Child Development Act,
122, 123
Congress: and budget deficit, 202–3, 250;
and divided government, 237–9, 274;
and foreign policy, 68, 73, 82–4,
145, 146, 224–6; fragmentation of
power within, 158–9; 'New Politics'
Democrats within, 134–5
Connally, John, 101, 131, 132
Conkin, Paul, 29
Conservative Caucus, 179
Coolidge, Calvin, 174, 205
Coors, Joseph, 177
Cotton, Norris, 82
Council of Economic Advisers (CEA), 9,
11, 35, 97, 177
Crane, Philip, 184
Cuba, 24, 28, 80, 146, 194
Culver, John, 180
Cuomo, Mario, 200, 261

Daley, Richard, 126
Danforth, John, 255
Democratic Leadership Council, 209, 262
Democratic Party: divisions over Vietnam, 32, 34, 52–5; and economic
policy, 11, 106–7; and foreign policy,
71–2, 83–4, 85–6, 140, 243–4; neoliberals within, 163–4, 262, 273; and
New Deal coalition, 12–14, 56–7,
129–30, 156–7, 165–6, 232–3, 234–5;

New Politics and, 124–8, 134–5;
presidential nomination contests of,
52–4, 127–8, 135, 164–5, 235–6,
236–7, 261–2; southern wing of,
18–19, 237, 255, 262, 273
Deng Xiaoping, 146
detente: 24–5; concept of, 58–9, 61–3;
decline of, 76–86
Dewey, Thomas, 14, 184
Diem, Ngo Dinh, 29
Dixon, Alan, 261
Dodd, Christopher, 163
Dolan, Terry, 179
Dole, Robert, 133
Dominican Republic, 24
Douglas, Paul, 13
Duarte, José Napoleón, 220
Dukakis, Michael, 163, 231, 234, 236–7,
262, 263
Duke, David, 255

Eagle Forum, 180
Eastland, James, 18
economic policy: and monetarist doctrines, 95–6, 177–8; and new economics, 35–40; and Nixonomics, 95–104;
and party divisions over in 1970s,
104–7, 272–3; prior to 1965, 8–11;
and supply-side doctrines, 178–9, 187–
90
economy: in postwar era, 3–8; in 1960s,
36–7; in 1970s, 88–95, 151; in 1980s,
199–202, 204–6; in 1990s, 250–2; and
stock market crashes, 98, 202, 213
Edsall, Mary, 55, 117, 234
Edsall, Thomas, 55, 117, 135, 234
Edwards, Edwin, 255
Egypt, 78–9, 144–5, 241
Ehrlichman, John, 69
Eisenhower, President Dwight D., 9–10,
17, 26, 64, 238
Elections: congressional, 41, 129, 131,
134, 166, 181, 185, 230, 230–1, 237,
260–1; presidential, 10, 11, 13, 41–2,
52–7, 106–7, 126–30, 132–3, 164–9,
229, 230, 231, 233–7, 261–7
Ellsberg, Daniel, 60, 124
El Salvador, 142, 220, 224

energy crisis, 91, 131, 152–3
environmental policy, 115–6, 213–4
Equal Employment Opportunities Com-
mission, 121, 217
Equal Rights Amendment (ERA), 122,
123, 132, 133, 162, 172, 180, 184, 218
Ethiopia, 81, 146, 221
European Community, 88, 101

Fair Deal, 16
Falwell, Jerry, 182
Family Assistance Plan, 112–14, 161, 210
Family Support Act, 209, 210
Federal Reserve, 30, 97, 98, 102, 151,
152, 154, 199, 204
Feinstein, Diane, 261
Felstein, Martin, 177
Ferraro, Geraldine, 235
Firefighters Local Union No 1794 v *Stoots*
(1984), 216, 217
Florio, James, 163
food stamps, 43, 114, 168, 190, 211; *see
also* welfare
Ford, President Gerald: 50, 76, 83, 191,
237; economic policy of, 104–7, 200;
reelection campaign of, 85, 132–3
Forrestal, James, 15
Fraser, Steve, 12
Friedan, Betty, 121
Friedman, Milton, 95–6, 97, 176, 177,
208
Fulbright, William, 32
Fullilove v. *Klutznick* (1980), 162

Gaddis, John, 58
Gantt, Harvey, 254
Garthoff, Raymond, 63
Gatlin, Rochelle, 123
Gephard, Richard, 261
Gergen, David, 247
Germany (Federal Republic), 2–3, 100,
101, 204, 240, 243
Gerstle, Gary, 11
GI Bill of Rights, 5, 265
Ginsberg, Benjamin, 201
Goldwater, Barry, 15, 41–2, 132, 168,
172, 174, 186
Gorbachev, Mikhail, 226–7, 241, 244

Gore, Albert, 261
Gorusch, Anne Burford, 214
Gramm–Rudman–Hollings, 203, 224, 249
Great Society: 42, 160, 257, 272; antipoverty policy of, 43–7; and Vietnam War, 31, 40, 45; neo-conservative criticism of, 110, 130
Green v. *New Kent County School Board* (1968), 117
Greenberg, Stanley, 264
Greenspan, Alan, 252
Grenada, 197, 222, 223, 230
Griggs v. *Duke's Power Co.* (1971), 215, 254
Griswold v. *Connecticut* (1965), 122–3
Guatemala, 24
Gulf of Tonkin Resolution, 31, 68
Gulf war, 240, 242–4, 245–6, 248, 267

Haig, Alexander, 223
Haiti, 142, 220
Haldeman, H. R. (Bob), 64
Hamby, Alonzo, 110
Hargrove, Erwin, 138, 160
Harkin, Tom, 247, 261
Harriman, Averell, 15
Harrington, Michael, 47
Hart, Gary, 134, 163, 169, 235, 236, 262
Hatch, Orrin, 143, 186
Haynsworth, Clement, 118
Healthcare policy, 16, 17, 43, 161, 250, 265, 275
Heller, Walter, 11, 35
Helms, Jesse, 133, 186, 254
Helsinki Accords, 74, 133, 143
Heritage Foundation, 177, 178, 208
Hesburgh, Theodore M., 130
Hess, Stephen, 261
Hibbs, Douglas, 154
Hill, Anita, 260
Hill, Patricia, 260
Hodgson, Godfrey, 1, 2
Hoover, Herbert, 157
Hoover Institution on War, Revolution and Peace, 177
Hoover, J. Edgar, 69
Horton, Willy, 234

Humphrey, Hubert: 13, 134, 135, 235; in 1968 election, 54–7; in 1972 election, 127–8
Humphrey-Hawkins Full-Employment Act, 106, 151
Hussein, Saddam, 242, 243, 244, 245

income levels, 4, 5–6, 37, 92–3, 205–6, 252, 256
Independent Federation of Flight Attendants v. *Zipes* (1989), 254
Indonesia, 24
inflation, 10, 36–7, 91, 92, 98, 103, 104–5, 150, 151, 154, 199
Iran, 24, 79–80, 142–3, 152, 222–3, 225, 227; hostage crisis in, 148–9, 164, 245
Iran-Contra affair, 174, 225–6, 230
Israel, 77, 78–9, 144, 222, 241, 244
Iraq, 225, 227, 240, 241, 242–3, 245
Italy, 24

Jackson, Henry, 85, 127, 135, 140, 146
Jackson, Jesse, 209, 235–6, 257, 261
Jackson–Vanik Amendment, 84
Japan, 88, 89, 100, 201, 204–5, 243, 247
Javits, Jacob, 185
John M. Olin Fund, 177
Johnson, President Lyndon B.: 156, 157, 159, 160, 173, 186, 217, 274; economic policy of, 36–40; and 1964 election, 41–2; and Great Society, 42–5; and Vietnam war, 29–35
Johnson v. *Transportation Agency Santa Clara County* (1987), 217
Justice Department, 162, 195–6, 216, 217

Kaiser Aluminum and Chemical Corporation v. *Weber* (1979), 162
Katznelson, Ira, 46
Kavanagh, Dennis, 271
Kegley, Charles, 22
Kemp, Jack, 185, 186, 257
Kennan, George, 22, 219
Kennedy, Anthony, 218, 259
Kennedy, Edward, 54, 95, 155, 164–5, 169

Kennedy, President John F., 11, 13, 26, 29, 35, 36, 169, 229, 238, 246, 274
Kennedy, Paul, 227–8
Kennedy, Robert, 32, 53–4, 124–5
Keyserling, Leon, 9
King, Martin Luther, 32, 49, 53, 141, 235
King, Rodney, 256
Kirkpatrick, Jeane, 177, 194, 220
Kissinger, Henry: 26, 59–60, 133, 186; and concept of detente, 61–3, 77; and Vietnam War, 65–8, 69, 75; and Yom Kippur war, 78–9
Korean War, 5, 9, 23, 25, 53, 223, 243
Krauthammer, Charles, 243
Kristol, Irving, 110, 140, 175
Krogh, Egil "Bud", 69
Kuwait, 222, 240, 242, 243, 244, 245

Labor Unions: 34, 37–8, 128, 235; and Democratic party, 13, 14, 56, 124, 126, 127, 136; relations with management, 7–8, 91–2
Ladd, Everett, 169, 228
LaFeber, Walter, 62–3
Laffer, Arthur, 178–9
Laird, Melvin, 102
Laos, 65, 68, 76, 81
Laxalt, Paul, 186, 211
Lebanon, 24, 144, 222, 224
Lekachman, Robert, 204–5
LeMay, Curtis E., 56
Leuchtenburg, William, 5, 166
Libya, 222
Life Amendment Political Action Committee, 180
Local 28 Sheet Metal Workers v. *EEOC* (1986), 217
Long, Russell, 160
Lorance v. *AT&T Technologies* (1989), 254
Los Angeles Riot, 256–7
Louvre Accord, 202
Lovett, Robert, 15
Lundborg, Louis B., 38

McCarthy, Eugene, 52–4
McCarthy, Joseph, 26

McCormick, Thomas, 84
'McGovern, George, 127–30, 137, 166
McIntyre, Thomas, 181
McNamara, Robert, 34, 67, 220
Magaziner, Ira, 264
Marshall, George C., 26
Marshall, Thurgood, 253
Martin v. *Wilks* (1989), 254
Mead, Lawrence, 209
Meany, George, 124
Medicaid, 43, 211
Medicare, 43, 44, 47
Meese, Edwin, 217
Middle Americans, 48–9, 51, 233
Mitchell, John, 112
Mondale, Walter, 232, 235–6
Moral Majority, 182
Morton, Thruston B., 32
Moynihan, Daniel: 110, 111; and welfare reform, 46, 112, 210
Mozambique, 80
Mundell, Robert, 178
Murray, Charles, 209
Muskie, Edmund, 13, 116, 127

Nathan, James, 139
National Abortion Rights Action League, 260
National Advisory Commission on Civil Disorders, 48, 50
National Energy Act, 153
National Governors Association, 210, 211
National Highway Safety Administration, 115
National Organization for Women, 121, 235
National Right to Life Committee, 259
National Security Act, 22
National Welfare Rights Organization, 112, 114
NATO (North Atlantic Treaty Organization), 24, 147, 220
Nelson, Gaylord, 180
neoconservatives, 110–1, 174–5, 193–4
neoliberals, 163–4, 235, 236, 262, 273
New Deal: 8–9, 12–13, 46, 236; compared with Reagan Revolution, 228–9
New Directions, 86

New Federalism, 116–17, 210–12
New Republic, 113
New Christian Right, 140, 181–3
New Right, 179–81, 183, 184, 185, 195
Nicaragua, 142, 194, 221, 224–6, 241–2
Nitze, Paul, 177, 241
Nixon, President Richard: 173, 191, 213, 233, 238, 244, 245, 253, 273; background of, 59–61; and civil rights, 117–20; downfall of, 130-1; economic policy of, 10, 11, 95–104; foreign policy of, 61–3, 65–8, 72–3, 74, 77, 86; and presidential elections, 54–7, 110–2, 128–30; and welfare reform, 112–5
Noriega, Manuel, 242
Norwood, Janet, 253
NSC-68, 23
North, Oliver, 226
Nunn, Sam, 261, 262
Nye, Joseph, 244

Occupational Safety and Health Administration (OSHA), 115, 213
O'Connor, Sandra Day, 196, 259
Office of Economic Opportunity, 43
oil: Arab embargo of, 79, 91, 101; OPEC price hikes of, 80, 19, 101, 152, 153, 154; US consumption of, 89, 152–30
Okun, Arthur, 36
Oliver, James, 139
O'Neill, Tip, 191
opinion polls: 25, 32, 34–5, 48–9, 55, 57, 70, 87, 107, 128, 149–50, 13, 156, 157, 164, 165–8, 223, 230, 231–2, 242–3, 248, 242, 268–9, 274; Gallup poll, 67, 68, 131, 157, 165, 182, 224, 226, 247–8, 259; Harris poll, 47–8, 50, 51, 86; National Opinion Research Center poll, 167, 168
Organization for Economic Cooperation and Development (OECD), 204, 265, 267
Organization of Petroleum Exporting Countries (OPEC), 79, 80, 91, 141, 152, 154, 204

Pakistan, 143, 221, 241

Palestine Liberation Organization (PLO), 79, 144, 146, 222
Panama, 242
Panama Canal, 133, 143–4, 160
Peele, Gillian, 210
Pentagon Papers, 69
Perkins, Carl D., 130
Perle, Richard, 177
Patterson v. *McLean Credit Union* (1989), 254
People's Republic of China (PRC) 24, 61, 70–1, 146, 220–1, 245, 246
Perot, Ross, 261, 267–70
Peterson, Peter G., 91
Peterson, Wallace C., 252
Philippines, 24, 143, 220, 224
Phillips, Howard, 179
Phillips, Kevin, 110–1, 131, 132, 185
Planned Parenthood of Southeastern Pennsylvania v. *Casey* (1992), 259
Podhoretz, Norman, 140, 175
Polenberg, Richard, 207
Political Action Committees (PACs), 159, 176, 184, 238
Pomper, Gerald, 239
poverty; 6, 20; in 1960s, 42–7; in 1970s, 94–5; in 1980s, 206
Price Waterhouse v. *Hopkins* (1989), 254
Progressive Policy Institute, 264
public interest, 175

Quayle, Dan, 181, 257, 267

RAVCO, 179
Reagan, President Ronald: compared with Franklin D. Roosevelt, 174, 218, 229, 239; economic policy of, 156, 187–91; 199–207; and foreign policy, 85, 133, 140, 149–50, 173, 191–4, 219–28, 245, 246; and judiciary, 196, 218–9, 253; and party politics in 1980s, 228–39, 273, 274; political beliefs of, 171–4, 183; presidential campaigns of, 131–3, 165, 166, 168, 229–30; and national morale, 196–7, 230, 240; and racial issues, 168, 216–7; and regulatory government, 116, 212–4; and social issues, 194–6

Regan, Donald, 193
Regents of the University of California v. *Bakke* (1978), 162
Rehnquist, William, 218, 253, 259
Reich, Robert, 264
Reichley, James, 95–6
Reilly, William, 214
Religious Roundtable, 182
Republican Party: 16, 159; in Bush era, 255, 267; emergence of right within, 131–3, 183–7; law-and-order concerns of, 50, 123–4; in postwar era, 14–15, 17–18; in Reagan era, 228–31, 238, 273; views of on detente, 83–4, 84–5; views of on 1970s economic policy, 106–7
Reynolds, William Bradford, 216
Rizzo, Frank, 128
Robb, Charles, 262
Roberts, Paul Craig, 179, 188
Robertson, Pat, 182–3, 267
Robertson, Willis, 19
Robison, James, 182
Rockefeller, David, 141
Rockefeller, Nelson A., 10, 132, 133, 184
Roe v. *Wade*, 122, 136, 258, 259
Rogers, William P., 60
Roosevelt, President Franklin D.: 8, 10, 62, 100, 156, 157, 164, 165, 234, 243, 246; compared with Bill Clinton, 270; compared with Ronald Reagan, 174, 218, 229, 239
Roth, William, 185
Rusher, William, 132
Russell, Richard, 18
Russia, 244, 247

Sadat, Anwar, 78–9, 144
Saudi Arabia, 77, 242
Savage, James, 156
Savimbi, Jonas, 221
Scaife, Richard Mellon, 177
Scalia, Antonin, 218, 259
Schlafly, Phyllis, 180, 260
Schlesinger Jr, Arthur, 160, 172
Schneider, William, 262
Schulzinger, Robert, 79
Shafer, Byron, 126–7

Shafter, Martin, 201
Shultz, George, 120, 221, 224
Simon, William, 176
Smith, Gaddis, 139, 149
Smith, Howard, 18
Smith, Howard K., 98–9
Soares, Mario, 274–5
Social Insurance, 16, 20, 44–5, 114, 232; Reagan administration reforms of, 207–8
Somalia, 81, 146, 247
Souter, David, 253, 259
South Africa, 80, 142, 225
South Korea, 143
Soviet Union; 11, 22, 61, 88, 220, 240, 245; and detente, 61–3, 72–3, 77, 80–1, 84; in Middle East, 78, 144; retreat from Cold War by, 226–8; and Vietnam war, 65, 66, 74, 81
Sprinkel, Beryl, 189
Stein, Herbert, 95, 103
Stevens, John Paul, 259
Stigler, George, 177
Stockman, David, 179, 189, 202
Strategic Defense Initiative (SDI), 177, 219–20, 226–7
Supreme Court: 50–1; and abortion rights, 122–3, 163, 259; and civil rights, 19, 117–18, 119, 216–17, 254
Swann v *Charlotte-Mecklenberg Board of Education* (1971), 119
Syria, 78, 144, 222, 245

Taft, Robert, 25, 26
Taiwan, 24, 70–1, 221
taxes: 39–40, 176; George Bush and, 184, 232; Ronald Reagan and, 172, 173, 188–90, 202–3, 204, 206, 231, 232; supply-side doctrine and, 178–9; and "tax revolt", 166–7
Terkel, Studs, 48
Thatcher, Margaret, 157, 212, 271
Thieu, Nguyen Van, 75
Thomas, Clarence, 217, 253, 259, 260
Thornburgh v. *American College of Obstetricians and Gynecologists* (1986), 218
Thurow, Lester, 98
Tobin, James, 40, 207

Truman, President Harry S., 9–10, 16, 21–3, 25, 26, 194, 229, 243, 245, 246, 274
Tsongas, Paul, 163, 169, 247, 262–3
Ture, Norman, 188
Turkey, 245

Uganda, 142
unemployment: in 1970s, 93–4, 97, 105, 154–5; in 1980s, 199–200; in 1990s, 252–3
United Nations (UN), 227, 242–3, 244, 245–6, 248

Vietnam war: 23, 24, 28–9, 158, 221; antiwar opinion and, 32–3, 65, 67–8, 68–9; economic effects of, 37–8; ending of, 75–6, 81; and Great Society, 31, 40, 45; Lyndon Johnson's policy towards, 29–35; Richard Nixon's policy towards, 64–8, 74; US casualties in, 33, 65; US Congress and, 31, 68, 82, 83
Vance, Cyrus, 141, 145, 146
Viguerie, Richard, 179, 180, 182
Volcker, Paul, 199
voting trends, 12–14, 41, 55–6, 129–30, 134, 136–7, 156–7, 165–6, 167–9, 229–32, 233, 234–5, 268–70

Wallace, George, 55–6, 117, 127, 135, 168
Wallace, Henry, 25
Wanniski, Jude, 177–8
Wards Cove Packing Co v. *Atonio* (1989), 254
Warnke, Paul, 145
War Powers Act, 82–3, 224
Warren, Earl, 19, 50, 253
Watergate, 60, 78, 84, 107, 130–1, 158

Watt, James G., 177, 213, 214
Wattenberg, Benjamin, 175
Wayne, John, 143
Webster v. *Reproductive Health Services* (1989), 258, 259
Weidenbaum, Murray, 177, 212
Weinberger, Caspar, 192, 221, 224
Welfare: 20, 161; and Great Society, 43–7; and new federalism, 210–11; Nixon administration reforms of, 112–15; popular views of, 48–9, 113, 168; and workfare, 208–10, 266; *see also* Aid to Families with Dependent Children, Food Stamps, Medicaid, Poverty
Westmoreland, William, 33
Weyrich, Paul, 179, 180, 181, 182
Wheeler, Earl, 33
White, Byron, 259
Wilkins, Roger, 118
Will, George, 184
Willkie, Wendell, 14
Wilson, James, 174
Wilson, Woodrow, 141, 160, 243, 246
Wirth, Tim, 163, 164
Wittkopf, Eugene, 22
Wofford, Harris, 247
women: and electoral politics, 235, 239; and ERA, 122–3, 162; in employment, 121, 218; and feminism, 120–1; poverty among, 6, 45, 95, 206

Yankelovich, Daniel, 87, 167, 253
Yeltsin, Boris, 244
Yom Kippur war, 78–9, 83
Young, Andrew, 141, 146
Yugoslavia, 24, 245

Zaire, 81, 142
Zimbabwe, 142